TAUNTON'S COMPLETE GUIDE TO

Growing
Vegetables
& Herbs

TAUNTON'S COMPLETE GUIDE TO

Growing
Vegetables
& Herbs

FROM THE PUBLISHERS OF
FINE GARDENING & KITCHEN GARDENER

Edited by Ruth Lively

The Taunton Press

The Taunton Press

Inspiration for hands-on living®

The Taunton Press, Inc., 63 South Main Street,

PO Box 5506, Newtown, CT 06470-5506

e-mail: tp@taunton.com

Editors: Ruth Lively, Carolyn Mandarano

Copy editor: Seth Reichgott

Indexer: Heidi Blough

Jacket/Cover design: Carol Singer

Interior design: 3&Co.

Layout: Annie and David Giammattei

Fine Gardening® is a trademark of The Taunton Press, Inc., registered in the U.S. Patent and Trademark Office.

The following names/manufacturers appearing in *Taunton's Complete Guide to Growing Vegetables and Herbs* are trademarks:
20 Mule Team® Borax, ACQ®, BioNEEM®, Dawn®, Deer Away®, Deer Off®, Ferry-Morse® Seed & Nursery Co., Garlic Barrier®, Green Light® Neem Concentrate, Gurney's® Seed & Nursery Co., Harris® Seeds, Henry Field's®, Hinder®, HotKaps®, Ivory®, JMS Stylet-Oil®, Johnny's Selected Seeds®, Joy®, K-Mag®, Lexan®, Miracle-Gro®, Organica® Neem Soap Concentrate, Palmolive®, Perk®, Polygal®, Seeds of Change™, Stokes®, Sul-Po-Mag®, Sunspray® Ultrafine Oil, Titebond II™, Trex®, Tubtrugs®, Volck® Supreme Oil, Wall-O-Water®.

Library of Congress Cataloging-in-Publication Data
Taunton's complete guide to growing vegetables and herbs / publishers of Fine Gardening & Kitchen Gardener ; edited by Ruth Lively.
      p. cm.
  Includes index.
  ISBN 978-1-60085-336-4
  1. Vegetable gardening. 2. Herb gardening. 3. Gardens--Design. I. Lively, Ruth. II. Title: Complete guide to growing vegetables and herbs.
  SB321.T36 2011
  635--dc22

                  2010047880

Printed in the United States of America
10 9 8 7 6 5 4 3 2 1

ACKNOWLEDGMENTS

Thanks to the many contributors—authors, photographers, illustrators, and editors—to *Kitchen Gardener*, published from 1996 to 2001 by The Taunton Press, Inc.

CONTENTS

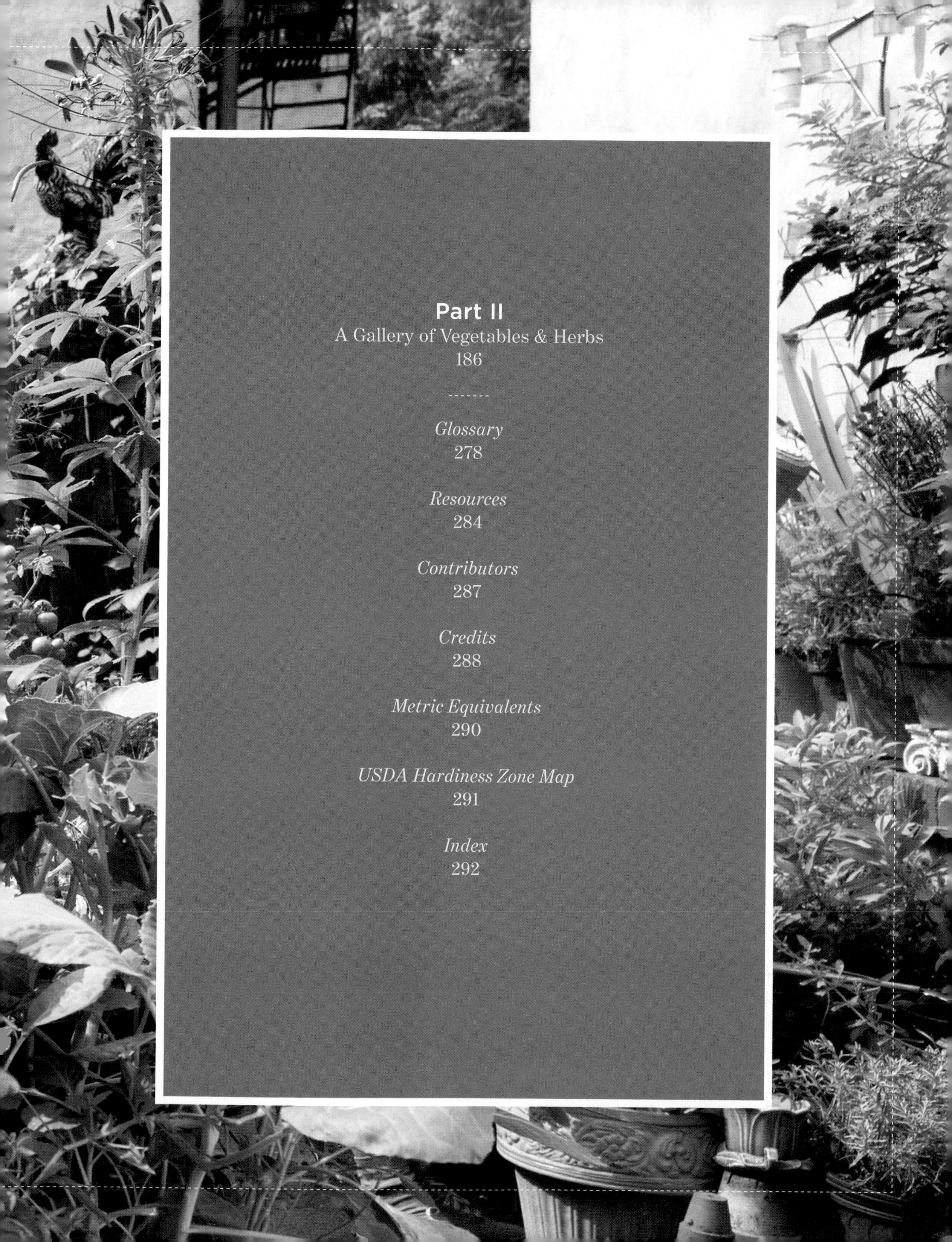

Part II

INTRODUCTION

I DON'T REMEMBER MUCH ABOUT MY FIRST GARDEN. When I was five, my mother let me have a corner of my own in the family garden, and I got to pick out seeds—radishes and marigolds. When I planted my first all-on-my-own garden 20 years later, radishes were again my first crop. I still remember the thrill of pulling up the bright red balls, rinsing off the clinging soil, and delighting in their peppery crunch.

What is it that so excites us about vegetable gardening? Maybe it's the basic act of nourishing ourselves. Growing food, after all, is perhaps the one activity that truly justifies itself. That elemental thrill of growing and eating our own vegetables is common to us all, and it never wanes.

Gardening isn't only sustaining, it's compelling. It gets into your blood. And food gardening is growing—pun intended. Challenging economic times have more and more people wanting to grow their own vegetables to save on their food bill, as well as to have more control over what they put in their mouths.

Kitchen Gardener magazine, published from 1996 to 2001, was entirely dedicated to edible gardening. Now for the first time, we've collected that valuable information and condensed it into a single volume. This book contains all you need to know to grow a bountiful and beautiful vegetable garden, from design and layout to hardscape and structures to fundamentals like soil improvement, watering, and fertilizing to managing pests and problems. And of course there are the crops themselves: the whole range of vegetables and herbs that are good to grow and eat. The expert information in these pages comes from scores of first-rate gardeners from all over the continental United States and southern Canada. Whether you're a first-timer looking for a lot of guidance or a veteran gardener wanting to learn some new techniques, you'll find a lot of useful material in this book.

As I write this, I sit looking at my own garden, which lies just beyond our patio. It's not huge—a fenced area about 32 ft. square. Beds line the fence on three sides, with a space in the middle of one side for a garden bench. In the center are six raised beds. Altogether I have 325 sq. ft. of beds. There are dwarf apple trees espaliered against the fence, and one corner holds rhubarb. The paths are grass. There are two gates, one with an arbor over it with climbing roses and a clematis, the other just a basic gate that's convenient to the compost piles in one direction and the tool shed in the other. The patio holds another bench, some chairs, a small table under an umbrella for alfresco dining, a grill, and a fireplace. A plum and a cherry tree grow nearby.

I've been gardening this plot for nearly 20 years. It started very small. We moved into the house in May and by June I'd dug up some ground and planted tomatoes and herbs. The next year I doubled the size of the garden, and in year three I doubled it again. The fourth year I built the raised beds. In year five, we replaced the flimsy wire fencing with a real fence. Then came the refinements—the arbor, a bench, various structures for climbers. This year, I'll make a new cold frame before chilly weather arrives in fall, to replace the one that's falling apart.

Vegetables can't get any fresher than those picked right outside the kitchen door. My garden sits as close to the kitchen as possible and smack dab in my center of vision from the house. When it's too cold or too hot or too rainy or I'm too tired to work in the garden, I can sit indoors and observe my little agricultural enterprise.

I have never used pesticides in this garden, and yet I've never had many insect problems. Aphids attack my plum tree and roses, but ladybugs come to the rescue. Pretty soon the plum tree is crawling with ladybug larvae, chomping away on aphids. I let the cilantro go to flower so these beneficial insects have some nectar to feed on when they've polished off the aphids.

While there's definitely a low season, there's scarcely a time when I can't harvest something. I pick kale well into winter, and I dig leeks from fall through spring. And my cold frame keeps fall salad greens going well into December. From the season's earliest harvest (chives and mâche) to the last (kale and leeks), the garden is a joy.

I tell you all this to emphasize the points made in the pages that follow—that gardening is fun, not tedious, especially if you start small and add on as interest and knowledge increase; that your garden can easily look great, not just utilitarian; that using sustainable techniques really does work; and that even a small garden can make a big difference in your life and in your diet.

Gardening is a lesson in humility and in patience. Mixed in with the triumphs will be the occasional disaster. When that happens, just focus on what is doing great and ignore what is doing terribly. There's always next year.

—RUTH LIVELY

PART I
The Basics of Vegetable Gardening

CHAPTER 1
DESIGNING YOUR GARDEN

There are all kinds of vegetable gardens. They run the gamut from tiny to immense, basic to elaborate, rustic to fancy. Regardless of size and style, a well-tended plot full of healthy, productive plants is a thing of beauty. What's important is that your garden is right for you—the right size, the right style, filled with the right kinds of vegetables.

So, the first thing to do before buying seeds or digging in the soil is to think about what you want from your garden. Do you want to grow enough to supply the daily table during the gardening season or have extra for putting up? Do you want to grow just a few favorites so you can experience the joys of eating what you grow? Do you envision your garden as a place to relax, possibly to entertain, as well as a place to grow food? Do you want the vegetable garden be an attractive design feature on its own merits?

Besides having a vision of what you want your garden to produce, you also need to have realistic expectations of the work and money involved. Once the garden is established, how much time per week will you have to spend in it? Will anybody be helping you tend the garden? How much money do you have to spend? A garden of any kind is defined largely by budget and time, so if you don't have much of either, make a garden that is small and simple. As you gain experience, and as desire and need dictate, you can increase the size and make it more elaborate.

Let's start with practical considerations.

The design of this front yard garden is practical as well as beautiful. The layout makes space for vegetable beds to frame the rustic wooden fence, while paths leading to the front door surround raised beds and a chicken coop.

Texture and color add subtle design features to this garden, from the filmy carrot greens to the tall-growing corn and onions to the mounding lavender and sweet alyssum.

LOCATION, LOCATION, LOCATION

When choosing a site for your vegetable garden, you'll need to consider several factors.

Sun is probably the first consideration. Ideally, a vegetable garden wants 8 to 10 hours of sun a day. In truth, though, you can get by with much less (for more on that, see p. 107). Fruiting crops that depend on sugars to taste good—things like tomatoes and peppers, melons and winter squash—need maximum sun. If the only suitable spot gets just a few hours of sun, you will still be able to grow beautiful leaf and root crops, plus many herbs. If nearby trees on your property are casting shade on your ideal garden spot, limbing them up can dramatically improve the light situation underneath them.

Vegetables, herbs, and fruit trees are just outside the back door in this urban garden. A hose is just down the path, making watering easy.

Access to water is critical. Is there a hose spigot nearby? If not, you'll be limited to what you can keep going with a watering can. That will work for a collection of containers and possibly a small in-ground bed, but more than that and watering will become a tedious and easy-to-overlook chore.

Another practical consideration is proximity to a utility area. You'll need a place to keep tools—spade, shovel, garden fork, rake, and hand tools, at the very least. A garden cart or wheelbarrow will come in handy for hauling things in and out of the garden. If possible, you'll want to have a suitable spot for composting close by.

Level ground is ideal. If the site slopes, you'll need to manage erosion, either by using beds that are contoured to the terrain or terraced beds. You may need a fence to keep out animals or uninvited visitors. If your site is windy, a hedge or a solid or semisolid fence can act as a windbreak.

Will you garden in raised beds or in-ground beds? Which you choose should be dictated by your climate and soil. If summers tend to be dry and hot, in-ground beds are probably better. In the spring, the soil in raised beds heats up early and helps crops along, but come summer, the beds will drain quickly and overheat. If your summers are moderate in temperature and not overly dry and your soil is heavy clay, raised beds will definitely help you get better soil quickly. However, they take work and can be expensive to construct. A note as you plan: You can always add raised beds later.

The closer to the house, the better

Having said all this, there's another important factor in choosing a location—proximity to the house. The old adage "out of sight, out of mind" explains one of the main reasons many gardeners suffer some degree of disappointment. Putting a vegetable garden behind the garage, around the corner, behind a fence, or in some other obscure spot almost guarantees unsatisfactory yields or compromised quality. Problems that go unseen for just a short time—like insects, diseases, weeds, lack of water, foraging wildlife, and even your own pet—can wreak havoc on your best intentions.

It's true that gardeners who keep their plots in a visible location get higher yields of top-notch vegetables than those who, either intentionally or inadvertently, hide their garden. Perhaps it's a matter of pride—the desire to excel and perhaps a little friendly competition with other gardeners—that makes highly visible gardens successful and productive. Perhaps it's simply because the proximity of the garden means the gardener spends more time in it. Having the garden near the house also makes it convenient to run out and harvest herbs and vegetables for the table, which, after all, is the whole point.

In addition to being visible, a vegetable garden should be an integral part of the home landscape. It should add to the appeal of the home and surrounding garden. Rather than just a place to till, hoe, and grow a few things, a vegetable garden should also encourage fun, relaxation, and family togetherness.

HOW BIG A GARDEN?

The size of your garden will be a function of the time, energy, and space you have available, as well as what you want to grow. Before you decide on size, think about what you want to eat. Make a list of vegetables and herbs you simply must grow, then look up their space requirements. If you have room for everything on your list, great. If

not, trim your expectations. If this is your first garden, you might be wise to start small and see how you like it. If you've got the space, you can always make next year's garden a little bigger.

If your garden isn't going to be a design feature in your landscape, once you've made these decisions you can pick up your spade and start digging. On the other hand, if you want your vegetable garden to be a special and beautiful space, you've got more planning to do. The fun is just beginning, and the only limit is your creativity.

Think before You Dig

- How many hours and dollars do I want to spend gardening?

- What do I really want to grow?

- Do I want enough produce to freeze, can, and preserve?

- How will I integrate my kitchen garden into the overall landscaping?

- What site makes the most sense in terms of appearance, sunshine, competing plantings, microclimates, and access to water and equipment?

- Do I need to fence the garden?

- Do I want raised beds or a garden at ground level?

AESTHETIC DECISIONS

Let your garden reflect your style, whether that is formal or informal, structured or natural, fancy or plain, traditional or quirky. If the garden will be visible from above, say from an upper-story window or a deck, incorporating a design will add interest. A formal layout of geometric patterns combined with permanent structures such as a fence and arbor and the sculptural effects of a few carefully placed perennial plantings can visually carry a garden through the winter months, making it a place of beauty even when there are no crops growing. Although more labor-intensive and costly upfront, a formal garden with hardscape elements will most certainly decrease your maintenance down the road and make it easier to keep the garden looking beautiful. Keep in mind that a garden of patterns doesn't necessarily have to be formal; just take a look at "A Garden in the Natural Style" on pp. 22–23.

If you like, include some feature areas in your design—a big pot of flowers, a birdbath, a gazing ball, a birdhouse, or a quirky scarecrow—as visual exclamation points. More than anything else in your garden, they can help define your style. Do you desire elegance and tradition? Build a tuteur and top it with a copper cap. If an element of fun and spontaneity is more your style, how about painting the fence pickets or the tomato stakes a variety of colors? Hang a wind chime in the garden so you can work to its

The owners accessorized their garden with a collection of birdhouses to invite nesting couples to start a family and feed their young on insects from the garden. The downward slanting fan of sharp objects keeps four-legged predators from reaching the houses.

gentle music. Put up a birdhouse or two—they will look nice and attract garden helpers who will consume insects for you. Be sure to include a place for a seat of some kind, so you can take a well-earned rest or simply sit and contemplate the results of your labors.

For more ideas on personalizing your garden, see "Designs to Inspire and Instruct" on pp. 14–33.

Later in this chapter are nine examples of beautiful gardens in various styles to help inspire you. Check around to see what's on view in your region or in the area where you're traveling. Many public gardens have display vegetable gardens. First, though, a little historical perspective is in order.

The gardener's style is evident from these two examples: A traditional-looking raised bed, woven from saplings and iron bands, and contemporary use of recycling painted oil drums for an urban garden.

Gardens with a four-square layout, like this reconstructed garden at The Ephrata Cloister in Pennsylvania, are simple in form but provide plenty of opportunity for originality and personality.

The four-square garden

The four-square garden is a simple design, as the most enduring designs often are: four raised vegetable beds surrounded by a perimeter herb bed, with a fence around the whole thing. The pleasures and virtues of the form include a dramatic architectural presence, a comforting sense of enclosure, and an efficient layout that facilitates planting and crop rotation. The garden's picket fence sets it apart as a destination. When you walk through a four-square, everything seems right and orderly, even on a bad-weed day. A four-square garden makes you wish the rest of your life were as well structured and under control.

The four-square garden was the preeminent kitchen-garden form of the American colonies, but its roots stretch back over centuries. The cloister garden of medieval European monasteries was the quintessential four-square. Bisecting paths represented the Christian cross, and at the center was a basin of holy water. Renaissance gardeners took the four-square design to new heights by using the form to create colossal pleasure grounds. The Italian villa gardens, in particular, set standards of excellence. Significantly, the laborers who worked in the cloister gardens or in the villa gardens brought the four-square design back home to their own vegetable patches.

When these European working-class gardeners came to the New World, they brought along their heirloom cabbage and turnip seeds, and planted them in four-square gardens, just as they had always done. In Lancaster County, Pennsylvania, the form flourished among the Amish and other Pennsylvania Germans.

A four-square garden retains its formal beauty year-round. This Pennsylvania German garden shows off its architectural bones even under snow.

From Europe to America, immigrants brought the four-square tradition with them. The reconstructed kitchen garden at The Ephrata Cloister in Pennsylvania looks much as it did in the 18th century.

The four-square garden began to disappear, though, early in the 20th century. One reason was that this design has always been best at taking advantage of small garden spaces, like those in crowded European villages. In America, we had room to spare. So square, raised beds were eventually replaced with long, flat rows. For contemporary gardeners faced with limited time and space, the traditional four-square garden still makes sense.

In a four-square, the center, where the two main paths cross, is the most important feature area. Traditional treatments include planting a yucca or a rosebush here, or putting up a martin house or a sundial. The center of the garden is also an ideal spot for a dipping cistern. Eighteenth-century gardeners stored rainwater in the garden in aboveground containers. This tradition can be recreated with something as simple as a whiskey barrel, surrounded by wooden buckets and gourd dippers, in a bed of herbs or flowers.

The midpoint of each perimeter herb bed is another ideal spot for a feature area. This is the place for a shaded bench under an arbor of pastel antique roses, a piece of sculpture, or an arrangement of your best potted herbs on a barrel pedestal or an étagère.

A 4-ft. picket fence is the classic enclosure for a four-square. Pointed pickets are historically correct, and in the early days, points were incorporated to keep roosters from perching on the fence to scan the garden for strawberries.

Two bisecting paths neatly divide this garden into four large beds for annual vegetables. The narrow outer beds are home to perennial herbs and flowers. The paths provide access to the beds and lead to feature areas: potted plants to the left, a barrel of manure tea to the right, a sitting bench straight ahead. At the center, a yucca awaits bloom time.

Simple elements allow for endless variation. This Pennsylvania German four-square garden features a martin house in place of the traditional yucca plant.

DESIGNS TO INSPIRE AND INSTRUCT

The nine case studies that follow present gardens of differing sizes and personal styles, in a variety of climates. Each can provide inspiration, both for overall design as well as for solutions to specific challenges. The main takeaway here is that a garden is personal, so let your own needs and wants drive what you create.

Formality and surprise in a four-square garden design

The owner of this Maine coastal garden is a professional gardener, which leaves her little time for working in her own plot. She needed a garden that would reflect her design capabilities, produce a summer's bounty of vegetables and herbs, and give her a place to experiment with new varieties. And the maintenance required had to be just two to three hours a week.

An alcove set in the perimeter bed opposite the main entrance is just the spot for a French antique iron bench, a resting place for a contemplative gardener and guests.

Four Views of the Garden's Form

FIELD VS. GROUND
A formal geometry borrowed from the classic four-square kitchen garden ensures the garden has a discernible pattern. The raised beds can be seen as solids, or field, and the paths as void, or ground. The center garden reads as a solid in plan, though in three-dimensional reality, it's so low it could be considered path, or ground. This ambiguity adds to the interest of the design.

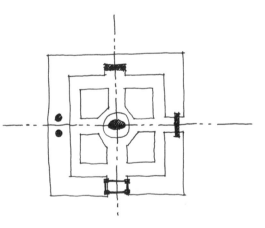

STRUCTURAL ELEMENTS
The formal geometry of the garden is reinforced not only by such hard features as the fence and the beds, but also by key plantings (most of them perennials) that mark corners, entries, and edges. With these stable elements holding down the visual fort, the annual plantings can vary, and plants can take on the rambling habits of a cottage garden, all without destroying the garden's essential form.

An archway marks the main entrance to the garden. Its ample depth gives visitors a sense of passing through an enclosure and into a room that's distinct from the world outside.

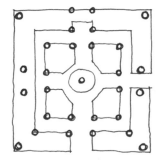

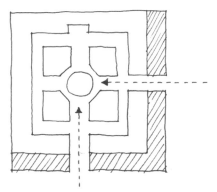

AXIS AND FOCAL POINT

The garden is laid out on two central axes that pass through an entry and cross at the center of the garden, each establishing a sight line. From the main archway entry, the primary axis ends at a wrought-iron bench, set in a break between two raised beds, suggesting a third entry. From the side entry gate, the secondary axis ends at two tall tomato tepees. The center garden prevents you from walking straight across the garden on axis, causing you to experience the garden as larger than it is.

ENCLOSURE AND ENTRY

The beds placed outside the fence on two sides of the garden room mark a break with the four-square tradition. These outer beds, filled mostly with tall plants, serve as a backdrop to the inner beds when seen from inside the garden. The tall plants in the outer beds also help conceal the garden from the outside, heightening its sense of enclosure. In addition, the outer beds combine with the inner perimeter beds to double the width of the archway and gateway, subtly enhancing your experience of the entries.

Raised beds are an integral part of the design. The four inner beds are just 10 in. high to help accentuate the 12-in.-high beds along the fence.

A fence reflects both the formality and the hidden pleasures of the garden as a room. Working with a local fence company, the author designed the scalloped pickets and the posts with colonial finials.

She wanted the clarity, planting coherence, ordered appearance, and ease of harvest and maintenance that a formal garden design offers. Yet she also loves the informality and spontaneity of the English cottage garden, with herbs and flowers that spill over walls and beds into pathways, softening hardscapes and fusing colors and textures.

In a break with the traditional four-square form, she added two long beds of perennials outside the fenced area. From inside the garden, these tall, colorful plantings form a backdrop for the mostly shorter edibles in the raised beds. From outside, the exterior beds help conceal the garden, providing a sense of enclosure and mystery and heightening the sense that you are entering a room when you enter the garden.

To achieve a cottage-garden effect, she planned ample space for flowers along with the food crops. The structures—raised beds, fence, gates, and arbor—allow her to let some of the plants run wild, all without diminishing the coherence of the garden.

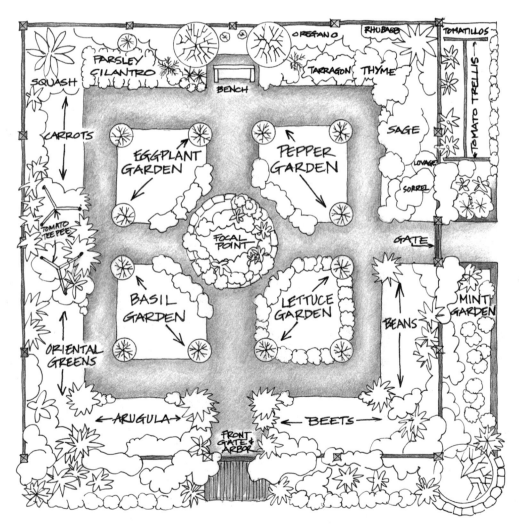

Planning Ahead

A detailed working plan drawn up before digging helps determine the form of the garden as well as the placement of the plantings.

Structures and exuberant plantings create a lush garden

This garden in a suburb of Portland, Oregon, is another variation on the traditional four-square style. Instead of rectangular beds in the quadrants, the owners designed L-shaped beds. And rather than a picket fence, an open hedge of upright, narrow arborvitae embraces the garden, giving it a feeling of seclusion. Otherwise, this garden has all the traditional four-square elements: a cruciform design, raised beds, perimeter beds, and ornamental features at the center and in the middle of each side.

The owners designed and built this garden themselves over a span of two years. In the first year, they dug the area (a former pasture) and put in the beds, a drip irrigation system, and gravel paths. In year two, they built the four arbors, one at the center of each side of the garden. Three of the arbors frame entryways and are planted with climbing roses and clematis. The fourth, which shelters a bench, is festooned with a climbing rose and wisteria, a mistake they regret because they wrangle with the rose every time they prune the wisteria. At one of the entry arbors there's an outdoor sink, which is a handy place for working and a wash-up area for vegetables. Trellises crafted of copper plumbing pipe, which provide permanent support for climbing crops, are easily picked up and moved from bed to bed as crops rotate.

The outer beds hold taller plantings, including corn and, on the copper trellises, pole beans, peas, and cucumbers, plus fragrant sweet peas and bright morning glories. Also in the outer beds are blueberry and currant bushes. They plant tomatoes, eggplants, and all forms of peppers in the middle rank of beds, using a four-year crop rotation. Two of the innermost beds are home for perennial herbs, and two hold annual herbs and lettuce.

As in the garden on pp. 14–17, the formal layout serves as a perfect foil for luxuriously bountiful plantings. Plants billow into the paths, softening the straight lines of the beds, but there remains always a sense of order.

Rose-covered arbors frame each of the entryways to the garden, softening the strict formal lines and lending an air of romance and generosity.

The first year, the couple built raised beds, laid irrigation lines, and put down gravel paths. The next year, they added the arbors.

The pea trellis, fully strung, looks ready to make music. The gardeners made several such trellises from copper plumbing pipe, in different sizes and shapes. The trellises can be moved from spot to spot.

Site Plan

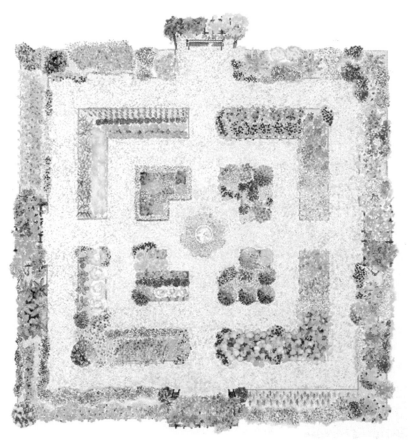

Having the garden next to the house encourages the gardener to monitor the health and progress of his plants. This garden began with raised beds, and then the deck started to grow around them. The result is a neat, productive garden with almost no weeds.

A deck garden close to home

By placing his garden as close to the house as possible, this horticulture-professor gardener created a deck garden that he can easily maintain during the hot Texas summer. He began by building a raised-bed garden just outside the house. Then, bit by bit, he created a deck surrounding the beds, using a mix of surfaces for interest—wood, brick, and bark mulch. He varied the direction that the decking and bricks run and included a few diagonal lines to keep things from being boring. The deck eliminated the need to weed, edge, and mow the spaces between the beds.

In Texas, gardens depend on frequent irrigation. But in this area, the local groundwater is high in sodium, which eventually can build up in the soil, causing plants to turn sickly and yellow. The owner designed a system that collects and stores rainwater from the house roof, and at the turn of a faucet, sends it to the garden via a drip system. A small electric pump supplies water to all the beds through a network of 1/2-in. PVC pipe and T-tape. Each box has its own valve, so it's easy to tailor the watering to the needs of each crop.

Roof runoff is a valuable resource that homeowners should take advantage of, and it's not hard to set up a collection system. In this garden, a large tank is positioned under a downspout that drains half the roof. A fine-mesh fiberglass screen filters debris from the runoff and excludes mosquitoes. The original translucent 250-gal. fiberglass tank wasn't big enough and encouraged algae growth inside the tank, so the homeowner replaced it with a true cistern. The 800-gal. cylindrical steel tank holds plenty of water, and because it's opaque, there's no algae problem.

Rainfall of 1 in. easily fills the cistern. When it doesn't rain, a garden hose is used to fill the cistern with groundwater. On the bright side, because the soil in the beds is so porous, excess salts leach out readily. A float valve inside the top of the cistern lets the gardener leave the faucet open with a hose leading into the cistern. When the water level drops, the float valve opens and the cistern fills automatically.

Not only has the cistern made watering simpler, more resource-efficient, and cleaner, but it also has eased plant-feeding chores. The homeowner simply adds 1/2 cup of a balanced soluble fertilizer to the tank every couple of weeks. When he turns the system on, his plants get the nutrients they need to ensure healthy, vigorous growth.

The owner leaves a different box unplanted each year and uses it for in-situ composting, adding plant material throughout the season. Every couple of weeks, he turns it in with a mini-tiller.

With a gas grill and outdoor cooking station at hand, the deck garden has become an extension of the house—and an important part of the owner's lives.

The compost bin is always nearby. Each year the homeowner improves the soil of one bed by using it as a compost pile.

A cistern collects and stores rainwater. The tank is connected to a drip irrigation system that carries the water directly to the garden beds. Nourishing the plants is easy, as soluble fertilizer is added to the tank every so often. The original fiberglass tank shown here has been replaced with a steel cistern.

Not only are the pathways maintenance-free, but the homeowner used three materials—decking, bricks, and wood chips—and varied the angles and levels of the walkways.

A garden in the natural style

The owners of this garden, on an island off the coast of Maine, contend with heavy soil, a short growing season, and strong prevailing ocean winds. To create a snug microclimate, they planted two rows of raspberries on one side of the garden area and roses and lavender on the other. These mini-hedges create a sheltered space for the vegetables. Copious amounts of homemade compost each year have transformed the native soil into a fertile platform for a healthy garden. In fall, they apply an over-wintering mulch of rinsed seaweed, hauled from the shore.

The seaweed adds nutrients and protects the hard-won fertile soil from erosion by wind and rain.

In the center of the garden, four raised beds shaped like wedges of pie and filled with alpine strawberries form a circle. From there, brick paths stretch from the heart of the garden outward, dividing other raised beds. Over time, the original rectangular beds have given way to a sprawling, natural-style garden that follows the gentle contours of the site. Below a retaining wall of local granite is more garden space.

The original rectangular wood-framed beds gave way to a natural style. Now the garden sits lightly on the land, flowing in and out of its contours.

The heart of the garden holds four beds of alpine strawberries. From there, brick paths extend out-ward, defining more raised beds.

The gardeners follow no-till practices. To loosen the soil before planting, they simply drive in the tines of a garden fork and wiggle them back and forth. Year-round mulching keeps weeds suppressed.

This garden fits its location on an island in Maine beautifully. A hedge of rugosa roses buffers the prevailing winds. A retaining wall of local granite and a rustic bough tepee are right at home.

Site Plan

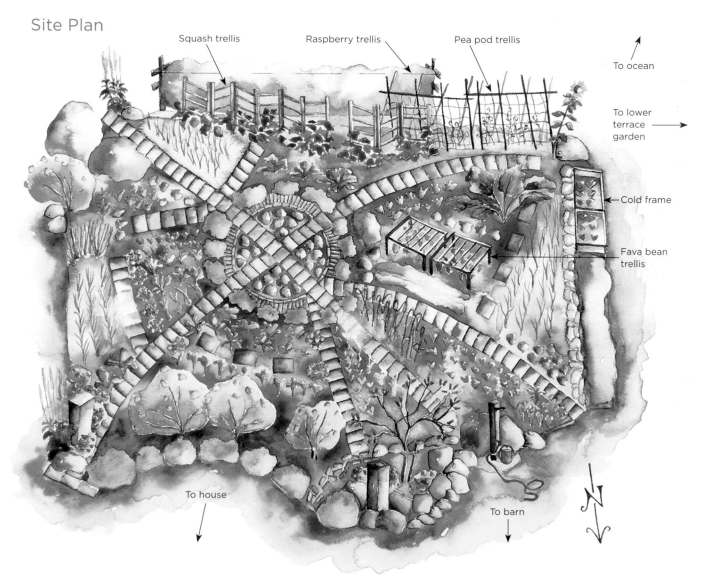

Squash trellis

Raspberry trellis

Pea pod trellis

To ocean

To lower terrace garden

Cold frame

Fava bean trellis

To house

To barn

N

Rooftop refuge in the asphalt jungle

This New York City rooftop garden is testament to two truths: You can garden almost anywhere, and you don't have to spend much money to have something visually delightful.

Splendor in the city. This rooftop garden is an exuberant blend of vegetables, herbs, and flowers. Old brick arches along one side of the rooftop provide an artful backdrop.

To turn an empty, sunny rooftop into her personal Eden, the gardener, an artist, became a scrounger. She raided her local nursery's dumpster for black plastic pots and discarded dirt. On the streets she found plenty of interesting objects to use as containers—an old sink; empty 5-gal. spackle buckets; discarded fan covers that, lined with moss, would become hanging baskets; and wooden wine crates. Spruced up and planted, her collection of found objects adds a unique beauty to her rooftop garden.

The first hurdle to rooftop gardening is access. Everything—pots, soil, benches, lumber—has to be carried up a flight of stairs and maneuvered out through a door with a 1-ft.-high sill that keeps rainwater from flooding the apartment. To minimize the burden on the roof, the gardener uses a lightweight soil mix—equal parts topsoil, peat moss, dehydrated cow manure, and vermiculite. To distribute the weight of the pots, everything sits on boards or pieces of plywood. Boards laid in the pathways also provide something to walk on when the tar is hot and squishy in the summer. Plants growing in containers don't have access to the wealth of minerals in the ground, so every spring she refreshes the old medium by dumping it in a big mixing tub and adding new soil and amendments. She gets compost at a local community garden.

A garden this lush requires regular feeding to keep container plants growing strong. Once the season gets under way, the gardener applies Miracle-Gro® every two weeks.

Recycled cast-offs and thrift-store finds create a quirky, rustic charm. A plaster cupid hovers under the aegis of an iron votive wheel. The blue "medallion" is an old enameled pot lid, but the green wire settee was a real sacrifice—$20 at an antiques shop.

On a rooftop, where the microclimate features baking sun and drying wind, containers dry out even faster than on a patio. Daily watering is a necessity. Even on rainy days, she can't assume her plants are actually getting enough to drink, especially when their leaf canopies get large. Because nutrients are flushed out of a container at every watering, this gardener is diligent about feeding. She uses a time-release fertilizer when potting up, and during the growing season boosts the plants with liquid fertilizer every two weeks.

Throughout the garden, other people's castoffs have come to roost, creating an eclectic, quirky place of beauty and bounty.

The house salad, please. In spring, the gardener harvests lettuce, sorrel, spinach, herbs, scallions, and edible flowers.

A completely different style of city garden

This 1950s bungalow in Vancouver came with an ugly jungle for a backyard. When they had to replace the drainage system, the owners took the opportunity to excavate the entire landscape, a bold stroke that gave them a clean slate to design a new garden. A network of concrete paths forms the key element of the design. Placing concrete paths requires careful thought, because once they are poured, the layout is cast in stone—literally.

With the paths laid and new soil brought in, the next step was to add structures—an arbor, posts and wires on which to train espaliered fruit trees, and a tall wooden fence along the street side. They installed a ground-level deck in a protected corner under the dining room window and relocated a small greenhouse to a concrete pad. They also built another, larger lean-to greenhouse with the floor sunken 3 ft. below grade. A basement door opens into this new greenhouse, making it a cozy spot for breakfast on sunny winter mornings.

With the two greenhouses, there is plenty of room to start seedlings, overwinter tender fruit trees, and ripen heat-loving peppers and eggplants in the cool Pacific Northwest summers.

The homeowners created a beautiful, productive four-season garden with vegetables, herbs, and fruit.

A glass house showers plants with extra heat. The 6-ft. by 8-ft. greenhouse gives peppers a better chance to ripen in cool summers.

During renovation

A thoroughfare offers easy garden access. Concrete paths are easy to build and maintain, and prevent the soil from being compacted by foot traffic.

Site Plan

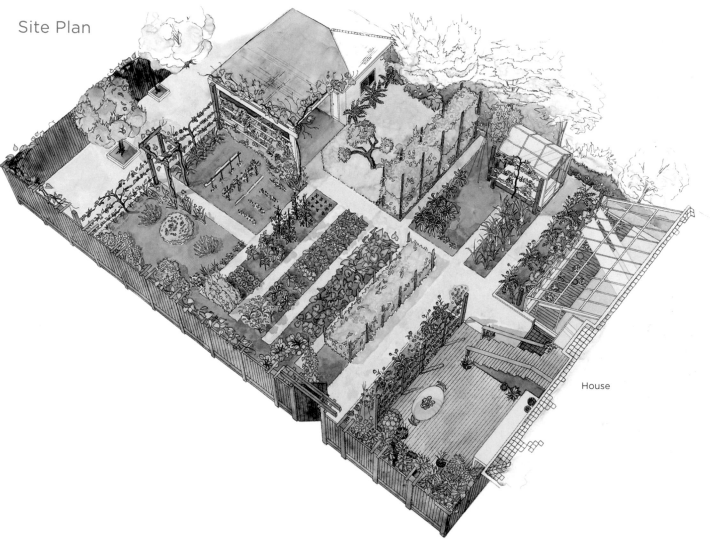

House

Building a garden around an existing shade tree

Geometric raised beds overflow with a riot of herbs, flowers, and vegetables in this Northern California garden. In the crook of the garden's arm stands a large California live oak, with outstretched limbs that spread shade over some of the garden beds. It's an integral part of the garden landscape, not an unappreciated neighbor, though when the garden was begun it would have been easier to cut the tree down and start from bare ground.

The design of this garden involved several important considerations. One was the size of the oak tree and the shade it throws. In the Northern California wine-country climate, certain plants, like lettuce and basil, benefit from some shade, so the homeowners planted shade lovers in beds northwest of the tree and full-sun lovers in the

Site Plan

To house

Oak tree

The garden gate leads to the kitchen door. Easy access from the kitchen is the result of deliberate design. In seconds, the cook can be in the garden picking peppers and curly parsley for dinner.

beds with little or no shade, those in the northern and eastern sections.

Another consideration was to maintain the health of the tree. California live oaks are susceptible to root pathogens when subjected to constant dampness. The pathogens lie dormant in the winter, when the region gets most of its rain, so typically they aren't a problem, unless an area has to be irrigated during the warmer months, as it does in a vegetable garden.

Since planting directly around the tree was ruled out, the owners circled it with a patio and took full advantage of its stateliness and shade. Another consideration was proximity of the vegetable garden to the kitchen door, allowing them to pick edibles at the last possible moment.

The L-shaped garden embraces the oak without encroaching upon it. Within the enclosed garden are raised beds, perimeter planters both inside and outside the fence, and potted bay trees. Adding an angle to some of the corners of the beds keeps them from looking utilitarian. Small ledges on the beds give a finished look and are great places to rest tools. In addition to the potted bay trees, artichokes, climbing roses, and lilies contribute important vertical elements, breaking up the horizontal nature of the garden.

Raised beds, pea gravel paths, and topiary bay trees in clay pots create a formal atmosphere. Pains were taken to work around the majestic California live oak. In the heat of summer, salad greens thrive in the shade cast by the great tree.

Tradition gets an update in the heart of Virginia's horse country

The combination of strong lines, octagonal shape, green textures, and brilliant colors—reds, purples, yellows, oranges, pinks, and whites—in this striking garden creates an impressionistic vision against lush, rolling hillsides where fox hunting and steeple chasing are still a part of life for many.

This is an eminently practical garden, thoughtfully put together with extra-high raised beds and paths wide enough for easy movement of wheelbarrows or other garden accoutrements. And it is chock-full of rich plantings destined for the table.

The original concept was a round garden defined by a picket fence. But round would have been prohibitively expensive, requiring bending wood for the fence. The gardener, working with a designer, settled on an octagonal shape because, "square would have been boring, the expected thing to do."

The site for the garden was originally a gently rolling sweep of lawn and walnut trees. To let in more sun, a few trees were removed. The area was graded, drain tiles installed, and landscape cloth laid down.

The picket fence, lined with wire mesh to keep out rabbits, supports vining crops and serves as a backdrop for flowers. Inside are a series of raised beds 2½ ft. high, perfect for preventing an aching back. They are laid out in rectangles and odd angles, contrasting with the curves of the terraced perennial garden that surrounds the gardener's 1731 log house. The raised beds are essentially open-bottomed boxes on legs driven into the earth like fence posts. Rubble and stone fill the bottom of the beds, with about 2 ft. of soil mixture on top. Bluestone covers the paths.

Outside the fence are inkberry hollies and rhubarb. Four tuteurs stand at symmetrical spots just outside the fence, which lets the gardener grow runner beans, moon-vines, and morning glories without casting shade on the

The high sides of the raised beds not only help to better visually separate them from each other and the paths in between but also help to make weeding less back-breaking.

Site Plan

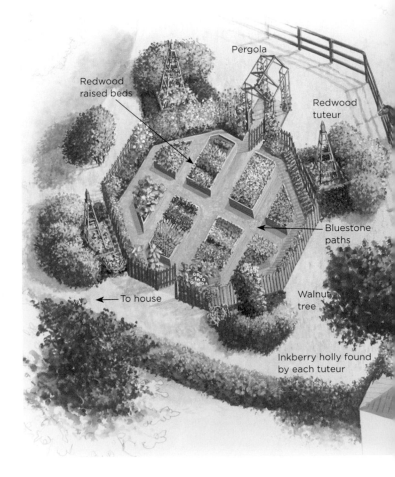

Pergola

Redwood raised beds

Redwood tuteur

Bluestone paths

To house

Walnut tree

Inkberry holly found by each tuteur

vegetables or taking up prime garden real estate. Pots and barrels—abundant in the owner's perennial gardens—spill over here with basil and rosemary. This garden is planted for cooking, fragrance, making arrangements for the house, and attracting birds, bees, and butterflies.

The garden's combination of beauty and practicality, of ornament and functionality, is firmly rooted in Virginia's history and tradition, dating back to plantation farming. Two of the best known gardens of this type can still be seen at George Washington's Mt. Vernon and Thomas Jefferson's Monticello below.

Tuteurs are graceful accents on four sides of the octagon and also free up space once claimed by sprawling plants inside the garden proper.

Thomas Jefferson's Ornamental Farm at Monticello

About 70 miles and two centuries away from the garden here lies Thomas Jefferson's Monticello. Jefferson's 1,000-ft.-long garden provided food for the family at Monticello, and during his presidency, for the White House dinner table as well.

Jefferson's goal at Monticello was a *ferme ornée,* or ornamental farm—a combination of beauty and function. He was engaged in every aspect of the effort, recording his successes, failures, thoughts, and plans with enthusiasm and meticulous detail. He terraced his vegetable garden into the protected south side of the mountain and divided it into 24 growing plots, where he tried out more than 250 varieties of vegetables, documenting their performance every year in his quest "to select one or two of the best species or variety of every garden vegetable, and to reject all others."

An architect and lover of beauty, Jefferson designed a brick pavilion from which to admire his garden; planted cherry trees beside its long grass walk to add spring blossoms as well as shade; and set out rows of purple, white, and green broccoli for visual effect. He also devised an arbor entirely devoted to different shades of scarlet runner bean.

Jefferson left gardeners an inspiring legacy, not only in the deeds that created his ornamental farm but also in the words: "The greatest service which can be rendered any country is to add a useful plant to its culture."

Pest control is incorporated into the design of this garden. Practically invisible black netting keeps deer out of the garden and birds out of the blueberries.

Deer control was a primary concern, and fencing the property was the only answer. They used a combination of 6-ft. fencing and inexpensive deer netting strung 7 ft. high. On the west side, to preserve sunset views, they installed lower fencing and topped it with netting and wires to keep deer out.

The cedar raised beds are two boards high. The gardener attached copper tape to the top of the lower board to exclude slugs. It's very effective, and it provides an attractive touch.

The weed barrier underlying the whole garden (except in the blueberry beds) completely eliminated moles, as well as major problems with existing perennial weeds. The solid fencing offers additional weed control by excluding

Pest control by design

The owner of this rural Oregon garden did constant battle with deer, slugs, moles, birds, and even her cat, who thinks a newly planted bed makes a great litter box. When she decided to relocate the vegetable garden to the back of her property, she designed the new garden to eliminate or minimize as many of her pest problems as possible. She also wanted the garden to be easy to care for, and, perhaps most important, attractive enough to lure her out to the "back forty," and to hold her there with its beauty.

The gardener and her husband got a neighbor to clear the area with a tractor and then hired someone to till and level it. They then covered the entire space with professional-grade weed barrier, built the new beds on top of this surface, and filled them with a mixture of purchased topsoil and mushroom compost.

Copper tape placed along the tops of the lower boards of the raised beds is effective at keeping slugs out. To prevent them from crawling in on overhanging foliage, the gardener doesn't let plants grow into the paths.

much of the seed that would otherwise blow over from the neighboring Christmas tree farm. The new gravel paths are less hospitable to weeds than her former bark mulch paths.

Bird netting draped over trellises keeps birds out of the blueberries. Netting stretched over newly planted beds keeps both birds and cat out. When seedlings are a few inches high, the netting comes off.

Because some of the structures in the vegetable garden would be visible from a Japanese-influenced area of their property, they included several Asian-style features in the design. They made bean and raspberry trellises out of wood and bamboo (see "A Simple Yet Elegant Bamboo Trellis" on p. 62), and they built torii-style tops for the gate posts and the blueberry trellises.

Bird netting draped over newly planted beds keeps cats and birds from scratching around. A stick in the center holds the netting above emerging seedlings.

A Well-Protected Garden

When the blueberries start to ripen, the trellises above them are draped with netting to keep out birds.

A 4-ft.-high solid fence excludes small animals but doesn't block the view of lovely sunsets.

The gardener tested two methods of deer control. Black netting suspended from a wire hangs behind the fence and the gate. On this half are several strands of nylon fishing line. Both are effective.

Throughout, Asian-influenced design elements in the wooden structures visually tie the kitchen garden to the Japanese garden nearby.

Twin bamboo trellises flanking a dwarf cherry anchor the north end of the garden. Four dwarf apple trees grow just inside the fence.

CHAPTER 2
STRUCTURES AND HARDSCAPE

Structures and hardscape—those manmade elements in the garden—serve dual purposes. At their most basic, they are practical solutions to a need or a problem—a frame to hold soil for a raised bed, a trellis to support climbing plants, a simple enclosure to keep out rabbits, a gravel path to keep you out of the mud while you work. But they also are part of the garden's design, simply because you can see them. So it's worthwhile paying attention to form as well as function.

Whether you do the building yourself or hire the work out, these are probably the most expensive parts of the garden. Hardscape features in particular—those more or less permanent things like paved pathways, walls, fences, arbors—tend to be costly. But the money spent pays dividends for years in reduced maintenance, and well-designed, well-made structures make your garden look great.

RAISED BEDS

Gardening in raised beds can put you on the fast track to solving several garden problems, from terrible soil (or no soil), to minimizing irrigation and protecting your plants (and soil) from the ravages of pets and toddlers. In short, raised beds let you grow more food from better soil in less space and with less water. They also can enhance your garden design by defining the space.

The trellis at the back of the garden provides climbing vegetables with support, while the paver pathway makes negotiating a garden cart easy.

The raised beds in this Asian-influenced garden were designed for beauty and practicality.

The benefits of raised beds

By completely separating the growing areas from the paths, raised beds allow you to concentrate your soil improvement efforts where they do the most good. Any fertilizer, compost, and amendments you add stay right there in the same soil where your plants grow, instead of spilling out into the paths. It's the horticultural equivalent of all your charity dollars going directly where they're needed. If you have truly awful soil, you can fill your beds with purchased topsoil and compost and have a good garden the very first year. And if you don't step into the beds, the soil will remain fluffy and well aerated, allowing plant roots to grow freely.

The same efficiency applies to watering. If you use drip irrigation, soaker hoses, or a bubbler or soaker head on your hose, you can water only the beds, not the paths. The end result is you'll use less water.

You can custom design your beds to suit your site and your landscape. If your site slopes, terraced beds will give you a level gardening surface. If you want to sit on the edge of the bed, you might want to have a 6-in. board or "cap" around the edge to make sitting more comfortable. (This does make it just a bit more difficult to turn the soil, though.) In areas where gophers, voles, or moles are pests, you can tack hardware cloth across the bottom and several inches up the insides of wooden beds, giving your garden a gopher-free zone in one swoop. You can use beds to divide your garden into "rooms," sometimes quite formal in design.

Material options

Lumber is the most common material used for raised beds. Brick or stone beds are more expensive and labor intensive to install, but they last a lifetime if well built, and they can be used to retain small slopes. You can even make unconstructed raised beds simply by raising the level of the soil, shaping it into a flat-topped mound with sloping sides. The advantage to this system is it's free; the disadvantage is that the beds need reshaping every season. However, if your soil is in pretty good shape and you only want to raise it a few inches, unconstructed beds work well. By keeping the layout of the beds the same year to year, you can still reap the same benefits of focusing your soil-building activity.

Raised beds with trellising not only allows climbing plants multiple opportunities for a place to go but also means harvesting is easier on the back.

Lumber. Since you'll most likely choose to build your raised bed from lumber, it is wise to check into a native wood species whose heartwood is decay resistant. Black locust, red mulberry, osage orange, and Pacific yew show outstanding longevity, though none of these might be available where you live. Other highly rot-resistant species include catalpa, Arizona cypress, juniper, mesquite, and several species of the oak family, namely bur, chestnut, Gambel, and Oregon white. Call around to see what your lumberyards or home centers carry.

Once you've decided on your material, find out what dimensions it comes in. Most boards are sold in 8-ft. lengths, but 10-ft. and 12-ft. boards may also be available. Making the length of your beds the same as readily available lumber will result in a minimum of cutting and no waste—good for your pocketbook and the environment.

How Material Options Stack Up

These common options, all of which have many years of decay resistance, are worth investigating as raised bed material.

- ACQ® pressure-treated wood: ACQ is a water-based wood preservative. Nothing in ACQ is considered hazardous by the EPA, and no ingredient is a known or suspected carcinogen. Look for ACQ Type D with built-in water repellent, and buy only wood with a retention rate of 0.40 for ground contact. If you're interested in ACQ but can't find a source, ask your local lumberyard to start stocking it.

- Cypress: The longevity of first-growth cypress is comparable to pressure-treated wood; second-growth cypress is moderately decay resistant. Cypress grows in the southeastern United States, particularly along the coast, in wet, swampy conditions. A compound called cypressene gives the wood its admirable rot resistance. As with other durable species, look for heartwood. Not widely available outside its range; visit www.cypressinfo.org for more information.

- Redwood: Lasts for 15 to 25 years. Heartwood is where the rot-resistant compounds are concen-trated. Avoid construction common grade, which contains sapwood, and like any nondurable wood, will last only a few years with ground contact. Construction heartwood is primarily a product of young-growth timber, not old-growth "guilt wood."

- Trex®: This manufactured lumber product is made from waste hardwood fiber and reclaimed plastic grocery bags. It carries a 10-year warranty against decay, splintering, or cracking due to weather. Trex hasn't been on the market long enough to decay, but in accelerated-age tests it racked up an ex-pected life of at least 28 years. It has a dense, even texture and is heavier than wood. Hot weather compromises rigidity, due to a plastic content of about 50 percent and a lack of continuous wood fibers running the length of the boards. A company engineer recommends reinforcing the long sides of a raised bed by placing stakes every 2 ft. to 3 ft. to prevent bowing.

- Western red cedar: Lasts for 15 to 25 years. Knotty cedar is considerably less expensive than clear grade but quite suitable for garden use.

The width of your beds should be based on how far you can comfortably reach and work with your hands. Make them no wider than twice your comfortable reach. For most people, that's about 4 ft., providing you have access from both sides. You can make the sides of a 4-ft.-wide bed from 8-ft. boards with a single cut per board and no waste.

Height is more personal and depends on several considerations. First, in what position do you want to garden? Will you stand, kneel, or sit? Second, what is your soil like?

If it's really awful—compacted and full of debris, for example—you may want higher beds, which will give you a greater depth of really good soil. But higher beds will need more irrigation. If you want to sit comfortably on the edge of the bed to garden, make the beds 15 in. to 18 in. high and wide enough to perch on. If you don't want to sit down to garden, a depth of 8 in. to 10 in. will give you ample room for soil improvement. If your soil is pretty good and you just want to boost the drainage a little, 6 in. may be enough.

Building a Raised Bed Step-by-Step

1. To make the corner posts for your raised bed, measure and cut an 8-ft. 4×4 into four 24-in. lengths.

2. To make the long sides of the bed, nail or screw three 8-ft. 2×6s one at a time to two corner posts; you will have boards stacked three high. The bottom board should be flush with the bottom of the post while the top board should end approximately 7½ in. short of the top of the post. Repeat this step to form the second long side. Cut three more 2×6s in half so you have six 4-ft. 2×6s for the ends.

3. Stand the two lengths with posts up, parallel to each other, approximately 4 ft. apart. Nail or screw the 2×6 end pieces to the corner posts, three to each end. They should be aligned flush with the posts. Don't sink the 4×4s into the ground because they will rot faster.

4. If desired, staple a 4-ft. by 8-ft. piece of ½-in. hardware cloth across the bottom of the box. This allows drainage and root growth but keeps the critters out.

The final design will be a give and take between the lumber available and your needs. For a sit-on-the-edge bed, use three rows of 6-in.-wide boards or two rows of 8 in. wide. (Remember, actual lumber width is slightly narrower than the nominal width; a 2×6 is really only 5½ in. wide, for example.)

You'll need sturdy corner posts sizable enough to attach the boards to with screws. (Don't use nails; moist soil, especially when frozen, will put a lot of outward pressure on the boards and can push the nails out of the posts.) You can use either 2×2 or 4×4 stock for posts. The 4×4s will give you more room for fasteners; remember, you'll be drilling or nailing from two different directions. If you live in a mild climate where the ground doesn't freeze, you can get by without sinking the posts into the ground. Where the ground freezes hard, beds that aren't anchored are liable to shift around a bit over winter. This might not be a problem for you, but if keeping the beds in their proper places is critical, you'll want to anchor them by allowing the corner posts to extend 6 in. or so into the ground. The posts can extend above the bed, too, if you wish (this can be handy if you need to drape bird netting over the bed, for example), or simply cut them off flush.

If you live in a temperate climate and don't need to install corner posts for stability, consider creating a raised bed using interlocking mortise-and-tenon construction.

The 4-ft. width of the raised beds allows you to reach the center from either side.

Position the mortises a few inches from the ends of the board to prevent splitting. Mark a rectangle the correct size 3 in. to 4 in. in from the ends of the board and centered between the two edges of the board. To get rid of most of the wood inside the marked line, use a drill fitted with a large bit to bore numerous holes. Don't bore too close to the line, though. Then use a chisel to clean out the excess and square up the mortise. Use a saw to cut the tenons. Once you've tested and refined the fit, put the boards together and mark the hole for the pin on the tenon just where it protrudes from the mortised board. You'll want a snug fit. Disassemble the bed, and drill a ³/₄-in. hole for the pin. Make the pins from ³/₄-in. dowels.

White cedar planks are joined with mortises and tenons, held fast with wooden pins—easy to put together, solid, and elegant. This design works for beds that are no more than one board high.

This method works for beds that are only a single board high. No nails or screws are needed—just a mallet to bang in the wooden pins that lock the corners together. This method of construction is beautiful in its simplicity. The effect is a little rustic, perfect for a country garden or one in a historical setting.

To make the joinery, you cut a mortise (or slot) in either end of two boards that will form opposite sides of the bed. The other two boards get their ends shaped into tenons, which fit through the mortises. The mortise should measure the same width and half the height of the boards you're using. So, if your board is 1¹/₂ in. thick and 6 in. wide, your mortise should be 1¹/₂ in. wide by 3 in. long. (As noted previously, be sure to measure your boards, because lumber is typically narrower and thinner than its listed dimension: a 2×6 is 1¹/₂ in. by 5¹/₂ in.)

This bed was built right on top of exposed granite ledge. The property is on the site of an abandoned granite quarry, so usable stones were plentiful. The 8-in. concrete cap provides visual relief from the stone. Because the bed sits right on top of solid granite, crucial drainage is provided by a 4-in. drain set into the bed at the lowest corner of the underlying granite ledge.

This kitchen garden with gracefully curved stone beds fits the aesthetics of the landscape.

Stone. Stone beds are beautiful and can work well in urban and very rural settings. Typically in an urban location, space is limited, and you'll likely combine the raised bed with a patio, stone or brick walkway, or terracing. In very rural areas, stone looks very natural, so can help raised beds tie in to the surrounding environment.

Regardless of where you live, using stone or the like can be challenging in a number of ways. You'll need to make sure the stones are adequately secured so that they don't fall into the garden if you step or lean on them as you're tending your plants. Individual stones can also be heavy, and if you don't have enough flat stone, you'll need to bring it in.

Unlike lumber, stone offers an opportunity to add some natural design elements to your raised bed garden, including small sculpture. You can also enhance your stone raised bed by planting rock-climbing annuals and perennials, which will provide color and texture to the entire space.

PATHS

A path invites us into the garden, bestowing the freedom to wander and enjoy the results of our labors. On a more practical level, paths allow easy access for performing those labors. Pathways also define the style of a garden, creating a mood of formality or casualness, framing the plantings, and establishing viewpoints.

You have a lot of choice about how to treat the paths, whether you are gardening in traditional in-ground beds or in raised beds. The first decision is how wide to make the paths. Do you want to be able to maneuver a garden

In this garden, the structure of the paths and symmetry of the plantings are balanced by the informality of shimmering corn stalks, hot-colored dahlias, and rustic tepees wrapped in netting.

cart or wheelbarrow between the beds? If so, make them 3 ft. wide. If they will be grass, you'll need to get a mower in there as well. If space is limited, you can get by with narrower paths. A wheelbarrow needs about 18 in., but you'll need to take care when turning it. Paths 1 ft. wide give you room to walk and stand or squat.

Materials for paths

There are many options available as the base for a path, and choosing one depends on how the path will be used. Since some options are longer lasting than others, it's a good idea to think long term before making a decision.

Straw, bark, or pine needles. A path mulched with straw, bark, or pine needles works well, and any of these materials is inexpensive. While paths made from these materials will keep your feet clean, they will continue to be compacted as you walk on them. Narrow paths can be covered with boards, which will not only keep your feet dry and clean but will also prevent compaction. However, all of these path coverings provide places for soil pests like slugs and snails to hang out. You'll need to flip the boards from time to time to slow down decay and to keep them from cupping. If you're not using boards, you'll want to turn over the mulch occasionally to get rid of sneaky pests.

Grass. Grass paths are nice underfoot and pleasing to look at, but they require the same care as the rest of your lawn: mowing, edging, fertilizing, and weeding. This last chore is best done by hand because you should not use herbicides where you're growing food. Also, any plants spilling over the beds onto the path get in the way of mowing and trimming. Moreover, the spreading plant may eventually kill the grass underneath. If your garden is on a slight slope, grass can be a real plus; it won't go sliding downhill, as mulch or gravel would, and you don't have to worry about grading the area, as you do with paved paths.

Gravel. If you're going to edge your path with something that stands a bit higher than the ground, then gravel can be a good solution—if you choose the right kind of gravel. Crushed gravel packs together well enough to form a fairly stable path; unfortunately it's not very attractive. Pea gravel looks fantastic, but it doesn't pack down, which can create challenges. It can be difficult to keep in place, because it tends to pop into the beds. If pea gravel is more

Grass paths and wood edging help to keep this garden tidy. The paths are the width of the mower, so they can be cut in one pass.

Beware When Choosing Pea Gravel

While pea gravel makes a great-looking path, weeds sprout easily. The good news is they're easy to control. There are several methods to keep weed seedlings from growing through the gravel. One is to rake with the flat back of a metal garden rake to dislodge the seedlings; then simply pull them up and throw them in your compost pile. Another is to lay transparent plastic over sunny paths for a couple of hours to fry the unwanted plants. This works only in full sun. A gravel path is also an excellent place to use a propane-fired blowtorch weeder.

than a couple of inches deep, it's more effort to walk on it, and anything with wheels, like a garden cart or wheelbarrow, is apt to get bogged down in it.

➥ *For more on pea gravel, see the facing page.*

If your raised beds are framed with wood or masonry walls, then the beds themselves can provide the coping to contain the gravel. If your beds are unstructured, you'll need to use something—bricks, stones, plastic or metal edging, or boards set in the ground on edge—to keep the gravel in place.

Bricks, pavers, and flagstone. Paving the paths with something hard like brick or flagstone is the most permanent solution. You can set these materials right in the soil and let bits of grass, herbs, or small flowers come up in the cracks, which gives a charming, though somewhat

The brick path in this backyard garden is one of the only spaces without edible plants springing forth.

unkempt, look. For the most enduring paths, lay the material on a thick bed of stone dust. This solution is considerably more expensive than grass or mulch but results in beautiful, maintenance-free paths for years if the material is correctly installed.

Paved paths will warm up your garden, which could be either positive or negative, depending on your climate. If your summers get really hot, mulched or grass paths might be more comfortable for you. On the other hand, if your growing season tends to be cool, having paths that absorb and reflect the heat might be a good thing.

Bricks come in several different types, lots of different colors, and even different sizes. For a pathway, it's essential to use hard brick rather than the softer types made for indoors, especially if you're in an area where the ground freezes in winter. Before you make a big buy of bricks, you might want to bring home 20 or so to play with patterns. The most common patterns are basketweave, herringbone, or straight rows laid jack-on-jack or in a running bond (see the sidebar on p. 49). Keep in mind that

Beds are linked by gravel-filled pathways edged by boards. The paths are wide enough to allow a wheelbarrow to fit comfortably.

if you're using multiple shades of brick, the random mix of colors will tend to hide any pattern in the design. Cast concrete pavers come in a variety of shapes and colors. Some of them are hard to distinguish from real stone, except they have the advantage of being regular in shape, which makes them easy to work with. Flagstone is gorgeous but

expensive. Colors vary with the type of stone; go to the sales yard and see what appeals to you. You can also mix materials: a flagstone path lined with brick, for example.

Calculate your square footage (multiply length of path by width); if you have multiple paths that cross each other, be sure to count the area of each intersection only once. Buy 5 percent more paving material than is needed to cover your square footage. That will give you enough to make allowances for any that are imperfect or that break badly. If you run out and have to buy more brick or pavers, the color might not be exactly the same.

Here's an important tip: If you want to add plumbing to your garden, be sure to do it before laying the paths.

Building a stone-edged gravel path

A gravel path bordered by a cobblestone curb is adaptable to many garden styles and is relatively easy to build and maintain. This style works well in a formal geometric garden, but it can also be designed to wander with the landscape. The same style would work even in a rustic setting if you replaced the top couple of inches of gravel with bark chips.

To build this type of path, you begin by digging a shallow trench, lining it with weed-barrier fabric, then filling it with an inch of gravel. You then stand cobblestones on edge atop the gravel base layer, adding or subtracting gravel underneath until the cobblestones form a smooth, even line. Once the stones look good, you tamp soil behind the cobbles and fill the path with additional gravel until just a couple of inches of the stone project above the ground. For stability, the cobbles must be buried to approximately three-quarters of their depth.

Few special tools are needed, just a 4-ft. builder's level, a tape measure, stakes, and string. A sturdy wheelbarrow is a must for moving the gravel, and a pointed shovel is the best tool for digging into it. You'll also need a dirt rake for smoothing the gravel and for tamping and smoothing the

---

Estimating Quantities of Path Materials

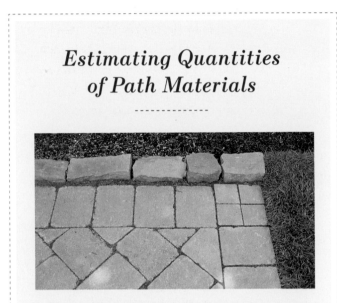

Before ordering materials for a paver walkway, take into account any design that might impact quantity.

Brick and pavers: Figure the square footage (length x width) of your paths.

Sand and gravel: Both are measured in cubic yards. To arrive at cubic yards, start by determining the square footage of your project. Next, divide that by 12, then multiply the result by the required depth of the material, in inches, to get the cubic footage. Divide the cubic footage by 27 to get cubic yardage.

Example: 3 ft. wide x 127 ft. long = 381 sq. ft.

381 sq. ft. / 12 = 31.75

(381 sq. ft. / 12) x 3.5 in. gravel = 112 cu. ft.

112 cu. ft. / 27 = 4.2 cu. yds. gravel

(381 sq. ft./12) x 2 in. sand = 63.5 cu. ft.

63.5 cu. ft./27 = 2.4 cu. yds. sand

Small beds are outlined with barely raised edging pavers, helping to keep the look of this garden informal while containing the pea gravel to the paths.

soil behind the cobbles. Building a path is labor intensive; getting help and pacing yourself will make the job manageable and enjoyable.

Select stone and gravel. Cobblestones can vary in size, but the ones used in this example—8 in. wide, 11 in. long, and 4 in. thick—are a good size for curbing. When shopping for stones, take a good look before you buy. The cobblestones should be very close to rectangular and of even thickness. If the cobbles vary a lot, they'll be hard to fit together and form into a smooth line.

The best gravel for covering the path is pea stone. The stones are about the size of jelly beans. Pea stone is the coarsest gravel that can be easily shoveled and shifted by hand, an important consideration when setting the cobblestones in place. The coarseness of the pea stone also gives the path texture, encourages drainage, and discourages weed growth. If you want, the top few inches of material can be different from the underlying pea stone foundation.

Since even a small project will need several tons of gravel, try to have it delivered close to the garden. If at all possible, dump the stone on a paved surface or on plywood sheets. A gravel pile dumped onto grass gets

Design Rules for Paths

Only a few basic rules pertain when designing a gravel path, but they're important. Ignoring them will make construction difficult and the path awkward to walk on.

- The path can go up or down a gentle slope with a rise or fall of up to 1 in. per foot. On a steeper slope, the gravel will shift and gradually work its way down hill. Steeper slopes are best handled either by creating level runs joined with steps, or by zigzagging across the slope's face.

- For easy walking, the path should be level from side to side. For the path to run across sloping ground, recontour the slope to create a level terrace for the pathway. Make the terrace wide enough to leave 6 in. of level ground outside the cobblestones before continuing up or down hill.

- Because cobblestones can't be cut to size, avoid designs for which the stones have to fit exactly into place. When the stones must fit against a fixed object, start at the fixed end and work away from it.

- Main paths should be at least 3 ft. wide between the outside edges of the cobblestones. If you want the paths to accommodate two people side by side, make them a minimum of 4 ft. wide. Side paths can be a little bit narrower, but try not to drop below 30 in. wide or you'll find them restricting.

- If you are going to finish the ends of the paths with cobbles laid straight across, the path will need to be an even number of stones wide, but a path doesn't have to end by being simply squared off. The stones can make a half circle or expand into a larger circle or square, creating an accent in the garden's design.

Building the Path from Start to Finish

Mark the path with stakes and string set 8 in. out to give yourself room to work. Dig the path 1 in. shallower than the height of the stones. Lay weed-barrier cloth in the bottom of the trench and cover with 1 in. of gravel. Place the stones, then backfill with soil along the outside. Fill the path with more gravel and rake smooth.

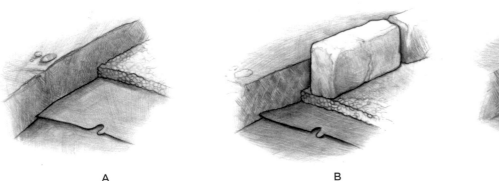

A
Lay weed-barrier cloth and 1 in. of gravel.

B
Put the stones in place, making sure they're even.

C
Fill the path with gravel and rake it smooth.

tangled in the lawn, making the last few inches nearly impossible to pick up. What gravel you do recover will be loaded with stems and dirt.

Lay out the path. Lay out the path with stakes and string or by laying lengths of wood lath (1-in. by 3-in. wood strips) on the ground. Using wood lath works especially well because it gives you a clear visual sense of how the finished path will appear. For a winding path, use lengths of garden hose to outline the path's edges.

If you find that the ground needs to be recontoured to keep the path level crosswise and only gently sloping over its length, now is the time to do your major earthmoving. This can be heavy work, but don't skimp on this step. Getting the ground properly contoured will make installing the cobblestones much easier, and the finished job will look better and be more comfortable to walk on.

Build the path. Once you have the ground contoured and the edges of the path outlined, hammer in a set of stakes 8 in. out from the edge of the path, and run a string taut

from stake to stake. This will give you a stable reference point for digging, since the inner stakes or hose will need to be removed for digging the trench. Excavate about 1 in. shallower than the width of the cobblestones; a 7-in.-deep trench would be right for 8-in.-wide stones (remember that the stones will be set on edge, so their width becomes their height). At this depth, with 1 in. of gravel underneath the cobblestones, the finished curb will be 2 in. higher than the ground. Determine the depth by laying a board across the width of the path and then measuring downward.

The width of the trench should be a couple inches wider on each side than the final width of the path. Digging the walls to 6 in. from stakes set 8 in. out will give you the extra width you need to place the stones and ensure that there is a full layer of gravel under them. As you dig, set aside the top couple of inches of soil to be used later as backfill against the outside of the stones (the rest of the soil is waste). It is best to do all trenching at one time; after that, cobbles and gravel can be installed a section at a time.

Once the trench is dug, pack down any loosened soil to prevent later settling. Then lay the weed-barrier fabric, making sure it completely covers the width of the trench. Next, spread a 1-in. layer of gravel on the fabric and rake it out level (see section A of the drawing on the facing page). Now you're finally ready to start laying the cobblestones.

Begin by placing four or five cobbles in a line down one side of the path. As you place each stone, wiggle it and press down. The stone will settle into the gravel an inch or so and become fairly fixed and stable. After you've set this first group of stones, step back and check their alignment. They should be even in height, a couple of inches above ground level, forming a straight line or smooth curve as needed, 8 in. in from the outer stakes (see section B of the drawing). Readjust the stones until they look right.

Continue setting stones down one side of the path, checking the alignment as you go, until you've gone 8 ft. to 10 ft. or you've come to an intersection. Now go back to the beginning of the path and start setting the opposite curb's stones in place. Use a level to make sure the new stones are set at the same height as the opposite curb. Use a tape measure to keep the width of the path even. For convenience, you can cut a length of lath the width of the path to use as a gauge. Make sure the stones on each side stay even with each other. If one curb is running a few inches longer than the other, you'll run into problems at intersections.

Because cobblestones are irregular, setting them and getting them to look right is more art than science. Trust your eye and readjust until everything looks right. For complex layouts, you should have all the cobblestones laid in place and adjusted before you backfill with soil and gravel.

Once you are satisfied with the layout of the stones, backfill the soil, packing it firmly behind the stones. After the backfill is in place, the only remaining step is to fill in the path itself with more gravel, raking it and the soil outside the curb to even up the exposure of the cobblestones (see section C of the drawing).

Neat, attractive brick paths are a highlight of this garden.

Creating a path from bricks, pavers, or flagstones

Installing a permanent path is a lot of work, but if you have a strong back and like to work with your hands, it can be a rewarding experience. Plus you'll save money by doing it yourself. And one of the best benefits is low maintenance. You'll only need to pull the occasional weeds and sweep some sand in the cracks in the spring to replace any lost to rains.

Good preparation is important. Successful installation of a dry-laid brick, paver, or flagstone path lies in proper preparation of the foundation. You could lay paving in sand right on top of level, compacted soil, but the path will become uneven relatively soon and weeds will be a bigger—and ongoing—problem.

Accurate measurement and attention to construction details are important as you work on the layers of the sandwich: subbase (the ground beneath the path), base (a layer of crushed rock), sand bed, and paving material. Just as important is the edging, which must be put in place around the perimeter of the paths before you begin paving. Dry-laid pavers will shift without an edging to contain them; consider brick, stone blocks, concrete curbs, boards, or strips of steel or PVC. If your raised beds are framed with wood or masonry, the beds themselves can serve as edging.

Cut bricks to size with a brick set and hammer.

Establish an elevation. Use a string level (also called a line level—a small level hooked onto a length of string) hung between stakes driven into either end of each path to mark out the elevation. Chances are your garden site isn't perfectly level. If not, you'll need to grade the path so it slopes evenly from the highest point to the lowest. Keep the string in place as you work, and check the distance frequently. Where the path ends meet another walking surface—lawn, patio or deck, or another walkway—you'll want them to be at the same level to avoid creating a hazard.

Ideally the bricks should be at grade level. Making a smooth transition from grass to path might require some creative finagling.

Excavate the paths to the necessary depth (the exact measurement will be a sum of the thickness of your paving material plus 2 in. of sand plus 3 in. to 4 in. of gravel), removing all the topsoil and getting them as level as possible. (Call the electric and water utility companies before you begin to be sure that your digging won't damage underground cables or pipes.)

Prepare the subbase. Put down a layer of heavy landscape fabric (to keep the gravel from being compressed into the soil), then add about 3 in. of crushed gravel and stone dust (called aggregate or hardpack). Spray the aggregate with water to keep dust down while you work. Level it as best you can with a rake, and then pound it with a tamper to compact it. If a hand tamper is too much work, you can rent a motorized plate compactor to do the

job quickly. A plate compactor is noisy (ear protection is a must) and heavy, but simple to operate. Run it over the surface twice in each direction to be sure the material is adequately compacted.

Repeat with a second layer of aggregate. It's important to get the subbase as level as possible (within 1/4 in.) because the paving will eventually settle to conform to the subbase's contours. The plate compactor will not radically change the level of the excavation, but it may cause some uneven settling. If you use this machine, check the grade again and add more gravel where necessary.

When you're satisfied with the gravel layer, add 2 in. of sand and run a screed over it to create a level bed. A screed

With the bricks in place, spread sand over top then sweep it into the crevices to ensure the path is firm under foot.

You'll almost certainly need to cut some of the paving material. You can use a common brick set or chisel. If you have a lot of cuts to make, consider renting a brick saw. A brick chisel creates a reasonably straight cut. To begin, position the brick for size and note the length needed with a scratch of the chisel. Then set the brick on a board (any firm, flat surface that can absorb a blow will do) and score a line all around with firm hammer blows on the chisel. Once the line is scored, continue tapping the chisel around the brick until it fractures cleanly.

Sweep in sand. The last step is easy: Sweep dry sand over the surface to fill in the gaps between the bricks or stones. If you've rented a plate compactor, you can run it over the sand-covered paths to firm up the sand, but this isn't necessary.

is a straightedge you make from a board (you can make it from a 2×4) notched at either end. When dragged over the sand, the screed leaves a level surface at the proper depth. You'll need smooth and level edges on either side of the excavated pathway for dragging the screed. You can create these by laying lengths of 1-in. pipe or 2×2s on either side. Whatever you use, be sure the pieces are level and at the proper height before you screed. Screed an area and move the pipes or 2×2s along as needed. Once the sand is screeded, you mustn't disturb it until you place the paving.

Lay the paving material. Starting at one end (it's a good idea to begin at the location that will be the most noticed), set your paving material in according to your chosen pattern (see the sidebar at right for options). Position the brick or paver or stone over the sand and then place it carefully, to keep the sand bed level. Pay attention to spacing; you'll want to keep it as even as possible (some materials have built-in spacers).

Pick Your Pattern

Below are the most common designs for brick pathways. You can choose one of these or combine two or more patterns to create a design unique to your garden. The jack-on-jack and running bond designs, if set lengthwise along the walkway, are very directional, so they lead the eye and make paths appear longer. Herringbone and basketweave patterns break up space and make paths appear shorter. You can use these patterns for other rectangular paving materials, too

Jack-on-jack   Running bond   Herringbone   Basketweave

Picket fences can be individualized in many different ways. The pickets in this one imitate birdhouses, with entry holes, perches, and roofs. The only thing missing is the rest of the birdhouse!

FENCES

Not every garden needs an enclosure, but if you need to keep out animals—be it deer, rabbits, the family dog, or uninvited two-legged visitors—a fence can do the job. Fences can also help to protect your plants from prevailing winds or to screen an eyesore. And of course they also can be primarily ornamental. What you're trying to accomplish will inform what kind of fence you install.

If all you need to do is keep the dog or the kids from running through your plants, or if you just like the idea of an enclosed garden, your options for fencing are wide open. Your limitations will be primarily those of what you like and what you want to spend. Wood picket fences offer an enormous range of styles, from historic (think Colonial, Federal, Victorian) to sedate to eclectic and just plain fun. Wood can also be combined with other fencing material, like wire.

A wood and wire fence combines good looks and practicality. The wire tends to disappear visually, giving the garden an open feel even though it's thoroughly enclosed.

Fencing against deer

The deer population in the United States is higher than ever; some biologists speculate that whitetail numbers exceed 20 million nationwide. The impact of deer on vegetable gardens and landscape plants is particularly severe in suburban areas where there is some woodland habitat and not enough deer hunting to keep numbers down. There are two styles of fencing that work, depending on how much of a problem you have.

For moderate to high foraging, the best solution is often a simple, one-strand electric fence. An electric fence is not a complete physical barrier; instead, it works through behavior modification, producing an electric shock that conditions animals to avoid the fence. To a deer, an electric fence is an unfamiliar object. A deer investigating the fence for the first time may touch it with its nose. If the deer receives a sufficient shock on this first encounter, it usually stays clear of the fence afterward.

To create a deer-proof electric fence, run a wire 4 ft. off the ground, supported every 10 ft. or 12 ft. with a post or on a tree. Electricity is supplied by a 6- or 12-volt battery- or solar-powered transformer that puts out high voltage at a low current. To attract deer to the fence, wrap adhesive tape around the wire in 3-in. sections at 2-ft. to 3-ft. intervals. Then coat the tape with peanut butter. Cover the bait with aluminum foil flaps, which make the fence highly visible. When a deer approaches the bait, it will touch the foil with its tongue. The resulting buzz of voltage will not hurt the deer, but it will teach it to stay away. An advantage to electric fencing is that it can be configured to keep out a variety of other garden raiders, such as rabbits, woodchucks, and raccoons, and it requires surprisingly little maintenance.

Children need to be warned of the uncomfortable consequences of touching an electrified fence. Contact with a live fence will cause a minor buzz of electricity but no damage. One solution is to turn the fence off during the day, when deer are less likely to forage. Pets quickly train themselves.

To keep the deer out, a combination of heavy fishing line (to the right of the birdhouse) and nylon netting (to the left) was hung between 8-ft. fence posts.

Before building an 8-ft. fence, check your local code to be sure such a height is allowed. There are various ways to arrive at an effective 8-ft. barrier. You can stack two 4-ft. widths of strong wire fencing. Use 12-ft.-high posts, and fit the bottom of the fence tightly against the ground, or deer will slink under it.

Another option is a webbed polypropylene fence, which is inexpensive and can be strung between posts or trees. It, too, should be 8 ft. high to keep the deer from leaping over it. The fencing comes in two weights; the heavier one is more suitable for deer. The lighter version works for deer as long as they sense its presence and don't try to jump through it. If you use the lightweight version, hang something reflective or light-colored on it—old compact disks, strips of aluminum foil, or strips of white cloth—so the deer see it's there. You should also be prepared to repair or replace sections of it.

A deer-excluding fence doesn't have to look utilitarian. If you already have a standard 4-ft. to 6-ft. fence in place, or if you like the look of that height but want to exclude deer, you can simply add a round of deer netting on top of an existing fence. If you're planning to install such a fence, plan to make the corner posts, and at least some in between on long runs, 8 ft. high. Then hang the necessary depth of netting from a sturdy wire, strung tautly from post to post. Attach the bottom of the netting to the top of the fence in the same way. One caveat: birds won't see the netting and so will try to fly through it. An alternative to the netting is to run multiple strands of heavy fishing line or wire from post to post, spaced 10 in. apart. This will keep out the deer but not hinder birds (see the photo on p. 51). You can deer-proof a gate in a similar manner. Hang a panel of netting from tall posts on either side of the gate, so the netting hangs down on the outside of the gate. Weight the netting with a length of wood. You can lift the netting to get through, but the deer cannot.

Fencing against rabbits and woodchucks

Rabbits and woodchucks, aka groundhogs, are both common suburban mammals, and cute ones, too—unless they're foraging in your garden. Rabbits can squeeze through amazingly small spaces, especially when they're wee bunnies. Woodchucks are known as one of the garden's biggest marauders. Protecting crops against these foes is a significant challenge.

Both are also diggers, especially woodchucks, so in addition to installing a fence, you'll need to make sure the barrier extends below ground. To make matters worse, woodchucks can climb fences.

It is possible to fence them out. The fencing should be at least 3 ft. tall and made of tight wire mesh, such as chicken wire, or special rabbit fencing that has spaces no more than 1 in. high. To guard against the animals tunneling under the fence, bury it in the ground a minimum of 1 ft. deep. An additional measure is to angle out a section

A good fence to protect gardens from woodchucks consists of a tight wire mesh at least 3 ft. tall. The top can be bent at a 45-degree angle away from the garden to deter climbers.

This arbor is anchored around the garden with 2×4 frames and lattice inserts. Wire-coated mesh also helps to keep out rabbits.

Fences for screening

To hide a bad view or to create a windbreak, you can use either a fence or well-placed plants such as evergreens or fast-growing vines. If you choose the planting approach, keep in mind that large plants like evergreens can compete with your vegetables for water and nutrients, and can block sunlight. To screen with fencing, you'll need something that is solid, or nearly so. If you want to block strong prevailing winds, an almost-solid fence is better than something truly solid, which can create areas of turbulence. Choose a design that leaves small spaces between boards or that is solid on the bottom and allows for air to flow at the top, like a solid fence topped with lattice panels.

Sometimes elegance is the best defense against ugliness. To distract the eye from an eyesore—in this case, a dilapidated greenhouse next door—a series of freestanding planters are each backed with a lattice panel constructed of wood and copper plumbing pipe. Between every two planters is a larger panel of the lattice. Fast-growing vines will make an effective screen. An edging of concrete pavers around each box gives a finished look.

of the underground portion of the fencing to create an L-shape. Curving the top of the fence outward will deter bold woodchuck climbers. Be aware, however, that these opportunists will seek out any weakness, such as a swinging gate or an overlooked chink in the wire, and gain entry, so you'll need to be vigilant.

Electric fences will provide the same or better protection but will require two strands of conductor, usually at 4 in. and 6 in. to 8 in. above ground. This configuration allows easy access to the garden and doesn't detract terribly from a garden's aesthetic quality.

Swelling fruits like these watermelons will need support on a trellis; an old T-shirt makes a perfect sling.

TEPEES, TUTEURS, TRELLISES, AND ARBORS

Structures add a lot of appeal to a garden, and they have plenty of virtues: They save space in the garden, make it easier to plant and harvest, and serve as decorative accents. Structures can define a garden as a room or even a series of rooms. The bigger your garden space, the more it will benefit from having some vertical elements, but even a small garden needs movable supports for growing climbing crops. Structures should be a primary consideration when you plan your garden. And when you can make them ornamental as well as practical, so much the better.

The first step in determining the size, number, and use of vertical structures is to develop a list of vegetables you want to grow and select those crops you feel will need support. Then consider what kind of support is best suited to the crop, taking into account growth habit, vigor, length of season, and ornamental value of the crops. For example, pole beans, Malabar spinach, and peas need moderate support. Beans and Malabar spinach climb by twining around something; they can climb almost anything: string, wire, laths and branches. Peas and cucumbers have thin tendrils that wrap around anything they touch; thin things like string, wire, or small branches work well. Plants with vigorous growth and heavy fruit— winter squash, melons, and gourds—need sturdy support. (The individual fruits of squash and melons will need support as well—slings made of netting or fabric—to prevent stems breaking under the weight.)

Not only does your structure need to be sturdy enough to support the intended crop, but it also needs to be firmly anchored in the ground. A breezy day can wreak havoc on a trellis or tepee that is inadequately stabilized. A stiff breeze or a sudden gust of wind can topple a bean-covered trellis if its base isn't firmly planted in the ground.

The versatile tepee

The typical tripod, known as a tepee, is relatively easy to build and will support a wide variety of vining plants. Tepees can range from the simplest of structures, used only for utilitarian purposes, to intricately composed designs. For elaborate structures, select a plant with only a moderate growth habit, so as not to completely hide the design. Vigorous plants with aggressive vines and large leaves will quickly shroud the architectural detail of a structure. They are better suited for simple, sturdy designs.

The legs of the tepee are the most important structural feature. They support and stabilize the entire vertical mass. The fewer the legs, the stronger each needs to be. Also make sure each leg is driven into the soil. This will ensure good stability throughout the season. You can expect a well-made tepee to keep its structural integrity for one to three years. The life of a larger tepee built of durable materials can be extended by repairing weathered lashing and less-durable components.

Materials are everywhere. Tepees can be made from a variety of materials, including items on hand and those collected locally. Commercial 2×2×10s work well for the simplest tepees, but they aren't very attractive. Natural materials, like sticks gathered from the woods or saplings cut from overgrown fields, are good. Materials for more delicate tepees are usually easier to find. Water sprouts, those vigorous shoots growing straight up from the trunk or main branches of fruit or flowering trees, work well because of their sturdy growth habit.

The use of bamboo for garden structures is almost unlimited. It's readily available in a variety of lengths

This tomato tripod is ornamental thanks to the border of marigolds.

from commercial suppliers. Red or white cedar poles also provide a pleasing natural appearance. They're available from specialty lumber suppliers in different lengths and diameters. They are very rot-resistant, which can extend the life of the structure for many years.

Whatever material you select for the structure, weave cut vines through it to soften the lines. You can use flexible pieces of grapevine, bittersweet, Virginia creeper, or rose canes. Remember that while functional, these structures can be a personal work of art. Imagination and vision are the most useful skills in building structures.

How to make a tepee. To make a tepee, place three or more stakes of similar size equidistant into the ground to form the outline of a circle. The diameter and length of the leg supports determines the overall height and strength of the tepee. Place the legs according to the following width to height ratio: For taller, heavier crops needing more support, use a ratio of 1 ft. to 1½ ft. or 2 ft. This means 1 ft. in distance between the legs for every 1½ ft. or 2 ft. in height. This makes for a very stable tepee.

You can use many variations in the width-to-height ratio. For a stronger vertical accent, use a ratio of 1 ft. to 3 ft. or 1 ft. to 4 ft. to create a narrower tepee. The ratio is often dictated by the site or the materials available for construction. After you determine the height and width, draw the tops of the supports together, one at a time, all overlapping in the same direction, and fasten them with earth-toned, natural-fiber string, bailer twine, or nursery sisal.

➥ For more information on tying together supports, see Lashing for Gardeners on pp. 60–61.

Elegant tuteurs

Tuteurs, multisided towers with flat, angled sides, are plant supports with Old-World style. They serve the same purpose as a tepee but are more refined and much longer lasting, 15 to 20 years if made from red cedar or heart

Two Easy-to-Build Tepees

To build these tepees, you'll need hand pruners, a handsaw, a shovel, a drill with a $3/32$-in. bit, a hammer, $2^3/4$-in. siding nails, twine, a tape measure, and a stepladder. It's best to build the structures in place, early in the season, when there is ample working room in the garden.

A word of caution: If the soil is wet, stand on planks or plywood while working to help prevent unnecessary soil compaction. Always loosen the soil near the base of the tepee with a digging fork or spade before adding plants.

FINE-SPIRALED TEPEE

The fine-textured spiral tepee is a favorite for less-vigorous vines. Because of the lightweight materials used, this tepee is short-lived, usually lasting one season. Use this structure for peas, half-runner beans, full-runner beans, and Malabar spinach. With these crops, architectural detail will be enhanced and not covered completely.

Materials
• 20 to 30 freshly cut water sprouts, 5 ft. to 6 ft. long
• Lightweight garden twine

1. Start by marking a circle in freshly prepared soil. The diameter of the circle will depend on the length of the water sprouts; keep in mind the desired width-to-height ratio. Push the butt ends of the longest and sturdiest water sprouts into the soil 8 in. to 10 in. deep and 8 in. apart in a circular pattern. The number will vary according to the width.

2. Add more sprouts until you have a full-looking tepee. Gather the tops together and tie them several inches below the juncture of all the sprouts.

3. To achieve the spiraling effect, attach a piece of twine at the base and spiral it around the tepee several times before reaching the top.

4. Adjust the twine, keeping it uniformly spaced from top to bottom. You may want to attach the twine to the sprouts temporarily at a few points to keep it from slipping as you create the permanent spiral.

5. Then attach long, thin sprouts, end to end, following the predetermined spiral created by the twine. Work your way to the top, tying each sprout to the vertical members and removing the twine as you go. Securing the spiraling sprout to each support member in a number of places will strengthen the entire structure.

6. Re-tie the tops securely with twine.

MODIFIED TRIPOD

The modified tripod uses decorative crossmembers for added sturdiness. This larger, more rugged design is perfect for crops with vigorous growth, bearing heavy fruit—winter squash, melons, gourds, pole limas, and cucumbers.

Materials
- 3 main support poles, about 3 in. by 10 ft.
- 9 cross members, 1½ in. to 2 in. by 4 ft.
- 9 cross members, 1 in. to 1½ in. by 3 ft.
- 9 cross members, ¾ in. to 1¼ in. by 2 ft.
- Bailer twine or nursery sisal
- 1 lb. 2¾-in. siding nails

1. Start by digging three holes in a triangular pattern for the main support members. Holes should be 12 in. deep and about 40 in. apart. Place the larger ends of the support poles in the holes and backfill. Do not firm the soil at this point. Allow the members to stand straight up before bringing the tops together.

2. Tie the three members together loosely about 12 in. to 18 in. from the top. Stand back and visually assess the basic form. Look at the structure from all angles, and make any necessary adjustments. When the structure is straight and the location is correct, bind the support members securely together and firm the soil at the base of each pole.

3. Then attach crossmembers to the main support poles. Either hold or tie crossmembers in place temporarily. Start with the larger diameter crossmembers at the base. Work toward the top, using the thinner-diameter materials.

4. Use three crossmembers per group and attach three separate groups of crossmembers, equally spaced on each side of the structure.

5. Drill a small pilot hole in each crossmember and nail the crossmembers to the support poles. Trim the crossmembers to the proper length. They will look best if allowed to hang 3 in. to 4 in. beyond the support members.

6. Put additional lashings at the top to visually balance the crossmembers.

Make a Tuteur

This tuteur was made from workshop scraps. Lower horizontals are slightly closer together than the upper horizontals for stability. Diagonal braces add strength and also give vines additional support as they ramble up the structure.

MATERIALS

- 24 linear ft. $^5/_4$ x 6-in. cedar or redwood (this is a couple of feet more than strictly necessary, to allow for error)
- $^5/_4$ x 8-in. x 8-in. cedar or redwood (for pyramid base)
- $^1/_2$ lb. 4d galvanized shingle nails
- Six 8d galvanized common box nails
- 18-in. x 20-in. piece copper flashing

CUT LIST

Legs
- Four, $1^1/_8$ in. x $1^1/_8$ in. x 7 ft.

Vertical braces
- Four, $1^1/_8$ in. x $1^1/_8$ in. x 6 ft. 4 in.

Horizontals
24 total, from top to bottom, in the following sizes:
- Four, $1^3/_8$ in. x $^1/_2$ in. x 10 in.
- Four, $1^3/_8$ in. x $^1/_2$ in. x 15 in.
- Four, $1^3/_8$ in. x $^1/_2$ in. x 20 in.
- Four, $1^3/_8$ in. x $^1/_2$ in. x 25 in.
- Four, $1^3/_8$ in. x $^1/_2$ in. x 29 in.
- Four, $1^3/_8$ in. x $^1/_2$ in. x 35 in.

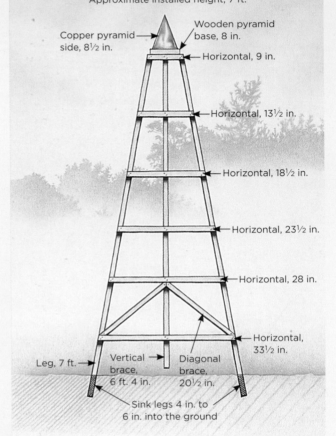

Approximate installed height, 7 ft.

Copper pyramid side, 8½ in.

Wooden pyramid base, 8 in.

Horizontal, 9 in.

Horizontal, 13½ in.

Horizontal, 18½ in.

Horizontal, 23½ in.

Horizontal, 28 in.

Horizontal, 33½ in.

Leg, 7 ft.

Vertical brace, 6 ft. 4 in.

Diagonal brace, 20½ in.

Sink legs 4 in. to 6 in. into the ground

Diagonal braces
- Eight, $1^3/_8$ in. x $^1/_2$ in. x 22 in. (lengths allow for approximately $^1/_2$-in. overhang on each end of the horizontals, to be trimmed once in place.)

redwood and about 5 to 8 years if made from white pine. Tuteurs are fun to make and they create unusual height and an interesting focus in any garden. Top it off with something ornamental—a copper pyramid, birdhouse, or fancy finial.

Tuteurs can have as few as three sides or up to six (more than that is overkill). If you have basic woodwork-ing skills you can easily make a simple tuteur from standard cedar or redwood lumber, flashing, and nails (see the drawing above). Take the time to mark the placement for the horizontal members carefully. Any that aren't parallel will be noticeable, at least until the whole tuteur is over-taken by plants.

Latticeworks of different heights and configurations make the garden feel like a series of rooms.

Trellises and ladders

Whereas tepees and tuteurs are designed to be viewed from all sides, trellises are more about offering one or sometimes two planes of climbing surface. Depending on its height and sturdiness, a trellis can support any kind of climbing crop. For a basic, workaday trellis, string a frame with twine or fill it with netting for peas, beans, cucumbers, and tomatoes. For an ornamental trellis, use something sturdy and pretty, like bamboo, reclaimed saplings, or copper pipe.

Wooden ladders, another kind of support panel for vegetables, can also be cobbled together pretty easily

and inexpensively. A series of ladders can function as a wall, fence, backdrop, shade structure, or focal point. A zigzag line of them makes a good tomato support. You can assemble a triangular tower using three ladders to corral vigorous squash, melon, and cucumber vines. Or attach panels of vinyl-coated fencing anchored around the top and bottom rungs to provide support for growing peas, runner beans, pole beans, and nasturtiums.

Bamboo. Bamboo is a wonderfully versatile building material and one of the world's most renewable resources. It's lightweight, strong, and flexible, and it looks at home in most gardening schemes, whether you live in town in a centuries-old home or in the suburb in a contemporary. Another plus is that bamboo can last 8 to 10 years before showing signs of deterioration.

One of the benefits of designing and building your own trellises is that you can determine their size and add whatever visual interest you desire. Bamboo can be mail-ordered in bulk to save money and to have extra on hand for other projects. With an investment of only a few hours and not much money, you can have a custom-made trellis for your garden.

Saplings and twigs. Trellises from natural materials work well in any landscape, since the supporting material comes from nature. Most any type of wood will work, so long as the branches are larger than about 1 in. in diameter. While spring tree pruning can offer an opportunity to reuse branches, look around you as well—scour your yard and woods for fallen branches. Gather more branches than you think you'll need, so that you have choices as you design and create your trellis. You can even strip the bark and sand the branches if you want a smoother look.

When using these materials, keep in mind that the structure will be rustic, so a few flaws are OK. Plus they will be covered by vines as your plants grow. And don't expect these types of structures to last for more than one season.

Lashing for Gardeners

While there are a lot of ways to tie some sticks together, a genuine lashing is more efficient, more fun to tie, and usually stronger than making it up as you go along. The methods shown here are based on those in Scouting handbooks.

For tying bamboo of a finger's thickness to a square wooden stake to serve as a tomato trellis, cotton or nylon string works fine. To lash together three stout saplings for a bean tepee, something on the order of thin clothesline works best.

Most of the lashings done by the book start and finish with a *clove hitch*, though a diagonal lashing starts with a *timber hitch*. Whether you're lashing big spars or little—the sticks you lash together are called spars—and whether you're lashing at right angles or on a diagonal, the key to a taut lashing is to make two or three or even four really tight turns, known as frapping turns, around the rope itself before tying off the lashing. Do not overlook the value of frapping turns; they are key to a good, sturdy lashing.

Allow about 1 yard of string or rope for each inch of the combined diameters of the spars you're lashing together. For lashing a roughly ¼-in.-dia. bamboo spar to a 1-in. by 2-in. wood spar, give yourself a good 6 ft.

The drawings here are based on the *Boy Scout Fieldbook* and on the 1968 edition of *Handbook of Knots & Splices*, by Charles E. Gibson.

1-2

3

CLOVE HITCH

1. Pass the rope around the spar and over itself.

2. Pass the rope a second time around the spar, below the first turn, then bring the rope under itself.

3. Push the loops close together and then pull hard on the rope ends to tighten.

1-2

3

TIMBER HITCH

1. Wrap the rope around the spar, then under itself and over, then pass the rope through the loop that has formed.

2. Twist the end of the rope a few times around the part of the rope to the front of the spar.

3. Push the timber hitch against the spar, then pull hard on the rope to tighten the hitch.

SQUARE LASHING

1. Start by tying a clove hitch to the vertical spar, just below where the horizontal spar will be.

2. Twist the end of the rope around the vertical part of the rope for a clean look, then wrap the rope around the horizontal and vertical spars, binding them together.

3. Continue by wrapping the rope three or four times around the vertical and horizontal spars.

4. Make two or three frapping turns between the spars, around the rope itself. Pull these frapping turns very taut. Finish by tying a clove hitch to the horizontal spar.

DIAGONAL LASHING

1. Start by tying a timber hitch around the crossing of the two spars.

2. Wrap the rope three times around the spars alongside the timber hitch, placing the rope turns side by side, not on top of each other.

3. Wrap the rope three more times around the spars, crosswise to the first turns. Be sure to pull each turn taut.

4. Make two or three frapping turns between the spars, around the rope itself. Pull these frapping turns very taut. Finish with a clove hitch tied around the most convenient spar.

TRIPOD LASHING

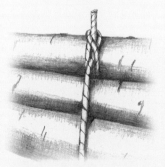

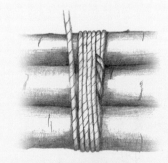

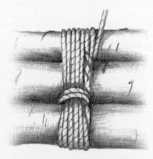

1. Place three spars side by side. Tie a clove hitch to an outside spar.

2. Wrap the rope, loosely, seven or eight times around the spars.

3. Next make two tight frapping turns between each of the spars, around the rope itself.

4. Finish with a clove hitch tied around an outside spar. Stand the spars upright and spread them apart to form a tripod.

Copper. Copper trellises provide great permanent supports for peas, cucumbers, and green beans and acquire a beautiful patina with age. You can move them easily around the garden from year to year.

These trellises are easy to make from copper plumbing pipe, which comes in ½-in. and ¾-in. sizes, with fittings to match. The ½-in. pipe is good for smaller trellises. When designing the trellises, keep in mind the available fittings are Ts, sleeves, and 45-degree and 90-degree angles. With these as the only limitations, you can create great works of art to support your vines.

Arbors are permanent

An arbor is ideal for framing an entrance, whether or not there is a fence, and if you've got a sitting area in your garden, an arbor makes for a shady spot to rest and enjoy the view.

A Simple Yet Elegant Bamboo Trellis

Function and beauty go hand in hand in this Asian-inspired bamboo trellis. The outer frame and diagonal support pieces in opposing corners are made from cedar. Bamboo stakes fill in the interior vertical and diagonal sections. The frames are designed to slip over the ends of 8-ft.-long wood-framed beds, and are attached to the beds with wood screws. The bottom horizontal section of the frame rests on the top of the bed and provides additional stability.

Prior to assembling the frame, pound in 2-in. finish nails at measured points along the top and bottom of the frame (and sides for the diagonals), leaving about 1 in. of nail projecting. Then assemble the frame, attaching the components with wood screws sunk through predrilled holes. The diagonal bamboo pieces are too short to have enough flex to go in later, so add them as you assemble the frame. After the frame is complete, the flexible bamboo uprights can be slipped easily onto the nail extensions.

This striking trellis supports heavy crops and provides easy access for harvest.

MATERIALS

• 5 cedar 2x2s, 8 ft.
• 12 bamboo stakes, 6 ft.
• Wood screws
• 2-in. finish nails

DETAIL

Nail

Bamboo slips over nail.

Cedar 2x2

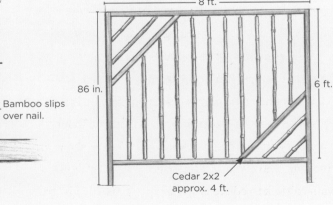

8 ft.

86 in.

6 ft.

Cedar 2x2 approx. 4 ft.

A copper pipe trellis supports sweet peas and is topped by a wooden finial. The curved top is made from pliable copper refrigerator pipe, shaped by hand.

While you'll want to be able to move your vining crops from bed to bed each year, an arbor gives you the opportunity to grow permanent climbers. Roses, clematis, wisteria, and honeysuckle are popular choices. You can make endless beautiful combinations of roses and clematis, and the flowers complement each other. (Don't pair roses with anything that needs lots of pruning, like wisteria, though, or the rose thorns will eat you alive.) Annual vines give you the option of changing the scene from year to year. The combination of morning glories and moonflowers is a classic; both open their blossoms for only a matter of hours each day, but between the two, you'll get a lovely show both morning and evening (and longer on cloudy days). If you want to stick to edible crops, grapes or hardy kiwifruit

are perennials; for an annual vine, plant runner beans for showy flowers and delicious harvests.

For arbor supports, use sturdy posts—4×4s or even 6×6s, if the arbor is especially large or carries a lot of weight on top. The top can be as simple as 2×4s running from side to side with small crosspieces on top, or as fanciful as your creativity and pocketbook allow. The sides can be left open or enclosed with crosspieces, lattice, or wire panels—whatever is suitable to the type of plant you want to grow.

Arbors can do more than give you a place to grow climbers. Set at a garden entry, an arbor is a prime spot to build in some simple bench seating. Just be sure to leave plenty of room to pass through with a garden cart or wheelbarrow. Elsewhere, arbors can shelter other conveniences, like a potting bench, or an outdoor sink. A plant-draped arbor isn't good over a grill, though—you'll sear your vines. For anything cooking related, a structure with a solid roof is a better choice.

Rustic benches on either side of this rose-covered arbor frame the garden and provide a peaceful resting spot.

One-Day Garden Bench

This trestle-style bench is an easy project that requires simple tooling. You could build it with hand tools, but that requires some skill and it certainly would take longer. Even a beginning woodworker can start this project in the morning and sit on the new bench by sundown.

Red cedar is an excellent decay-resistant wood species, but in some parts of the country it's often hard to come by and certainly not cheap. Shop around—you might find a great buy.

MATERIALS

- 4 vertical supports, 2x4 x 17 in.
- 4 horizontal supports, 2x4 x 16 in.
- 1 bottom stretcher, 2x4 x 43 in.
- 2 top stretchers, 2x2 x 43 in.
- 1 median seat support, 2x2 x 13 in.
- 5 seat slats, 5/4x4-in. deck lumber x 48 in.
- $1\frac{1}{4}$-in. and $2\frac{1}{2}$-in. outdoor wood screws

CUTTING THE PARTS

Cut the parts on a tablesaw outfitted with a dado head. You'll also need a sharp 1-in. chisel.

1. On the tablesaw or by hand, cut the vertical and horizontal supports from 2x4 cedar. You'll need four vertical members, each cut to 17 in., and four horizontal members cut to 16 in.

2. Cut the bottom stretcher from 2x4 lumber to a length of 43 in. The top stretchers can be cut to the same length from a 2x4 and then ripped in half to form two $1\frac{1}{2}$-in. sections. (Remember that a nominal 2x4 is actually $1\frac{1}{2}$ in. by $3\frac{1}{2}$ in.)

3. Cut the median seat support from either 2x2 or 2x4 lumber (ripped in half) to a length of 13 in.

4. Cut the seat slats to length from 5/4x4 deck lumber, or rip 5/4 boards to $3\frac{1}{2}$ in. wide and crosscut them to 48 in. long.

    Install a dado head in your table saw and allow for maximum width, since you will be cutting joints $3\frac{1}{2}$ in. wide. Raise the blade to a height of half the thickness of the vertical and horizontal members (approximately $\frac{3}{4}$ in., but measure to get a more accurate setting). Mark off the lap joints.

5. Make multiple passes over the blade with the horizontal members until you form a lap the width and half the thickness of the vertical members. A stop block installed on an auxiliary miter fence will help make consistently accurate cuts.

6. Cut the half lap in the vertical members in the same fashion.

7. Create the notches in the top horizontal stretchers with a handsaw. The notch is half the thickness of a nominal 2x2 (that is, $\frac{3}{4}$ in.).

8. Cut the tenon on the bottom stretcher with a handsaw (or a bandsaw, if you have one). The tenon is $1\frac{1}{2}$ in. long (the thickness of the 2x4 vertical member) and 1 in. thick.

9. Cut the angle on the top and bottom horizontal supports, either by hand or on the table saw. The

ASSEMBLING THE BENCH

It's a good idea to use glue in addition to screws to hold the parts together. Choose a good water-resistant PVA glue such as Titebond II™ or polyurethane glue.

1. Glue the half laps of the trestle supports (vertical and horizontal members) and reinforce with at least three $1\frac{1}{4}$-in. outdoor wood screws in each joint. Offset the screws for added support.

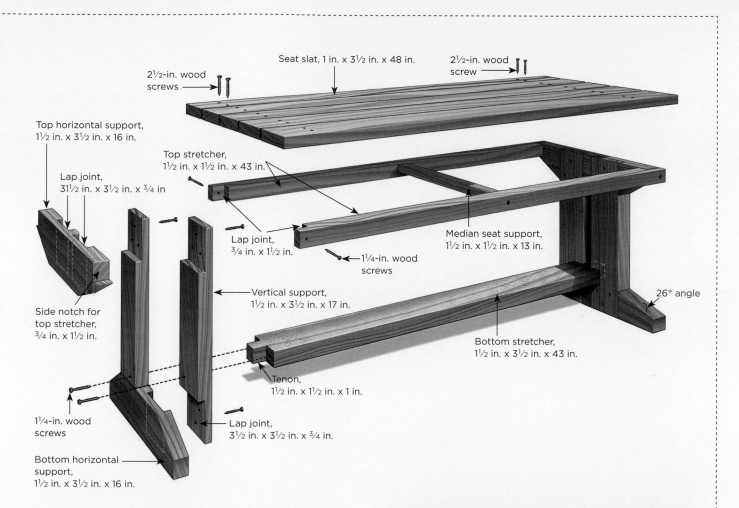

Seat slat, 1 in. x 3½ in. x 48 in.

2½-in. wood screws

2½-in. wood screw

Top horizontal support, 1½ in. x 3½ in. x 16 in.

Top stretcher, 1½ in. x 1½ in. x 43 in.

Lap joint, 31½ in. x 3½ in. x ¾ in

Lap joint, ¾ in. x 1½ in.

Median seat support, 1½ in. x 1½ in. x 13 in.

Side notch for top stretcher, ¾ in. x 1½ in.

1¼-in. wood screws

Vertical support, 1½ in. x 3½ in. x 17 in.

26° angle

1¼-in. wood screws

Tenon, 1½ in. x 1½ in. x 1 in.

Bottom stretcher, 1½ in. x 3½ in. x 43 in.

Bottom horizontal support, 1½ in. x 3½ in. x 16 in.

Lap joint, 3½ in. x 3½ in. x ¾ in.

2. Slip the tenon of the bottom stretcher between the two vertical members and install the two top stretchers in the notch created in the horizontal support. Glue and screw the top stretcher into the upper support (with a 1¼-in. outdoor wood screw). Drive screws through each vertical support into the shoulders of the bottom stretcher.

3. Install the median seat support between the two top stretchers and secure with a 2½-in. outdoor wood screw from each side.

4. Drill pilot holes and countersinks for two 2½-in. outdoor wood screws at either end of the five seat slats. Drive in the screws.

Most woods will weather to an attractive gray without any finish, and film finishes require a lot of maintenance. A coat of teak oil will give it some protection, if you prefer.

Simple construction and a minimum of materials make this bench quick to build and easy on your budget.

CHAPTER 3
GARDEN FUNDAMENTALS

The key to having a good garden is good soil, and to get good soil, you have to tend and nurture it. By deeply cultivating the soil and adding plenty of organic matter and natural fertilizers, you will increase the production of your garden. No matter whether your growing space is ample or in short supply, you can achieve good results.

BUILDING SOIL

Soil is a complex living environment, an ecology of fine rock particles, partially decomposed organic matter, roots, water, air, worms, minuscule soil creatures, and micro-organisms that are mostly benign.

Three kinds of minerals make up soil: sand, silt, and clay. Sand particles are between 2.0 mm and 0.05 mm in size, so large they don't retain water well. Sandy soils are easy to work and dig. They warm up quickly in the spring and dry out fast. They're generally low in nutrients.

Silt is composed of soil particles between 0.05 mm and 0.002 mm in size. And clay particles are so minute (less than 0.002 mm) that they pack together tightly, causing drainage and water infiltration problems. But clay soils are usually rich in nutrients.

The ideal loamy soil is a balance of sand and silt, with some clay and a lot of humus. Loam is porous and spongy, nearly perfect in texture. It makes a ball when squeezed but crumbles easily. Whether you're starting out with

glacial grit in northern Maine, sand in Arizona, or clay in Kansas, if you don't have the near-perfect texture, overall conditions can be improved by adding organic matter.

Dig the soil but don't turn it over

Soil is a vibrant ecosystem that suffers if it's exposed to too much light and air. If you're making a new bed in unbroken ground, use a spade to cut the edges. Then loosen the ground with a digging fork, thrusting it as deep into the soil as you can. Rock the handle back and forth to loosen

A bean tepee made from recycled tree dahlia (*Dahlia imperialis*) stalks proves that anything can be used to support edibles and ornamentals.

Before planting in spring you'll need to clean up your garden if you didn't get to it in the fall. Be sure to get rid of old plant matter, add compost, and top-dress the soil.

and lift the soil, but try not to turn the soil over. Just wiggle the fork around to make it easier for roots to penetrate. Deep cultivation will encourage roots to grow downward, allowing you to grow plants closer together and get more plants in the bed. If you can dig your bed only 6 in. or 8 in. deep the first year, don't worry. Earthworms and plant roots will penetrate even further, loosening the soil so you can dig a little deeper the following year.

If possible, don't use a rotary tiller to loosen the soil. Excessive mechanical tilling can destroy organic matter by overaerating the soil. It can also create a layer of compacted soil in the subsoil just below the depth where the blades reach. Roots will have a tough time growing down into such hard soil. Besides, tillers are tricky to maneuver in a small space. A better alternative to a rotary tiller is a specialized tool called a deep digger.

→ *For more information on tools, see p. 100.*

Break up soil clumps and rake out the grass. Use a cultivator or a rake to work over the bed, giving it a rough shape, breaking up clumps of soil, and pulling out grass as you go. A long-handled 3- or 4-tine cultivator does a good job and will allow you to reach to the middle of a 4-ft.-wide bed.

You'll need to loosen the soil and break up clumps each year in preparation for planting, but it doesn't take as much effort as it will the first year.

Feed the soil with organic matter

Now you begin to be a farmer of soil microorganisms. Your aim is to encourage as much life as possible. The bacteria, fungi, actinomycetes, and other organisms that inhabit your soil will convert the food that you give them (compost, manure, organic fertilizers, plant residues) into nutrients for your growing plants. As they release nutrients, these organisms are also creating humus (minuscule particles of decomposed organic matter) and binding soil particles into irregular clumps. Over time, the regular

There's no doubt that poor soil can benefit from organic matter, becoming "black gold," as evidenced by the soil on the right, which was amended with chicken manure, compost, and top soil.

addition of organic matter will improve the structure of your soil. It will help sandy soil hold water and nutrients longer, and will help clay soil drain faster and allow roots to penetrate more easily.

The first time you prepare a bed, add at least 3 in. of compost. That works out to about a cubic yard for every 100 sq. ft. You can use homemade compost, livestock manure, commercial compost, mushroom compost—whatever is cheap, abundant, and available. Since this initial amending will require a lot of matter, it pays to shop around for a material that you can get in bulk rather than bagged. Avoid sawdust, even the kind that has been dosed with chemical nitrogen. The high carbon content of wood products tends to reduce the availability of nitrogen in the soil. Check with local stables—horse manure is low in cost, high in organic matter, and decomposes quickly.

In following seasons you'll need to add only an inch or two of organic matter. Remember, however, that no two years are alike in weather or in the crops you choose to grow. So be adaptable and pay close attention to your soil. If it begins to lose its crumbly structure or gets hard or sticky, you can add organic matter in the spring and again in the fall. A warm summer combined with moderate watering and intensive planting can use up organic matter quickly. It's as though the soil were a furnace that you have to keep stoked with fuel. After a few years you will find yourself holding a handful of soil and watching it teem with life. Well-cared-for soil has an unmistakably whole-some, earthy smell.

Rake the manure out evenly over the bed and cut it into the top 3 in. to 4 in. of soil, using either the cultivator or the fork. If you use a digging fork, stir in the compost with a twisting motion. If you find it awkward to reach to the center of the bed with a fork, lay a board across the bed to give you a place to stand without compacting the soil. Finally, use a rake to blend the manure in evenly and shape the bed surface. Now you're ready to add fertilizer.

With a well-prepared bed, direct-sown seed has a better chance of germinating and producing.

Improve Your Soil Every Year

- Loosen the soil as deeply as you can, but don't turn it over.
- Break up clumps of soil.
- Add plenty of organic matter.
- Chop in nitrogen-rich fertilizer.
- Keep on the paths and out of the beds to avoid compacting the soil.

FERTILIZING

The three basic elements critical to plant health are nitrogen (N), phosphorus (P), and potassium (K). Nitrogen allows plants to produce the proteins needed to build living tissue for green stems, strong roots, and lots of leaves. Phosphorus helps move energy throughout the plant, especially important in maturing plants. Potassium aids plants in adapting sugars needed in growth and is especially helpful in root crops. Together, these three elements form that magic formula N-P-K, the backbone of all fertilizers, man-made or organic. Knowing the analysis of a fertilizer, its N-P-K formula, is important in determining how much of what element to apply.

One of the most important distinctions among fertilizers is how soluble they are, a concept critical to protecting groundwater.

Plants absorb oxygen, hydrogen, and carbon dioxide from the air. Fueled by sunlight, plants use these elements to manufacture carbohydrates through the process of photosynthesis. But that's just a part of what they need. In order to make vital proteins and amino acids, they require 13 other elements.

There are the primary nutrients (nitrogen, phosphorus, and potassium), the secondary nutrients (calcium, magnesium, and sulfur), and the micronutrients (zinc, iron, manganese, copper, boron, molybdenum, and chlorine). Each plays a vital role in plant growth, and if any one of them is deficient, the plants will suffer.

Nitrogen gets the most attention

Nitrogen is the fuel that makes plants go. It's used to synthesize amino acids, proteins, chlorophyll, nucleic acids, and enzymes. Plants need more nitrogen than any other element. It's the nutrient that most often needs to be applied.

The good news is that nitrogen is in plentiful supply in nature; it comprises 78 percent of the earth's atmosphere. The bad news is that plants cannot extract nitrogen from the air. In fact, whether in the air or in the soil, nitrogen cannot be absorbed by plants in its elemental form. For nitrogen to be absorbed by plant roots, it must be converted, or "fixed," into nitrates (NO_3) or ammonium (NH_4) ions.

That transformation occurs naturally in the nitrogen cycle. Some nitrogen is fixed in lightening strikes and delivered via rainfall. But most is converted from organic matter in the soil with the aid of microorganisms, which transform the nitrogen to nitrates. This transformation can be a slow process. But the richer the soil, the higher it is in organic matter and microorganisms, and the faster the nitrogen is made available.

Until about 100 years ago, this natural nitrogen cycle was the only way nitrogen was converted to nitrates. We farmed and gardened under the restrictions of time and nature and in harmony with the nitrogen cycle, applying manure and wastes and allowing them to break down over time, thus providing a steady stream of nitrogen. In those days, virtually all nitrogen fertilizers came from natural sources: manure, plant residue, and bone and blood meals.

That all began to change in the late 19th century, with a breakthrough discovery that nitrogen could be fixed artificially by combining atmospheric nitrogen with hydrogen to form ammonia. That ammonia could then be used to produce nitrates. The result? The nitrogen cycle was speeded up dramatically, and the synthetic fertilizer industry was born.

This breakthrough changed the way we looked at fertilizer. Unlike in natural fertilizers, the nitrogen in these synthetics was available to plants almost as soon as it hit the ground. We could practically watch the plants green-up and grow before our eyes. But there was, and is, a downside to these fast-acting, water-soluble synthetics. They are also very mobile in the soil. They can rapidly wash out of the reach of plant roots and into groundwater. So they must be used carefully and applied frequently. If you apply too much at one time, the excess nitrates can leach into groundwater and pose a health hazard; too little and plants suffer.

Phosphorus and potassium round out the big three nutrients

Phosphorus is second only to nitrogen in the amount required by plants. It is a vital element early in the season, as it stimulates early shoot growth and root formation. When phosphorus levels are low, plants grow slowly and may have poor fruit or seed development. Phosphorus is especially important in cool weather. That's why most starter fertilizer contains high amounts of it.

Vegetables can be easy and satisfying to grow if you prepare the soil well, fertilize carefully, sow the seed lavishly, and thin them conscientiously.

The problem with phosphorus is the opposite of that with nitrogen. Soils generally contain a good supply of it, but it is not readily available to plants. Phosphorus is extremely immobile in the soil. It does not travel in the soil solution, and plant roots must be in contact with phosphate ions to absorb them.

All phosphate fertilizers originate from phosphate rock, generally in the form of francolite. But in its natural form, it takes forever to become available in the soil. However, in 1842 it was found that treating phosphate rock with sulfuric acid would greatly speed the release of phosphorus. The result was superphosphate.

Superphosphate (0-20-0) is produced by reacting finely ground phosphate rock with sulfuric acid. Concentrated, or triple, superphosphate, containing as much as 45 percent phosphate, is formed if phosphoric acid is used.

Finely ground phosphate rock (0-30-0) is still used as a natural source of phosphorus, as are colloidal phosphate (0-20-0) and bone meal (0-12-0). They all release their nutrients very slowly. No matter what type of phosphate fertilizer you use, the key is location, location, location. Make sure to work the fertilizers into the root zone of the soil. Add the required amount of phosphorus in fall or early spring. Don't bother to side-dress during the year.

Applying a slow-release fertilizer in spring and fall keeps nutrients available.

Potassium fertilizer comes in several forms. Potassium chloride (0-0-60), also known as muriate of potash, is the most common. Derived from sylvanite ore, it is available to plants almost immediately. However, potassium chloride is rather acidifying, and some crops, notably beans, potatoes, and tomatoes, have a low tolerance to chlorides.

Potassium nitrate (13-0-45) is produced when potassium chloride reacts with nitric acid. Its advantage is that it does not acidify the soil and does provide nitrogen as well as potassium. However, it leaches from the soil rapidly. Sulfate of potash magnesia (0-0-21), sold as Sul-Po-Mag® or K-Mag®, is derived from the mineral langbeinite. It is in a form that is available to plants rapidly.

Potassium sulfate (0-0-50), another mined product, provides sulfur as well as potassium. Other common sources of potassium include greensand, from the mineral glauconite (0-0-6), wood ashes (0-0-10), and granite dust (0-0-7).

Small amounts of other elements aid plant growth

The secondary nutrients—calcium, magnesium, and sulfur—are not required in great quantities by plants and are often present in the soil in adequate amounts. Also, some nitrogen and phosphorus fertilizers contain small amounts.

Calcium must be present in plants for the construction of new cells, where it strengthens the walls and membranes. The soil usually has sufficient quantities, except in alkaline or very dry conditions. Calcium deficiencies show up as tip burn on young leaves, or abnormally green leaves. Limestone is a good source of calcium, as are calcium nitrate and superphosphate fertilizers.

Magnesium is an essential element in the process of photosynthesis. It may be deficient in sandy soils and it

If the soil is cold, use a liquid starter fertilizer containing ammonium phosphate. The nitrogen in the formula seems to make the phosphorus more readily available.

For more information on sidedressing, see p. 283.

Potassium, the third primary nutrient, also encourages root growth and helps plants resist disease. It helps increase the size of vegetables and improves cold hardiness. Signs of potassium deficiency include weak plants, slow growth, small or shriveled fruit, and leaf burning at the tips and margins. As with phosphorus, only about 1 percent of the soil potassium is available to plants.

will show in yellowing of leaves. Dolomitic limestone is a good source of magnesium. You can also provide magnesium with magnesium sulfate, epsom salts, and sulfate of potash magnesia (Sul-Po-Mag).

Sulfur is necessary for protein synthesis. Much of it is absorbed through the air and from the soil. When sulfur is deficient, plants are small and spindly, and the youngest leaves are light green to yellow. To supplement, apply Sul-Po-Mag, gypsum, or superphosphate.

An even smaller set of dietary elements also influences plant development. We call them micronutrients, and plants need only traces of them. For example, just ¾ oz. of 20 Mule Team® Borax, the laundry detergent, provides all the boron necessary for 100 square feet of garden.

Zinc, manganese, and copper contribute to the formation of enzymes and hormones in plants. Iron and chlorine are necessary for the formation of chlorophyll. Boron regulates the metabolism of carbohydrates in plants. Molybdenum helps convert nitrates to amino acids. Most of these micronutrients are available in chelated forms, formulas that dissolve easily, making them readily available. Properly fed soil with well-adjusted pH should require no added micronutrients.

➡ *For more information about pH, see p. 282.*

Though it's fine to add the three primary nutrients to your garden soil as a matter of course, the secondary and micronutrients should not be applied unless indicated by a soil test. Over-application may cause more harm than good by contributing to a mineral imbalance in the soil.

Organic or synthetic?

As all organic gardeners come to understand, organic fertilizer is bulky, occasionally inconvenient, sometimes sloppy, and often smelly. But it works as long as you don't expect instant results. If you're patient and have time to build up the soil, organic fertilizers pay dividends over the long run. If you work into the soil about 1 bushel of manure per 100 sq. ft. of garden early in the year, every year, you will be providing virtually all the nutrition most plants need. The residual organic matter means that the plants never starve, and you won't overfeed or underfeed.

However, we often don't have the luxury of time. Or after years of building the soil in our garden, we pull up stakes and move and must start all over again. Or the pepper plants lag just when the compost bin runs out, and you can't lay your hands on some mellow, aged manure.

Another approach is a compromise between strictly organic and synthetic. There are many gardeners who would never consider using just a touch of synthetic pesticide but who will occasionally supplement organic fertilizer with a synthetic pick-me-up. The important distinction is not whether a fertilizer is organic or synthetic but whether its nitrogen is water insoluble or water soluble. Water-insoluble nitrogen is released gradually for steady feeding, whereas water-soluble fertilizers are here today and gone tomorrow. Not only do you have to reapply them regularly but there is also a danger of harmful nitrates leaching into the groundwater.

Some of the newer synthetics mimic the slow-release quality of organics. Some, such as sulfur-coated

For more about calculating how much fertilizer you need, see p. 79.

You need to keep in mind the actual amount of the ingredients, not only to get the biggest bang for your buck but also to determine how much to apply to different crops. You want to avoid overdoing it with the fertilizer and risking groundwater contamination.

Organize the garden around feeding plants

Different plants have very different fertilizer requirements. Potatoes, for example, require about four times as much nitrogen and potash and twice as much phosphorus as beans. A 100-sq.-ft. patch of potatoes needs about $\frac{1}{2}$ lb. each of actual nitrogen, phosphorus, and potassium per year for good growth. That's about 5 lb. of a 10-10-10 fertilizer.

Root crops and leafy vegetables, such as lettuce, cabbage, and spinach, need about $\frac{1}{3}$ lb. of actual nitrogen, $\frac{1}{4}$ lb. of phosphorus, and $\frac{1}{3}$ to $\frac{1}{2}$ lb. of potash per 100 sq. ft. Fruit crops, such as tomatoes, cantaloupes, and peppers, need $\frac{1}{4}$ lb. of actual nitrogen and phosphorus and $\frac{1}{3}$ lb. of potash per 100 sq. ft., while legumes, such as beans and peas, require only $\frac{1}{10}$ lb. of nitrogen, phosphorus, and potash for the same amount of space.

Trying to meet the diverse needs of a whole garden full of crops could make your head spin. But there's an easy way to keep the meal plans straight. You can plant your garden primarily according to the feeding needs—basically the nitrogen requirements—of the plants. Here's how.

Potatoes, the heaviest feeders of all, get their own bed. Group the medium-feeding fruiting crops—tomatoes, peppers, melons, cucumbers—in another bed. Root crops get a bed, and so do the greens and legumes. This way, you can apply the same amount of fertilizer to a single bed, and know that every plant in it is getting the optimum amount of nutrition.

urea, come in a shell that breaks down to release the nutrients over time. Others, like isobutylene urea (IBDU) or methylene urea, contain nitrogen forms that are less water soluble, relying on temperature and microorganisms to release the nitrogen over time. They eliminate the need to constantly reapply fertilizer, but they offer none of the soil-building qualities of organics.

When shopping for fertilizers, read the label carefully. It will list the percentages of water-soluble and water-insoluble nitrogen. The bag, of course, will show the amount of other nutrients in percentages. A 100-lb. bag of 10-10-10 fertilizer has 10 lb. of each of the nutrients, with stabilizers making up the rest. If you need 20 lb. each of nitrogen, phosphorus, and potassium, you would need two bags of the fertilizer.

Potatoes require luxurious amounts of nutrients, but manure that isn't well-aged can promote disease problems.

A fertilizer doesn't have to be natural, but using it has to feel natural to you. That is, it must be in a form you feel comfortable with and one you will use faithfully because you need to feed. If you feed the plants properly, regardless of whether they're heirlooms or hybrids, they will reward you with a harvest that's everything you expected.

Fertilizer au naturel

Manure is gardener's gold. Whether it's from cows, horses, goats, rabbits, or birds, manure makes for good growing.

In addition to the three basic elements of nitrogen, phosphorus, and potassium, manure also contains large amounts of humus, a wonderful soil amendment. Humus is simply the bulky, fibrous material that comes from plant fibers and animal remains and is valuable in several ways: It gives better tilth to clay soils; supplies food for soil flora and fauna; preserves moisture during dry spells, while

assuring good drainage during wet times; and is a storehouse for nitrogen in the soil. In short, humus acts like a reservoir, allowing nutrients to work.

Manure quality will vary from farm to farm and from time to time, depending a great deal upon the amount and type of bedding collected with it. Testing manure may be the only way to determine for sure what its nutrient content actually is. So keep in mind that the references made here to nutrient levels in different kinds of manure serve as only a general guide.

All animals produce manure, but only livestock produce it in sufficient quantity and in a limited enough location to be of use to gardeners. And in case you're wondering, it's not a good idea to use manure from household animals like dogs and cats. Their feces are more likely to contain pathogens harmful to humans. Stick with the droppings from barnyard animals like those mentioned above. One note of caution: Individuals with compromised immune systems, such as those with the HIV infection, should talk with their doctors about eating food from gardens fertilized with manure.

Horse and cow manure is humus-rich. Because cows and horses are grazers, most of what they consume is in the form of roughage like grass or hay, which produces a bulky, humus-rich manure, but one with relatively low levels of the three essential elements. Cow manure, depending on bedding amounts, weighs in at a dismal 0.5 percent nitrogen, 0.5 percent phosphorus, and 0.5 percent potassium, low in all three elements. Be sure to cure cow manure by giving it plenty of time in your compost pile.

Horse manure usually scores slightly better in all categories with a 1.5–1.0–1.5 N-P-K rating and a shorter

Choosing Your Nitrogen Source

Not all sources of nitrogen are created equal. The synthetic sources of nitrogen carry a high percentage of the fertilizer and offer a quick boost to plants. But they do nothing to build the soil and may leach into groundwater. The organic sources contain less nitrogen but last longer and contribute to a healthy soil matrix.

Fertilizer	% Nitrogen	Tendency to Leach	Period of Availability in Soil*
NON-ORGANIC			
UREA	46	high	2 weeks
SULFUR-COATED UREA	38	moderate	6 months
UREAFORMALDEHYDE	38	moderate	3 months
AMMONIUM NITRATE	33	high	1 month
ISOBUTYLENE UREA (IBDU)	31	low	9 months
METHYLENE UREA	28–41	moderate	6 months
AMMONIUM SULFATE	21	high	1 month
NITRATE OF SODA**	16	high	3 months
CALCIUM NITRATE	15	high	3 months
POTASSIUM NITRATE	13	high	3 months
ORGANIC			
BAT GUANO	11	low	3 months
BLOOD MEAL	10	low	1 year†
FISH MEAL	10	moderate	3 months
COTTONSEED MEAL††	6–8	low	1 year†
ALFALFA MEAL	5	low	1 year†
COW MANURE (DRY)	2–3	low	1 year†
POULTRY MANURE	2	low	6 months†
SEAWEED (DRY)	2	low	9 months†
HORSE MANURE (FRESH)	1	moderate	1 year†

*Assumes ideal soil conditions of neutral pH, moderate moisture, and warm temperature. **Though a natural product, not necessarily certified as organic. †Available 2 weeks after application. ††May contain pesticide residues. Sources: *The Encyclopedia of Organic Gardening* (Rodale); *Knott's Handbook for Vegetable Growers* (John T. Wiley); *Western Fertilizer Handbook* (Interstate Press).

composting time. However, unlike cow manure, you can't buy it bagged. Although horse manure breaks down faster than cow manure, it still should be well composted before using it on a garden during the growing season.

Sheep and goat manure is easy to handle. Sheep and goats produce better manure than cows and horses. For one thing, they're neater, producing pelletized droppings that are easily gathered and distributed. And in the case of milk goats, which are often kept in stalls with bedding, the urine is captured along with the droppings, thus greatly increasing the value of the manure by retaining more nitrogen. Both animals produce around a 1.5–1.0–1.8 rating on the nutrient chart. An added advantage is quick composting because the pelletized form of the droppings allows more air into the compost pile and makes for greater surface area and quicker drying. Also, goats and sheep produce a manure that is virtually odorless if gathered in cool weather. And, since it comes in pellets, it is simple to spread and till into the garden.

To gather sheep manure, you can actually use a broom and flat shovel to sweep it up and then dump it into a wheelbarrow. It's quick and much easier than the back-breaking work of mucking out cow or horse stalls.

Rabbit manure scores high in nitrogen. Resembling the droppings of goats and sheep, only smaller, rabbit manure looks like it was made for gardeners. But the big bonus from bunnies comes in the nutrient level, which rates an impressive 3.5 percent in nitrogen. The other elements are also slightly higher than in manure from goats and sheep. The difference, of course, is quantity. Rabbits, like all herbivores, eat a tremendous amount of food for their size, but for an average rabbit, that might mean 100 lb. of feed a year. You can expect somewhat less than that weight to be returned as manure. But because it is twice as nutritious as the other manures mentioned thus far, you get more for your money.

Bird manure is premium stuff. Of all farm animals, birds produce the most valuable manure of all. Pigeon guano, for instance, has been prized in Europe as a super-manure since the Middle Ages, when folks kept dovecotes and pigeon lofts atop their houses, growing the squabs for food and using the manure to fertilize gardens and fields. Pigeon manure rates higher than other fowl at 4.2 percent nitrogen, 3 percent phosphorous, and 1.4 percent potassium. It is harder to find and gather than other manures, and is best if composted thoroughly before using.

Let manure mellow in your compost pile

Commercially packaged manure comes composted, but if you collect fresh manure, you'll need to compost it before applying it to your plants. How long depends on the type of manure and the season.

Add the manure slowly to the compost pile over several days or weeks, allowing plenty of air to circulate in the compost bin. Add other organic matter like grass clippings and leaves to break up the manure and speed curing. Turn the compost regularly as you add more manure. Stop adding the manure two months before you plan to use it in the garden. You'll know the manure is well composted when it produces no heat and loses most of its objectionable odor when dry.

While it's okay to add manure directly to garden soil in the fall (farmers do it all the time), it's best to compost cow, horse, and bird manure first. On the other hand, sheep, goat, and rabbit manure are easy to spread directly. Broadcast the pellets evenly and work them 1 in. to 2 in. into the soil. Then add another layer on top of the soil. This keeps the manure distributed, an important step in curing manure because it creates a larger surface area and combines the manure with the existing soil. This allows for easy decomposition over the fall and winter months.

Finding your own source

It's ironic that with all these types of fertilizer, only cow manure is readily available in most garden shops. But there are alternatives, and with a little reading and a few phone calls, you can locate a hot spot for manure that's much better than bagged cow manure and probably free to boot.

How do you find other manures? Farms are the most logical place to begin. You generally won't find them in the phone book, so try looking instead in the classified sections of local newspapers. Once you locate someone in your area selling livestock, call and volunteer to clean out stalls. Or, if you're a real salesman, you might simply arrange to be handy as a free hauling service after the stalls are cleaned.

If you're interested in the better stuff, however, you might again try the paper or the extension agent in your county. Ask the agent if he or she knows anyone in the area who raises goats or sheep. You will probably be surprised to find that there are folks within an hour of your house who have these ruminants. Remember, you get double the nutrients in half the manure and with a third the work.

Rabbits present a different problem because few people raise them in sufficient quantity for manure except pet stores and a few breeders. So start with your local pet store and ask what they do with all their manure and if they work with local breeders. If they don't hang up on you, they'll probably be more than happy for you to come by and pick up the manure after they have already scraped it themselves. Be nice. Provide the bucket. But make sure it's rabbit manure you're getting; you don't want droppings from dogs, cats, or reptiles.

Pigeons, too, are not as rare as some might think. Call your local extension agent or even your local Chamber of Commerce (perhaps there's a pigeon club in your area) and ask if they know of anyone raising pigeons. Since immaculate lofts are important for healthy birds, most pigeon fanciers are religious about cleaning out lofts; as with rabbit manure, provide your own bucket.

With the emphasis these days on recycling and chemical-free gardening, manure is a perfect answer for many people. With a phone call or two and a few hours of work, you can provide your soil with natural, organic nutrients that enrich your garden at little or no cost.

CALCULATING FERTILIZER BEFORE YOU CULTIVATE

When it comes to fertilizers and soil amendments, too much of a good thing, or the wrong thing, may decrease yields, waste money, and potentially harm groundwater. A few uncomplicated formulas and a trick or two will help ensure your garden gets what it needs.

How big is my garden?

Before you call up the dairyman to buy his manure or go to the garden center, you need to know the size of your garden. Determine the area of square and rectangular gardens by multiplying the width times the length. Separate odd-shaped plots into more manageable sections. A rectangle, triangle, and half circle comprise the garden in Figure A on p. 80.

Calculate each area separately using the formulas in the diagram. If you have a quarter circle, divide by 4 instead of 2. The value of pi is 3.14, but multiplying by 3 is close enough. Add all three areas to get your total.

The garden in Figure B (p. 80) is serpentine. To determine the length of the curved sides, edge them with a hose, straighten the hose, and measure. Flattened out, the garden becomes the trapezoid in Figure C (p. 80).

Even the most bizarre shapes break down into rectangles, triangles, and circles. Sketching the garden's shape may help.

How much stuff do I need?

It's important to get a soil test, a service offered through most state cooperative extension offices. You must find out what your soil needs before you can apply any amendments.

➦ *For more information on testing soil, see p. 81.*

Once you've computed the area, it's time to figure out how much muck you need to throw on it. Topsoil and mulch are usually sold by the cubic yard and spread 1 in.

How Many Cubic Yards of Top Soil and Mulch Do I Need?

Depth (in.)	Sq. ft. covered by 1 cu. yd.
4	80
3	110
2	160
1	320

to 4 in. deep. The chart above converts cubic yards to approximate areas at different depths.

To determine the amount needed, divide the total area of the garden by the conversion factor for the recommended depth. For example, if you have a 1,120-sq.-ft. garden and want to cover it in 2 in. of amendments, divide 1,120 by 160, which is the square footage figure corresponding to 2 in. on the chart. You'll need 7 cu. yd. of amendments.

Manure, however, is often sold by the pound. The chart below shows roughly how much area will be covered by a 40-lb. bag of manure at various depths.

How Many Pounds of Manure Do I Need?

Depth (in.)	Sq. ft.
4	25
3	38
2	50
1	100

The calculation for computing pounds of manure works almost the same way as the one for figuring cubic yards. If you have a 1,000-sq.-ft. garden and want to cover it with a 2-in. layer, it will take 800 lb. because 1,000 divided by 50, the square footage covered by one 40-lb. bag, is 20. And 20 times 40 lb. is 800 lb.

Buying the right amount of N-P-K

So let's say you did the wise thing and sent off a soil sample for testing. Your soil test results indicate you need to add 30 lb. of phosphorus.

The numbers on a fertilizer bag are percentages of nitrogen, phosphorus, and potassium in the bag. The bigger the number, the higher the percentage of nutrient. A 100-lb. bag of 10-10-10 contains 10 lbs. each of nitrogen, phosphorus, and potassium. The other 70 lb. is filler used to stabilize the nutrients and make application easier.

You'll need 300 lb. of 10-10-10 to get 30 lb. of actual P. But you'll also get 30 lb. each of nitrogen and potassium you don't need and 210 lb. of filler. Instead, buy a fertilizer high in the requisite nutrients.

To calculate the amount needed, divide 100 by the percentage of the nutrient on the bag, then multiply the result by the amount of nutrient you want. For example, how much 0-20-0 (called superphosphate) do you need to get 30 lb. of phosphorus? Divide 100 by 20, which is 5. Then multiply 5 times 30 lb., the amount of phosphorus you want, and you can see you need 150 lb. of superphosphate.

A bag of 0-20-0 may cost twice as much as 10-10-10, but you need only half as much. You won't be adding unnecessary nutrients and filler to the soil, and you'll be maintaining your garden's health.

Although the amounts of nutrients in organic fertilizers are less uniform, the calculations are done in the same way. For example, chicken manure has a 3-4-2 rating for N-P-K, while cow manure is 2-0-3, according to the *Master Gardener's Handbook* put out by the University of New Hampshire

Cooperative Extension. But the amounts can vary by as much as 2.5 percent, depending on the source. Labels on all packaged fertilizers should include a nutrient analysis.

The recommendations from soil tests come in various forms. Some offer amounts of specific nutrients and others suggest amounts of certain types of mixed fertilizers. This math will better equip you to respond regardless of the form the recommendation takes.

Getting the Lay of the Land

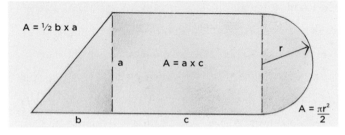

FIGURE A
The area of an odd-shaped plot is just the sum of its parts, in this case, a triangle, a rectangle, and a half-circle. For the half-circle, calculating pi at 3 instead of 3.14 is close enough.

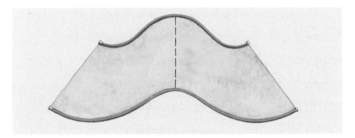

FIGURE B
Don't let a curve throw you. Trace the border of this wavy shape with a rope or hose. Then straighten the lines into a more manageable figure.

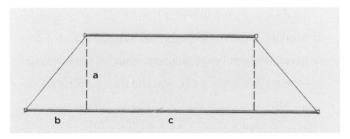

FIGURE C
This trapezoid can be divided into two triangles and a rectangle that are easy to measure using the equations in the top diagram.

What about small gardens?

Most bags of amendments give directions in pounds per 100 sq. ft., but how do you estimate an application rate for a tiny garden? Most people either guess or assume they can convert pounds directly to cups. But pounds measure weight and cups measure volume. A pound of limestone fills 1 cup, but a pound of shredded leaves fills buckets. Convert pounds to cups easily using a bathroom scale, a large plastic tub, an old measuring cup, and a waterproof marking pen.

Place the plastic tub on your scale and reset it to read zero so you're not weighing the tub. Keeping track of the number of cups, add the product to the tub until the scale reads 10 lb. Most bathroom scales aren't accurate below this amount. If 20 cups of fertilizer weighs 10 lb., then 1 cup weighs ½ lb. (10 divided by 20 is ½). Write the weighed equivalent on the bag with the marker. You might also want to record it in your garden journal (for more on this see p. 107) so you don't have to go through this the next time you buy the product. Repeat the process for each amendment you use.

If your product label recommends a rate of 3 lb. per 100 sq. ft., use the same conversion to figure how many cups to add; in this case, ½ lb. equals 1 cup, or 6 cups per 100 sq. ft. So if your little garden is 20 sq. ft., or a fifth of 100, then divide 6 cups by 5, which equals 1.2. Simply apply a little more than 1 cup of product to your garden. Approximations are better than guesses, and applying this math will improve the chance your soil will be productive.

SOIL TESTING SAVVY

Dedicated gardeners say they grow soil, not plants. To grow great soil, you've got to know what you're working with—the type of soil, its pH, and the major nutrients present or lacking.

The pH indicates how acid or alkaline the soil is. If pH is too high or too low, your plants won't be able to use the nutrients around them, no matter how naturally rich the soil is or how much fertilizer you add. Many gardeners ignore soil testing, relying on over-the-fence wisdom that can be far off the mark. Unless you test your soil, you won't know how much lime or fertilizer is needed. Many gardens are overfertilized or given the wrong ratios of the well-known trio N-P-K.

Getting ready to test

There are three options for soil testing. Do-it-yourself kits are available, but the information is not always accurate. Commercial labs provide soil-testing services that can be tailored to your needs. The turnaround time for receiving results may be only a few days. Or you can get your soil tested through your local cooperative extension office, listed in the phone book under state or county offices. Prices for testing vary with each state, and in some states it's free. Your county agent can explain the procedure and give you the proper paperwork and container. It might be a small paper bag on which you fill out your name, address, county, and intended crop. Be specific about anything that has special requirements, such as acid-loving crops like blueberries or rhododendrons.

The pH is rated by numbers: 7 is neutral, while numbers below that are acidic and numbers above are alkaline. Most soils will fall in a range between 4.3 and 8.5. Most plants want slightly acidic soil. The acid-lovers mentioned above (blueberries and rhodies) do best in a range of 4.5 to 5.0; potatoes and rhubarb like 5 to 6, and most other veggies and flowers like a pH range of 5.5 to 6.8. Gardeners in areas with a lot of rain, like the eastern United States and the Pacific Northwest, tend to have soils on the acidic side. In the western half of the continent where rainfall is low, the soil tends to be alkaline.

Dried, labeled, and ready for testing, this soil sample will undergo analysis for its pH and constituents.

Taking a sample

Any time the soil isn't frozen is fine for taking a soil sample. It's best to test in late summer or fall, though, since additives to correct pH take several months to work. Also, you'll avoid the spring rush at the extension office.

You want your sample to be representative of all the soil in the growing area, so you need a bit of soil from five or six spots in your vegetable, herb, or fruit garden. Don't take samples around walls, fences, stone piles, and compost bins or near spilled fertilizer or other chemicals. These sites are full of minerals that will throw off the reading.

To take a sample, remove any surface debris in the bed. Use a clean trowel to dig 6 in. deep and pull out an evenly sized slice from the top to the bottom of the hole. Put the sample in a clean plastic bucket and proceed to take four or five more, adding them to the bucket. Mix the samples thoroughly, removing any sticks, gravel, worms, or bugs. Keep your hands out of the soil.

Pour a cup or so of the soil into the bag or box provided by the extension office. If no container is provided, use a zip-top bag. The test results generally come back in a few weeks, telling you major and minor nutrients, pH, and best of all, making recommendations for additions or corrections.

The ABCs of N-P-K

Your soil test report will most likely tell you how much of what blend of fertilizer to add to your garden. These reports are easiest to use if you're buying bagged fertilizer. If you want to customize your fertilizer—say with your own compost, rotted manure, or other ingredients such as blood or bone meal, wood ashes, greensand, granite meal, or Epsom salts—consult your county agent to figure out how much of each to add. Each ingredient has its own N-P-K ratio that can affect your soil's pH. Manure, peat, and compost, for example, are typically acidic. Once you know what you have, you're on the way to turning your soil into a thriving ecosystem of nutrients and microorganisms.

TRY DOUBLE DIGGING FOR GREAT SOIL

The immediate way to completely revamp your soil is to double dig it. This requires lots of elbow grease but creates fertile, well-drained soil right away.

Double digging involves removing the top soil layer, exposing the subsoil (or hardpan) beneath, breaking it up, adding organic matter, and replacing the topsoil that was initially removed. This allows roots to reach deeper into the earth, where better-draining subsoil makes it less likely they'll become water-logged or oxygen-deprived. Deeper roots mean plants don't have to be watered as often. And more plants can grow in the same area because they don't have to rely on the topsoil alone for moisture and nutrients.

While the technique is simple, double digging isn't necessarily easy—digging through hard subsoil is tough work! Fortunately, double digging a bed is a one-shot deal

More Dirt on Soil

If you really want to dig in, get a copy of the Brooklyn Botanic Garden Handbook #192, *Healthy Soils for Sustainable Gardens*. You can order it at www.bbg.org or by calling (718) 623-7280.

Preparing your soil properly, which could include double digging, will increase your chances of having a productive garden.

COMPOSTING: THE BEST THING YOU CAN DO FOR YOUR GARDEN

A single handful of finished compost contains millions of participants in a fertile microcosm: fungi, bacteria, enzymes, sugars, and nutrients. Millipedes, earthworms, and sow bugs are the visible denizens of compost, but it's the unseen army of microscopic creatures that does most of the work of breaking rough stuff into compost. The end result is dark, crumbly, sweet-smelling compost and its benefits to the garden are huge. No wonder gardeners call the stuff "black gold."

Making compost is probably the single best thing you can do to improve your garden. The benefits are innumerable, from improved tilth to a revitalized soil ecosystem. Composting turns organic waste—which is arguably not waste—into a soil conditioner. Nutrients aren't lost; they're just moved around. Composting is ecologically sound, simple, and cheap. And there are a number of ways to go about it.

you'll never have to repeat. And this low-tech process requires only a couple of tools, the most important of which is a short-handled, square-tipped spade (rather than a round-tipped shovel, which is meant for digging holes, not beds). The spade allows you to make flat, sharp slices through the dirt, and the short handle forces you to bend your knees while digging, thus taking the strain off your lower back. You may also need a garden fork for loosening subsoil and a wheelbarrow for hauling organic matter to work into the bed. The wheelbarrow can also serve to move topsoil from the first trench dug to the last; a tarp would work, too.

For more information on double-digging, see p. 84; for more information on garden tools, see p. 100.

To prepare the soil for planting, follow this sequence. First spade the edges of the bed using a garden fork and cultivator to loosen the surface soil and then using the garden fork again or a deep spading fork to loosen the subsoil; mix amendments into the bed with the fork; then finish the bed by shaping and grading it with a level-head rake.

When double digging a bed, start at one end and move backward. Once the soil is loosened, turned, and aerated, you don't want to step on it again, as compaction defeats one of the purposes of double digging.

From the initial input of chopped leaves and grass (upper row) comes partially decomposed, then finished compost (lower row).

Double Dig a Bed Step-by-Step

1. Dig a trench across the width of the bed, removing the topsoil and piling it at the end of the bed on a tarp or in a wheelbarrow. The trench should be the width and depth of your spade.

2. Put several inches of organic material in the trench. Fresh manure or any rough, nonwoody plant matter like leaves, grass, old cornstalks or sunflower stems are good. Save your compost to mix in the topsoil once you've finished digging the bed. If you don't have a source of organic materials, commercially bagged compost or manure will do.

3. Loosen the soil to another spade's depth, chopping or turning the organic matter into the subsoil. If it is very rough and rocky, work in 2-in. to 3-in. sections at a time. Remove large rocks as you go. You want to break the hardpan into small chunks interspersed with organic matter, providing channels for water to drain and roots to grow into. A soil fork might work better than a spade on this bottom layer.

4. With the first trench dug, start another parallel to and just behind the first, one spade-width wide and one spade-depth deep. Throw the topsoil from the second trench on top of the first trench's mixture of organic material and subsoil. Repeat the process by tossing a layer of organic material into the second trench, and digging and mixing it into the subsoil.

   Keep double digging trenches down the length of your bed. When you get to the end of the bed, you will be one layer short of topsoil. Get the topsoil from your first trench, and spread it on the last trench.

5. Rake smooth the top of the bed, and add some fine compost or other soil amendment.

Hot and cold composting

At the ends of the composting spectrum are two methods: hot and cold. A *cold composting* system is one in which organic waste is simply dumped in a pile. The gardener expends little or no energy managing the pile and just waits for it to decompose. *Hot composting* requires managing the pile so as to raise temperatures high enough and for a long enough time to destroy weed seeds and plant pathogens. This requires some work on the part of the gardener, both up front with careful layering of materials and later on by turning or aerating the pile. In between the two techniques are numerous degrees of intervention.

Actually, the term cold composting is a misnomer, as even in an untended pile, temperatures rise. Gardeners use these terms to differentiate between active and passive composting. A cold pile may be as sophisticated as a three-bin system or as simple as a heap of leaves. The beauty of cold composting is that you just pick a spot to toss your organic refuse and then add to it. Cold composting takes longer to produce finished compost.

A three-bin system with removable front slats makes it easy to turn one pile into another. The top flips down to keep out large critters.

The hot method requires monitoring the moisture content and temperature of the pile, aerating to keep oxygen-hungry microbes fueled, and adding brown and green material in proper ratio. The result is fast decomposition, with temperatures high enough to destroy most plant pathogens and weed seeds.

A bin isn't an absolute necessity. You can make either cold or hot compost in an open pile. Bins have a number of advantages, however. A bin encloses organic material and allows better control of compost temperature, as well as tidying up your yard. In dry climates, an enclosed bin will reduce evaporation and water loss. In wet climates, an enclosed bin keeps material from getting too sodden (a tarp will do this as well). An enclosed bin will also deter unwelcome scavengers, although a determined rodent can eat through plastic. Heavy-duty hardware cloth will keep them out.

There are numerous compost bins available commercially. Most are not suited for hot composting because they're too small and usually not designed for easy turning of compost. Compost tumblers take a lot of the ache out of

A large compost tumbler holds about as much as a 3-ft. by 3-ft. by 3-ft. bin. A crank makes it easy to turn the compost material in this enclosed system.

Creating Healthy Compost

Theoretically, anything of organic origin can be put into a composting system, but in an open bin, meat, fish, poultry, or foods with added fat are too likely to attract pests, are slow to break down, and can be odorous. If you have a closed system and want to add animal bones or food scraps, bury them in the center of the pile and cover with brown material; you should also have a layer of brown material around the outside. Deterring rodents has to do as much with how you manage the bins as with their contents and the construction of the bin itself.

Pesticides. Evidence indicates that pesticides and herbicides break down into innocuous components during hot composting. Nevertheless, many gardeners avoid putting treated grass clippings in their compost.

Animal manure. Fresh manure provides a large input of nitrogen. Use 1 part fresh manure to 4 parts brown organic matter. Give it plenty of time to break down. Horse, cow, rabbit, and poultry manure are all good additions.

Keep cat, dog, and human feces out of your bin, as they may contain harmful pathogens. Bird cage waste typically includes numerous weed seeds and possibly diseases, so is best kept out. Any manure can contain pathogens. The concern is not only whether pathogens will break down in the compost, but also that you may come in contact with pathogens when handling waste to put in the bin. This is of less concern with manure from herbivores.

Paper. Most newspapers are printed with soy-based inks and are safe to add to your pile. Use them in moderation and shred them first. If you run out of

Make sure you mix brown and green material and completely cover food waste with brown matter.

brown matter during the winter, paper is a good stand-in. Do not add shiny, colored magazine paper, because the ink may contain heavy metals.

Weeds and diseased plants. Do not add diseased plants to compost. If you're certain you have your pile cooking at 150°F to 160°F for at least a few days, weed seeds will be destroyed. Certain pernicious weeds may persist in any but the hottest compost piles.

If you're new to composting, keep it simple. Stick to kitchen waste and backyard clippings.

Good compost requires management. When the center of the pile reaches about 155°F, it's time to turn it. Mixing air into the pile brings the temperature down, but within a day it will climb back up.

aerating compost. Most of them, however, are smaller than the ideal 27-cu.-ft. capacity.

A homemade bin can be as rudimentary as a circle of welded wire fencing or as advanced as an enclosed, multi-bin structure made of rot-resistant material. (Don't build a compost bin out of pressure-treated lumber, however; the organisms in compost will cause treated wood to decay and chemicals to leach into your compost.) Be sure your bin or pile is 1 cu. yd. or larger; otherwise, there's not enough mass to hold the heat given off by microbes during decomposition. This heat is important, even if you're composting via the cold route.

For hot composting, you'll need a fork for turning the pile. You can use a regular garden fork, but a compost fork or a manure fork, both of which have long handles, makes the job easier. A composting auger can help aerate deep piles, but you'll still need to do some turning. If you want to be sure your compost reaches temperatures high enough

A thermometer will let you know when your pile is really cooking.

to kill pathogens, you'll need a thermometer. While a 20-in. compost thermometer is nice but not necessary, you can simply use a meat thermometer. Just be sure to stick the probe deep into the center of the pile.

Compost accelerators are unnecessary. Leaves, grass clippings, plant debris, and food scraps come with bacteria and inoculants to spare. The best primer is a shovelful of freshly made compost, teeming with microbes ready to devour fresh organic matter.

Making hot compost

Hot composting requires a balance of green (nitrogenous) and brown (carbonaceous) ingredients. The latter provides microbes with energy to carry out their work, similar to the way carbohydrates provide humans with energy. Nitrogenous material provides microbes with the energy needed for growth, similar to the function of protein for humans. In a composting system, carbonaceous material tends to be brown: dry leaves, stalks, twigs, wood chips and sawdust (from untreated wood only!), and torn-up newspaper. Nitrogenous material has a higher water content and is typically (but not always) green: grass clippings, fresh plants, food scraps, coffee grounds.

The ideal carbon to nitrogen ratio is three to one by volume (unless you're making special compost for compost tea). Eyeballing the volume works, but if you want to be more precise, use one container for measuring everything you put in; a 5-gal. bucket or one of the flexible Tubtrugs® is ideal. Add one measure of green matter for every three of brown matter.

Try to mix a whole pile at a time. To get it up to temperature and keep it there, you need a mass that measures at least 1 cu. yd. Moisten the pile as you make it so that it is damp but not wet. An easy way to tell is to pick up a handful of the material and squeeze it as hard as you can; only one or two drops should be squeezed out. Less than that, add water; more than that, let it dry out.

Once the pile is made, you can add kitchen scraps as they accumulate. Bury them in the center in different places to help maintain heat in the pile. Small additions don't upset the ratio. If needed, you can balance the green additions with shredded newspaper or wood shavings.

Compost Bin Options

Before buying or making a compost bin, you should first decide how devoted to composting you're going to be. The time and effort you're willing to make, as well as the amount you have to compost, will influence your decision. In addition, think space, location, and cost.

When it comes to composting, gardeners fall into three categories: casual composters, serious composters, and high-production composters.

For casual composting, a compact plastic bin. This is a good choice if you have a small garden, don't have a lot of leaves, and mainly want to recycle kitchen waste, grass clippings, and plant refuse. Any of the compact plastic bins sold in garden centers and by mail-order suppliers qualify. Holding between 10 cu. ft. and 12 cu. ft. of material, these small bins don't take up much space and are fairly unobtrusive. The better ones have vents to allow the air to circulate, a lid to give them a neat appearance, and a sliding door to make shoveling out the compost easier.

For serious composting, a large single bin plus a wire leaf bin. This combo is a good choice if you have a good-size garden, want compost to use both as humus and as mulch, and don't mind spending a few minutes at the end of a day in the garden maintaining a manageable pile. Corral the leaves in a wire holding bin, and use them as you build the pile, adding them to the compost bin along with kitchen scraps, garden prunings, and grass clippings.

For production composting, a three-bin setup. If you want a steady supply of black gold, you need three bins that are 3 cu. ft. to 5 cu. ft. each. Smaller than that, and the pile isn't large enough to hold heat. A pile larger than this range is too big to allow air to get to the center, and it's too big to turn easily. The lightweight wire three-bin system you can buy is suited to leaf piles, but for an actively managed compost operation, which requires turning the piles, you'll need to construct sturdy bins. You can make them quickly and cheaply from discarded shipping pallets, or build wood or wood and wire frames. You can also just use cylinders of heavy-duty welded wire fencing.

A good compost pile really cooks. The pile will heat up right away, as microorganisms start breaking down the material. The pile must stay between 135°F and 160°F for three days. At 135°F, weed seeds, human pathogens, most plant pathogens, and most root-feeding nematodes are killed. The pile shouldn't go above 160°F, because at that temperature large numbers of the beneficial organisms begin to be killed.

Within a day or two, the center should reach 135°F. Measure the temperature with a long-stemmed thermometer. Take two or three readings from several areas of the pile each day for the first week when you first start making compost, so you get a feeling for what is normal. If you make the same mix again and again, after several batches you won't have to monitor quite so closely.

When the temperature gets to about 155°F, turn the pile with a pitchfork or a garden fork. This mixes the cooler materials on the outside to the center and brings air into the pile, preventing anaerobic conditions. Within a day or so, the pile will be back up to 155°F and you'll need to turn it again. Expect to turn the pile every day or two for about the first week to get it and keep it in the 135°F to 155°F range. After that, you can leave it alone, maybe turning it once or twice more during the next few weeks.

As the compost matures, the temperature will drop gradually until, after six to eight weeks, the center of the pile is cool or barely warm to the touch. Once the material is adequately broken down, the fodder for the various bacteria will be depleted and the temperature will fall to ambient levels. When this happens, the compost is done. The pile will be about half its original size, and the contents will have broken down to a beautiful, rich-brown, friable substance.

Though the compost appears ready, it's good practice to let it sit for two weeks to allow soluble salts to leach out. Salt-sensitive plants such as cress or melons can be harmed if salt levels are high.

A Worm Bin Makes Great Compost

Worm composting, also known as vermicomposting, was developed as a four-season system to recycle kitchen waste. But in addition to kitchen scraps, worms will also eat torn-up newspapers. The worms excrete an odor-free, nutrient-rich, organic compost called worm castings. Worm castings contain five to ten times more available phosphorus, nitrogen, and potassium than the compost you get from your outside bin.

You can buy a worm bin along with worms—red wrigglers are the ones you want. They have a high metabolism and digest their food with amazing speed.

In about eight weeks, red wriggler worms will have turned household kitchen scraps and shredded newspaper into castings.

Harvesting worm castings is simply a matter of screening out the worms. The worms go back in the bin, and the castings are great for the garden.

WATERING THE GARDEN

In some areas—and in some years—watering a vegetable garden can be as easy as watching the rain. But the heavens usually aren't so dependable. Vegetables need regular moisture to thrive. Turning on the hose only after the ground has turned dry and plants have started showing signs of flagging is an excellent way to have a disappointing garden. What you want to do is quench your plants' thirst without overdoing it.

Watering in sync with the weather

You've probably heard the irrigating rule, "an inch of water a week." But why water the same amount every week when the weather is always in flux? Each day, your garden loses water by evaporation from the soil surface and by transpiration from leaves. The amount lost is affected by humidity, sunlight, wind speed, and temperature, and also by how much the plant's canopy covers the soil. A hot, windy August afternoon might cause your garden to lose nearly five times the moisture as a cool, humid April morning. Likewise, a garden in a hot, dry area might need three times the water during the same week that one in a cool, moist climate would need. Paying attention to the weather and the soil moisture will help you water wisely.

Try to think in terms of replacing lost moisture rather than of adding water. Irrigating works on the same principle as sleep: You can't store it, and it's much better to get what you need regularly than to play catch-up. Ideally your soil should be as moist as a wrung-out sponge. If you start with that as a baseline, then you need to replace only the moisture that's been lost to weather or used by plants. Refer to the chart on p. 94 for recommendations about how much to water in various weather conditions.

Get to know your soil. What kind of soil you have makes a difference in how frequently you need to water. Clay-laden soil presents special watering challenges. Clay has an electrical charge that draws water, pulling it away from plant roots. In dense clay, little room exists for passages that permit the exchange of essential gases with the air above ground. Clay also drains slowly. Water flows more easily through sandy soil. But if it's too sandy, water drains too quickly, leaching dissolved nutrients with it. Both clay and sandy soils can be turned into a preferred loam by mixing in organic material, such as compost.

You can check how fast your soil absorbs water using any type of cylinder, such as an empty coffee can with the bottom removed. Push one end into the soil an inch or so. Fill the can with water and let it drain completely. Fill it again, and then see how long it takes for the water level to drop 1 in. If it takes more than four hours, you've probably got a drainage problem that could harm plant roots. Raised beds may be the solution if that site is your only option for a garden.

Keep water percolating in the zone. The top 1 ft. of soil is far more important for water and nutrient absorption than anything below. That's where the vast majority of a vegetable plant's roots are. Even deep-rooted plants like tomatoes have their fine network of feeder roots in the upper portion of the soil. Vegetable roots occupy an

Soon to be covered with mulch, this soaker hose will adequately moisten the plants in this small raised bed.

area much wider than the plant's foliage; watering just around the plant under its foliage canopy isn't enough. If you garden in wide beds, water the whole bed area. If you garden in long rows with narrow paths in between, water the entire garden.

Water before you mulch. Mulch helps conserve water in your soil by shielding the ground from the hot rays that burn off moisture. But it's a good idea to soak the soil before you lay on that first layer of mulch. Just as the mulch hinders evaporation, it also slows penetration of moisture to the roots. It's more efficient to get the water down first, then mulch.

Read the leaves. Don't let leaves fool you. If they're drooping in the hot, midday sun, you need not necessarily be alarmed. The plants may just be protecting themselves by exposing less surface to the sun and conserving water. If the same plants are drooping in the morning or at night, that's an indication you need to water. There's no reason to water the leaves. That can encourage a variety of fungi that develop in moist conditions, causing mildew and blight.

Choose your time wisely. Early morning, late afternoon, and evening are usually best for watering because the cooler temperatures mean less water will evaporate. Limiting your watering to these times is a particularly good idea if you use overhead sprinklers. Under bright sunshine, water droplets intensify the rays and can singe the leaves. It's also safer not to water at night, as the leaves will remain wet, which may encourage disease. In arid places, however, some people decide to risk night watering to give the water longer to soak into the soil and cut evaporation from the sun.

Know when to say when. Divining how much the garden is actually getting is tricky. You can estimate by using a rain gauge to track precipitation. Position the gauge near the garden but where water splashing off pavement or overhangs won't affect the reading. If you water via a sprinkler, the rain gauge can also tell you how much water you're delivering to plants, as long as it's positioned in the sprinkler's path but where the plants themselves don't interfere with the spray pattern. An inexpensive flow meter attached to the garden spigot is the most accurate

With a drip system, the moist areas on the surface at left are only the tip of the iceberg. As water spreads out underground (see the drawing on the facing page), the wet areas merge to form a zone of continuous moisture.

way to measure and about the only way if you're using soaker hoses or a drip system. It works like a timer: Set it for how much water you want to deliver to your garden and it automatically shuts off when it reaches the set volume. About 60 gal. will provide the proverbial 1 in. of water over 100 sq. ft.

Methods of watering

There are myriad methods to deliver the water. Some gardens are small enough to water by hand. The large size of others or a lack of time may require more elaborate arrangements, including sprinklers, soaker hoses, or drip irrigation systems. You have to balance your commitment with the needs of the plants and the results you expect.

Hand watering. If your garden is small and you have the time, this can be a good way to water. Because you are right there with your plants, you have the chance to observe them carefully and to notice any problems as they surface. You can customize easily how much water each crop gets. Those are the pros. The cons are first, it takes more time to water a garden this way, and second, it's easy to err in giving too much or too little, particularly if you're pressed for time. If you do water by hand, use a wand with a gentle shower head.

Sprinklers. Sprinklers are great for lawns but they're not the best for vegetables. There are lots of different types of sprinklers on the market. Pulsating ones can damage nearby plants; with rotating ones, it can be hard to get even distribution. Oscillating sprinklers are probably best. But even so, you're wetting the plant foliage every time you water. Any fungi on the plant or soil surface is just going to get splashed around. Yes, when it rains this happens, but if you use overhead watering, you're guaranteeing that it happens 100 percent of the time the garden gets irrigated. It's also difficult to position a sprinkler so taller plants don't block the spray pattern.

Soaker hoses. Soaker hoses are a low-tech method of drip irrigation; they are much more limited than a real drip system, but they are cheap and fairly easy to use. Typically made of recycled rubber, a soaker hose leaks water slowly through its many pores. In order to work correctly, it must be installed over a level surface—otherwise water leaks unevenly—and you must use very low water pressure. Lay the soaker hose right on top of the soil; it will loop and coil, so you'll need to use earth staples of some sort (pieces of clothes hangers bent to a U-shape work) every couple of feet to keep the hose on the ground. Don't bury the hose,

How the Moisture Zone Forms below the Surface

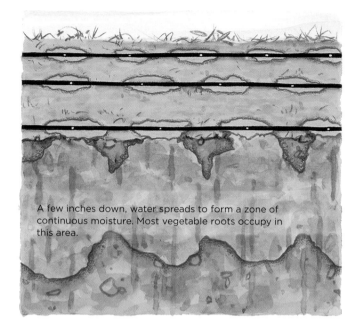

A few inches down, water spreads to form a zone of continuous moisture. Most vegetable roots occupy in this area.

but once it's all in place you should cover it with mulch. This not only hides the hose but also prevents loss of moisture to evaporation and lengthens the life of the hose by protecting it from UV degradation.

You can't make sharp turns with a soaker hose (if you do, water will trickle out at the curve much faster than elsewhere) but you can make gradual curves. You also can cut the hose and make angles with hose fittings and hose clamps. To get continuous coverage in the root zone, lay hoses about 2 ft. apart.

Drip irrigation. Drip irrigation is really the best way to make gardens flourish, even in fairly rainy areas. This is one way you can make your gardening life much easier.

Some gardeners resist putting drip irrigation in their vegetable gardens because they change what they plant and where they plant it every year. When you irrigate the entire bed, however, it doesn't matter what your crop rotations are; all vegetables will get the water they need because drip irrigation lets water seep directly into the

soil. Water comes out through emitters, small gizmos that regulate the water's flow to a mere dribble—$\frac{1}{2}$ gal. or 1 gal. per hour. They're built into flexible tubing, which is strung throughout the garden. Water is regulated, filtered, and turned on and off by a few parts attached to an outdoor faucet. Because drip irrigation trickles moisture slowly, most of the soil's pores don't flood, and they remain aerobic.

If you look at an unmulched, drip-irrigated bed, you'll see a series of dark, moist circles separated by dry soil. But underground, the wet spot balloons out. Put the emitters close enough together and the wet spots merge below ground to form a continuous zone of irrigation, even though much of the surface remains dry. Drip irrigation, with its many points of application, keeps the soil moist

In-Line Emitters: The Way to Go

In the early days, emitters were justifiably criticized for clogging. Now, the best emitters, tortuous- or turbulent-path models, are virtually clog free. A complex, twisted pathway inside the emitter makes the water take many turns. Each turn forms an eddy that keeps the sediment suspended so it doesn't settle and clog the emitter.

The emitters are manufactured right inside tubing, so you don't install them yourself, and there's nothing to break off. All you see is a tiny weephole or a colored dot where the emitter is.

You can get emitters that each drip $\frac{1}{2}$ gal. per hour (gph) or that drip 1 gph. You can also choose tubing with emitters spaced every 12 in., 18 in., 24 in., or 36 in. The best combination for most gardens is $\frac{1}{2}$ gph emitters spaced 12 in. apart. Laid out correctly, this type of line will quickly give you full-root-zone irrigation in any soil.

right where the roots need water the most. This promotes better foliage and blooms and therefore higher yields. Plus, you'll have fewer problems with weeds and diseases, and you'll use less water. And, once your system is in, you'll spend little time or energy watering.

There are different types of drip systems, but the easiest to use is one with in-line emitters. To install it, just roll out the tubing, join any pieces together with plastic connectors, and anchor the lines to the ground with wire pins.

If you're just getting your feet wet, consider starting with a kit, which has all the parts you need. It's also heartening to know that the companies that sell drip supplies have knowledgeable staff who will help you figure out what you need and how to put it together (see Resources starting on p. 284). They will even design a system for you if you send them a plan of your garden.

As for cost, it's true that you'll spend more on drip irrigation than you would on a sprinkler and a hose. But the system pays off in increased yields, water savings, and, if you connect a timer to it, the convenience of programmed waterings.

How Much Should I Water?

The chart below has guidelines based on what your recent weather conditions have been. It assumes no rain has fallen and that you have one ½-gph emitter per square foot. If you want to irrigate more often than weekly (some people water daily), simply divide the number of minutes in the third column by 7 to get the daily ration, and then multiply that by how many days it's been since you last watered. If it rains, wait until the soil dries out to its ideal moisture level before starting the cycle again.

If you don't have a drip system, this chart can still be useful to you as long as you have a flow meter. Multiply your garden's square footage by the appropriate number of gallons, given recent weather, then set the meter to deliver the total amount of water.

Weather conditions, temperature	Amount of water needed per square foot per week (gal.)	Length of time to run the system per week
Humid, below 70°F	0.4	45 minutes
Dry, below 70°F	0.6	1 hour, 15 minutes
Humid, in the 70s	0.8	1 hour, 45 minutes
Dry, in the 70s	1.0	2 hours
Humid, in the 80s/90s	1.3	2 hours, 30 minutes
Dry, in the 80s/90s	1.5	3 hours
Humid, over 100°F	1.75	3 hours, 30 minutes
Dry, over 100°F	2.0	4 hours

Bird's-Eye View of a Drip Irrigation System

In a wide-bed garden, treat each bed as a separate, closed-circuit unit.

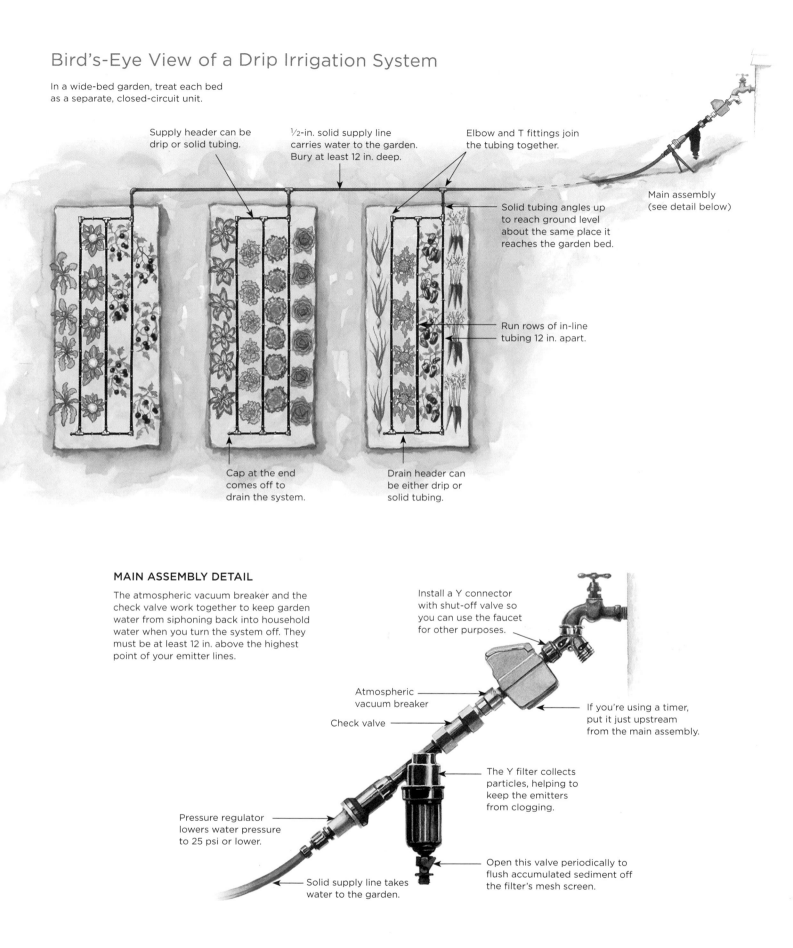

Supply header can be drip or solid tubing.

½-in. solid supply line carries water to the garden. Bury at least 12 in. deep.

Elbow and T fittings join the tubing together.

Main assembly (see detail below)

Solid tubing angles up to reach ground level about the same place it reaches the garden bed.

Run rows of in-line tubing 12 in. apart.

Cap at the end comes off to drain the system.

Drain header can be either drip or solid tubing.

MAIN ASSEMBLY DETAIL

The atmospheric vacuum breaker and the check valve work together to keep garden water from siphoning back into household water when you turn the system off. They must be at least 12 in. above the highest point of your emitter lines.

Install a Y connector with shut-off valve so you can use the faucet for other purposes.

Atmospheric vacuum breaker

Check valve

If you're using a timer, put it just upstream from the main assembly.

The Y filter collects particles, helping to keep the emitters from clogging.

Pressure regulator lowers water pressure to 25 psi or lower.

Open this valve periodically to flush accumulated sediment off the filter's mesh screen.

Solid supply line takes water to the garden.

MAGNIFICENT MULCH

Mulching—covering the surface of the soil with something—is good for your garden, good for your plants, and
good for you, the gardener. Here are some of the ways
mulch helps your garden.

A mulched garden looks better and performs
better than one without mulch.

- **Mulch suppresses weeds and reduces the need for
cultivation.** A thick layer of mulch shields the soil from
sunlight and prevents weeds from germinating. Those
weeds that do poke through are easy to pluck because
the soil below remains loose and friable. You can drop
those weeds on top of your mulch, where they simply
turn brown and become part of it.

- **Mulch stabilizes the soil.** It retains soil moisture,
discourages soil erosion, and insulates the soil from
temperature swings. Some mulches reduce evaporation from the soil by as much as 50 percent. During hot
spells, the soil beneath mulch can be 10°F cooler than
exposed earth. And because water percolates slowly
through mulch, the soil below runs less risk of being
washed away by a heavy rain.

- **Mulch prevents some plant diseases.** Mulched plants
are splashed less by pelting raindrops than plants in
bare soil. Because all soil harbors disease microbes
that can harm vegetation, unsplashed plants tend to be
healthier than muddy ones.

- **Mulch provides nutrients.** It creates an environment
that encourages healthy microbiological activity. Microorganisms consume humus, then release valuable nutrients back into the soil. This explains why mulching has
been described as "sheet composting." Because mulch
boosts fertility naturally, your soil needs less added
fertilizer. A well-balanced, organically rich soil produces
healthier plants that don't need as much treatment with

herbicides or pesticides. And because healthy soil tends
to strike a balance between alkalinity and acidity, seek-
ing a neutral pH, it needs less lime or other agents to
sweeten it.

- **Mulch can improve the look of your garden.** Some
mulches are better looking than others, so consider
appearances when making your choice, especially if your
garden is in full view from your windows, porch, or
patio. A well-conceived kitchen garden, neatened,
protected, and improved by decorative mulch, is landscaping at its best. Moreover, you can move around in a
mulched garden, even on the wettest days, and not come
away with gobs of mud stuck to the soles of your shoes.

The best mulch is airy, dry, and weather-worn

The right mulch for you will depend on several factors. Do you want an organic material that will break down and can be turned into the soil or added to the compost bin at season's end? Do you prefer something that will last for several years? Are looks important? Sometimes the choice is dictated by what is available nearby for free or almost free.

Organic mulch materials include leaves, hay, pine needles, marsh grass (rinsed if it's from a salt marsh), newspaper, cardboard, burlap bags, and even old boards.

There are numerous man-made mulches that you can buy, from heavy-duty woven polypropylene mats sturdy enough to last many seasons to lightweight weed fabric made entirely of recycled plastic bottles. Aluminum foil as mulch can discourage insects like aphids (and thereby cut down on aphid-transmitted diseases like viruses) because it reflects light onto the normally shaded undersides of leaves. Black plastic works well to suppress weeds, but unless it is perforated, it prevents rain or water from overhead sprinklers from reaching the soil. Red plastic mulch has been shown to increase yields on tomatoes and peppers. These inorganic mulches contribute nothing to the soil, and when they start to deteriorate, you'll want to remove them to keep the garden from looking very shabby.

The best mulch materials are rich, texturizing organic ones like hay, leaves, and marsh grass. Other such mulches include pine needles, dried manure, leaf mold, peat moss, sawdust, seaweed, weathered wood shavings, even coffee grounds. Although you need not be too fussy about what to use as mulch, you should take care to avoid a few risks associated with some mulches.

Heavy mulch can inhibit water percolation and reduce aeration. Matted leaves, for instance, can form an all but impervious layer. The ideal mulch is light and open enough to permit the passage of water and air.

Avoid fresh mulch, which can rob nitrogen from the soil. Nitrogen is a vital ingredient of the decomposition process and a critical plant nutrient, but it can't be both at the same time. As fresh mulch decomposes, it ties up nitrogen that would otherwise be feeding your plants.

Lawn clippings and marsh grass are good mulches, but be careful to give these wet, fresh, and very green mulches a chance to dry out before putting them in your garden. Clumped together undried, fresh marsh grass, like fresh lawn clippings, becomes a greasy, smelly mess, the antithesis of what mulch should be.

Hay can be a good mulch if you stay away from the first spring cutting, which tends to be loaded with seeds, all of them liable to sprout and grow into weeds. Try to find spoiled hay that was harvested late in the summer. In most cases, seed pods had not yet formed on this second-cut hay. Older hay that's been wet and is no longer useful as feed is ideal for mulch—it has already started to decay, and most of the weed seeds are dead.

Old mulch is better than new. The weathered hay at left is light and loose enough to allow air and water to pass through. The cut grass on the right is too wet and matted.

Apply mulch selectively

Although mulching is a good practice, it's not always necessary. Young plants need sunlight and air. Quick-growing plants often crowd out weeds on their own. You probably don't need to mulch vegetables that stay in the garden for a relatively short time, like lettuce, spinach, or other leaf crops. If slugs and snails are a problem in your area, be aware that mulch provides an ideal home for these voracious pests.

On the other hand, plants that remain in the garden for much of the season benefit from mulch, once they are established. These include tomatoes, peppers, melons, pumpkins, squash of all sorts, broccoli, cabbage, Brussels sprouts, onions, and perennial edibles such as asparagus, rhubarb, strawberries, raspberries, and blueberries.

But don't be too anxious to mulch in the spring. The risk of damping-off, a moldy condition that can inhibit or kill young plants, may be heightened by mulching them

Bring On the Hay

A permanent deep mulch of hay has a lot of advantages, especially for working gardeners who either have no time or are absent from their gardens during the week. A hay mulch smells wonderful after a rain and is readily available. It's also easy to pull apart and mold to make rows, squares, holes, or other openings for planting, and it's clean and comfortable to sit or kneel on. Permanent deep hay mulching is an important part of the no-till gardening technique.

Be patient with permanent mulch. The advantages of permanent mulch aren't immediately apparent. It takes time for the hay to establish its cycle of suppressing weeds and luring those good garden helpers, garter snakes and spiders. Snakes adeptly control slugs and like to spend the winter in any hay bales you have stockpiled.

Apply hay twice a year, in spring and in fall, spreading a layer about 12 in. deep. The depth will diminish to about 4 in. as the hay decomposes, which it does quickly.

Buying enough hay to maintain this kind of mulch may seem costly at first, but the savings down the road in time and effort make this expense and trouble worthwhile. Before you buy, examine the bales closely for seed pods or any other undesirable debris.

Permanent mulch asks little, gives much. This kind of mulching means there's no need for tilling. Weeds are held down, and expired plants become part of the mulch, so there's nothing to turn under. This makes for easier gardening and doesn't disturb the top few inches of soil where all the good microbes reside. In addition, mulch keeps the ground cool and traps moisture, which allows you to cut down on watering in the summer. And it improves the texture of the soil and adds nutrients.

Unfortunately, as mulch rots, it robs the soil of nitrogen, so you must add some. Although any legume plant adds nitrogen to the soil as it grows, this alone isn't the solution. A straight nitrogen fertilizer (46-0-0) is the easiest way to provide the needed boost. Spread about $1/2$ oz. per square yard on top of the mulch. Some granular types of nitrogen must be soaked into the ground two or three months before planting in order not to burn tender plant tissue. If you use this type, be sure to apply it in plenty of time.

too soon. Give the soil ample opportunity to warm up in direct sun, then give young plants a chance to get growing. You should mulch when the weather warms up and when drought threatens.

To loosen and aerate the soil, it's a good idea to cultivate around plants before you mulch them. This should be the last time you'll need to do this. Leave some room for the young roots to breathe, then gradually move the mulch closer to the plants' main stems.

It's counterproductive to spread mulch too thin. It will disappear fast and weeds will replace it. Don't be afraid to experiment. Just take a little care, and the benefits of mulch will far outweigh the potential risks. You can hardly go wrong.

Hay used as mulch keeps a garden pretty and productive.

Hay makes a fine nest for plants. When you're ready to plant, push the mulch apart to reach the soil. You can make narrow rows or squares about 4 ft. wide, depending on what you intend to plant. Fill the spot with compost to hold the hay back, the weeds down, and the moisture in.

With this kind of mulch, you can let plants like peas, cucumbers, and tomatoes sprawl, if you have the space. The fluffy hay allows good drainage and air circulation, so you don't really need to stake them, and you can sit down to pick the produce.

Potatoes grow great in this mulch. In early spring, sow whole or half potatoes on top of the hay remain-ing from the previous year and cover them with 2 in. to 3 in. of hay. As they grow, and green leaves poke through, toss on even more hay until there is a cover-ing of a foot or more. Harvesting is easy, and the potatoes are clean.

Hay-flanked vegetable plants produce fabulously. Fruits that don't turn out well can be left to rot. If a spot looks messy, simply cover it with hay. At the end of the season, leave everything to decay; by the following spring, most things will have disappeared. If anything endures intact, such as corn stalks, just push them under the hay in an area that is to be-come a path.

Some tools for working the soil include, from left to right: level-head rake, deep spader, cultivating fork, D-handle fork, and D-handle spade.

To prepare the soil for planting, you're mostly likely to follow a sequence that involves spading the edges of the bed, using a garden fork and cultivator to loosen the surface soil, using the garden fork again or a deep spading fork to loosen the subsoil, mixing amendments into the bed with the fork, and then finishing the bed by shaping and grading with a level-head rake.

D-handle garden spade

This tool, with a strong ash handle and a forged-steel blade, is designed for serious digging, but its flat blade also cuts a clean, crisp edge. The shaft is short, about 36 in., and ends with a handle shaped something like a "D." The D-shape allows you to push and pull the tool with the least amount of strain to your wrist. The short shaft allows you to put your weight on top of the tool for leverage. And the 11-in. hardened steel blade cuts through the soil easily and holds up to any amount of leveraging. In double digging, you use the spade to cut a chunk of soil and lift it carefully onto your loosened subsoil, setting it down like a piece of cake. The flat blade allows you to dig to a uniform depth.

For more on double digging, see p. 82.

Because its blade is straight rather than curved like a pointed shovel, a spade can make neat corners and even vertical sides. It's also useful when transplanting young trees and shrubs. Its long blade gets under the roots and allows you to lift a rootball. It's equally useful for dividing clumping perennials.

ESSENTIAL TOOLS FOR WORKING THE SOIL

Since tools are extensions of the hand, it makes sense to look for simple and strong tools that keep you in touch with the ground you're working. Of the following five tools, four of them are pretty much essential to prepping your garden beds: a spade, a fork, a cultivator, and a level-head rake. If your subsoil is impenetrable, the deep spader should be on your list, too.

The flat blade of the D-handle garden spade is ideal for edging beds.

Besides loosening and aerating soil, the D-handle garden fork is perfect for mixing in soil amendments like fish meal.

D-handle garden fork

This tool is a gardener's right hand. You'll almost never leave the garden shed without it. Built like the D-handle spade with its short ash handle, the fork features a forged steel head with four 11-in. tines. Use a garden fork for many jobs: to loosen, cultivate, and aerate the soil; to mix soil amendments into the surface of a bed; to break up large clumps of soil; to prepare planting holes for perennials; to lift refuse out of the wheelbarrow onto the compost heap; to aerate compost; and to dig potatoes. In a garden with wide beds and narrow paths, the short D-handle allows you to twist and lever the fork in tight spaces.

After edging a bed with the spade, use the fork and a cultivator to break up the soil in the bed. If the soil is friable, the fork is sufficient to work it into plantable shape. (If it's tough, use the cultivator first.) The fork is especially handy to loosen, but not turn over, the subsoil. Work the fork into the soil as deep as it will go, using a back and forth motion, then pull back on the handle to pry and loosen the deeper soil. This improves drainage and gives future roots some breathing room. Don't try this around irrigation lines, however.

Garden forks are available in various lengths to match the stature of the gardener and are made of various materials to suit the pocketbook. Beware of garden center versions with rolled steel tines, which won't hold up well in tough soil.

Cultivator

Built like a large hoe with flat tines instead of a single blade, the cultivator works like a muscle-powered roto-tiller. With this tool in hand, you can quickly plow through the soil, dislodging weeds, breaking up compacted surface soil, loosening, mixing, and generally getting a bed ready for planting. One common variation has three pointed tines, a good design for breaking up tough soil. Even better, though, is one with flat, chisellike forged-steel tines with which you can either chop or chip away at the soil.

When tackling a weedy, neglected bed, use the cultivator first. After working your way through the bed,

you can simply rake out the weeds. Another pass with the cultivator will prepare the bed for amendments or for deeper cultivation with either the garden fork or the deep spader. When adding manure or compost to the bed, use the cultivator to chop and mix.

Deep spader

When you need to loosen the soil deeply, deeper than you can go with the garden fork, for planting tomatoes or potatoes or any other deep-rooted summer vegetables, you need a deep spader. It requires heavy lifting to use this thing—it weighs in at about 25 lbs.—but for serious, large-scale gardening you can't beat it for breaking up the subsoil.

Shaped like a large fork with a handle made of 1-in. pipe, a tubular crossbar, and four 16-in.-long pointed triangular blades, the deep spader is built to penetrate tough soils easily, even those that haven't been deeply cultivated before. You get the benefits of double digging without the backaches.

To use the deep spader, carry (or drag) it to the bed you want to work and heave the tines into the soil. Hold onto the handle and stand on the bar to which the tines are attached, as if you were getting on a pogo stick. As you rock the tool back and forth and side to side, the tines will sink into the earth. When they won't go any deeper, step off backward and pull the handle toward you. As you pull, the spader will break up the subsoil without exposing it to too much light and air. Lift the giant fork out of the ground and repeat as many times as necessary. Although it's a workout, you can spade a lot of ground in a surprisingly short time, and the deep cultivation is worth the effort.

When it comes to breaking up soil, the chisel-like forged tines of this cultivator are stronger than the rolled steel tines of the more common three-pronged cultivators.

The labors of Hercules might have been easier with this heroic fork. To loosen the soil deeply, thrust it into the ground, stand on the crossbar, and then step off backward and pull the handle toward you, really putting your weight into it.

The back of a level-head rake is just the thing for smoothing out garden beds.

Level-head rake

When a bed has been shaped, dug, and cultivated, it's time to use a level-head rake to finish it, to give it a final shape, to smooth its surface, and to pulverize or rake away any large dirt clods. This gives a fine surface for broadcasting seeds or transplanting. (After broadcasting small seeds such as carrots and beets, use the rake once again to lightly chop the seeds into the soil.)

A bow rake seems to flex when you're breaking up soil, but a strongly attached level-head rake transfers more force to the ground. You can use the back of the rake to smooth surfaces and make hills and raised beds. Use the back to clean paths between beds. A level-head rake also does an excellent job of mixing soil amendments into the top few inches of the soil.

CHAPTER 4
PLANNING AND PLANTING

You might think that putting your garden to bed in the fall or winter is the end of the gardening year. In fact, it's just the opposite. Fall is—or should be—the beginning of the gardening year, since you are not only preparing the garden to face the winter but also readying it for an early start come spring.

The fun really begins, though, when you start looking at catalogs that arrive in the bleak winter months. Those, coupled with the journal of last year's garden, will start you on the journey of thinking about what you want to do with this year's garden.

STRATEGIZE YOUR VEGETABLE GARDEN

Good soil, plenty of nutrients, and adequate water are good starting points for a productive vegetable garden, but there are other things you can do to maximize your garden's output. Two important steps are planning ahead and then staying organized about where and when you plant. Whether your goal is a very high-output garden that will keep you in vegetables and herbs all season or just enough bounty to make the most of your efforts, practicing the following techniques can make you a better gardener.

Even a small space can hold a mix of vegetables, herbs, and ornamentals, as evidenced by this front-yard garden. The trick is to have a solid garden plan from the get-go.

Become a planner

If you don't have a scale drawing of your vegetable garden, you should make one. Twenty minutes spent with pencil, paper, and ruler will pay big dividends year after year, both when you're figuring out a planting scheme and when you're calculating how much fertilizer or soil amendment to add. Graph paper makes it easy to draw the beds to scale, but all those squares get in the way later. The solution is to make the first drawing on graph paper using a dark, heavy pen. Then lay plain paper over the graph paper and trace the outline of the beds. Note somewhere in the margin the square footage of each area. This second drawing is your master plan (toss the graph paper). Make photocopies and use these to plan your plantings.

The best time to start planning next year's garden is late summer or fall (for more on this see p. 137). Not only are the current year's plantings right there before

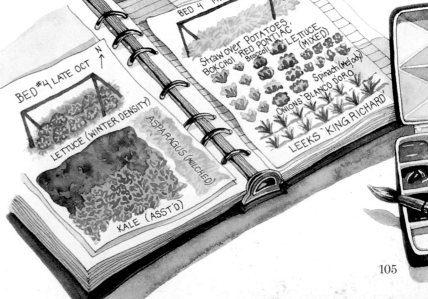

your eyes, instead of a distant memory, but crops that bridge two growing seasons, like garlic and salad greens that are planted in fall and come out the following spring or summer, affect where you plant next summer's crops. Sometime in August, sit in the garden with that year's plan and make notes that give an accurate reflection of reality, because there are always things that didn't go according to plan. Good things to make note of include diseases and pests (including the four-legged kind), weather issues, plants spaced too close together, whether you actually liked the crops you grew, and anything else that will help inform your decisions about next year's garden. Next, pull out a clean master plan sheet and pencil in where you think next year's crops should go.

Keep your garden plans from year to year (put a date on each one). They will not only help you track recurring issues that need to be dealt with but also help you rotate your crops without having to rely on memory. This is especially important if you're not following the simple leaf/fruit/root/legume rotation described on page 114.

Play the numbers game

For the most part, a garden is an escape from things like math (great news for many of us), but some numbers are critical: your frost-free dates, and the length of your growing season, and the number of days to maturity of the vegetables you grow.

Your gardening season. Most gardeners know or have an idea when their last frost in spring is likely to occur, but what about the first fall frost? This is critical information if you want to grow long-season crops like pumpkins or winter squash, and particularly if you want to squeeze in a late planting of a quick-maturing crop or if you plan to garden through the fall. You can find frost dates in an almanac, from your county extension service, or on the Internet. The number of days between the last frost in spring and

first frost in fall is the length of your growing season. Memorize your frost dates, but keep in mind they are not cast in stone; they are *averages*. Be sure to add these dates to your yearly master plan as well.

Days to maturity. Most catalogs and seed packets note a crop's days to maturity. This indicates how long it will take the plant to produce something harvestable, counting from germination for direct-seeded crops, and from transplanting for crops started indoors. As with frost-free dates, consider the number of days to maturity as a *guideline*—the actual number will vary depending on your climate and growing conditions. For example, if you plant warm-season crops before soil and air are adequately warm, they'll take longer than normal to bear fruit. Likewise, if you plant them later than normal, when summer is in full swing, they'll mature earlier than the listed time. A cool summer slows things down; a hot one speeds them up.

Create a gardening calendar

The third prong in your garden-planning strategy is to keep a garden calendar. Every January, get yourself some kind of calendar—a desk calendar, a wall calendar, or a day planner—and use it to schedule sowing and transplanting tasks. When your seeds arrive, sit down with the calendar, your planting plan, the seed catalog, and the seed packets. Make notes about when to start what indoors, when to transplant, and when to direct-sow other crops. For certain crops, you might want to note when they should be ready to harvest and when to take them out to make room for another planting. Block out any lengthy planned absences from the garden, like vacations or business trips, at the beginning of this process so you can schedule around them. During the growing season, make notes on the calendar about when you start and finish harvesting a crop, rainfall data, and other significant events, like weather extremes.

Keep the calendar handy, because if it's out of sight and not being updated, then it won't be useful in the long run. You may never do *everything* that's on the calendar, but it will help you to remember to do things on time.

SUN VS. SHADE

Sunlight is, of course, what makes the garden go 'round. In the process of photosynthesis, green plants capture the sun's energy and transform it into a form they can store and use. The more efficient the plant is at this extraordinary process, the more shade it can handle. Plants with broad, flat, all-green leaves that tilt at various angles are ideal solar collectors—and the more abundant the leaves, the better.

One characteristic of plants that do well in shade is that they don't manufacture large, sweet fruits—like tomatoes. A trait in common is their acidity, with tangy-tasting leaves and fruit.

The quality of sunlight varies. Partial sun in June is more intense than partial sun in September. Furthermore, an hour's sun in Seattle hasn't the candlepower of the same hour of sun in Miami. That's because the sun's rays strike straight down at the equator, then become increasingly oblique, or milder, as the sun moves farther north or south.

You can remove low-hanging tree branches to increase the light under a tree, making it a suitable place to grow some edibles. But take note: Growing plants under trees means they'll have competition for water and nutrients from the tree's roots. Also, irrigating moisture-loving

A Journal Tells the Story

Keeping a journal will help you find your garden's unique patterns. Although the most important thing is to simply record information in your journal, there are three essentials that will make it most useful.

- Log the **weather** carefully: first and last frosts, dates and amounts of precipitation, and average night and day temperatures.

- Record your **soil preparation and amendments.**

- Note the **source of seeds and plants** so you can weed out unreliable suppliers.

Beyond those basics, you can record all manner of events, insights, and level of detail. Did that touted tomato type grow vigorously, withstanding pests and disease? Did the new broccoli planting form heads before that early freeze? How long did it produce usable side shoots? Which beds are due this year for manure? When was each variety sown, transplanted, set out, and harvested? Make a special effort to record the elements of this last question on the relevant day in the calendar.

As you build your journal, it will come closer to a perfect planting guide for your microclimate. This is important if you're trying to figure out how to manage succession planting.

➤ *For more information on succession planting, see page 115.*

Let the garden past lead to the spring ahead. Fall offers a good time to consider the successes so you can begin heading off potential failures next year. A well-kept journal can provide a good shopping list and, more important, a day-by-day planting timetable for the coming year.

Vegetable Gardening in the Shade

STUDY THE SHADE PATTERNS

The first step in developing your shady area into a garden is to track the shade patterns. Take a look several times a day and make a rough sketch of the sun's progress at key hours. The shade patterns will vary from dense to dappled at different times, which will create shade zones. Use the same technique if structures rather than trees are casting shade, but keep in mind that structures create drier and more solid shade.

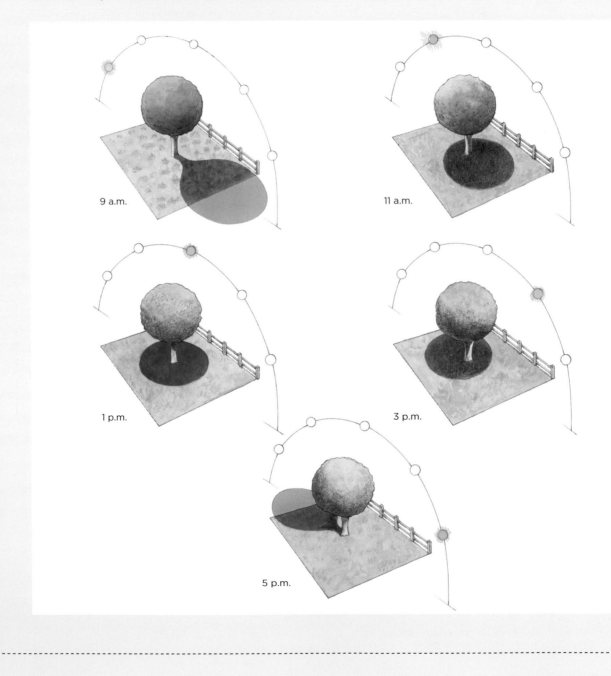

9 a.m.

11 a.m.

1 p.m.

3 p.m.

5 p.m.

FIND THE ZONES

If you overlay the effects of the sun's movement throughout the day, you'll see shade zones emerge. The diagram below shows these zones based on patterns formed at two-hour intervals from 9 a.m. to 5 p.m. The zones are a bit oversimplified because morning sun is weaker than afternoon sun, but the number of hours of sun a day is a good guide for deciding what to plant where.

CHOOSE YOUR PLANTS

The chart below lists just a smattering of the edibles that will live in a shady garden. The first zone shown for each plant is its preference, the second the shadiest it will tolerate. In selecting plants, remember the role your climate plays. Plants that appreciate afternoon shade in Atlanta may need all-day sun in Vancouver.

Zones determined by shade patterns

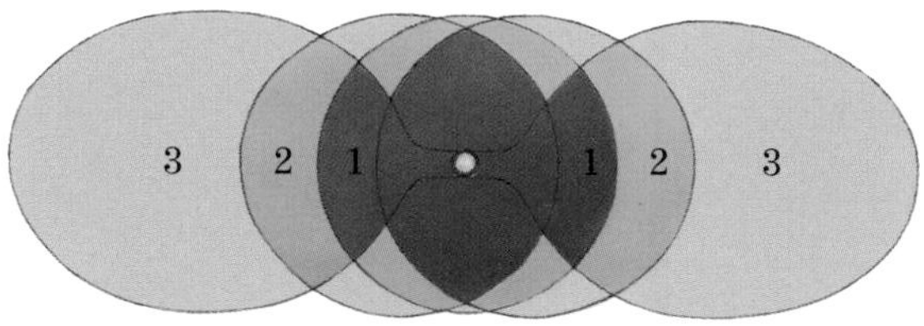

Hours of Sunlight Per Zone

Zone	Hours of Sun
1	0-2 hours
2	3-4 hours
3	4-5 hours

Take Your Pick of Plants	Zone
A DOZEN VEGETABLES	
Amaranth, arugula, asparagus, bok choys, Chinese cabbages, garland chrysanthemum, mustard greens, spinaches	3, 2
Chicories, endives/escaroles, kales, lettuces, sorrel	3, 1
A DOZEN CULINARY HERBS	
Anise hyssop, common and garlic chives, lemon balm, lovage, mitsuba, perilla, pineapple sage, sweet bay	3, 2
Bergamot/bee balm, chervil, horseradish, true mints, parsley	3, 1

The owners of this garden interspersed many edible flowers in with vegetables not only to beautify the garden but also to use in cooking.

plants like vegetables isn't always in sync with the tree's needs, so be sure you are informed before you plant a garden under the drip line of a tree.

PLANTING SCHEMES

How you arrange the various crops you grow can make a difference in the health and productivity of your garden. If you're not keeping track of where you grow different crops year to year, you may not be getting the most out of your garden—or giving your vegetables all they need. And you may be making needless work for yourself.

Rotate crops for a healthy garden

Moving plants around from year to year is one of the best techniques to minimize disease and bug problems and to maximize soil fertility. Various rotation plans are popular. The simplest is to not plant the same thing in the same place three years in a row. This strategy is designed to ward off pests. For example, if cabbage looper pupa nestles down in the cabbage debris in October and reawakens the following spring to more cabbage, that's instant sustenance. But if you've moved the cabbage, the looper may die trying to find its food.

To minimize disease and insect problems, many gardeners rotate their crops based on plant relationships within a plant family. The major plant families—there are others besides those listed here—are alliums (onion, leek, shallot, garlic, and chives), brassicas (broccoli, Brussels sprouts, cabbage, cauliflower, kohlrabi, mustard, and turnip), composites (lettuce, endive, and artichoke), cucurbits (melons, zucchini, squash, and cucumber), and nightshades (tomato, potato, pepper, and eggplant). Rotating crops within one family is a good system, but it can require subdividing your garden into lots of different beds, since there are so many plant families involved.

There's a simpler system that's easy to remember and implement. It separates crops based on their nutritional requirements. It so happens that plants fall pretty neatly into leafy crops, fruiting crops, and root crops. A fourth division is for legumes—peas and beans—which technically are fruits, but get their own plot because they actually add more nutrients to the soil than they take. By default, this system separates families and so helps to diminish pest problems. Leaf/fruit/root/legume is a workable crop rotation plan, with no detailed list of plant relationships and no bookkeeping necessary.

To follow this system, divide the garden into four sections and plant each with one of the following groups: leaf, fruit, root, legume. Every year, rotate the plantings so the leaf group moves to where the legumes grew the season before, and the other groups all move over a section.

Having four areas of roughly equal size makes this system work, even though you'll probably want to grow more of one kind of crop than another. If you make each division big enough to hold the largest group you grow, you can fill the empty spaces in the smaller rotations with cover crops. If the areas aren't the same size, when it comes time to put the largest group—say, the fruits—into a too-small space, you'll be tempted to sneak some extra tomatoes or peppers in where they don't belong. And then your nice, neat system has been breached.

➡ *For more information on cover crops, see page 115.*

Leaves love nitrogen. Plants like lettuce, spinach, herbs, cabbage, and broccoli need plenty of nitrogen to build strong stems and leaves. Nitrogen is the most readily soluble of all the nutrients and therefore the hardest for the soil to hold onto. So it's important to grow leaf crops in soil that's had a fresh infusion of nitrogen. Manure or green manure (see "Using Cover Crops" on p. 115) is the cornerstone. During the growing season, you can also sidedress the plants in the leaf bed with alfalfa or fish or blood meal, and if necessary spray them with a fish emulsion solution.

➡ *For more information on sidedressing, see page 283.*

For fruits, use phosphorus. Tomatoes, squash, cucumbers, peppers—everything that develops as a result of a flower being pollinated—are fruits. These crops need generous amounts of phosphorus to set blossoms and develop fruit. If the soil is very rich in nitrogen, the leaves will be luxurious, but flowers and fruits will be few. Bone meal and rock phosphate are the best sources of phosphorus. Bone meal breaks down sooner and needs to be renewed more often. Rock phosphate takes a year to become fully available, but one application lasts for five years.

Muskmelon
Cucumis melo

Practicing Crop Rotation: The Same Bed over Four Years

If you rotate crops according to their nutritional requirements, then you can add soil amendments in rotation, too. This illustration, showing the same bed over four years, indicates how different types of crops take up different nutrients.

FALL OF PRIOR YEAR **YEAR 1: LEAF CROP** **YEAR 2: FRUIT CROP**

Roots rely mainly on potassium. Onions, garlic, turnips, carrots, radishes, and other root crops are heavy potassium users. At the same time, they need even less nitrogen than fruits. That's fine, because by the third year, most of the nitrogen has been used up, but the leisurely potassium is ready and waiting to go to work. Greensand is a great potassium source because it also yields dozens of trace minerals and helps break up clay soil. Wood ashes, gypsum, kelp, and granite dust are also good sources of potassium.

Legumes put nitrogen back into the soil. Beans and peas pull nitrogen from the air and store it in their

roots. Grow these in the last year of the cycle because when their roots decompose in the soil, the nitrogen becomes available for next year's leaf rotation. And the spent plants, when turned into the garden, add organic matter.

Rotate amendments, too. Another big benefit to this rotation system is that it's easy to remember when and where to add soil amendments. Every fall, amend only the bed that will hold next year's leaf rotation. First test your soil, and then add manure and whatever amendments the test results recommend: lime, rock phosphate, greensand.

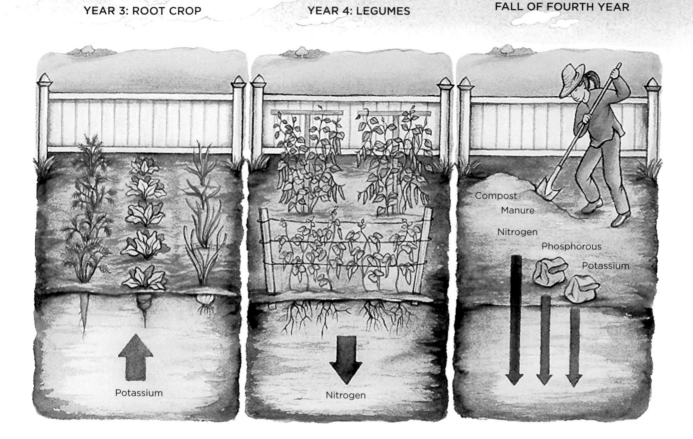

YEAR 3: ROOT CROP   YEAR 4: LEGUMES   FALL OF FOURTH YEAR

Compost
Manure

Nitrogen

Phosphorous

Potassium

Potassium

Nitrogen

At this time, you should also spread compost over the entire garden. This program is based on using organic amendments, which stay in the soil longer than nonorganic fertilizers. If you're not cover cropping, you'll need to add manure to every bed every year.

➺ *For more information on testing your soil, see page 81.*

Every rule has exceptions. Some of the crops that don't fit neatly into this rotation system include corn, potatoes, and garlic. Corn is a heavy user of nitrogen so it's best grown in the leaf rotation, even though it's a fruiting crop. You can plant corn seed right into your lettuce patch; the growing corn shades the lettuce and takes over when the lettuce is finished.

Potatoes are roots, but they are also in the nightshade family, same as tomatoes, peppers, and eggplants. Potatoes tend to suffer more pest problems when they follow their relatives. A solution is to plant potatoes in the legume bed, which keeps them two years away from their kin.

Finally, garlic is a little awkward because its growing season stretches from fall to summer. Plant garlic in October in the fruit bed, which will be the root bed the following year.

Following the Planting Beds through the Year

This chart shows examples of vegetables you can grow over a year in each rotation.

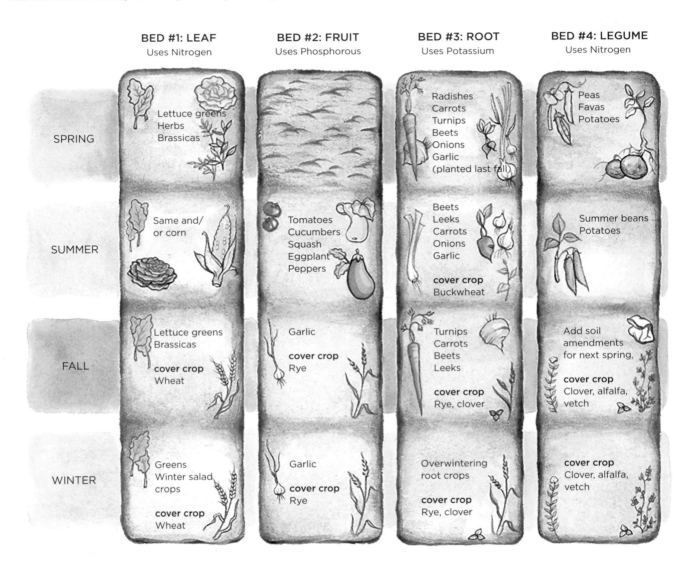

	BED #1: LEAF Uses Nitrogen	BED #2: FRUIT Uses Phosphorous	BED #3: ROOT Uses Potassium	BED #4: LEGUME Uses Nitrogen
SPRING	Lettuce greens Herbs Brassicas		Radishes Carrots Turnips Beets Onions Garlic (planted last fall)	Peas Favas Potatoes
SUMMER	Same and/ or corn	Tomatoes Cucumbers Squash Eggplant Peppers	Beets Leeks Carrots Onions Garlic **cover crop** Buckwheat	Summer beans Potatoes
FALL	Lettuce greens Brassicas **cover crop** Wheat	Garlic **cover crop** Rye	Turnips Carrots Beets Leeks **cover crop** Rye, clover	Add soil amendments for next spring, **cover crop** Clover, alfalfa, vetch
WINTER	Greens Winter salad crops **cover crop** Wheat	Garlic **cover crop** Rye	Overwintering root crops **cover crop** Rye, clover	**cover crop** Clover, alfalfa, vetch

LEAF   FRUIT   ROOT   LEGUME

CROP ROTATION OVER FOUR YEARS

Every year, each group moves to the next space. Every four years, the groups are back in their original spots.

Plant for productivity with succession planting

If you're like most gardeners, you plant in spring, harvest in summer, and clean up your garden in the fall. But to get the most production out of a garden, you should practice succession planting. Succession planting combines two techniques: interplanting quick-maturing crops with slow and small-stature crops with large, and replacing spent plants with fresh, vigorous transplants. Done throughout the growing season, succession planting can give you two or three crops in the same space rather than one.

Succession planting requires that you work in close association with your calendar and that you use transplants whenever you can. You cannot garden this way without soil that is fertile and in prime condition. So use lots of compost and add amendments: rock dust for trace minerals, oyster shell for calcium, and kelp for a balance of minerals and nitrogen.

Two planting techniques are key. Interplanting is essentially mixing different crops in the same bed. You can interplant fast-growing crops amidst slower ones and smaller crops among larger ones. For example, surround cabbages and broccoli, which grow slowly to a large size, with onions and spring greens, which are smaller and grow quickly. As the onions and greens mature and are harvested, there's more room left for the brassicas. Or grow lettuces close to tomatoes. By the time the tomatoes are getting large, you'll have cut the lettuces.

When planning to interplant, it's important to think about the growing habits of the different crops. Do they grow upright, bushy, or trailing? How large will they get? How long will they take to mature? When will you need the bed space for the next rotation?

Replacing harvested plants with transplants is succession gardening in its purest form. Sometimes you might fill a hole with the same type of plant. Lettuce is a typical

---

Using Cover Crops

Cover crops are plants grown to enhance production, reduce weeds, and stimulate soil activity. When turned under, they compost right in the soil, which is why they're also called green manure. Cover cropping is standard practice for farmers, but small-scale home gardeners can use this technique, too. You can grow cover crops during the off-season when you're not growing vegetables, and also use them to fill blank spaces in those smaller crop rotations.

Try to match the cover crop to your rotation plan. Sow legumes—clover, vetch, or alfalfa—in the legume bed and also in the leaf bed, which benefits from the extra nitrogen. After the leaf crops are harvested, sow wheat, which discourages diseases and nematodes that might plague next year's tomatoes and peppers. Mow or cut the wheat when it's about 8 in. tall, leave it on the bed over winter, and turn it under in spring.

After the fruiting crops are finished, broadcast rye over the empty bed. Rye grows more mileage of roots than any other cover crop. The decaying rye roots leave the ground fluffy, perfect for growing shapely carrots and beets. In the hiatus between spring and fall root crops, plant buckwheat, a grain that thrives in summer heat. Buckwheat discourages weeds and also loosens the soil. Take care to mow buckwheat before it flowers or else it will become a weed. After the fall roots are harvested, you're back to legumes.

example. If you keep a supply of lettuce seedlings on hand, you can fill in spaces left after cutting out mature heads. Other times, you might fill the hole with something else. For example, you might replace winter chard or beets with tomatoes and spring greens, or put summer squash where you've just harvested a cabbage.

The crops to direct-seed are those which cannot be transplanted, like carrots, turnips, and beets. Summer bean crops can be sown right in among the pea vines. Having healthy transplants on hand at the proper time is critical, and that means starting them yourself. Otherwise you won't be able to find the seedlings you want when you need them.

Plan for your seasons. As discussed earlier, becoming familiar with your gardening year is important to a successful garden. This is particularly critical if you'll be practicing succession gardening. Use the calendar you created to remind you of times for sowing seed and setting out transplants. Timing is critical, particularly for the fall garden. As soon as your summer crops are in, start thinking about starting seedlings for fall crops.

Pay attention to how long it takes the varieties you're growing to mature. This will help you plan ahead. For fall growing, choose varieties that mature quickly. Count back from your fall frost date the number of days or weeks to maturity—that's the date you need to have the plant settled in the garden. Now count back another six weeks. That's the date you should sow the seed in flats.

Start small, then expand. If you're new to succession planting, start with one bed of a manageable size, say 3 ft. to 5 ft. wide and 10 ft. to 14 ft. long. This will give you room to experiment with a variety of plants. Once you're familiar with the techniques, you can expand into additional beds. It also helps to start with easy crops, like lettuces, tomatoes, peas, and beans. These are all fast growing and rewarding. Leave the more difficult crops like brassicas until you've gained some experience. In time, you'll develop a rhythm of sowing, transplanting, and harvesting that will become second nature to you.

You can devote one area of the bed to lettuces, replacing the harvested heads each week or two with new seedlings. Each month start as many plants as you'll use in that amount of time (say 40 lettuces for a family of four). In another area, set up a trellis where you can grow early spring peas. Just when the leaves start to yellow, poke bean seeds between the pea vines. When the beans are about 3 in. or 4 in. tall, cut the peas at ground level and compost the vines.

SEED-STARTING STRATEGIES

What's the best reason for starting your own seeds? Selection! The range of varieties offered by specialty seed catalogs makes the selection at a nursery seem like a limited menu. When you start your own seeds, you alone are in charge of the criteria, whether it be taste alone or whether you consider other attributes like productivity, disease tolerance, or adaptation to local conditions.

Plan to start your seeds so they are at the proper stage of development to set out at the optimum time (see "Timing Is Everything" on p. 118). For northern gardeners, this is crucial because the growing season is short, and good timing increases your production. For mild-weather gardeners, it can mean getting two or three crops in a season by removing the remnants of a harvested crop and planting three-week-old seedlings in their place. Perfecting this technique requires good timing and seed selection, understanding your climate and soil, and some practice in starting seedlings.

Find seeds

Your first step is to acquire seeds, whether you order from a catalog or select packets from a seed rack. If you want to grow plants from your own seeds in the future, be sure

When first starting out with vegetable gardening, try a couple of raised beds. Even when they're a modest size, like 4 ft. wide by 8 ft. or 9 ft. long, there's plenty of room to experiment with different crops without getting overwhelmed.

to use open-pollinated or heirloom seeds. Seeds from a hybrid, which is the result of crossing two plants, will not produce a plant identical to the hybrid. Talk to gardening friends and county extension agents to find out which varieties do well in your area. You can also search the website of your state land-grant university, which has an agriculture department (see Resources, p. 284). Buy some tried-and-true varieties and do some experimenting as well.

Try to resist the temptation to order more seeds than you're likely to use in a year. That's hard to do in midwinter, when the seed catalogs come and every variety sounds like a winner. But seeds don't keep forever. Even in unopened packets stored under ideal conditions (cool, dark, and dry), germination rates diminish with each

passing season. The germ rate of leftover seed in opened packets goes downhill even faster. For more details on how to store leftover seed, see p. 124.

Select the right containers

You'll need containers that have drainage holes and a tray to catch excess water. The range of potential containers is wide. Plastic plant 6-packs and 4-in. containers will serve most of your needs, and you can reuse them. Pressed peat pots and peat pellets, which you plant right in the garden with the seedling, are good for crops whose roots you shouldn't disturb. Peat pots tend to restrict the progress of the seedlings' roots; peat pellets work a little better. There are even pressed pots made from composted cow manure— a biodegradable container with a little fertilizer built right in! Just be aware that the organic pots dry quickly and need to be monitored for moisture. You can even use paper cups, which are great for sharing seedlings with friends.

You can make a long-lasting, wooden, 12-in. by 16-in. seedling box (see the bottom photo on p. 119) that fits under standard grow-light tubes. You can also buy a gadget that compresses soil into blocks or one that molds newspaper into biodegradable pots. A cheap but effective container is a disposable foil baking dish with holes poked in the bottom; use a second one as a drip tray to catch excess water.

Whatever you use, be sure it's clean. Wash recycled containers in a weak solution of laundry bleach to sterilize.

Use a good, sterile, soilless mix

Next, you'll need a starting mix. There are some great seed-starting mixes on the market. Look around for one that fits your budget, or mix your own. A starting mix should be a sterile, lightweight medium that will stay moist without compacting. Standard ingredients for achieving this are vermiculite, perlite, peat moss, and sphagnum moss.

Using a soilless mix lessens the chance of a common seed-starting disease called damping off, which rots stems

Timing Is Everything

Resist the urge to start seeds too soon. Seedlings that languish inside, waiting for settled weather, become leggy and weak. Check your last date of frost and group your seeds according to the starting date.

Label your varieties and their starting dates. And remember that some seeds take longer to germinate than others. Here's a rough estimate of the lead time for popular seeds.

Crop	When to Start Seed Indoors	When to Set Plants Out
CABBAGE, BROCCOLI, COLLARDS	4 to 6 weeks before setting out	2 to 4 weeks before last frost
CUCUMBERS, MELONS	2 weeks before last frost	When soil is warm and night temperatures are at least 55°F
EGGPLANT	6 weeks before last frost	2 to 3 weeks after last frost, when soil temperature is at least 60°F
LETTUCE	3 to 4 weeks before setting out	4 to 5 weeks before last frost
ONIONS	8 to 10 weeks before last frost	2 to 4 weeks before last frost
PEPPERS	8 to 12 weeks before setting out	2 to 3 weeks after last frost, when night temperatures are at least 60°F
TOMATOES	6 to 8 weeks before setting out	When soil is warm and night temperatures stay above 45°F

and topples seedlings. So does cleaning containers and tools in hot, soapy water with a tad of bleach. A thin layer of perlite on top of the soilless mix will keep moisture away from emerging stems. Some slow-to-germinate seeds benefit from being covered with plastic to maintain moisture. If you do this, be careful not to produce a jungle environment, because too much moisture and warmth will promote fungal growth. Uncover the container as soon as the seeds have sprouted.

Stay away from unsterilized soil, compost, or worm castings until the seedlings are ready for transplanting. And if the seedlings must remain in the container for a while, fertilize with a weak solution of fish or seaweed emulsion.

Make sprouting successful

Fill your container with 3 in. to 4 in. of starting mix, up to about ½ in. from the top. Moisten thoroughly with warm water; this eliminates the need for top watering immediately after sowing so the seeds won't be displaced.

Next, take a look at the size of the seeds; this will dictate how deep and how far apart to plant them. The three-seed rule applies whether starting seed in a pot or in the ground. Place three seeds in a line. The length of this line is how deep you should plant the seed. For example, plant peas about 1 in. deep; spinach seeds, ¼ in. deep.

Tiny seeds like lettuce and parsley should be broadcast (sprinkled) across the top of the soil or planting medium and then covered ever so lightly. When broadcasting, be sure not to sow too many seeds, or they will be difficult to separate later. The ideal distance between seeds will provide enough space so the resulting seedlings and their roots do not touch or intertwine. Basically, the longer you plan to leave the seedlings in their first home, the farther apart the seeds should be sown.

Once the seeds are planted, you must keep the planting medium moist and warm. Place freshly planted containers on a heated seed-starting mat or in a warm spot in the house. Any place the cat likes to hang out will be appropri-

This homemade flat will last through many growing seasons. The screen mesh on the bottom keeps soil in but allows excess water to pass through.

Seed Starting Step-by-Step

1. Use containers that have drainage holes like old plastic plant containers. Or make a home-made flat with screen mesh on the bottom to keep the soil in but allow excess water to pass through.

2. Use a soilless mix and, as a general rule, space seeds three lengths apart and three lengths deep.

3. Transplant seedlings after they have at least one set of true leaves. Grasp the seedling by a leaf rather than by its stem to avoid damaging the stem.

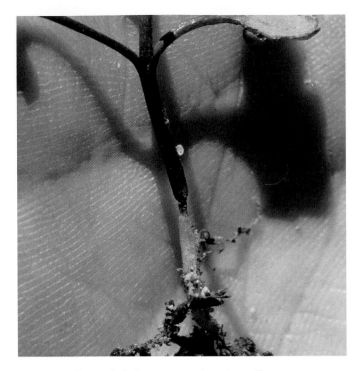

Using a soilless mix helps prevent damping off, a fungus that attacks a seedling's stem where it meets the soil.

ate, or try the top of the dryer, near a heater, on the gas stove, or on a windowsill. Individual varieties have different temperature requirements for germination. Some seed packets will furnish this information, but you can figure most will germinate between 60°F and 80°F. Seeds need warmer temperatures to germinate than young seedlings need for growth, so after the sprouts have true leaves, move them to a cooler home. Some seeds need light to germinate, so check the packet for this information, as well.

For more information on true leaves, see p. 282.

Letting the potting mix dry out or allowing soil temperatures to fluctuate widely will reduce your germination rate. Check the containers daily to be sure the mix is moist. It's preferable to water from the bottom; simply set the containers in a shallow pan of cool—not cold—water.

Let there be light

Once the seedlings emerge, they need a lot of light; spindly growth will tell you they're not getting enough. Incan-

descent lights won't do because they don't provide the full spectrum of light that growing plants need. Use grow lights or fluorescent lights instead. Place seedlings under them for 12 to 16 hours a day. Longer than that, and the plant won't be able to go through the metabolic processes required for growth.

The key to using lights is positioning the plants at the right distance from the source—nearly touching when the plants are newly emerged, increasing up to 4 in. later. Plants in a sunny window can grow leggy reaching for the sun, so rotate them a quarter turn each day to keep them straight.

Seedlings need room to develop healthy roots and stems. Overcrowding will diminish air circulation and light. Even with the best effort at careful spacing during planting, you may have to remove some plants. Pinch them out or use small scissors to nip stems at the soil line; this makes for less root disturbance to remaining seedlings.

Pot on and pinch back

Whether you start your own seeds or buy seedlings, chances are they'll need to be potted on before you can get them in the ground. This is especially true of those crops that can't be planted until the soil has warmed up, like tomatoes, peppers, and eggplants. Cramped, crowded roots will send seedlings into quick decline. So move them up to larger pots where root growth can continue to progress with leaf development, a process known as potting on. Four-in. pots are a good size for little plants that have outgrown 6-packs. If you're separating seedlings started in a flat, gently tease apart roots with your fingers or a pencil. Handle the seedlings gently, holding the plants by a leaf to prevent damaging the stems.

Given good conditions, seedlings grow quickly. The plant hormone auxin is present in a seedling's terminal bud and assists in growth by making cell walls more elastic. Auxin, however, suppresses growth at a seedling's

Make Your Own Soilless Mix

THE RECIPE

1 part peat moss
1 part perlite
1 part compost
1 part good garden soil

OPTIONAL

A handful each of:
Garden lime
Soybean meal
Rock phosphate
Kelp meal

Moisten the ingredients to make mixing easier. Place a 1/2-in. mesh screen over a garden cart or other large container, and sift all ingredients to remove any large particles. Mix thoroughly.

The handfuls of garden lime, soybean meal, rock phosphate, and kelp meal (any of which can be omitted) provide extra nutrients that enable this mix to feed plants for a year or two without additional fertilization.

lower lateral buds. If you pinch out the terminal bud, and thus the auxin, side shoots will grow. This results in bushy, many-branched plants and eventually more flowers and fruit. Once seedlings are 3 in. or 4 in. tall with a good supply of true leaves, pinch them back. You can use scissors or pruning shears, but thumb and forefinger work just fine.

While your seedlings are growing indoors, you can toughen them up by regularly running your hand gently over the tops of the little plants or by shaking the flat or tray to mimic the stress that breezes create on stems and leaves.

Harden off

Before planting seedlings in the garden, you'll need to harden them off, or acclimate them to the tougher conditions outdoors—strong sun, wind, and more extreme temperatures. The timetable for hardening off plants depends on outdoor temperatures as well as on the crop. Your seedlings should be ready to harden off once they have two or three true leaves. Place them in a shaded cold frame or in dappled shade for about five days, and then move them into a sunny location for another five days before transplanting them into their new home.

For more information on hardening off, see p. 280.

Be sure to label seedlings properly. If you have the tenacity to keep a record book, you will learn quickly from both your successes and errors. If keeping a record book is not for you, then use small plastic or wooden stakes (tongue depressors make excellent plant labels) and write on them with a permanent marker. Write the variety on one side and the date you started the seedlings on the other. Transplant the stakes along with the seedlings. This is also a simple way to keep track of how many days a plant takes from sowing to harvesting.

Plant outside on an overcast day

A cloudy day is best to plant seedlings in the garden. If it's lightly drizzling, all the better. If the forecast is for sun, avoid planting seedlings in midday. Get an early start in the morning, or wait until the end of the day.

Slip the seedling out of its pot and gently loosen the roots if they've become pot-bound. If your seedling is in a peat pot, peel away as much of the pot as possible without disturbing the root ball. It's especially important to remove the portion above the soil line to prevent the peat pot from wicking moisture away from the plant's roots.

Give seedlings some protection from sun and wind for a few days after they've been transplanted. Overturned baskets, row covers, or shade cloth will shelter them temporarily while roots settle in. Water the seedlings every third day, or more often if it's unusually hot, until they become established.

Depending on the plant, you may need to provide protection from insect predators. Cutworm collars are advisable for most seedlings. Cole crops (crops that are part of the cabbage family—cole is an old term for cabbage and is where cole slaw comes from) are vulnerable to the larvae of cabbage butterflies and other moths; covering the seedlings with floating row covers prevents moths from laying eggs.

➡ *For more information on row covers, see p. 127.*

Be on the lookout for slugs and remove debris that gives them a place to hide. If you suspect slug damage, check the beds at night with a flashlight and hand-pick the culprits.

Thin direct-sown seedlings for a healthy crop

Most vegetables sown directly in the soil, rather than transplanted, will need thinning. Root and salad crops are not so sensitive to root disturbance, but it is a good idea

Four weeks after sprouting, an escarole seedling is ready for the garden.

to thin when the soil is damp rather than dry. Plants slip out more easily then, and the ones you leave behind stand less risk of having their roots exposed to air pockets in the soil. If it's dry when you thin, irrigate the garden as soon as you're done to resettle the soil around the roots of the survivors.

Some root crops also can be thinned by harvesting. Tiny radishes, barely ½ in. in diameter, can be used whole in salads. Baby turnips the size of a dime steam up in just a few minutes, and the leaves can be left on. If you want baby turnips, however, be sure to grow a variety intended for that purpose. Standard turnips, such as 'American Purple Top', don't size up until the plants are quite large. They will need to be thinned early, before the roots have formed. The young greens can still be eaten, though.

No matter how delicious those young greens may be, you need to know when the crop has been sufficiently thinned. Think about the mature size of the plant or root. If you want a 2-in. beet, leave that much space between seedlings. If you want a lettuce with a wingspan of 12 in., give it 6 in. on all sides. Carrots, which are delicious even if skinny, can be left at a spacing of ½ in. to 1 in.

Once bean seedlings have their first set of true leaves, they're ready to be thinned so that each plant is 4 in. apart.

A few plants, most notably beets and chard, grow from compound seeds—actually multiple seeds that are fused together and therefore produce several plants growing from the same hole. Both crops must be thinned to prevent the plants from being spindly.

It's far better to have one-tenth of the crop flourishing than the whole lot malnourished and spindly. You don't need to go to extremes in seeding, taking care to place the tiniest seeds just so in the ground to avoid thinning later. And thinning needn't be a backbreaking task. Many crops, such as radishes, carrots, and beets, can be thinned with a garden rake. When the plants are an inch tall, drag the garden rake lightly through the row or bed on the diagonal, first one

With some plants, such as beets, the seeds come in clusters that resemble a ball of tiny oysters. Thinning is required even if you plant just one of the compound seeds.

direction and then the other. The rake's teeth will uproot just enough of the plants, leaving the rest nicely spaced.

Methods vary with the plant. It's important to not apply one thinning method to all plants. Not all crops should be thinned by yanking excess plants out of the ground, even with a rake; see some specifics below. The same advice goes for weeding. If weeds have gotten a bit out of control, cut them off instead of pulling them out.

- Peas, beans, and all members of the cucurbit family—cucumbers, melon, and squash—have fragile roots. Pulling up one plant is likely to damage the neighbor on both sides because their roots will be intertwined. Thin them immediately after they germinate, before the roots have spread too far. If you procrastinate until they are a couple of inches tall, thin with a pair of scissors, snipping excess plants off at soil level.
- Lettuce, spinach, arugula, and other salad greens can be thinned with the rake technique. However, you might like to thin these crops by hand when the leaves are large enough to use in the kitchen. Several light thin-

Know the Leaf Area Index

A seedling should produce many leaves that enlarge quickly to maximize light absorption. But how many leaves should a plant have? A practical rule is that the total leaf area in a plant canopy should be four times as large as the ground area enclosed in the circle of the drip line. This ratio, known as the leaf area index, is the most important factor determining light interception. It is controlled by plant spacing and the leaf area per plant. When the index is 4, all sunlight is absorbed and none reaches the ground. If the index exceeds 4, the lower leaves will be too shaded for photosynthesis. If the index is less than 4, some sunlight is wasted because it reaches the ground and is not used for photosynthesis.

The rate of leaf expansion and the number of leaves per stem is controlled genetically, and plant breeders incorporate these traits when selecting cultivars. Seed growers consider the leaf area index when making recommendations on spacing plants. When seedlings or seeds are planted in the garden, the spacing between plants and rows controls the competition among plants for sunlight.

Spacing recommendations printed on seed packets should be taken seriously. Seed growers already have figured in the light interception requirements for photosynthesis, which varies from plant to plant. Peas can be seeded 1 in. apart because the leaves are small. Summer squash seedlings should be thinned so they are 30 in. apart because the foliage will turn out to be quite large.

nings, rather than one heavy one, will provide salad ingredients for several weeks.

- Beets must be thinned so that they don't produce all tops and no roots. The rake method works well for thinning.
- Chard that's not thinned will grow many small, spindly leaves and no large one with those delectable crunchy ribs.
- Carrots, when thinned, will release carroty perfume throughout the garden, attracting carrot flies. The carrot fly, also called the carrot rust fly, lays eggs near the crown of the plant; these hatch into maggots, which tunnel through the roots. Be careful to take the thinnings out of the garden rather than throw them on the ground. You also can cover the carrot patch with a floating row cover for several days after thinning to thwart the fly until the scent dissipates.

SEED SAVING

There are a variety of reasons to save seeds. You might do it to save a plant that is unique, or you might save seeds to select a certain trait, such as flavor or disease resistance, or to perpetuate a variety that is particularly successful in

Once bean seedlings have their first set of true leaves, they're ready to be thinned so that each plant is 4 in. apart.

your garden. Two other big reasons: to save money or to preserve the memory of the gardener who first gave you the seed.

It's important to identify your goal and save accordingly, since the reason you choose to save seeds will likely impact what you save and how you save it. If your goal is to maintain or increase the stock of a particular variety, then save the seeds from at least a dozen plants, because the more genetic diversity the better. If you want a particular trait, save seeds from as many plants that show that trait as possible. In either case, look for healthy plants growing in good soil. Mark the plants whose seed you plan to harvest, or simply pull out the plants you don't want.

Unless your plants are growing a far distance from other gardens and therefore safe from visiting pollinators loaded with foreign pollen, you may prefer to save the seeds of self-pollinating plants. These are much less likely to cross unexpectedly with a neighbor. Crops that fall into this category include tomatoes and beans, where each flower has both male and female parts.

The only way to be sure that the plants you raise from the seeds you save will resemble their parents is to save seeds from nonhybrid or open-pollinated varieties. If you save the seeds of hybrids, crosses between two highly inbred plants, the seeds may be sterile or, if not, the plants you grow from them may resemble one or the other parent variety. Some crops are tricky. Corn is wind-pollinated and therefore hard to isolate from cross-pollination. Melons, squash, pumpkins, and cucumbers cross easily and therefore need to be hand-pollinated to assure they'll come true from the seed you save.

Harvesting and cleaning techniques

How you harvest the seeds depends on how they are produced. Fleshy fruits such as tomatoes, peppers, eggplants, and watermelons can be handled alike. When the fruits are very ripe, harvest them, split them open, and

Make Your Own Seed Packets

Use the template at right as a starting point in designing your own personalized seed packets. Get as creative as you want with artwork and embellishment, or cut plant photos from catalogs for reference. Use the filled packets as package tags during the holidays or to accompany other garden gifts like pickles and jams. Three or four seed packets tied together with a pretty ribbon or raffia make a special gift in their own right.

1. Photocopy or trace the pattern at right. You can use different types and color of paper, as long as it's thin enough to fold.

2. Cut along the solid black line.

3. Fold along the dotted lines.

4. Fold over the large flap first (A). Glue flap B down with rubber cement, then flap C.

5. After the rubber cement has dried, you may wish to decorate your packet. Remember to leave room on either the front or back of the

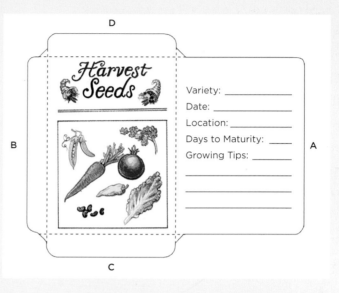

packet for plant information: variety, where it was grown, date seed was collected, days to maturity, and any helpful hints you can pass along with your seeds.

6. Fill the packet with your seeds. Fold the last flap (D) down and glue.

remove the seeds. Spread the seeds on an old window screen or a wire mesh strainer and clean them with a water sprayer. Spread them out and leave them until they feel very dry, then seal in jars or plastic bags, labeled with the year of harvest, variety, and a brief description. The germination rate and disease resistance of tomatoes improves if you squeeze the seeds and surrounding gel into a container and let them ferment for a few days. Wash any mold away on a fine screen, let the seed dry, and store.

For lettuce, carrots, parsley, cilantro, and leeks, let the plants go to flower and gather the seeds as they dry.

Take a paper bag into the garden, bend the seed heads into the bag, and shake and rub until the dry seeds fall into the bag. You can separate the chaff by pouring the seeds back and forth between two bowls in a light breeze.

When the seeds of chard and beets are dry and brown and beginning to fall from the stalks, strip them by hand into a paper bag and dry them in the sun for a day or two. They are a bit prickly, so you might want to wear gloves.

Beets can be dug up in the fall and inspected. Save the best ones for replanting in the spring and then let them set seed. Onions can be treated this way, too. Harvest in early

Most seed companies put basic growing information on their seed packets. A few stop at the barest basics: planting season depth, spacing, and days to germination and to maturity. Having dated seed packets is important if you don't use a whole packet in one season or if some packets go unopened. Dates are required on packets sold off seed racks, but not on those sold by mail. If your mail-order seeds arrive undated, write the year on the packets so you'll know how old the seed is, if you end up not sowing all the seed this year.

Ferry-Morse®, Henry Field's®, Irish Eyes, Gurney's®, Harris®, Johnny's Selected Seeds®, Seeds of Change™, and Stokes® all provide quality seed and detailed growing information on the packets. It is worth calling attention to the extras. Territorial Seed lists the usual life of the seed, which, along with a dated packet, is of real value. Ferry-Morse gives outdoor planting dates for different zones. Perhaps most enlightened of all is Irish Eyes Garden Seeds, which includes not only pest control, but also seed-saving directions for open-pollinated varieties. The hands-down winner, though, is Stokes, whose packets give as much information as a magazine article and often have a drawing of a new seedling for identification.

summer, select the healthiest specimens, put them in mesh bags, store them, and, after they sprout, replant them in the fall. This becomes your seed crop the following summer.

You can let podded seeds such as beans, peas, okra, broccoli, and arugula dry on the plant until the pods are brittle and split easily. Then crush them into a bag or bucket and separate the chaff. Before storing bean seeds, put them in the freezer for three days to kill any bean weevil eggs. You can't see the eggs, but the hatching larvae can turn your most carefully planned bean-seed-saving project to dust.

Label your seeds carefully with the date, the crop name, and variety (like 'Anasazi' bean), or if you don't know the variety, at least a description (Uncle Joe's Italian onion).

Seeds vary in longevity. Properly dried and stored in airtight containers, lettuce, eggplant, and broccoli seeds should remain viable for five years; tomatoes, peppers, beets, and chard for four years. Beans, peas, leeks, and carrots will last about three years; onions will last for one to two years. Heat and moisture severely shorten the seed life. Ideal storage conditions are cool, dark, and dry. It's a good idea to put a packet of silica gel desiccant (available at craft stores) in the container to help keep moisture low; you can also use raw rice.

PLANT PROTECTORS AND SEASON EXTENDERS—ROW COVERS, TUNNELS, AND CLOCHES

The urge to garden usually strikes before the last spring frost has hit and often stretches past the first cold snap in fall. Fortunately, it's easy to extend the season at either end. If you're just getting started, consider investing in some lightweight spun-bonded row cover fabric, which can give your crops a little cold protection but also be used during the summer to keep out some of the more notorious insect pests. If you're gardening in a cold climate, plastic row covering or individual protectors like cloches,

HotKaps®, and water-filled protectors can make it possible to grow crops that wouldn't otherwise mature in your area. The ultimate season-extender is a cold frame, which you can use for hardening off seedlings, wintering over tender plants like rosemary, and even protecting an entire winter salad garden.

Row covers

Row covers offer multiple protection for plants: from wind, frost, and flying and leaping pests. They'll even protect from marauders like rabbits and woodchucks, who could chew through the fabric but are too dim to recognize the opportunity. These fabrics are ideal for covering seeds or plants because they are porous to air and water. Sunlight penetrates a row cover to warm the air and soil, creating a benign microclimate for germination and growth. In a row cover tunnel, cool-weather transplants get a significant boost, and warm-weather transplants can be set out two or more weeks earlier than usual.

There are several brands; some are made from spun-bonded polyester, while others are made from spun-bonded polypropylene. Their fibers are not woven but pressed together, and they are very strong. The lightest version, intended as a summer insect barrier only, weighs a mere 0.4 oz. per sq. yd. and transmits 90 percent to 93 percent light. Also for use as an insect barrier as well as light frost protection is a version weighing $\frac{1}{2}$ oz. per sq. yd., which transmits 85 percent of light, and provides 4°F of frost protection. For more cold protection, choose between a medium-weight fabric (1.5 oz. per sq. yd.), which transmits 50 percent available light and gives 6°F to 8°F of frost protection, and the heaviest type (3 oz. per sq. yd.), which transmits 40 percent available light and gives a whopping 10°F or more of protection.

Row covers can be purchased at garden centers and from many mail-order companies (see Resources on p. 284). The fabrics typically come in lengths of 20 ft., 50 ft., 100 ft., and 250 ft., and in widths of 5½ ft. or 6 ft. and 12 ft. The width you need depends on how your garden is laid out and the height of plants you need to protect. The larger width can be used to create a hoop house.

If your garden is sheltered from the wind, you can apply a row cover without supports. You'll need rocks to hold down the edges, but the plants themselves will support the fabric, hence the term "floating row cover." But an unsupported row cover can seriously abrade the plants under it if the wind chivvies it too long.

To make a hoop-supported tunnel, cut the fabric the length of the bed plus about 48 in., to have some slack to gather at each end. You can buy hoops to hold the row cover up, but it is far cheaper to buy 9-gauge or 12-gauge

A row cover stretched over hoops takes only about 15 minutes to install and won't abrade plants when the wind blows.

Thin wire hoops every 2 ft. support row covers.

Stretch the row cover fabric snugly over the hoops. Gather the surplus on the far side and hold it down with rocks.

Pull the ends of the fabric taut. Push the end hoops in to maintain tension, and secure the fabric with more rocks (above left). The tomato transplants (above right) are shielded from a late frost under a tunnel of spun-bonded polyester fabric.

wire and make them yourself, especially if you can find a hardware store or fence supplier that sells the wire by weight. To hold down the fabric, use fist-size rocks, bricks, or simply soil. Weighting the fabric makes more sense than using fabric staples (wire pins), which puncture the fabric.

Except when you pull back the fabric to weed or water, your transplants remain under cover as they grow. Remove it altogether when the need for protection is past, or in the case of insect-pollinated crops like squash, cucumbers, and melons, when flowering commences.

When the fabric is no longer needed, check it over, mend any holes and tears with duct tape, clean off any mud, roll it up, stuff it in a bag, and store it out of the way of mice. With care, row covers are reusable for three or more seasons.

Plastic tunnels

If you want to jump-start the growing season by warming the soil and air around your plants but you're not concerned with frost protection, you can use a perforated clear plastic film instead of spun-bonded row covers to make your tunnel. This kind of product is especially good for northern gardeners who want to grow heat-loving crops that need lots of light, like melons, winter squash, peppers, and eggplants. The clear plastic transmits nearly full light, and warms the air inside by about 10°F more than a row cover. The perforations allow for air circulation, so the interior doesn't get too hot or too moist. It may keep some insects out, but doesn't give complete protection, due to the perforations.

Individual plant protectors

There are numerous ways to protect individual plants when you set them out early. Cloches are a classic method, dating back to at least Victorian times, when they were made of heavy glass and were vented by being propped up on one side. These days they're made from practical, high-impact, UV-stable plastic and have a vent at the top. You can also fashion your own from large clear or translucent plastic bottles—1-gal. milk jugs, juice bottles, plastic carboys, and even 2-liter drink bottles. Cut the bottoms off, place the bottle over a transplant, and press it down into the earth. To anchor it securely against wind, you can punch or melt holes near the base and secure the cloche with earth staples made from pieces of coat hanger.

There are other commercially available individual plant protectors. HotKaps have been around for years. These are heavy wax paper domes with slits in the top for ventilation. As the plant grows, the slits can be opened and the plant can grow right through the top. The smaller size

A cloche made from a plastic wine jug creates a snug microclimate.

is good for crops in the squash family; the larger ones work well for tomatoes, peppers, and eggplants. At the end of the season, you can compost the HotKaps.

There are several brands of plastic plant protectors which, when filled with water, act as a mini-greenhouse. The Wall-O-Water® is the original and best known, but other brands are good, too. Basically, these are double-walled plastic sleeves with vertical cells that are open at the top. You fill the cells with water, which absorbs heat during the day and releases it at night. Wall-O-Water provides lots of cold protection—to 16°F—so it can seriously advance your first harvest of tomatoes, peppers, and eggplants. These protectors can be used year after year; patch kits are sold in case you get a puncture.

COLD FRAMES

If you're not ready for the gardening year to end with the season's first hard frost, then maybe you're ready for a cold frame. This simple bottomless box with a removable glass or plastic lid protects plants inside from excessively low temperatures, wind, snow, and rain. In doing so, it creates a microclimate that is a zone and a half warmer than your garden. Your garden may be in Maine, but the plants inside your cold frame think they're in New Jersey. A cold frame in New Jersey provides Georgia weather. The result is a harvest of fresh vegetables all winter long.

A cold frame is an excellent tool for hardening off seedlings, wintering over marginally hardy plants, or protecting cold-tolerant crops like salad greens and root crops and thereby prolonging the harvest for months.

For this last use—providing a winter harvest—you must plan ahead. You can't wait until winter to plant the winter garden. The rate that plants grow diminishes with the shortening days of fall until it almost stops. By then, the plants need to have reached harvestable size. After that, they'll hibernate successfully in the shelter of the cold frame.

Cold frames don't need to be high tech or cumbersome. This lightweight cold frame cover is made of inexpensive materials.

A layer of 2x2s attached to the bottom keeps the frame itself out of contact with the soil, helping to ensure against rot.

A Bottomless Box with a Skylight

The beauty of a cold frame is that it's simple. It's a bottomless box typically made of 2× lumber, several inches higher at the back than at the front, and covered with glass frames, called lights (see "How to Make a Classic Cold Frame" on p. 134).

The back of the frame is cut higher than the front so the angled lights can catch the slanting winter sun. You'll want to site the frames with the lights sloping toward the south in a spot where they will have as much winter sun as possible. Some shade is tolerable, but full sun is best.

If you have access to old storm windows, you can use those as lights. If you don't want to build your own frame, however, you can buy a sturdy ready-made polycarbonate-glazed cold frame (see Resources on p. 284).

Grow cold-tolerant crops

One of the keys to success is to focus on vegetables that thrive in, or at least tolerate, the cold. While a cold frame isn't going to put vine-ripened tomatoes on your table in January, it will easily provide you with the best carrots you've ever tasted, firm-fleshed leeks and scallions, succulent cooking greens, and a host of salad ingredients.

Spinach is one of the best such crops. It yields all winter in the cold frame. So does chard. Scallions are good, too—even better from the cold frame than from the outdoor garden. Carrots are outstanding. Make a big sowing on August 1 and enjoy delicious, tender baby carrots all winter. A thick layer of straw applied in late fall protects them from temperature swings.

A cold frame is a bonanza for salad lovers. You can harvest lettuce from a cold frame until it finally succumbs to repeated freeze-thaw cycles. Mâche, frisée endive, radicchio, arugula, mustard and turnip greens, and others are good cold frame candidates.

Three ideal cold frame salad crops are actually cultivated weeds. One is claytonia, also known as "miner's

Window Cold Frame

Recycle an old glass-pane window and prop on top of hay bales for a quick-to-make cold frame.

lettuce" because it was eaten in Gold Rush days. The round, succulent leaves on thin stems have a fresh, sweet taste. Minutina, a relative of the plantain weed, has slender, lightly fringed leaves that have a salty taste and crunchy texture. And 'Biondissima Trieste', a nonheading chicory, can be planted thickly to yield abundant quantities of delicious, tender, round to finely indented leaves.

How many varieties you'll be able to grow in your cold frame depends on where you live. For gardeners in Zone 6 and south, a cold frame will guarantee bounteous harvests. In the frigid winters of Zone 3, there are only five crops—spinach, scallions, mâche, claytonia, and carrots—that you can dependably harvest all winter, and only mâche during the coldest periods. If you want to increase the number of things you can harvest, erect a plastic tunnel over the cold frame, which will make a quantum leap in protection.

A cold frame timetable

Probably the most important point in using a cold frame is to start your plants early enough. Northern gardeners will need to begin in mid-July, sowing seeds for slow-growing or heat-tolerant crops like scallions, chard, and

One sowing of spinach yields from fall until spring when grown in a cold frame. Harvest it leaf by leaf, cutting 1 in. above the crown.

One of the best cold frame crops is mâche, a European salad green. Harvest and eat the entire plant, which has a mildly nutty flavor.

parsley, and for winter greens such as escarole, endive, dandelion, and radicchio. On August 1, sow carrots. By mid-August, start seeding mustard and turnip greens. And in September sow all the salad greens that germinate in cooler soil: mâche, spinach, claytonia, arugula, and mizuna, as well as radishes.

Managing the cold frame

On a sunny day, a cold frame can quickly become a hot frame. You don't want to be saving your crops from winter, only to have them cook before you can harvest them. A cold frame can overheat, even on a cloudy day. Keep the temperature below 60°F during the day by opening the frame a little. If you're at home during the day, you can vent yours manually, but you'll need to be diligent. It's better to install temperature-activated ventilating arms to look after this task for you. The Univent control is solar

Salad greens thrive in a cold frame. Two lesser-known crops are claytonia, which has heart-shaped leaves (at lower left), and minutina, the grassy-looking row down the center.

Vent the frame to prevent overheating. Heavy glass lights must be vented manually. If you use a lightweight glass substitute, you can install an automatic device to do this job for you.

A min/max thermometer inside the frame is critical; be sure it's shielded from direct sun with a board.

powered and has a quick-release feature that allows you to open the light all the way. It's always better to err on the side of overventing. If you're going to be gone all day, or if you're unsure about the weather, vent.

A minimum/maximum thermometer inside the frame helps keep track of temperatures. In times of extreme cold, an insulated, reflective cover over the frames at night is helpful as long as it's opened during the day to let in the sun.

You can leave a new snowfall on the frame for a few days as insulation if it's bitter cold. Heavy wet snow, though (6 in. or more), could break glass panes. Remove the snow with a broom instead of a shovel to avoid breaking the glass.

Turn your cold frame into a hot bed

If you want to keep crops actively growing during the winter (as opposed to just keeping them stable and

Layers of a Hot Bed Frame

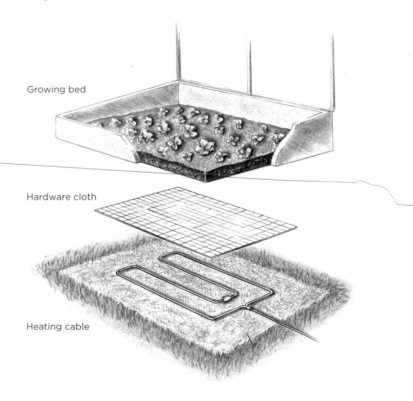

Growing bed

Hardware cloth

Heating cable

How to Make a Classic Cold Frame

This cold frame, consisting of a bottomless box and glass frames, called lights, is simple to build and designed to last for years. Use rot-resistant wood such as cedar, cypress, or redwood. The waste strips along the bottom are sacrificial. They keep the frame off the soil, and when they decay, you replace them instead of the entire frame. The lights have small wood stops at both ends. The stops keep the glass from sliding and enable water to run off freely, preventing ice build-up and rot.

To make a light, you'll need a table saw for cutting grooves and ripping stock lengthwise. Glazed with glass, each light will weigh around 35 lb., heavy enough to stay in place by itself but too heavy to be raised by an automatic venting arm. Glazed with a lightweight, insulated glass substitute like Polygal® or Lexan®, each light can be lifted with a venting arm, but will also need to be secured with hinges to keep it from blowing off in the wind.

MATERIALS

For each 8-ft. x 4-ft. frame
- Two 8-ft. x 12-in. boards
- One 8-ft. x 8-in. board
- One 4-ft. 2×2 for the brace
- Three 8-ft. 2×2s for the waste strips around the bottom
- 3-in. galvanized drywall screws
- 2½-in. drywall screws or 8d nails for attaching the waste strips
- Four 2-ft. x 4-ft. lights

For each light
- Two 4-ft. 2×2s for sides
- Two 21¾-in. 2×2s to rip for crosspieces
- 2 scraps for making the stops
- 3-in. galvanized screws
- 1-in. galvanized screws
- One 46½-in. x 22¾-in. sheet of glazing material (double-strength plate glass or polycarbonate glazing material such as Lexan or Polygal)

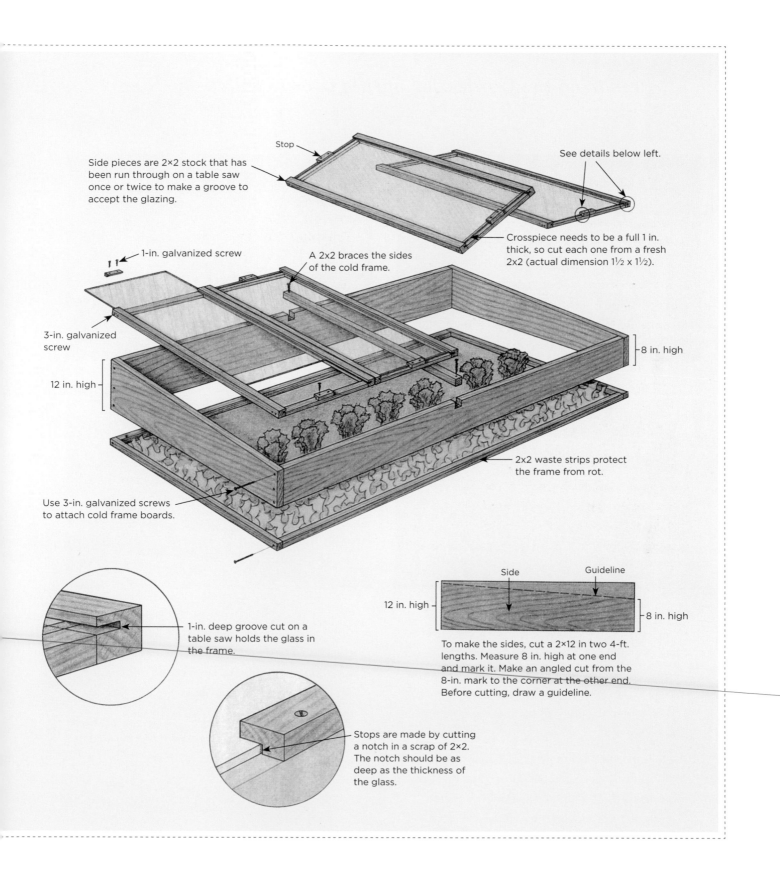

Side pieces are 2×2 stock that has been run through on a table saw once or twice to make a groove to accept the glazing.

Stop

See details below left.

Crosspiece needs to be a full 1 in. thick, so cut each one from a fresh 2×2 (actual dimension 1½ x 1½).

1-in. galvanized screw

A 2x2 braces the sides of the cold frame.

3-in. galvanized screw

8 in. high

12 in. high

2x2 waste strips protect the frame from rot.

Use 3-in. galvanized screws to attach cold frame boards.

1-in. deep groove cut on a table saw holds the glass in the frame.

Side   Guideline

12 in. high

8 in. high

To make the sides, cut a 2×12 in two 4-ft. lengths. Measure 8 in. high at one end and mark it. Make an angled cut from the 8-in. mark to the corner at the other end. Before cutting, draw a guideline.

Stops are made by cutting a notch in a scrap of 2×2. The notch should be as deep as the thickness of the glass.

Preparing the Garden for Spring Growing Step-by-Step

1. Mulch with autumn leaves. The most convenient way to enrich soil is to mulch the garden beds with leaves gathered from around the yard. The leaves decay slowly, keeping the soil sheltered for months. When turned under in spring, the leaves help aerate the soil.

2. Secure the leaves with netting so that they don't blow out of your vegetable garden and back under your trees. Bird netting is the perfect solution. Simply staple it around the perimeter of your raised beds.

3. Use hoops in the raised bed as an alternative to stapling netting to the raised bed perimeter. If your garden isn't divided into raised beds, you can stretch netting over large expanses of it and use the hoops as tie-downs.

4. Use lengths of 12-gauge wire, bent around a paint can to create hoops of uniform shape.

protected from frost), use your cold frame as a hot bed. A soil-heating, insulated electric cable attached to a mat of hardware cloth and buried 3 in. to 5 in. deep makes it possible.

Insulated soil-heating cables, available from garden supply houses, vary in size and quality, but all are equipped with built-in thermostats preset for 70°F or so. Follow the manufacturer's instructions to attach it correctly to hardware cloth.

In preparation for laying the hardware cloth, dig out the soil from inside the frame to a depth of about 5 in. Then put in the hardware cloth, making sure the cable side faces down. This will help protect against damage from cultivating tools. Cover it with the soil. Renew the soil from time to time with bags of topsoil.

For the electrical connection, dig a hole under one end of the frame so you can bring the plug end of the heating cable outside the frame. Connect it to a heavy outdoor power cord plugged into a protected exterior outlet. These outdoor outlets, which take a three-prong plug, are known in the electrician's trade as weatherproof receptacles. No further protection is needed at this end, but at the garden end, you should wrap electrician's tape around the plug and socket to keep water, snow, and ice out of the connection. To be on the safe side, though, consult an electrician about the codes applicable in your area for proper operation of outdoor appliances.

You can seed crops directly in the frame or use transplants, starting in early fall, but don't turn on the electricity until hard frosts come. September-sown crops of lettuces, arugula, beet greens, and spinach, can last into December and January. Put in new plants as necessary for late winter and early spring eating.

PREP FOR A SPRING GARDEN IN FALL

As soon as plants have quit producing or a hard frost has killed them, clear out all plant material and either compost it or, if it's diseased, send it to the trash. (Put the diseased plant debris in a kitchen garbage bag and dispose of it with your other refuse; never put diseased plant material in your compost pile.) Disassemble and store any plant supports that are best kept out of winter weather.

Fall is a great time to get your soil tested, because the turnaround time is quick. Add any slow-working amendments like manure, rock phosphate, and greensand that your test results indicate are needed. When leaves fall, gather and shred them (a mower works fine if you don't have a leaf shredder), and put a 2-in. to 4-in. layer over the beds. Use healthy tree leaves only and no other form of yard trimmings. The mulch of leaves greatly reduces spring weeding chores, and also encourages earthworms. The worms feed on the mulch, leaving behind a little fertilizer in the form of worm castings.

In late winter or early spring, when the ground becomes workable again, chop the leaf mulch into the soil, and rake the tops of the beds smooth. You're now ready to plant as soon as the soil and air temperatures are right.

CHAPTER 5
THE HEALTHY GARDEN

Laying the foundation for a healthy garden means following good gardening practices, creating an environment in which beneficial insects thrive, and conducting regular close inspections of your plants to see how they're faring. More than anything else, these things will help you have a successful garden.

First and foremost, rotate your crops. Growing the same vegetables in the same soil year after year pretty much guarantees you'll have disease and insect problems. One of the best methods of crop rotation for plant health is to group plants by genus. At the very least, don't plant members of the same family in the same space two years in succession. A three- or four-year break is even better, especially for the mustard family (cole crops, turnips, and radishes) and the nightshade family (tomatoes, peppers, eggplants, and potatoes), which suffer from more than their share of insect and disease problems.

➥ *For information on crop rotation, see p. 110.*

Second, practice good garden sanitation. Weedy beds and spent plant tops give insects a good hiding place. Throughout the season, remove diseased foliage as you see it and put it in the trash (hot composting will kill some pathogens but not all, particularly viruses). Do a thorough cleanup once a hard frost has killed plants, or better yet, do it bed by bed as soon as each crop is harvested or plants quit producing.

➥ *For information on cleaning up your garden, see p. 137.*

Mulch around lettuce and celery plants helps to keep them healthy.

Third, choose disease-resistant varieties, and make sure planting stock is disease-free. If you're planting saved seed, soaking it in very hot (122°F) water for half an hour will help kill fungus organisms. If you're purchasing seed potatoes, onion sets, asparagus crowns, or any other plant starts, buy from reputable sellers who can guarantee they're selling certified disease-free stock.

Finally, create the conditions your plants need for vigorous, unchecked growth. Unstressed plants are less prone to disease problems and better able to withstand insect infestations. Give them the right kind of soil, and provide adequate nutrition without overdoing it. Make sure they get the right amount of water at the right time. If you use drip irrigation, so much the better, because

Good soil, good plants, and a watchful eye toward pests and diseases are the foundation for a healthy garden.

you won't be splashing soil and wetting foliage. Give your plants elbow room. Proper spacing allows for good air circulation, which helps minimize diseases and makes it easier to monitor for insect pests.

For information on soil nutrition, see p. 69.
For information on watering your garden, see p. 90.
For information on plants' spacing needs, see
A Gallery of Vegetables & Herbs, starting on p. 188.

Of course, even if you do everything just right, trouble is bound to occur at some point. You'll have insect problems, disease will hit, and weeds can get out of hand.

When you see bugs on your plants, don't panic. Not all insects are harmful. Some of them are beneficial—they either eat the bad bugs or they parasitize them. Learn to recognize the good ones and the bad. Monitor for signs of disease. If you spot trouble, figure out what's bothering your plants and what, if anything, you should do about it. Weeds are a fact of life in the garden. Use nontoxic techniques to deal with them: mulch, cultivation, and if necessary, soil solarization.

No garden is pristine. A certain level of insect, disease, and weed presence can be tolerated. Learn for yourself where the tipping point lies. Finally, if you must use pesticides, take the least-toxic approach.

INSECTS

The graduated and multipronged approach to dealing with pests just described has a name—integrated pest management, or IPM. Gardeners who follow IPM practices have many options before they consider using a toxic pesticide. If you want to reduce pest problems in your garden, the best approach is to combine a number of strategies and then monitor regularly to see what's happening.

A monitoring toolbox might include a good bug book, a hand lens, and specimen jars.

Monitoring means regular observation

Most gardeners already monitor their gardens in an informal way, but often by the time they notice a problem, it may be too late to manage it in a nontoxic manner. Also, it is difficult to remember the exact conditions observed at a previous time. The key to effective monitoring of anything is writing down what you see. Keep a pest management log, either combined with other gardening notes or in a separate little notebook. If you created a garden journal, this is also a good place to make notes.

For information on creating a garden journal, see p. 107.

Simple tools of the trade. Many insects are tiny, so a hand lens is a great tool to have with you in the garden. Also, you may wish to stuff a pocket with some containers to hold collected specimens. Prepare a few empty pill bottles by pasting on a fresh label and making a tight cotton-ball stopper for each. Don't use the bottle's air-tight cap, which will cause the specimen to mold. A plastic bag or two might come in handy for larger samples of leaves or plant pieces that are showing symptoms of disease. Blow up the bag and close it tightly with a knot so air surrounds the sample.

Learn to read the clues. At times, it's hard to tell what's important and what isn't in the garden. In general, it's safe to say you are looking for creatures, large and small, that are out there on or around your plants. Also look for plants that seem to be doing poorly and have noticeable changes in the color or texture of their foliage.

Sometimes you'll see damage without knowing what caused it. But by careful observation you will learn to spot the clues. Slime trails mean slugs and snails, and pin size, round holes are probably flea beetles. Thrips rasp off the surface cells of the leaves, making them pale and slightly shiny. Cutworms sever very young seedlings at the base, leaving the tops lying nearby, and caterpillars and weevils often eat semicircles in leaf edges.

Now and then, you can guess the type of pest problem from the frass, or insect manure, left behind. For instance, thrips leave tiny brown spots on leaf surfaces, and lygus bugs leave smallish brown spots, but tomato hornworms leave relatively large fecal deposits. Eventually, as you

become attuned to the wildlife in your garden and keep notes you can refer to later on, you will become adept at linking plant damage with the critter responsible.

Put a name to a face. You may come across an unfamiliar insect and wonder if it is a plant eater or a beneficial insect that eats plant eaters. This is when you whip out your prepared, cotton-stoppered pill bottle. On the label, write the date and plant from which you collected the insect. Specimens you want to kill quickly and save can be put in the freezer overnight.

There are a number of good illustrated books to help you identify your specimen (see Resources on p. 284). Your library is another good source. Knowledgeable folks at the local garden club, plant nursery, community college, or cooperative extension office can help you decide what kind of an insect you have, even if they cannot put a species name to it. If you are lucky enough to have a master gardener program in your area, stop by the office with pill bottle in hand for help. Texas A&M University's Department of Entomology has a good website for identifying garden insects—both pests and beneficials—by name and photo, as well as by crop. The web address is http://vegipm.tamu.edu/imageindex.html.

Quantify what you see. If you think trouble is brewing, make an effort to quantify what you see. Often, quick action, like hand-picking insects, will prevent extensive damage. Drop the undesirables into a wide-mouthed jar half-filled with water and strong detergent. Count how many bugs you pick, either per plant, per yard or row, or per branch or leaf, and write it down. Following the same procedure a week later will tell you if the problem is getting better or worse.

The fun of monitoring begins when you go back to look the second, third, and fourth times. Now you have records that enable you to make comparisons with earlier conditions. You can begin to correlate the numbers of

You'll know right away what this beneficial is— a green lacewing—because of its beautiful wings.

pests you see with the damage they cause. But don't panic prematurely. A lot of plant-eating insects in the garden means a lot of their natural enemies will come around, too. So, there is no need to control anything unless you think the damage will become truly intolerable. If you wait, the predators and parasites of the pests may suppress them. Then you will have observed a great process at work—natural control.

Find out what works. By monitoring regularly you will be able to determine just how many pests it takes before action is required. And, since you'll be watching what's happening, you can catch the pests before their numbers build up. If you decide to take action, by spraying with insecticidal soap for instance, make counts before and after so you will know if the treatment worked or not. Ideally, a good monitoring program helps you figure out the least toxic approach to reducing pest damage in your garden.

Beneficial insects

There are a host of beneficial insects out there that feed on the bad guys eating your plants. The typical pattern starts with a buildup of plant-eating insects, followed by the arrival of their predators. If you use an insecticide, you'll kill good bugs along with the bad. To lure beneficial insects to your garden, first get to know your insect helpers, then give them the right habitat.

Grab your hand lens and a picture book of insects and take a rough census of your resident population. If you've avoided using pesticides and have a variety of plants growing, you may find many allies already present, most likely lady beetles, ground beetles, lacewings, hover flies, a couple of true bugs, and a few tiny wasps. These can be divided into two groups: those that eat their prey directly (predators) and those that deposit their eggs on or into their host (parasitoids).

Lady beetle larva

Lady beetles

Beetles. The two kinds of beetle that are most helpful are lady beetles (aka ladybugs) and ground beetles, both predators.

Lady beetles prey on aphids and other soft-bodied insects. The adults eat as many as 50 aphids per day. If you have enough aphids, and the beetles stick around long enough to lay eggs, each hatched larva will eat some 400 aphids before entering its pupal stage. There are many species of lady beetle that attack many different prey. The adults are independent, flighty creatures. If you buy and release some into your garden, be prepared to watch most of them fly away to your neighbor's yard. Those that stay, though, will be a big help.

Ground beetles don't fly much, preferring to run away when disturbed. You probably won't see them unless you uncover their hiding places. They're relatively large (about ¾ in.) and dark, with long, jointed legs. They're nocturnal hunters, rooting among leaf litter for insect eggs and larvae.

Soldier beetles feed on aphids. Mite-and-snail-destroying rove beetles inhabit piles of decaying organic matter.

Hover flies. With their striped abdomens, hover flies look like small bees, but they move through the air more like flies, zipping from plant to plant, hovering briefly before landing. The hover, or syrphid, fly is one of many predatory flies. They visit a variety of flowers in search of pollen and nectar, and they lay their eggs near aphids or other soft-bodied insects. The eggs hatch into hungry larvae that eat up to 60 aphids per day.

Lacewing larva

Lacewings

Ground beetle

Hover fly

Lacewings. When you see the fairylike green lacewing, you'll find it hard to imagine it in its fiercely predacious larval stage during which it devours aphids, caterpillars, mealybugs, leafhoppers, insect eggs, and whiteflies. It even eats other lacewings. Up close, the larva looks like a tiny (½-in.) alligator. If you keep a supply of flowering plants, adult lacewings may take up residence. If you decide to introduce beneficials to your garden, lacewings are the most effective predators you can buy.

Parasitic wasps. These very helpful creatures, ranging in size from small to minuscule, will defend your garden against caterpillars like corn earworms, tomato fruitworms,

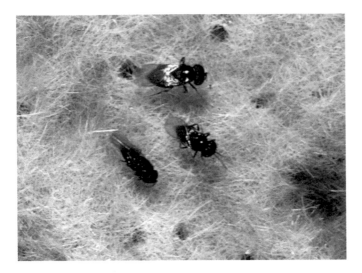

Trichogramma wasps

Paper wasps

Braconids parasitize aphids as well. If you're scouting with a hand lens and notice some mummified aphids with neat circular holes in them, you'll know a braconid was there—a young wasp developed inside the aphid and ate its way out.

If you can bear to let large paper wasps live around your property, they will eagerly control many caterpillars for you, possibly eliminating the need to spray with Bt. Paper wasps, *Polistes* spp., build toadstool-shaped nests, hanging down from trees and outdoor beams and eaves. The adults are calm, never bothering you as you move around the garden. They busy themselves flying back and forth collecting caterpillars to feed to their young in the nest. Learn to distinguish paper wasps from yellow jackets and hornets, who are far more irritable and make poor companions for small gardens, although they all catch pests.

Spiders. Deep, loose mulches encourage pest-eating spiders, especially the hunting spiders that hide by day and come out at night. Bare, cultivated ground is the least attractive to spiders because it does not afford the moist, dark hiding places with protection from temperature extremes that they need during the day. Spiders prey on thrips, catching hundreds of them in a single web. They're imperceptible in daytime, but if you go out at night with a flashlight and hold the light beam parallel to the plant, you can see them.

cabbageworms, and tent caterpillars. The smallest and perhaps most popular parasitic wasp is the trichogramma, a dust-size creature that lays up to 300 eggs in moth or butterfly eggs. You can buy them through the mail if you're expecting an infestation of caterpillars. They don't live very long, so timing their release to coincide with the presence of pest eggs is pretty important.

Braconid, chalcid, and ichneumid wasps are much larger than trichogramma and parasitize caterpillars directly, laying eggs in or on the caterpillar. The hatching eggs eventually either kill the host or disrupt its activities.

Pirate bug nymph

Pirate bug adult

True bugs. There are bugs and then there are true bugs. True bugs, like the minute pirate bug and the big-eyed bug, belong to the insect order Hemiptera. Many are plant feeders but many are predacious, with tubular mouthparts they insert like a straw to suck the juices out of their prey.

The minute pirate bug is a tiny ($1/12$-in.) predator with a wide-ranging appetite; it eats aphids, thrips, mites, whiteflies, and insect eggs. It lays its eggs on the leaf surface near its prey; nymphs hatch and begin feeding. The cycle from egg to adult takes only 3 weeks.

The other important true bug is the big-eyed bug. It's a little bigger than the minute pirate bug and has a similar diet. It also eats nectar and seeds, so it may stay even if it can't find an insect to eat.

You might come across some other common predatory true bugs, including assassin bugs, damsel bugs, thread-legged bugs, and a couple of species of stinkbug.

Turn your garden into an insectary

We're living in a bug-eat-bug world, and the greenest thing you can do for your garden is to keep it that way. To transform your garden into an insectary, a habitat where beneficial insects will feel at home, you need to do three things: Provide them with food, water, and shelter; keep the soil covered with organic matter; and avoid putting any harmful chemicals into their habitat.

Many of the predators and most of the parasites will use pollen and nectar for food. Growing a variety of flowers that bloom at different times will help to sustain them throughout the season. Since many of the beneficials are tiny or have short mouthparts, offer them tiny flowers with short nectaries, such as those on plants in the carrot and aster families.

Overhead sprinkling leaves puddles of water and wet leaves, giving insects something to drink from. If you use drip irrigation, offer them water in a saucer filled with pebbles, so they don't drown.

Beneficials need protection from heat and rain, and they need to hide from birds and insects who would make a meal of them. A variety of leafy plants offers protection. Ground beetles hide in low-growing ground covers and in mulch or leaf litter. Flying insects hide in shrubs, on the undersides of leaves, even among the petals of marigolds.

Insect allies hate dust. Keeping the soil covered at all times, either with mulch or with growing plants, conserves moisture, moderates temperatures, and eliminates dust.

Mulched paths give beneficial insects a good hiding place, and thus help combat bugs that might attack these pepper plants.

Creating a habitat for wild insects is a very imprecise activity. Your success will probably vary from year to year as the climate and vegetation change and new pests arrive. Expect the development of a habitat where pests and beneficials exist in a rough balance to be an effort of several years. And despite the presence of many beneficials in your garden, you may still find yourself from time to time having to hand-pick squash bugs or rub scale from the branches of the fruit trees.

Add plants to lure beneficials. Start luring beneficials quickly with annuals like alyssum, cosmos, zinnias, sunflowers, and marigolds. At the same time, set out perennial flowers and herbs, including golden marguerite (*Anthemis tinctori*), yarrow, lavender, mint, fennel, angelica, and tansy. Beneficials are also fond of dill, parsley, and cilantro flowers. When you've finished harvesting these herbs, leave the plants in the garden to flower.

Try to intersperse insectary plants with your vegetables. Add a patch here and there of alfalfa, buckwheat, or clover (all quite attractive to beneficials), and you'll be well on your way to establishing an arsenal of insect allies.

It also provides habitat for ground and rove beetles, as well as for nocturnal spiders. Try not to eliminate every weed. Leave some for the insects.

If you use selective insecticides to rid yourself of pests, you run a very strong risk of ridding your beneficials of prey. Nonselective pesticides could rid you of beneficials altogether. When you abandon chemical control for biocontrol, you may experience a sudden increase in pests. It may take a while for the beneficial insect population to expand to the point that you can relax your guard. In the meantime, you can rely on less-harmful botanical and natural controls to slow down the bad guys until the good guys show up.

Order bugs by mail. Many beneficial insects are available by mail. You might find it useful to buy a few to get a jump start on pests while your habitat is developing.

Green lacewing eggs

Perhaps the most effective and economical are lacewings, available as eggs, larvae, and adults. A thousand lacewing eggs is enough for 2,500 sq. ft. Lady beetles are widely available in garden centers or by mail. Remember to have some aphids and pollen around before you release them, and don't be surprised if many fly away.

When nature is in balance, you'll find a mixture of good and bad insects in your garden. A close look at the underside of a cabbage leaf reveals a whitefly infestation, hover fly eggs, and a hover fly larva, in the center, getting to work on those whiteflies.

A folding 10-power hand lens will help you tell the good bugs from the bad and keep tabs on who's winning.

Trichogramma wasps are available in the form of parasitized eggs glued to a card. In the event of a caterpillar invasion, you hang the card in the garden, the wasps emerge, and you're on your way to victory. It's important to consider, however, that trichogramma will attack butterfly larvae, too. Timing and accurate pest identification are very important. If you live where tomato caterpillar pests have several generations, then it is worth releasing Trichogramma when you notice high populations of caterpillars are present. If you garden in the North where only one generation per year is the rule and you had a problem the previous year with pest caterpillars, consider releasing

The tiny flowers of umbelliferous plants like fennel, parsley (shown), cilantro, carrots, and Queen Anne's lace are especially attractive to lacewings, but also to hover flies, parasitic wasps, and lady beetles.

Trichogramma early the following season to prevent a recurrence of the problem. Time the release when moths are laying eggs. Consult your county cooperative extension office for help in identifying which caterpillar species is present and when egg-laying begins.

Minute pirate bugs and big-eyed bugs are available, but very expensive. Minute pirate bugs can be released at any time in the growing season.

Insect-attacking nematodes

Nematodes are tiny, eellike, soil-dwelling roundworms ranging in size from microscopic to just barely visible to the naked eye. They play an important role in the biology of the soil and in the health of animals and plants.

The many species of nematodes are commonly divided into two groups: free-living forms that help in decomposing organic matter in the soil and parasitic forms that live off other organisms. This latter group concerns the gardener. In addition to those that parasitize plants, causing stunting and other signs of disease, an equally important subgroup parasitizes many insect pests of plants. These insect-attacking or beneficial nematodes provide a way to kill garden pests that spend all or part of their life in the soil, where their larval stages damage roots. Such pests include cabbage and onion maggots, carrot rust flies, potato tuber worms, thrips, mole crickets, root worms, wireworms, flea beetles, Japanese beetles, cucumber beetles, and black vine weevils.

Choosing the right nematodes. Species from just two nematode genera, *Steinernema* and *Heterorhabditis,* are commonly sold. Knowing a little something about how the nematodes from each genus act will give you insight into how best to use these beneficial organisms. You should also consult with your supplier.

Insect-attacking nematodes invade a host insect's body and infect it with bacteria, which multiply and kill the insect by releasing toxins. Once the host insect is dead, its skin disintegrates, and swarms of nematodes with the bacteria inside emerge to search out another host and give rise to more nematodes.

Steinernema nematodes enter through natural body openings of the host insect. The infested insect is killed within 48 hours. *Heterorhabditis* nematodes penetrate the insect's skin but can also enter through natural body openings. Because of this double means of attacking a pest, fewer *Heterorhabditis* than *Steinernema* nematodes are needed to kill a host, and they can better kill difficult-to-control pests such as root worms, various weevils, and other beetle larvae or grubs.

Insect-attacking nematodes are so tiny that 1 million fit on a small sponge or in a salt-shaker-size container, two common means of shipping them. Dilute them in water and spray or sprinkle them into moistened soil.

Using nematodes effectively. Releasing beneficial nematodes in the garden is not as simple as purchasing a package and sprinkling them about where you have problems. Applications should be made at points in a pest's life cycle and in locations where its larval stages are most susceptible. This is especially important because once activated by contact with water, nematodes won't survive long without a host.

With wireworms, for example, it is smart to use scrap carrots as monitoring traps before planting your crop. Push the carrots into the ground and leave them for a few days, then pull them up and inspect them for wireworms. By monitoring these trap carrots, you will be able to determine if wireworms are present and how severe the level of infestation is. In severe cases, the carrots can serve as a bait to attract high concentrations of wireworms, which you can then treat with a heavy dose of nematodes. By concentrating wireworms on the carrots, you increase the likelihood that the nematodes will succeed in their attack.

Japanese beetles can be controlled by applications to nearby turf areas where the larvae feed on roots. Peach tree borers, carpenter worms, squash-vine borers, and other insects that dig tunnels into trunks and stems can be controlled by injecting a liquid nematode solution into their burrows. Mail-order garden catalogs and some garden centers sell special syringes for injecting liquids into squash vines and the like.

While most caterpillars are best controlled above ground with Bt, there are several cutworm species (such as black, pale western, redbacked, or variegated cutworms) that live in the soil surface or in mulch. These are good candidates for the cuticle-penetrating *Heterorhabditis* nematodes.

Insect-attacking nematodes will also kill plant-parasitic nematodes, such as those that attack the roots of tomato plants. These nematodes that attack nematodes could be useful in small gardens where plant-parasitic nematodes are known to be problematic.

Plants seduce pollinators with fragrance and hue to ensure return visits.

Bees

Bees of all kinds perform a vital service in the garden: pollination. Whether it's the familiar honeybees, small, dark sweat bees, bluish-green carpenter bees, robust black and yellow bumblebees, or stout, dark leaf-cutting bees, all collect nectar. In doing so, bees brush against the flower stamens and cover themselves with pollen. As they go from flower to flower, pollen is transferred from stamen to stigma, where it fertilizes the embryo.

Bees pollinate at least 50 food crops, including apples, cucumbers, melons, plums, peaches, peas, peppers, and pumpkins. Although we harvest the roots or leaves of onions, potatoes, cabbages, carrots, beets, radishes, parsnips, lettuce, and spinach, without bees as pollinators there would be fewer seeds to plant next spring. Bees are even important to self-pollinated plants like tomatoes, which bear larger, higher-quality crops when they have been "sonicated," or buzz-pollinated, by bees.

Bee populations across the country have been badly damaged by parasitic mites. The mites attach themselves to the bees and suck their blood. A miticide has been used

A cluttered garden is asking for trouble since it creates a habitat for some pests who like to hide out in the debris. Always keep your garden clean.

successfully and has helped the bees recover, but there's always the risk that mites will develop resistance to the chemical.

If you've had plenty of flowers on squash, cucumbers, and tomatoes but little or no fruit, you've felt the effects of a diminished bee population.

To attract bees, add bee plants to your garden. Good ones include lemon balm, lavender, thyme, bee balm (*Monarda didyma*), catnip (*Nepeta cataria*), and borage (*Borago officinalis*). The flowers of nasturtiums, runner beans, sunflowers, poppies, and ornamental onions will bring bees to the garden. Perennial bee plants include pulmonaria, liatris, sedum, perennial sunflowers, phlox, asters, and goldenrod.

Home-garden pesticides that are extremely toxic to bees include carbaryl, diazinon (no longer sold or legal to use, but quite possibly still sitting on the shelf in many garages and garden sheds), and malathion. Rotenone, a biological control long considered safe in the garden, is moderately toxic to bees. If you must use these agents, be

Safe Aphid Sprays You Can Make

Here are two simple botanical sprays you can make to combat an outbreak of aphids. To be effective, the sprays must be applied thoroughly and directly on the aphids. These will break down quickly into harmless by-products. However, they kill most insects, including beneficials, so use with caution.

CITRUS OIL SPRAY

The peels of oranges, lemons, or other citrus fruit contain limonene and linalool. Steep the peel of 1 or 2 oranges in 2 to 4 cups of boiling water for 15 minutes. Turn off the heat, but let the peels continue to steep for 24 hours. Strain out the peels and cool the resulting oil.

GARLIC OIL SPRAY

Garlic contains allicin and sulfur. Soak 2 crushed garlic cloves in 1/2 cup of mineral or olive oil for 24 hours. Strain out the garlic. Add 2 teaspoons of the oil, plus a few drops of dish soap, to 1 quart of water. Stir and strain again.

aware that their toxicity usually lasts only for 3 to 6 hours after application, making it a good idea to apply them in the evening after bees have finished flying.

The bad guys

Just as you need to get acquainted with the good guys, those beneficial insects that will help keep your plants thriving, you also need to recognize the harmful pests that destroy plants. You must know what you're dealing with in order to arm yourself with controls—nontoxic, preferably—to keep them at bay.

Aphids. These tiny, pear-shaped, soft-bodied insects can be found in all gardens. They are typically green, whitish, or gray, but come in other colors, too, including red. Nearly all aphids feed by inserting their long, needle-like mouthparts into plant tissue. They're after the plant's sugary juices. The more nitrogen those juices contain, the more aphids are encouraged to multiply. Young growing plant tissue is usually high in nitrogen. So are over-fertilized plants, especially those nourished with chemical fertilizers. To avoid encouraging aphids, use slow-release nitrogen fertilizers such as well-aged compost, and save pruning chores for late winter when shrubs and trees are dormant.

Combatting aphids. Aphid predators include ladybird beetles, lacewings, big-eyed bugs, minute pirate bugs, and the larvae of aphid gall-midges, *Aphidoletes* sp. Some of the most important enemies of aphids are tiny members of the bee/wasp family, Hymenoptera, which lay hundreds of eggs under the skin of aphids. In a day or so, the eggs hatch and the larvae eat their hosts from the inside. The aphids change color and harden like a mummy, usually still attached to the plant.

Even with all these voracious insects around, some aphid colonies get out of hand. To keep the aphid population tolerable while you wait for the beneficials to take over, crush them with your fingers, or hose them off with a jet of water. Avoid pesticides that might damage natural enemies unless you're backed into a corner, and then confine their use to the precise area they are needed. Your aim should be to merely reduce the aphid population, not eliminate it. You want plenty of food around when the natural enemies do appear.

Since healthy seedlings are high in nitrogen, which they need for rapid growth, they can be very attractive to aphids. They're especially vulnerable because they have very little tissue to sustain them through an aphid onslaught. The simplest solution is to protect seedlings with a row cover.

Next, knock back aphids with plain old water. With sufficient pressure from a hose nozzle, water can break aphids' mouthparts and wash the insects to the ground. The fallen aphids may be captured by spiders or other predators, especially if a compost mulch under the plants provides habitat for ground predators. Water sprays can keep aphids from overwhelming plants until natural enemies arrive.

Watch for the arrival of beneficials. Be sure you can recognize the young of ladybird beetles and lacewings; they look so different from the adults they're sometimes taken for pests themselves.

Colorado potato beetles. A pretty, yellow-and-black-striped insect, the Colorado potato beetle feeds on potato, eggplant, and tomato plants. In spring, adult beetles

Observe the Cycle of Aphids and Beneficial Insects

If you discover aphids on one of your garden crops, you might want to try this experiment. Find a leaf with some brown and bloated aphids on it, as well as a number of tiny insect eggs. Put that leaf into a large jar, and place the jar in a cool place for a few days. A week later, examine the jar. If you haven't been using pesticides in your garden, chances are it will be teeming with other insects. The tiny eggs might have hatched into the predatory larvae of syrphid flies, aphid midges, and lacewings. The bloated aphids contained the eggs of tiny parasitoid wasps. The eggs will have hatched, and the young wasps will have eaten their way out of the aphids, leaving behind empty aphid "mummies."

Colorado potato beetle eggs are laid on the undersides of leaves (left). Fortunately they're food to ladybeetles. The larva (right) is preyed upon by the two-spotted stink bug.

emerge from hibernation in the soil and search out food plants for feeding and egg-laying. They lay yellow-orange eggs clustered in groups, usually on the undersides of leaves. The larvae, which look like fat, globular, slow-moving caterpillars, change from brown to pink as they grow, developing two rows of black spots along each side of their abdomen. When fully grown, in 20 to 24 days, the larvae burrow into the soil to pupate near the plants on which they were feeding. Emerging as adults, a week or two later, they start the process again. The second generation of adults remains in the soil until the next spring.

Combatting Colorado potato beetles. The Colorado potato beetle has become resistant to a large number of conventional pesticides, so a mix of alternative methods of control is your best strategy. The adult beetles are poor flyers and cannot easily travel far. For this reason, crop rotation is a traditional means of control. Unfortunately for home gardeners, the new plantings ideally should be at least 200 ft. away from the old site. However, it's still a good idea to rotate each piece of ground to a different plant family, because other pests, including soil-borne pathogens, remain behind from each year's plantings.

Handpicking can protect a small plot of potatoes. Picking is easiest early in the day when the beetles are cold and slow to move. Collect the beetles in a wide-mouth jar, coffee can, or deep baking pan, half full of soapy water. Place the container below leaves with beetles or larvae and shake the plant. The insects will fall into the container and drown. Larvae and egg masses also can be squished on the leaves. Gloves make the job easier. Another option is to vacuum up the beetles.

To prevent the emerging beetles from reaching early-sprouting tubers, especially in large plantings, dig a barrier ditch around your potato bed. A near-vertical-sided, plastic-lined, dry ditch 4 in. to 6 in. deep and 4 in. wide can trap migrating beetles. Row covers can also prevent migrating insects from reaching the plants. Anchor the covers securely into the soil because Colorado potato beetles are strong walkers and could move in under unburied row cover edges.

Planting very early or late can help avoid damage. For early planting, warm the soil with plastic sheets. Or, if your season length permits it, delay planting until late June or July. Another option is to plant an early potato crop as a trap crop. When the early crop is attacked, kill the beetles with a flamer. For a small garden, an ordinary hand-held propane torch works. Potato sprouts are fairly resistant to heat damage, and early sprouts attacked by the beetles will re-grow even if they've been damaged by fire. Don't use a flamer near mulch or flammable materials.

Planting potatoes in, or just beneath, a thick layer of straw mulch can reduce damage from a number of potato pests, including aphids and flea beetles, as well as Colorado potato beetles. Mulches attract predators, such as carabid ground beetles and hunting spiders, which feed at night.

A number of beneficial insects feed on or parasitize the Colorado potato beetle, including insect-eating nematodes, the tiny parasitic mini-wasp *Edovum puttleri*, and soldier bugs. There is now a commercially available soldier bug attractant to increase their numbers in the garden.

Btt (*Bacillus thuringiensis* var. *tenebrionis*) products have high selectivity for Colorado potato beetles and virtually no mammalian toxicity. Btt works best against the early larval stages, so must be timed properly. Wait until all the egg masses have hatched. Btt is different from the better-known Bt pathogen used to control caterpillars. Be careful to get the right product.

Beauveria bassiana is a commercially available fungal pathogen that is effective against Colorado potato beetles. *Beauveria bassiana* has a wider host range than Btt and works best under moist conditions. As with the Btt, it is most effective against the young larvae. However, it can also be sprayed directly on the beetles.

Cucumber beetles. Although this pest goes by many names—*Diabrotica,* rootworm, corn rootworm, striped cucumber beetle, spotted cucumber beetle, or just plain cucumber beetle—no matter what you call them, these flashy striped or spotted beetles and their larvae are double trouble. Adults attack primarily the blossoms of corn, cucurbits (summer and winter squashes, melons, pumpkins, and cucumbers), sweet potatoes, and the leaves of legumes.

Cucumber beetles lay their eggs in the ground; their larvae live in the soil, feeding upon roots, which is why the larvae are known as rootworms. The corn rootworm probably causes more agricultural loss than any other pest, and more insecticide is used against it than against any other. Nevertheless, the sight of cucumber beetles flitting about the garden is not always a signal that disaster is on the way.

Although cucumber beetles are common every year, their damage tends to be severe only some years. Heavy populations feed mainly on cucurbit blossoms, so if you have a surplus of squash, this might not be a problem. And not all squashes are equally susceptible to cucumber beetles in all areas.

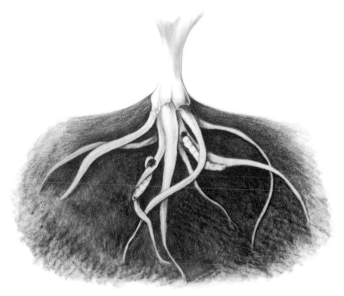

The cucumber beetle (left) and its larva, known as the corn rootworm (above), are both pests. Row covers, trap crops, and handpicking work best to stop the adult beetle. For the larva, try beneficial nematodes.

Deterring cucumber beetles. There is no effective pesticide against cucumber beetle adults available for the home garden, so you'll need to learn to tolerate a little damage.

Farmers sometimes plant a trap crop. Later, they plant the crop they mean to harvest beside the trap crop. When the beetles settle heavily on the trap crop, they can be vacuumed off, picked off, or sprayed, thus confining the insecticide to the trap crop and not the food crop. Some flowers, such as yellow and orange zinnias, make fine cuke beetle traps. When temperatures are cool and the cuke beetles are moving slowly, vacuum them up.

The cool of the day is also the best time to hand-pick. Jiggle the plant over a wide-mouth container half full of a strong detergent and water solution. The beetles will drop into the water. Leave them to die and then compost them.

Because seedlings are the most vulnerable to cucumber beetles, plastic or floating row covers, if carefully sealed with earth around the edges, can prevent the beetles from decimating new plantings. Be sure to remove the row cover at the first sign of female flowers, recognizable by the swelling behind the blossom.

Avoid using sticky traps, which will catch many beneficial insects as well as cucumber beetles. Insect-eating nematodes will help control cucumber beetles. Apply them to the soil around stem areas suspected of harboring cuke beetle larvae.

Mexican bean beetles. This pest will eat kidney, pinto, navy, adzuki, hyacinth, and soybeans, but it prefers snap beans, wax beans, or limas. These garden favorites are so tempting that they are used as trap crops to protect commercial crops of soybeans.

The Mexican bean beetle originated in Panama or Costa Rica, but today it munches happily throughout the eastern United States, from Florida to Canada, and also infests some western states. It is more of a pest in hot, humid climates, where there can be three generations a year. The 16-spotted, light-yellow to bronze-colored bean fiend looks suspiciously like some of its ladybug relatives.

Adults overwinter in leaf litter and underneath debris. They wander out of hiding in April or May, when warm spring days and rainfall trigger their appetites. After emerging, hungry adult beetles can live for 2 months, and waves of them will fly for miles looking for bean plants. Each female lays about 750 yellow eggs in clusters of 40 or 50 on the undersides of leaves. Between 8 and 10 percent of these eggs will survive to become adults.

The eggs hatch into spine-covered yellow larvae that feed on the undersides of leaves until only a lacy leaf skeleton remains. Most of the damage is done by the large larvae and by adults, and extensive defoliation can kill a plant. Complete development from the egg to the adult takes about a month, then the next generation begins. As long as bean plants are available, these beetles will not leave your garden. Beggarweed (*Desmodium tortuosum*) is the beetle's second choice of food.

Combatting Mexican bean beetles. A good garden cleanup in fall will destroy adult beetle homes. After harvest, destroy bean plants as soon as possible to kill any beetles that remain. Leaves and litter around the garden should be raked up and composted. If beggarweed grows in your area, destroy it to reduce the late-season food supply.

Purple-podded snap beans are more resistant than others. Choose varieties that mature quickly. Southern gardeners might be able to plant early and harvest a crop before the overwintering generation appears.

Try to hide your plants. Dense monocultures should be avoided, as these are especially attractive. If you plant bush beans in rows, keep the rows at least 6 in. to 8 in. apart. You can also alternate rows of beans with rows of corn or tomatoes. If cultural methods of protection are impossible or impractical, use row covers to protect your beans. Monitor your plants and catch beetles early. Crush any eggs you find and hand-pick larvae and adults, dropping them into soapy water to kill them. Hot weather or heavy rain will kill eggs and larvae.

Predators are more effective early in the season, when beetle populations are small. Soldier bugs are fairly good predators, and commercially available pheromones will attract these beneficials to your garden. Absolutely the best choice for biological control is the commercially available wasp *Pediobius foveolatus*. This parasitoid can give spectacular results. Like most parasitoids, it is extremely specific, attacking only the pest beetles and not beneficial ladybugs. It prefers to attack later larval stages, and turns yellow bean beetle larvae into brown mummies. The wasp reproduces every 2 to 3 weeks. Timing is important. Release the wasp when first-generation beetles are in early larval stages. Just 50 wasps can do the job in an average garden.

As a last resort, you might need to use some kind of spray. One possibility is the naturally occurring fungus *Beauveria bassiana,* which can kill most of a population. The fungus is commercially available and thrives in the same hot, humid conditions as the beetle. Apply as a foliar spray, making sure the undersides of the leaves are sprayed.

Another least-toxic option is neem seed extract. Neem is nearly nontoxic to mammals and has low impact on beneficial insects. After adult beetles appear, spray the undersides of leaves carefully every 7 to 10 days. Neem acts as an antifeedant and also stops larval development. If it is used on the first generation in the spring, fewer pests will be seen later in the season.

Other possibilities are insecticidal soap, insecticidal soap with pyrethrins, or a pyrethrins-oil formulation. Insecticidal soap will kill the soft-bodied larval stages if they are sprayed directly. Soap won't leave toxic residue and must be applied every few days. Insecticidal soap with pyrethrins leaves a repellent residue that will keep adult beetles from landing on your plants for a week or so. The oil in the pyrethrins-oil formulation smothers larvae, and the pyrethrins will kill and repel adults. Although they are natural products extracted from a type of chrysanthemum, pyrethrins are not entirely benign, as they can kill beneficial insects. If you have an organic garden, be sure to buy a formulation that does not contain the synergist PBO.

Cutworms. The larvae of certain night-flying moths are called cutworms. There are about 200 species, with slightly different eating habits. Most are gray-brown caterpillars, with the characteristic habit of curling up in the shape of the letter C when disturbed. Once you've experienced their damage, you'll have no trouble understanding why they're called "cut" worms.

Cutworms curl up into a C, spending daytime hours just below the soil surface.

CUTWORM
3.8 cm

Cutworms sleep by day just under the soil surface or occasionally in moist debris on the surface. Some make tunnels and feed just below or above the soil surface. These cutworms are the ones most likely to chop down seedlings. Other types remain in the soil and feed on underground stems and roots, causing plants to wilt. Some of these caterpillars are climbers that eat leaves or buds of larger plants or trees. All cutworms come out at night to do their devastating damage.

Deterring cutworms. The worst cutworm infestations in the vegetable garden generally occur where grassy areas have recently been broken up to create a new planting bed. If you're cultivating a new bed, allow at least 3 weeks before planting seed or transplants, to allow any cutworm larvae to grow up and move on in search of food. Mulching cleaned beds deeply in the fall keeps weeds down over

A toilet-tissue core makes a great collar for seedlings when cut in half. It helps to protect plants from cutworms and will eventually disintegrate. Be sure to push the collar into the soil slightly.

winter. If mulching is not an option, you can treat your garden with *Bacillus thuringiensis* var. *kurstaki* (Btk), which is effective against cutworms that feed below the soil surface as well as those that do a hatchet job on your seedlings. Since it's hard to determine when cutworm moth eggs are starting to hatch, spray Btk at weekly intervals while your seedlings are emerging and still small.

➡ *For more information on Bt, see p. 173.*

While sturdy seedlings with several true leaves are better able to withstand cutworms, protect their stems with a cardboard or plastic collar. Cutworms have many natural enemies. Most are too small to notice, like parasitic braconid wasps, tachinid flies, nematodes *Heterorhabditis bacteriophora* and *Steinernema carpocapsae,* bacteria, viruses, fungi, and protozoans. Others are more visible, like meadowlarks, blackbirds, toads, moles, and shrews.

Squash bugs. Although they're found throughout most of the United States, squash bugs may be less of a pest where its natural enemy, the tachinid fly, is present. Adults are gray or yellowish brown with flat backs. They lay orange-brown, elliptical eggs on stems and the undersides of leaves. Nymphs are yellowish green.

You can suspect squash bug presence when small specks develop on the leaves of squash and other members of the cucurbit clan. These marks may be yellow at first but soon turn brown. The plant may wilt from the point of attack to the end of the vine, turning black and brittle. Very young plants may be killed entirely.

Combatting squash bugs. Adults winter over in garden debris, so thorough autumn cleanup is paramount. Don't compost infested plants. Leave the raked ground bare of mulch for several weeks of cold weather, depriving squash bugs of winter protection. At this point, it's safe to spread a fresh layer of compost or mulch over beds.

Squash bug damage may cause plants to blacken and wilt.

Squash bugs (shown here, the larvae) feast on members of the cucurbit clan, including squash, cucumber, melon, and pumpkin.

ADULT SQUASH BUG
15-17 mm

Some plants are more attractive to squash bugs than others. Zucchini, cucumber, watermelon, and various types of muskmelon seem fairly resistant. Pumpkin and summer squash, such as yellow crookneck and straight-neck, are particularly susceptible. Skip growing these if you are overwhelmed with squash bugs each year.

The first squash bugs of the season will arrive as adults from wherever they spent the winter. If you can exclude them from the beds with row covers until plants are ready to flower, you've won half the battle.

Hand-pick adults in the cool hours of the day. While the plants are young and still covered with row covers, place boards on the ground near the squash beds to trap bugs migrating into the garden. Early or late in the day, turn over the boards, pick off the bugs, and drop them into a jar of soapy water. Remove and stack any boards used to trap squash bugs.

When you remove the row cover to allow pollination, start monitoring plants for adults and egg masses. You will find adults around the base of the plant and hiding in rough debris on the bed surface. Young nymphs hatch a week or two after eggs are laid. The adults continue to lay eggs until midsummer.

Squashing squash bugs (aka stink bugs) releases an unpleasant odor. Crush the eggs, but pick up the bugs intact and drop them into detergent and water. When they are dead, put them into a hot compost pile. Or capture them with a hand-held vacuum with strong suction. Insecticidal soap and homemade sprays are effective against adult squash bugs, but not against eggs, so you must still crush those by hand.

Squash vine borers. The larvae of squash vine borer tunnel into squash stems, causing the plants to wilt suddenly. Closely examine the main stem of the plant, or the portion of the vine that has died back, and you'll see one or more holes with a greenish, moist, sawdust-like material on the ground and within the hole. Slit open the stem near the hole, and you'll find a brown-headed, fat, white larva, about ¾ in. long. The wet sawdust material is excrement, or frass.

Squash vine borers attack many varieties of squash, pumpkin, and other members of the cucurbit family in parts of the United States east of the Rockies from Canada to South America. They winter in the soil, an inch or two below the surface, in tough black cocoons, then emerge as moths in the spring about the time the squash plants send out runner vines. These large, swift, daytime-flying, orange and black, clear-winged moths lay small, flattened, brownish eggs on squash stems and leaf stalks, especially toward the base of plants. The larvae hatch and enter the stems a week or two later. These borers tunnel along, eating the inner tissues of the stem for about a month, then they leave the plant and make cocoons in the soil. In the North, they stay in the soil until spring, but in warmer areas there may be a second generation later in the season.

Combatting squash vine borers. As with any insect that overwinters in the soil, crop rotation and good garden cleanup are critical. Put all squash debris in a clear plastic bag, tie the top, and set it in the sun for a week to kill remnant insects before adding the debris to your compost pile. After raking, turn the top couple of inches of soil so cocoons are brought to the surface. Over the winter, they will be killed by cold temperatures, especially alternate freezing and thawing. They'll also be exposed to birds, mice, shrews, and insect predators.

In spring, turn over the soil deeply, so any surviving cocoons are left at a greater depth than the usual inch or two. Deeply buried, the emerging insects will have a tough time making it to the surface.

If you live in a warm region, where two generations of squash vine borers are a threat, stagger your squash plantings over time; some of the plants will have a chance to grow large before the moths lay eggs again. Larger plants are better able to survive to produce fruit when borers attack. Pinch back young plants to encourage branching. With more stems, some will be spared attack by borers, and more will survive borer removal.

Protect young plants with physical barriers like row covers, making sure they are well secured and free from holes. When you uncover the plants for pollination, protect their main stems by winding them with nylon stockings or strips of aluminum foil, starting just below soil level and rising at least 6 in. up the stem.

When you see eggs glued to a stem, scrape them off with a dull knife or crush them. If you see a suspicious hole littered with frass, slit open the stem directly above it and carefully remove the borer with a knife or wire. Take care to injure the walls of the vine as little as possible. Then immediately cover the cut area of the stem with soil, and the vine will probably survive. Since many squashes can put out new roots from nodes along the stem, bury a few long trailing runners. That way, if there is dieback due to borer damage on some stems, you will have new plant sections already rooted.

Insect-eating nematodes kill squash vine borers. Inject a solution of the nematodes into plant stems with a syringe when you first see borer holes. Ask suppliers to recommend which species will be effective on squash vine borers and how much you'll need to get the job done.

Alternatively, inject squash stems with *Bacillus thuringiensis* var. *kurstaki*, or Btk, the bacteria that kill

If you suspect borers, carefully slit the stem and remove the larva with your knife.

Life Cycle of the Squash Vine Borer

The actual wingspan of the adult female moth is 1 in. to 1½ in.

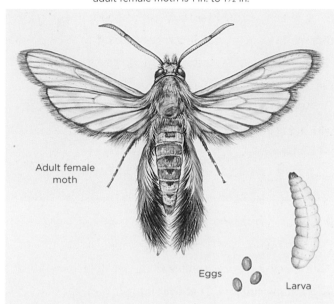

Adult female moth

Eggs

Larva

many caterpillars. Start by injecting Btk into the main stems within an inch or so of the soil, about the time blossoms start to open. Repeat in 10 to 14 days. Your goal is to bathe the inside of the hollow stems with the Btk solution. Any borers present will eventually die after eating stem material coated with Btk.

Scale insects. Scale insects can be serious pests for fruit and nut trees, currants, grapes, and raspberries. Citrus trees are especially susceptible to scale attack. Scale also attack bay trees.

For more information on scale and bay, see p. 221.

These sucking insects often look like small warts or outgrowths of plants themselves. Once settled, many species will not move again during their life, while others are still mobile as adults.

There are many species of scale insects. Most range in size from 1 mm to 3 mm and are circular or oval in shape. Their coloring runs from brown and black to red or orange; others are spotted or striped. There are two basic types—the so-called hard, or armored, scales and the soft ones. Soft scales often secrete honeydew, a sugary solution that is a condensed form of the plant sap the scales imbibe. Honeydew will grow a black fungus called sooty mold, which may coat leaves and twigs, and can interfere with photosynthesis. You can use insecticidal soap to wash it off.

Combatting scale insects. Most scale species don't become a serious problem because natural insect predators and parasitoids keep populations in check. Small populations of scale can be removed by hand with a scrub brush. Remove twigs and branches severely infested with scales. Wash the trunk and limbs with insecticidal soap and water when scale is present in the crawling stage.

If ants are present, wash them off and then put up a barrier of sticky tape. Ants feed on the secreted honeydew and act as caretakers for aphids, running off or killing ladybeetles and other scale predators. Spray with a refined horticultural oil, or brush it on if the plants are small. Depending on the type of scale you have, you may need to apply the oil in summer or winter.

Ugly, black, sooty mold on leaves and twigs may be the first noticeable sign of scale insects.

Hunting for slugs requires only a flashlight and a keen eye. Keep a bucket of soapy water close by for slugs you handpick from the garden.

The slug is a hermaphrodite, with both male and female sex organs. Although self-fertilization has been reported, cross-fertilization is the norm.

Be on the lookout for clear, pearl-like slug eggs, pictured, or similar-looking snail eggs. Snails lay eggs in masses averaging 86 eggs each. Slugs lay fewer eggs, which under dry conditions may remain un-hatched for long periods.

Slugs and snails. These mollusks damage plants by licking them with their radula, a tongue with thousands of teeth, leaving telltale ragged holes. Moisture is critical to slugs and snails, both of which have shells, although those of slugs are much reduced in size and hidden by the fleshy mantle on their backs. For much, if not most, of the growing season across the United States, rainfall, fog, or morning dew will provide enough dampness to encourage slugs and snails, and during dry spells, most gardeners water their gardens. Water management comes down to mitigating the effect of rainfall and watering.

If slugs and snails are a problem and you are watering overhead, do so early in the day so plants have a chance to dry off before nightfall, when these pesky mollusks move about and feed. Where appropriate, use underground drip irrigation or leaky hoses that leave the soil surface dry. And build raised planting beds to ensure good drainage of upper soil levels.

➧ *For information on drip irrigation, see p. 93.*
For information on raised beds, see p. 35.

A container cut in half, with the top inverted in the bottom, makes a low-tech yet effective slug trap. The slugs will drown in the beer on the bottom.

Combatting slugs and snails. Leave adequate space between plants so moving air can dry their surfaces. Reduce the area blanketed by dense ground covers, or relocate dense plantings away from the vegetable patch. Remove boards and other debris that will retain dampness at the soil surface (unless you are deliberately using them as traps). These provide protected cover during the day and moist places preferred by slugs and snails to lay eggs.

The next step is to grab a flashlight and go hunting. About 2 hours after sunset is the right time to handpick slugs and snails. Bring along a container filled with soapy water. Captured and drowned slugs and snails can be discarded in the compost pile or given a ceremonial burial in the garden, where they will decompose and provide nutrients for the next round of plants.

Handpicking may seem like an impossibly large job when you start, but by concentrating on the areas in most need of protection and by going out on as many consecutive nights as you can (slugs may not emerge every night), you can make a substantial dent in the population.

Augment your nighttime forays by setting traps and checking them by day. Some particularly attractive plants, such as mint or iris clumps, are traps in themselves. Visit these favored spots regularly and remove all the slugs and snails you find. Grapefruit halves, placed cut side down, and overturned, unglazed clay pots are attractive to slugs and snails. If you use clay pots, a crushed snail or two left inside will attract others as it decays. Place overturned pots on the shady side of plants so the pots stay cool in the daytime, and leave the ground uneven so snails can find entrance under the rims. Wooden boards, elevated from the ground with a pebble, also work.

Beer is a well-known attractant for slugs and snails because of the yeast it contains. Commercial yeast mixed with water can be used to the same effect.

Create some barriers around the areas from which you are removing slugs and snails. Neither likes crossing dry or caustic materials, so diatomaceous earth, ashes, or sawdust all work as a barrier, so long as they're kept dry. The catch is that the worst snail and slug problems arise when the weather is wet.

Copper is repellent to slugs and snails and makes a very effective and permanent barrier—until some vegetation droops or grows over the copper, creating a bridge. Everything from the most tender and mollusk-prone seedlings to entire planting beds to fruit trees can be ringed with copper strips (typically 2 in. to 3 in. high) to prevent snail and slug access. The copper oxidizing and turning green does not diminish its efficacy. A number of commercial products are now available through catalogues and nurseries.

If you must resort to chemical controls, use bait (typically Mesurol or metaldehyde) rather than sprays. Place the bait in containers that allow access only to slugs and snails, and position the containers in concealed locations where they cannot be picked up and played with by children or eaten by dogs.

To keep bait from contaminating your soil, place it in an empty can laid on its side. The slugs and snails will enter, take the bait, and die in the can. The dead bodies will attract more slugs and snails. In the vegetable garden,

Whiteflies often rest on the undersides of leaves and rise up like a snow flurry if disturbed.

WHITEFLY
Actual size, adult stage
1.5 mm

Whitefly nymphs have sucking mouthparts that damage plants and may spread disease. Encarsia formosa (center) is a tiny, parasitic wasp that lays eggs inside whitefly nymphs.

where young seedlings are the primary slug and snail victims, bait should be needed for no more than 1 to 3 weeks, while the seedlings put on some growth.

Whiteflies. Throughout southern and coastal areas of the United States, whiteflies feed on outdoor vegetable plants, like tomatoes, cucumbers, and potatoes, and many ornamental plants. Infestations of these tiny, white, mothlike flying insects are easy to spot—when you brush up against an infested plant, hundreds of whiteflies will immediately rise up in a cloud and then just as quickly subside. A close look might reveal their younger scalelike stages, called nymphs, lying flat like small oval bumps against the undersides of leaves. These nymphs may be translucent and hard to see without a magnifying glass, but they are fringed with very fine, white, hairlike filaments.

It is primarily the preadult stages of whiteflies that cause direct damage to plants through their feeding, although adult whiteflies can also be a menace. Whiteflies have sucking mouthparts, as do aphids and scale insects, with which they pierce plant tissues to suck out sap. Foliage on troubled plants may turn yellow and dry out, leaving plants weakened and susceptible to disease.

Also like aphids and scales, whitefly nymphs produce honeydew, a sugar and protein excretion, from the plant sap they ingest. Black, sooty mold may grow on the honeydew, interfering with plant photosynthesis and marring the fruit. But perhaps most seriously, these insects can transmit plant pathogens like viruses through the puncture wounds they make. This potentially makes whiteflies more severe pests than their numbers or fragility might initially suggest.

Combatting whiteflies. Many plants can tolerate low numbers of whiteflies without sustaining enough damage to warrant treatment. To determine if natural enemies are keeping whitefly numbers low, check the undersides of older leaves about 4 in. to 6 in. below the newest top growth on the plant. When you first spot preadult white-flies on the undersides of leaves, just pinch off the infested leaves. If you diligently do this when the plants are young, that alone may be sufficient to prevent a whitefly outbreak.

Your best protection against the build-up of large and potentially damaging populations of whiteflies in the garden is to have a wide variety, in small numbers, of both plant-feeding insects and their natural enemies present during the entire growing season. To maintain this diversity, keep pesticide use to a minimum. Spray only if whitefly numbers threaten to reach damaging levels. Yellowing or wilting plants are a sign of serious damage. Just seeing insects is not.

If natural or physical controls aren't sufficient to solve your whitefly problem, use a low-toxicity pesticide, such as commercial insecticidal soap, refined oil sprays, and pyrethrum products. Or you can use a homemade spray made from garlic, mineral oil, and soap.

For a recipe for a homemade spray, see p. 150.

When applying a pesticide, it's essential to focus on the undersides of leaves so the pesticide reaches the pre-adult whiteflies. To minimize impact on beneficial insects, spot-spray only those plants that have serious infestations.

Whiteflies favor warm climates and can be particularly troublesome indoors and in greenhouses. That's because their natural enemies are usually excluded from protected indoor environments. If you do get an infestation indoors, there are several management options. If just a few leaves are infested with whitefly scales, remove and discard the leaves. Or dab the preadult whiteflies with a cotton swab dipped in rubbing alcohol.

If a plant is heavily infested, give it a bath: Fill a bucket or dishpan with soapy water, wrap a cloth around the surface of the pot to hold in the soil, invert the plant, slosh the foliage in the soapy water, and remove the plant from the water. After a few hours, wash off the plant in clear water.

Tomato Pests

Unfortunately, a lot of insects like tomatoes as much as we do. By handpicking, squashing, or pruning off insect pests, they're not likely to multiply beyond control. Keeping branches off the ground by tying them up or clipping them off discourages ground-living pests like sowbugs, slugs, and snails from bothering plants. Here are the most significant tomato pests.

Tomato hornworm is a most impressive caterpillar but usually not the most damaging. There are several species in the United States, all 3 in. to 5 in. in length and green with stripes down the sides. A pointy red projection where you'd expect a tail on a mammal is the horn. Hornworms are the larvae of hawk moths, very distinctive large night

Hornworms (top) are scary looking but usually don't cause serious damage to tomatoes. They are the larvae of large hawk moths (bottom).

flyers. At dusk they may be mistaken for hummingbirds supping at flowers. The moths lay round green eggs on the undersides of tomato leaves. The eggs hatch in about 5 days. In the South, there may be as many as four hornworm generations in the summer, but in more northern latitudes one generation per year is the norm.

Despite their large size, hornworms are remarkably hard to spot. You may guess they're around if the top of a tomato plant is completely stripped of leaves. Another clue is their large fecal pellets, about the size of raisins, scattered in clumps on the leaves of interior stems. Look directly above the frass to find the caterpillar itself. Hornworms use their four pair of rear legs to hold onto leaves with a surprisingly strong grip. You can try pulling them off, but it may be easier to snip the caterpillars in two, leaving the halves for predatory wasps to clean up. Or just snip off the leaf supporting the worm and drop it in a bucket of soapy water.

Like all the caterpillars mentioned in this section, hornworms are susceptible to Btk, a naturally occurring pathogen that causes disease in the larvae of both moths and butterflies, but does not harm their natural enemies.

For more information on Btk, see p. 175.

Tomato fruitworms are truly damaging. They are also known as corn earworms when they bother corn. By either name, these worms are susceptible to Bt. Fruitworms feed on the tomato fruit itself, so a large infestation should be treated. You may need to repeat Bt applications every 12 to 14 days, since several generations can be present at the same time during serious outbreaks. For Bt to work on tomato fruitworms, it needs to be sprayed on leaves before caterpillars have become large enough to move from the leaves and enter the fruit. Damaged or fallen fruits should be gathered promptly and composted.

Tomato fruitworms feed on the fruit, so a large infestation is worth treating.

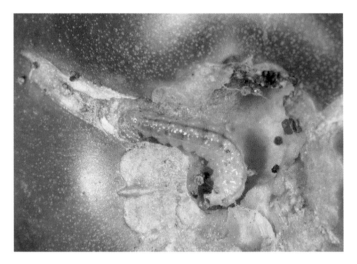

Tiny pinworms may tunnel into fruit before you even know they're around.

Pinworms are the worst of the caterpillar pests because they may tunnel into tomato fruit near the stem before you are even aware they are around. Some may tunnel into leaves as well. Pinworms are primarily warm-climate pests, so southern gardeners should check plants, looking for blotchy, translucent areas where these tiny miners are between the upper and lower layer of leaf cells. Remove infested leaves as fast as you notice them, crush the caterpillar in its burrow, and hot-compost the leaves along with any infested tomatoes. Bt is also effective on pinworms.

'Lacinato' kale holds a homemade insect repellent. The cotton ball in the vial was soaked with camphor oil to repel cabbage looper moths.

Thrips (the word applies to a single insect or many) are small insects that rasp off leaf surfaces, often causing a change in color. Their small, black fecal spots are sometimes noticeable. Thrips are as small as a hyphen on the printed page; the young are white, yellow, or translucent, and the adults are dark to the naked eye. Thrips are primarily a problem on fruit trees and tomato plants, mostly in the southwestern United States. They tend to cluster on the undersides of leaves along the veins. In addition to damaging plants, thrips can spread nasty pathogens.

Often thrips infest tomato plants that are too dry. Simply watering more may reduce even large thrips populations to insignificant status. If that doesn't do it, use the same approach that works with aphids, whiteflies, and mites—soapy water. Nocturnal spiders eat thrips, so keep a rough mulch around the plants to give the spiders daytime hiding places.

CONTROLLING PESTS

Nonchemical methods for controlling pests—crop rotations or handpicking, for instance—are best. But there are situations in which nonchemical methods are ineffective or unworkable, and in such cases, many gardeners choose to use a chemical pesticide, either biological or synthetic. There are valid arguments for and against pesticides. Some gardeners will never use them. Others will, and so it's important to focus on when, where, and how to use pesticides properly and on criteria for selecting them.

Use the least toxic approach to pesticides

The most important consideration is choosing the least-toxic product that will get the job done and using it only when necessary. Least-toxic materials are those that are least disruptive of natural controls, least hazardous to human health, least harmful to nontarget organisms, and least damaging to the environment.

Chemical pesticides, whether aimed at bacteria or bugs, share a common limitation: They rarely offer permanent control. In the short run, however, least-toxic chemical controls have their place. By temporarily shifting the balance between pest and natural enemy, the right chemical control used at the right time can pave the way for establishing long-term biological controls in the garden. Ladybeetles, lacewings, insect-eating nematodes, and other biological controls are commercially available. But if the pest population is already high, you must knock down the pest numbers before releasing beneficials.

You don't need to reach for a highly toxic pesticide to do this. Instead, use water sprays or an application of insecticidal soap or horticultural oil. The goal is to reduce the number of pests, not eliminate them. After all, you need to have some pest insects around to feed the beneficials when you release them or they fly in naturally.

Confine chemicals to intolerable situations

It makes sense to react quickly to vertebrate pests—deer, for example. But before you move fast against an insect pest, ask yourself two basic questions. Is it really necessary to control this pest? And if so, is there a simple alternative to insecticides? Don't overlook physical controls, such as handpicking the pest or pruning out portions of the infested vegetation. These nonchemical methods are often fast and satisfactory.

Use chemical controls for situations in which the damage involved is, or will soon become, intolerable. The presence of a few recognized pest insects is not enough to signal doom. On the other hand, a large population beginning to cause visible destruction may be a different matter. You should consider what you expect of the result. If the vegetable you're trying to protect is going right into the cooking pot, then who cares about a few holes or scars? Minor cosmetic damage is a sign that no poison residues need concern you.

If you observe your plants carefully, you will see that, even among those of the same kind, responses to insect pests vary. Make it a practice to treat only those plants that are severely attacked.

There are many ways to avoid using pesticides that kill nontarget organisms. The most obvious is to pick a material that either by its composition or its packaging is toxic to just one target pest. Bt is a good example, because it produces a disease specific to the insects listed on the label. Another example is insect growth regulators, which prevent molting in specific insects, such as whiteflies.

Bundle up no matter what pesticide you're applying. If wearing the equivalent of a space suit doesn't appeal to you, perhaps that's reason enough to seek a less toxic alternative.

Baits, if packaged to reduce attractiveness to and access by other animals, are another good way to confine a chemical control to the target pest. In some bait stations, the active chemical is combined with a pheromone attractant to bring a specific insect pest to the bait station.

Don't grab the first pesticide you see that mentions your pest. Study the label. You are looking for the least toxic—yet still effective—material that will leave no residue to harm beneficial wildlife or yourself.

Be sure the material is registered for use against the pest you wish to control. Also check to see if it can be used on vegetables right up to the harvest period. And you need to know what kind of protective clothing, gloves, goggles, or respirator you will need while applying the pesticide, as well as the recommended application equipment.

Always check the label for the toxicity rating. A rating of IV means the chemical is practically nontoxic. Category III chemicals are considered slightly toxic and are labeled "Caution." Make every effort to confine your use to materials no more toxic than this. Category II chemicals are moderately toxic and are labeled "Warning." Category I materials are highly toxic and are labeled "Danger—Poison," with a skull and crossbones. There should be no need to use Category I materials around the house or garden.

Use the least amount in the smallest area. Even a toxic material will cause little damage if you confine the pesticide to just the organism you wish to control. A good example of confining a pesticide to its target is using a soft paintbrush or a small piece of rag tied to a stick to wipe herbicide on the leaves or branchlets of a perennial weed.

When purchasing pesticides, buy the smallest amount that will do the job. Then mix up just the amount you need. The temptation is too great to use up the extra material by spraying it around places where it's not needed.

Protecting yourself. Even when using comparatively benign materials like insecticidal soaps or insect-specific diseases like Bt, be sure to protect yourself from chemical pesticides. The most common problem associated with careless use of a pesticide is a skin reaction, typically a rash or a burn. But you also need to avoid eye and lung exposure. Any vapor that enters the lungs will be rapidly absorbed into the bloodstream and distributed throughout the body. With some materials, there is a potential for damage to nerves or to body levels of the transmitter that enables signals to travel from nerve to nerve.

Wear gloves intended for handling chemicals, and store the gloves in disposable plastic bags between uses. The greatest hazard in applying chemical pesticides comes from spilling it accidentally on your unprotected clothing. Change out of contaminated clothing immediately. Spills or no spills, clothes worn while applying pesticides should be washed separately from the family laundry.

Be sure to store or dispose of the remaining materials properly. Never keep pesticides in unmarked containers or within reach of children and pets. Store all pesticides in their original package, but put paper or glass containers inside metal cans to avoid spills due to breakage or moisture. And bear in mind that leftover pesticides may lose effectiveness by the time you need them again.

If you have questions about a specific material, a good source of toxicity information is the EPA Hotline: (800)858-7378. You can also visit the National Pesticide Information center website at http://ace.orst.edu/info/nptn.

Repel garden pests

Unlike pesticides, which control pests by killing them, repellents deter pests from initially colonizing plants, and sometimes they even drive pests from infested plants. The challenge is determining what makes a good repellent. What works in one situation may not work in all circumstances because there are many complex factors that affect a pest's decision to adopt a plant as a host. Also, what appears repelling to us may actually draw in pests. For example, flea beetles are attracted to mustard gas. Hence, they often attack plants in the mustard family.

Many different home remedies have been touted to repel pests on plants. When making a home remedy, you must be careful that the solution is not phytotoxic to the plant (it must not burn a plant's leaves). Because ingredients in homemade remedies can vary greatly, it is difficult to know the phytotoxicity of a solution or guarantee plant safety. If a favorite repellent isn't mentioned here, there is no reason to believe it's ineffective. If you have a good track record with something that is not harming your plant but is deterring pests, you have a useful repellent.

Diligence is key in applying repellents. Most repellents are applied to plants as foliar sprays. In addition to thorough coverage, the secret to getting repellents to work is in your application diligence. Most repellents will not persist on plants after rainfall or beyond 5 to 7 days, so multiple applications over time are necessary for protection.

It is important to apply the compounds before the levels of pest damage are severe, because most repellents have a limited ability to reduce high pest populations. Many pests, such as Japanese beetles, have been shown to make plants more attractive to further pest visits once the plant has been fed upon.

Repellents for sucking pests. Because of their feeding habits (extracting fluids from plant tissues with a stylet rather than chewing on plants), their fast reproduction rates, and their ability to do extreme damage to plants, sucking insect and mite pests present a tough order for repellents to fill. The repellent must prevent the initial visitation by sucking insects or mites because once they arrive and begin to feed, the battle is soon lost.

Garlic is one of the most popular repellents. Most garlic oil repellents, like Garlic Barrier®, seem to work best against sucking pests such as aphids and whiteflies. Although these oils look and smell anything but palatable, some have no odor after the initial application.

Better known as insecticides, horticultural oils—also called parafinnic oils and stylet oils—can also work as insect repellents. Horticultural oils (such as Sunspray® Ultrafine Oil, Volck® Supreme Oil, and JMS Stylet-Oil®) have the ability to deter aphids from feeding on virus-susceptible crops. It is important to stop aphids before they attack the plant because once they feed, the plant may contract a virus from the aphids. As either a repellent or

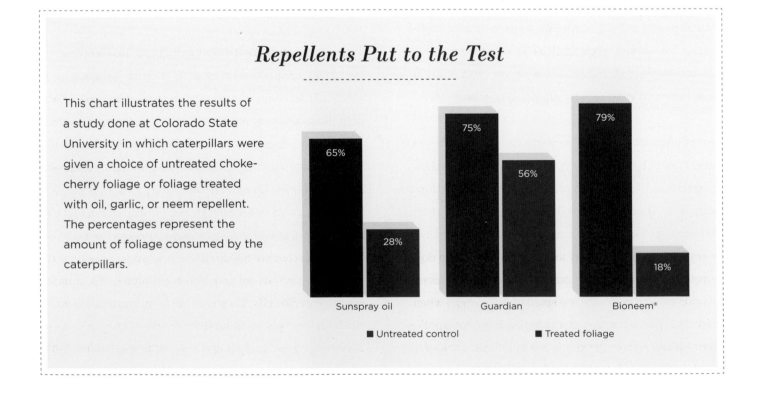

Repellents Put to the Test

This chart illustrates the results of a study done at Colorado State University in which caterpillars were given a choice of untreated chokecherry foliage or foliage treated with oil, garlic, or neem repellent. The percentages represent the amount of foliage consumed by the caterpillars.

65%   28%   75%   56%   79%   18%

Sunspray oil   Guardian   Bioneem®

■ Untreated control   ■ Treated foliage

an insecticide for sucking pests, horticultural oil represents a good choice. It does not persist in the environment long after application and so conserves the beneficial insects available in your garden to perform biological control.

Repellents for chewing pests. Many repellents perform well against chewing insects. Among them, neem oils (derived from the tree *Azadirachta indica*) are probably the best choice. The predominant compound in neem products is azadirachtin. Azadirachtin works in two ways. It is a growth regulator acting to disrupt hormone levels in insects, and it is a very potent insect repellent.

You can use neem products (like BioNEEM®, Organica® Neem Soap Concentrate, and Green Light® Neem Concentrate) to deter and control many different species of pests, such as caterpillars and sawflies, as well as many species of beetles. Although adult pests such as flea beetles will only be repelled by neem and not affected by its growth regulator action, neem may be mixed with other compounds, such as pyrethrum, to extend its punch and persistence as a plant protection agent. Remember that although neem has limited toxicity to mammals, it can pose a threat to certain beneficial insects, such as bees and parasitic wasps. Be sure to scout your garden first so you won't be hurting your biological control program with an application.

Repellents for deer and rodents. No pest receives more attention with regard to repellents than deer. Within a given region, deer will eat whatever is available if they are hungry. There are very few deer-resistant plants. Home-remedy repellent concoctions abound for deer and include everything from perfumed soaps to human hair to dog or coyote urine, and even rotten eggs. Ammonia salt compounds can approximate the smell of rotten eggs when initially applied, but the odor fades rapidly after application. Although many products are sold for deer deterrence (such as Deer Off®, Deer Away®, or Hinder®), they are also very effective at deterring rodents, such as voles and gophers. Their repellency against deer varies based on time of season and weather conditions. None is guaranteed, but any may work in your particular circumstances.

Available off your spice rack or as a prepared wax derivative labeled for use on plants, cayenne pepper can have superior effects as a repellent against a variety of pests, including deer. It is also a popular ingredient in many home-remedy recipes. To repel deer, apply the wax to desirable plants before damage is widely observed. The mixture remains in place to deter feeding for a limited time. Another popular use of cayenne pepper is to sprinkle a small amount near where ants are entering your house, which may prevent them from intruding.

When used with care, most repellents are safe to plants and people and are a great alternative to more dangerous pesticides. Trial and error will tell which repellents will be effective in your particular circumstances. Remember, if you decide to use home remedies, test your solution on a single plant or leaf before using it on your entire crop.

Horticultural Oils

Petroleum-derived horticultural oils have been used as pest-management tools since ancient times. For many years, oil treatments were largely restricted to applications on deciduous woody plants during the winter months, when they lacked foliage that could be burned by the oil. Hence the term "dormant" oil spray. By the 1980s, however, major improvements in oil-refining technology significantly lowered or removed leaf-burning contaminants such as sulfur and naphthalene. This resulted in new types of refined mineral oils that are highly effective at low application rates.

These new oils are known as horticultural oils, summer oils, or superior oils. They are relatively inexpensive and can be safely applied in summer or winter to a wide range of plant species—including many tender vegetables, fruits, berries, and ornamental plants—with little or no damage.

Superior oils can be applied while a plant is in leaf.

Most horticultural oils on the market are still derived from petroleum oil, but vegetable oils extracted from canola seed, corn, cottonseed, peanuts, soybeans, and sunflower seeds are slowly making their way into the marketplace. Some of them leave a heavier residue on plants than the petroleum oil products.

Because highly refined horticultural oils suited for summer applications on food crops are relatively new to the market, there hasn't been much research to determine which plants can tolerate summer oil sprays without damage. So far, various trials have shown that the following edible plants are compatible with summer applications of horticultural oil: asparagus, beans, beets, cabbage, cauliflower and other cole crops, celery, corn, cucumbers, eggplant, lettuce, melons, potato, radishes, peppers, squash, sweet potato, tomato, basil, lemon balm, and spearmint. Most fruit and nut trees and vines can also be sprayed in summer or winter.

The list of summer-oil-compatible vegetables may be larger than this, so gardeners are encouraged to conduct their own tests of oil tolerance on plants not listed here. Foliage burned by summer oil sprays initially develops light yellow blotches, which later become water-soaked, then darken and die. Damage from a dormant application of oil on trees causes dieback of branch terminal or lateral growth. Read the label on the package for the most updated list of crops that can be safely treated with oils.

Horticultural oils are effective against a wide range of pests. The most highly susceptible pests are soft-bodied insects like aphids, adelgids, caterpillars, leafhoppers, lace bugs, mealybugs, plant bugs, sawflies, and various scales, as well as spider mites. The corn earworm (also known as the tomato fruitworm) can be thwarted by adding 20 drops of mineral oil to the sweet corn silk just inside each ear 3 to 7 days after the silks first appear.

Scales on fruit trees, including citrus and avocado, can be treated with horticultural oils in spring or summer, when the scales are in the crawler stage, having just moved out from under the protective shell of the mother scale. To identify this key vulnerable stage, wrap sticky tape around a few branches where adult scales are seen. Monitor the tape weekly until you see the young scale crawlers stuck on the tape, then apply the oil.

Overwintering caterpillar eggs and pupae on fruit and nut trees can be suppressed by applying horticultural oils to the trunks and branches of trees during late winter, just prior to bud swell. Such treatments substantially reduce the summer populations of these and other pests, such as aphids, scales, and spider mites. When making winter applications, use the lighter-weight horticultural oils and apply them at a slightly higher rate, according to the instructions on the label.

Horticultural oils prevent the spread of plant viruses by controlling aphids before they can spread viruses like watermelon mosaic, squash mosaic, and potato virus Y. Oils also curb the spread of viruses that humans transmit by hands or tools, for example, tobacco mosaic virus.

Diluted horticultural oil mixed with baking soda also controls the powdery mildew fungus on roses, and research suggests that mildew-prone food crops, such as grapes, might also benefit from oil sprays, with or without additives like baking soda.

Several modes of action increase effectiveness.

Horticultural oils work on a broad range of insect pests in various life stages and under a wide variety of growing conditions. Oils can suffocate an insect by coating its entire body and blocking its breathing apparatus. Oils also appear to interact with insect fatty acids, disrupting cell membranes and metabolism. This is true of adult stages and eggs, which collapse when oil penetrates the shell and interferes with the functioning of cells and respiratory processes. Insects will also avoid plants coated with horticultural oil. Finally, oils act as an antifeedant. Some aphids, flea beetles, leafroller caterpillars, webworms, and whiteflies stop feeding when they encounter leaves coated with oil.

The benefit of multiple modes of action is that the target pest is likely to succumb to at least one of them. And the insect is unlikely to develop resistance to an insecticide that is effective in many different ways. Despite centuries of use, insect resistance to horticultural oil treatments has not yet been observed.

As with every insecticide, read the label carefully to determine which pests and plants can be treated with oil, and which application methods to use. Make applications in early morning on a cloudy day with low humidity (45 to 65 percent) to help speed evaporation of the oils and reduce any chance of leaf damage. Avoid applying oil sprays when the air temperature is below 40°F or above 100°F for 48 hours, since the oil will take longer to dry.

Apply dormant-season oils after insect dormancy ends in late winter or early spring and insects resume growth. This advice needs to be balanced against the precaution to avoid applying oil on newly emerging plant shoots in early spring to keep from burning them. In summer, leave at least a 2-week interval between treatments. Also, avoid oil treatments in the fall before true dormancy has taken place. Premature treatments can result in dieback of twigs and shoots on deciduous plants the following spring.

Horticultural oils show a low toxicity to humans and other animals, as well as to some birds and reptiles. However, they are toxic to fish. The impact of oil sprays on beneficial insects is usually minimal because these insects tend to disperse rapidly when oils are sprayed. (Beneficial insects are generally more mobile and faster than insect pests.) Unless they are actually covered with the oil, nontarget insects will escape harm. Since horticultural oil evaporates rapidly and when dried has little residual effect, beneficial insects can safely re-enter oil-treated areas. Careful spot-treatments of oil onto concentrations

Horticultural Oil Home Brew

You can make your own horticultural oil solution from familiar household products. Combine 1 tablespoon liquid dishwashing detergent or soap such as Dawn®, Ivory®, Palmolive®, or Joy® with 1 cup corn, peanut, safflower, soybean, or sunflower oil. Add 1 to 2½ teaspoons of this stock solution to 1 cup of water in a plastic pump-handled bottle. (The soap is needed to emulsify the oil in the water.) Agitate the mixture and spray it onto the undersides and topsides of infested leaves.

of pests will also help protect beneficial insects and other nontarget organisms.

Oils can be applied in combination with other low-toxicity insecticides such as Bt and insecticidal soap. Often these combinations increase the effectiveness of the treatment. For example, when combined with Bt, the oil apparently protects the living bacteria found in Bt from degradation by UV light and prevents chemical breakdown of the Bt protein toxin. When combined with insecticidal soap, horticultural oil acts as a synergist, helping to spread the compound over the insect's surface and speed up penetration of the toxin inside the insect's cuticle.

Monitor your plants as frequently as necessary to spot the arrival of insect pests or other problems early. If natural enemies or manual controls don't prevent pest numbers from increasing beyond your tolerance levels and a spray is needed, new horticultural oils are a promising alternative to toxic sprays.

Insecticidal soap

Soap sprays have been used to fight insects for several hundred years. But during the 1940s and 1950s, when using chemical pesticides became common agricultural practice, soaps fell from favor because they were perceived as less effective. Fortunately, a resurgent interest in organic, less toxic ways to control insect pests has led to the development of modern insecticidal soap. The active ingredients in soap are potassium salts of fatty acids and occasionally citrus oils, substances that occur naturally in the cells of some plants.

Insecticidal soap kills soft-bodied bugs by bursting their membranes and destroying their nervous systems. It works only on contact and thus is useless as a preventive measure. The bugs must be present when spraying occurs. Soap is effective against insects like mealybugs, spider mites, leafhoppers, earwigs, thrips, whiteflies, some types of scale, and especially aphids. It is not harmful to most

Scale insects can be effectively controlled with horticultural oils.

beneficial insects, including honeybees, ladybugs, and parasitic wasps. Furthermore, the crops on which it has been sprayed are safe for animals and humans.

Although it can be sprayed on crops up until the day of harvest, soap is not completely benign. If ingested, splashed in the eyes, or dumped in streams or ponds, soap can be just as toxic as any detergent. If you spray it on a sunny day, it can also burn the foliage. Some ornamental and succulent plants can't tolerate soap at all.

As with all pesticides, organic or not, you should first identify the pest, choose soap only if it is effective for that pest and plant, and then follow package directions carefully.

Biological insecticides

The list of least-toxic insecticides has been growing. Biological insecticides derived from plants are called botanicals; those derived from microorganisms like fungi, bacteria, and nematodes are called microbials. Like conventional synthetic insecticides, these products are most effective when used in combination with nonchemical methods and should be applied as spot treatments, when pest numbers threaten to exceed your tolerance level, rather than indiscriminately throughout your garden.

The biologicals mentioned here are currently registered by the U.S. Environmental Protection Agency for use on pests that attack both food crops and ornamentals. Since EPA registrations change frequently, check the label to ensure the product continues to be registered for use in the kitchen garden. Remember that biological insecticides may contain living organisms, so store them in a cool, dark area or refrigerate them. They will die if exposed to excessively cold or hot temperatures.

Neem oil is prepared from extracts of oils from seeds of the tropical neem tree, *Azadirachta indica,* native to India and the Asian subcontinent. Neem oil is effective against leaf-chewing and sucking insects, including aphids, beetle larvae, caterpillars, leafminers, leafhoppers, thrips, and whiteflies.

This product has several modes of action against insects. Primarily it acts as an insect growth regulator, meaning it prevents preadult insects from successfully molting from the juvenile to adult stage. Treated larval and pupal insects stop feeding and die without reproducing. It also inhibits pest feeding and contains ingredients that repel insects.

Neem products are applied as liquid sprays directly onto infested leaves. Thorough coverage, including the underside of leaves, is essential. If not washed off by rain or irrigation water, neem remains active on leaves for 2 to 7 days, sometimes longer.

Bacillus thuringiensis (Bt) is a microbial insecticide made from a naturally occurring bacterial pathogen. Bt is very discriminating in the species it affects. One of the strengths of this product from an environmental perspective is that it is toxic to only a narrow range of insects and does not harm beneficial insects or appear to impact humans or other animals, birds, or fish.

Bt affects only the larval stage of susceptible insects. It will not kill adult moths or butterflies. To be effective, Bt must be eaten by caterpillars or larval beetles. When ingested into the stomach, the bacteria releases a toxin that causes the insect to stop feeding and eventually die.

There are several commercially available strains of Bt and each kills a different insect group. Btk (k = kurstaki) and Btt (t = tenebrionis) are the most useful strains for the vegetable garden. Btk is specific to certain pests; see the sidebar on p. 175 for a complete list. Btt kills the larval stage of Colorado potato beetle. Bt is applied as a liquid spray onto upper and lower surfaces of plant leaves. It is best to apply these products when caterpillars or larval beetles are young and small and easier to kill. Since caterpillars have to feed on treated leaves to ingest a lethal amount of Bt, the younger the larvae, the less damage to plants. Treatments last up to 14 days if there is no rainfall to wash away the bacterial spores or if temperatures are not excessively high. You may have to spray again if pest populations are high.

VAM is short for Vesicular Arbuscular Mycorrhizal fungi. These products are made of beneficial fungi (genus *Glomus* and others) suspended in a powder. VAM spores in the soil move onto root surfaces, forming a protective mantle and stimulating physiological changes in the host plant that inhibit plant-attacking nematodes, root pathogens, and possibly other organisms that damage plants. The fungal threadlike mat expands the host plant's access to water and nutrients, thus increasing its resistance to stress, including pest damage and drought.

Powder laced with fungal spores is applied as a root-dip to transplants or is added to soil in the planting hole. It can also be applied in the garden as a water solution injected into the root zone of growing plants. Once mixed with water, the fungal solution must be used rapidly as lack of air kills the spores.

Pyrethrum-based insecticides from chrysanthemums

Pyrethrum is derived from the flower of *Chrysanthemum cinerariaefolium*. You might think that because it is derived from a natural source, a pyrethrum-based product is automatically safe. If you follow the directions for use on the package, it is relatively safe for people and pets, but it is unquestionably a true poison and will kill all insects it comes in contact with, both pests and beneficial insects alike. The most commonly available pyrethrum-based insecticides contain extracts from the flowers, called pyrethrins.

The advantage in the vegetable garden is that a pyrethrin insecticide is effective against a wide variety of hard-to-kill insects like aphids, beetles, leafhoppers, and certain caterpillars. Because pyrethrins degrade rapidly in sunlight, they usually disappear from the garden within 24 hours, allowing you to pick your produce not long after spraying.

Pyrethrum, pyrethrins, pyrethroid. You're not alone if you find the names of these insecticides perplexing. Understanding the terms is the first step in choosing the appropriate insecticide. Pyrethrum is the dried, powdered flower heads from the plant. It can be purchased as a powder in some garden centers. Pyrethrins are the active ingredients found in the dried flower heads. (Sometimes you will see the active ingredient referred to as pyrethrin, but there is more than one active chemical in the powder, so the active ingredient should be referred to as pyrethrins.) Pyrethrins usually come as a liquid that is put into solution with water and used in conventional spray equipment. Pyrethroids are the imposters—synthetic, man-made pyrethrins.

Pyrethroids are an example of how a chemical can be highly toxic even though it is based on a botanical source. Chemists have taken pyrethrum as a model and formed a whole group of poisons that have a structure similar to that of the natural compounds. The -oid suffix indicates "something like," so a pyrethroid is something like a pyrethrum. One of the most common pyrethroids is permethrin. The "per-" prefix means "chlorine," which is the key to the higher toxicity of permethrin. Gardeners with food crops should avoid permethrin since it has a residual life of 2 months or more and is more toxic than pyrethrum.

Products are marketed under various names, so check the ingredients to determine what you're buying.

Read insecticide labels carefully for EPA approval for use on food crops.

Target Pests of *Bacillus thuringiensis* var. *kurstaki* (Btk)

The following pests are susceptible to Btk, the most common commercially available species. Be sure to read all labels before treatment to make sure your target pest is included.

- Armyworm
- Bagworm
- Cabbage looper
- Diamondback moth
- Fall cankerworm
- Fall webworm
- Gypsy moth
- Imported cabbageworm
- Indianmeal moth
- Mimosa webworm
- Sod webworm
- Spring cankerworm
- Tent caterpillars
- Tomato/tobacco hornworm

Most of the world's supply of pyrethrum comes from eastern Africa, which has the right climate and the labor force to pick the flowers by hand. This makes the product relatively expensive compared with many other insecticides. In addition, some insects have the ability to break down the pyrethrins and recover from exposure to the chemical. To lower the amount of active ingredient (and thus lower the cost) while increasing the toxicity, manufacturers began routinely adding another component: piperonyl butoxide (PBO). It was assumed that PBO had little or no toxicity alone and merely made the mixture more potent, so it was considered a synergist.

The combination of pyrethrins and PBO produced greater toxicity against the same population of insects than the ingredients used individually. However, in this case 2 plus 2 did not equal 4, but 40 or 400 or more. The two components are believed to block different biochemical pathways in insects and thus overwhelm the detoxifying powers of an insect exposed to it, making it much more toxic to the insect.

More recently, PBO has been classified as an active ingredient. Although PBO is derived from a botanical source, many organic certification systems have been reluctant to include it among the permitted materials. Consequently, there are products with only pyrethrins as well as those with pyrethrins and PBO. The latter products are less expensive and more toxic than the pyrethrins alone, though not as toxic as a synthetic pyrethroid. If you cannot obtain the pyrethrins-only products, use those with PBO, particularly if the only other choices are more-toxic insecticides. If the package label is complicated to figure out, most nursery personnel will be able to help you. If no one can help you, it's worth avoiding the chemical until you have more information.

The ideal insecticide should kill the target pest without injuring nontarget insects, other wildlife, or you, the gardener. Pyrethrins are toxic to a wide range of insects, not to just a selected few pests, so they are not an ideal pesticide. But since they have an extremely short residual life, they kill only the insects present at the time of application, minimizing the number of nontarget pests killed, compared with most other commonly used poisons.

Pyrethrins have some selectivity with regard to mammals, since short-term (hours, days) exposure to skin or other parts of the human body does not lead to life-threatening or even health-threatening reactions. The only reported problems occurred with some people who were hypersensitive and who breathed in some of the material. These people may also have been reacting to various inert

The source of pyrethrum is the flowers of *Chrysanthemum cinerariaefolium,* also called the Dalmation flower.

ingredients in the product they were using, and not to the pyrethrum itself. The respiratory problems once caused by using the ground flowers ceased when extracted pyrethrin products appeared on the market.

It is possible that pyrethrum is one of the oldest insecticides known, and that in itself suggests its effectiveness and indicates acceptance by many people in many different situations. Because pyrethrum-based products have had many incarnations over time, it is best to be informed when buying and using them, as some are much more toxic than others.

ANIMAL PESTS

Unfortunately, harmful insects aren't the only pests you need to deal with. Four-legged types need to be minded as well. Other than deer, the two main animals you'll need to be on the lookout for are rabbits and voles. Although they're cute, they can be voracious, too.

Rabbits

If one morning you notice that it looks like someone took a pruning shear and snipped off the stems of young plants with clean, angled cuts, mowed your lettuces and beet foliage to the ground, or gnawed rings around the trunks of trees or vines, extending upward to about 2½ ft., your garden has likely been visited by a rabbit or two. To confirm your suspicions, look around for the ubiquitous ¼-in. to ½-in. round fecal pellets that rabbits seem to drop constantly. The presence of their characteristic footprints, consisting of an alternating pattern of small front feet and large back feet, is another clue to the identity of the culprit.

Vegetable gardens are highly attractive to rabbits, especially during droughts and long winters or where urbanization has reduced their wild habitat. Fortunately, there are practical ways to outwit rabbits without doing them harm.

Two groups of wild rabbits can become problems in the garden: jackrabbits *Lepus* spp., a type of hare, and cottontails *Sylvilagus* spp., a true rabbit.

Where food and cover are plentiful, rabbits tend to stay put. This characteristic combined with their frequent reproduction enables rabbits to quickly fill any empty habitat created when other rabbits are trapped and removed. That is why fencing gardens when you're in rabbit country is so important.

A 30-in.- to 36-in.-high fence constructed from woven wire with a mesh no larger than 1 in. is almost foolproof for excluding rabbits. The lower end of the wire mesh should be turned outward at a 90-degree angle and buried 6 in. in the ground to discourage rabbits from digging under the fence. Regular 20-gauge poultry netting supported by stakes can provide protection from rabbits for 3 to 5 years and is inexpensive to replace. Welded wire will protect for longer periods.

Rabbits (as well as raccoons and skunks) can also be excluded by electric fencing, which is portable and can be removed and stored when rabbit activity ceases or the growing season ends. Six strands of electric wire spaced 3 in. apart, with alternating hot and ground wires, should deter most rabbits.

➥ *For more information on fencing options, see p. 50.]*

By removing brush piles, weed patches, dumps, stone piles, and other debris where rabbits live and hide, you may induce rabbits near the garden to relocate voluntarily to more hospitable habitat. Although this won't totally solve your rabbit problem, it will help reduce rabbit populations close to the garden.

Commercial repellents can provide some protection to plants for short periods of time. Common ones include ammonium soaps, capsaicin (hot pepper), naphthalene (moth balls), and blood meal. These materials need to be reapplied to unprotected new growth, and after rainfall or sprinkler irrigation washes the repellent off plant leaves. They should not be applied to edible portions of the plant.

If all else fails, and if only a few rabbits are feeding in the garden, try live trapping and relocating. This is usually effective only with cottontails; jackrabbits are too trap-shy. In the warm season, bait the trap with whatever the rabbit has been eating—apples and fresh vegetables such as carrots, beans, or a cabbage leaf rolled tightly and held together with a toothpick. In winter, a dried corn cob, dried apples, and alfalfa are excellent baits.

Voles

The vole is a mouse with small ears. Quietly spending most of their time out of sight, voles commonly come to our attention when damaged bark is found at the base of valued fruit trees and ornamental plants.

Small and chunky with short legs and tail, voles are strictly outdoor mice. Usually they are brown or gray, but there may be a variation on the belly of white, yellow, or cinnamon. Many species are found from one end of the country to the other.

Voles like to nibble on the bark of fruit trees and ornamental plants. They usually eat grasses and weeds, but they also relish insects like gypsy moths, snails, and the remains of dead animals. In the fall, they gather and store seeds, bulbs, tubers, and rhizomes.

Voles are active day and night, year-round. Although they can carry a number of disease organisms transmissible to humans, they are usually not a public health hazard because we rarely encounter them in the wild. It is when they move into orchards and gardens that there is a potential for problems.

Other animals like rabbits can cause similar damage. The difference is in the size and uniformity of the gnaw marks. Vole marks are $\frac{1}{8}$ in. wide, $\frac{3}{8}$ in. long, and $\frac{1}{6}$ in. or more deep, and occur at different angles and in irregular patches. In contrast, rabbit gnaw marks are larger and not as distinct. Rabbits clip off small branches with clean oblique cuts. Voles nibble.

If chewing damage makes you suspect voles, the next thing to look for is their pathway system on the ground surface, where the voles have worn down grass and weeds. Pathways are 1 in. to 2 in. wide and can be quite extensive with numerous burrow openings.

Voles don't like to feed in the open, so the best way to manage them is to reduce the cover they need to protect themselves from predators. Cut down grass and other high vegetation. Pull mulch back 2 ft. to 3 ft. from the base of trees and shrubs. Leave the ground bare. Until the situation is under control, you may even need to remove mulch from garden beds.

Ploughing or tilling the soil is effective in destroying the voles' pathway and burrow systems. This is why voles are often less of a problem with annual crops, unless

Deterring Voles

One option for deterring rodents is this bent fence made from 18-gauge hardware cloth. Bury it in the ground to a depth of 8 in. to 10 in., with only about 4 in. above soil level (voles aren't climbers).

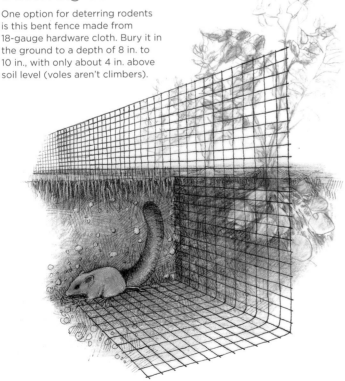

plants form a dense vegetative cover for a long period of time. If vole damage is severe in a home orchard, you can destroy their burrows with a rotary tiller by turning the soil under 5 in. to 6 in.

Place collars around the base of trunks of small trees and shrubs. You can use heavy wire such as hardware cloth; 1/4-in. mesh is necessary to prevent voles from biting through. Barriers must extend into the soil at least 6 in. and rise above it 8 in. to 12 in. Check the barriers a couple of times a year to make sure they're not restricting plant growth. You may need to stake the barriers if the soil is loose, or if you're not able to sink them deep enough into the soil.

Since most species of voles are poor climbers, it may be worthwhile to place a 1/4-in. hardware cloth fence around a garden bed you are trying to protect. The fence should extend at least 1 ft. above and 10 in. below the ground. Stake the fence at intervals to be sure it remains upright. Since vole populations fluctuate, extreme efforts like fencing might be necessary some years, but not others.

If other strategies don't work, try trapping with mouse snap traps baited with a paste of rolled oats and peanut butter. Set the traps on the ground, perpendicular to the vole pathway with the trigger end in the pathway. A pinch of rolled oats sprinkled in the pathway next to the traps may entice the voles, but be careful not to disturb the pathways or burrows. Make sure that traps are level and don't wobble. You don't want voles to be frightened away by movement, and you want the traps to perform properly so they'll catch instantly, killing the vole. To prevent birds from getting caught, cover traps with a length of cardboard bent in half. Leave enough space above the trap so the cardboard doesn't prevent the trap from springing.

Don't skimp on the number of traps. For a small garden, start with a dozen. For a large garden or orchard, you may need 50 traps or more. Also, it's essential to keep vegetation suppressed while you're trapping to deny cover to the voles.

Wear gloves when handling the captured voles. The most important thing to remember when trapping any rodent is to be persistent. If the population is large, it may take a while to make a difference.

➥ *For information on keeping deer out of your garden, see p. 51.*

DISEASES

As mentioned at the beginning of this chapter, you can keep plant diseases to a minimum by planting disease-resistant varieties, rotating crops, practicing good garden sanitation, giving plants adequate spacing to encourage air circulation, and avoiding overhead watering. For information on diseases that threaten a specific crop, see that crop entry in the Gallery section, beginning on p. 188.

Plant viruses

Viruses deserve some special attention, however. Since they're incurable, it's important to understand how they get transmitted, so you can do all you can to protect your plants.

All plants are susceptible to viral diseases. For example, potatoes are often infected by potato leaf roll virus (PLRV), which causes stunting, yellowing, and rolled leaves; by potato virus Y (PVY), which causes stunting and an irregular color pattern known as mosaic in the leaves; or by potato virus X (PVX), which usually shows no symptoms. All three viruses may be present in the same plant at the same time and all can reduce yield. Cucumbers, melons, and squash can be infected by cucumber mosaic virus (CMV), squash mosaic virus (SqMV), and zucchini yellow mosaic virus (ZYMV). All three viruses stunt growth, cause mosaic, and leave fruits deformed and mottled.

Some viruses infect only plants of a single family; others infect a wide variety of plants. In most cases, it is impossible to diagnose the specific virus by observing the symptoms because the symptoms often mimic other plant

Vegetable viruses may be invisible as they slip into plants and reproduce, but the trouble they cause with fruit is apparent. These zucchini show the disfigurement typical of viral infection.

problems. Luckily, plant viruses attack only the cells of their host plants. Plant viruses have no effect on the health of people or animals. You almost certainly have safely eaten virus-infected fruits and vegetables many times.

Viruses must catch a ride into a plant cell through a wound. Even the tiniest tear in a surface cell is enough, and routine gardening practices, even touching, can break open a cell. After handling a virus-infected plant, you probably have on your fingers some virus-laden sap, which you can spread to healthy plants.

Some viruses, such as tobacco mosaic virus (TMV), are extremely resilient. TMV can withstand the curing of tobacco and its processing into cigarettes. That means smokers should wash their hands thoroughly before handling plants. Wind also can help spread viruses, not through the air, but by causing leaves of neighboring plants to rub against each other.

A number of common garden insects, especially aphids, can spread plant viruses. They have piercing-sucking mouthparts that act like tiny hypodermic needles and transfer sap containing viruses from an infected plant to a healthy one. Similarly, some nematodes may carry viruses to a healthy plant when feeding with their sharp, hollow stylets.

Once inside a host cell, the virus spreads throughout the plant. Any part of the plant, including the leaves, tubers, fruits, or even the seeds within the fruits, may contain the insidious virus. The implications for propagation are serious. Any part taken from a virus-infected plant may itself be infected.

Recent advances have made testing plant material for viruses faster and more accurate. Tissue culture can be used to eliminate viruses from infected plants, so virus-free plants can be produced. Many companies offer seeds and propagative parts that are certified virus-free.

Methods to deter. To prevent infection, inspect new transplants or seedlings for signs of viral infection. Infected plants often stand out from healthy plants because they are stunted, yellowed, or show a mosaic pattern on the leaves. But some of these symptoms may reflect problems unrelated to viruses.

Any suspicious plants should be removed to avoid infection of nearby plants. Weeds can carry many common viruses, which is another good reason to weed regularly or to mulch. As tempting as it may be to try to protect your plants by killing potential insect vectors with insecticides, this usually isn't effective in preventing virus transmission. A single insect can inoculate a plant in just seconds.

Also, many seed catalogs offer cultivars with genetic resistance to the more troublesome viruses, so look for them if you have had problems.

WEEDS

Weeds manage to gain a foothold in even the most meticulously tended vegetable gardens. A "weed" is commonly defined as a plant growing in a place where it is not wanted. This designation is somewhat subjective, since the same plant species can be considered a weed in one setting and a wildflower, medicinal herb, or nectar source for beneficial insects in another. Nevertheless, there is a consensus on the weedy nature of certain plant species such as thistles, docks, crabgrass, and many others. These

---

5 Questions to Determine Your Tolerance Level for Weeds

While you don't need to tolerate all weed growth, a zero tolerance for weeds should not be your goal.

In setting weed tolerance levels it is important to ask at least five questions:

- Which weed species are growing in the garden?

- How aggressively do they grow and spread?

- Where in the garden are they growing, and how visible are they?

- How much damage to the crop plants, structures, or the overall aesthetics of the garden are they likely to cause?

- What positive contributions are they making to the garden?

These questions can be answered by monitoring the garden through the growing season and by learning the names and behaviors of the weeds found growing there. Be sure to record the information in your garden journal (see p. 107) for a season or two.

---

species share characteristics that enable them to take over garden habitats when conditions are right.

By gaining a better understanding of the conditions suited to weed growth and designing and maintaining your garden in ways that minimize such conditions, your battle with weeds will become briefer each year, and the need to resort to toxic weed control will be minimized or eliminated.

Weeds grow where the soil has been subjected to a disturbance at some point, leaving its surface bare of protective

Some garden weeds aren't all weeds. Thistle (left) has sharp prickles, and nightshade (right) has poisonous berries, yet both have deep roots that penetrate the subsoil, increasing openings for water flow and root movement.

vegetation. In most vegetable gardens, soil disturbance is a routine part of gardening. The mix of weeds that emerges is largely determined by the "seed bank" buried in the soil during previous seasons or by recently blown or flown in via wind or birds. The seeds of many weeds can remain viable in the soil for decades, just waiting for the right conditions, such as soil disturbance, to enable them to germinate.

Cultivating a tolerance for weeds

Although keeping weed populations to a minimum is definitely important to the growth and vigor of edible garden plants as well as to overall garden appearance, complete eradication of all weeds is neither feasible nor desirable.

Deep-rooted weeds like thistles, pigweeds, and nightshades are able to penetrate the subsoil, increasing openings for water and root movement and absorbing minerals such as phosphorous and potassium stored in the lower soil layers. Those minerals are brought up to the topsoil where they are made available to less aggressive plant species upon the death and decay of the weed that "mined" them.

Sometimes weeds assist the work of gardeners. For example, allowing weeds to develop among your onions

from July onward can actually assist the crop by using nitrogen and moisture, which the onions need in decreasing amounts as the bulbs enlarge. After the harvest, digging the weeds into the soil provides organic matter for the next crop.

Other weeds should be tolerated because they can assist the gardener by serving as trap crops for pest insects. For example, gardeners in South Dakota report that by encouraging weedy grasses and broad-leaf weeds such as the annual kochia (*Kochia scoparia*) to grow as a barrier between the garden and adjacent open fields, grasshoppers that normally migrate from the dry pastures into irrigated gardens in the summer stop instead to feed on the weedy trap crop.

The more adept you become at recognizing garden weeds, particularly in the seedling stage, the better you can judge which need immediate attention and which can be removed later or left alone. The easiest way to identify a weed species is to compare your live specimen with a good photo-illustrated narrative description of common weeds in your area. Some useful books for identifying common garden weeds are listed on p. 286. Another good reason for learning to identify weeds is that some act as indicators of relative levels of soil pH, salinity, moisture, and so on. By learning to recognize indicator weeds and what they say about soil conditions, the observant gardener can learn a great deal about general problems and/or opportunities in the garden.

Integrated weed management

Learning about the connection between weeds and disturbed soils often leaves gardeners wondering how they can maintain a vegetable garden without creating conditions that perpetually favor weeds. After all, isn't at least some tilling, mowing, hoeing, or spraying required to plant and maintain a garden? The answer is quite simple. In order to minimize weeds in the first place or to prevent their return, any tactic used to remove weeds must be combined with an action designed to modify the soil habitat so it becomes unfavorable for future weed growth.

Once you have acquired some biological background on the weeds that grow in your garden and have established realistic weed tolerance levels, you are ready to implement strategies that will rid your garden of excessive weeds and prevent new ones from taking their place.

This approach to weed management is often referred to as integrated weed management or IWM. IWM focuses on understanding the conditions that allow weeds to grow and on reducing those conditions. By addressing the basic causes of weed growth, not just treating the individual weeds themselves, you can help your garden develop weed resistance, keeping weed numbers low enough to prevent excessive competition with food crops, yet retaining the benefits of low numbers of certain beneficial weed species. An important feature of the IWM approach is that herbicides are rarely, if ever, necessary.

Weeds need life-support systems in order to grow. These include adequate soil type and condition, water, nutrients, sunlight for photosynthesis, and space for growth. When designing (or redesigning) your garden, you can build in weed-prevention components that deny weeds one or more of these essential life-support systems and thereby prevent unacceptable levels of weed growth.

For information on designing a vegetable garden, see the chapter starting on p. 6.

Defend paths against weeds. Many gardens have unpaved paths or paths covered with a permeable layer of gravel or loose bricks or stones. These paths are wide open to weed invasion. To prevent or reduce the likelihood of weeds growing through a permeable paving, you can place several layers of heavy building paper or roofing paper on the soil before installing the paving material. Tar-impregnated roofing paper is very durable and does not decompose rapidly. By blocking light, tar paper will prevent weed growth for many years. Synthetic weed barrier mats, discussed below, serve the same function, but tend to cost more.

For more information on designing and installing garden paths, see p. 40.

You can weed-proof unpaved paths by covering them with 4 in. to 6 in. of readily available mulch materials that deny weed seeds the light or nutrients needed to grow. Sawdust is a good mulch for garden paths. Not only is it usually free, but microorganisms attempting to decompose the sawdust tie up soil nitrogen, rendering it unavailable for weed growth in the path. In this sense, sawdust acts as a herbicide; be sure to use it only on paths, though, not on your planting beds. As a bonus, the rough surface of dry sawdust also helps deter slugs and snails, whose soft bodies are vulnerable to abrasion when they try to navigate over this material.

Tip the balance in favor of food crops. Disturbed soil is a highly favored habitat for many weeds, whose rapid germination and rate of growth enable them to get a head

Managing Weeds

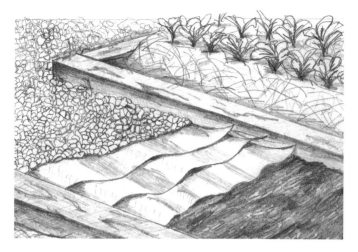

To discourage weeds from growing in your garden path, lay several layers of tar paper over the soil, then cover with gravel or other paving material.

start on slower-germinating food crops. Since soil cultivation is a regular activity when preparing beds for planting, disturbed soil is a common feature of most kitchen gardens. The trick to overcoming this seeming dilemma is to combine a number of horticultural strategies to tip the ecological advantage to the food crops instead of to the weeds.

- **Limit light.** Weed seedlings denied access to light will die without ever making an appearance above the soil. Mulch with a layer of organic plant residues, such as compost or weed-free straw or hay, or with a synthetic weed barrier fabric.

  Apply a mulch immediately after soil cultivation or other soil disturbance; for example, after pulling weeds or readying the soil for planting.

  On vegetable beds, apply organic mulches 3 in. to 6 in. deep. Around perennial crops such as artichokes, berries, grapevines, or fruit trees, be careful to keep the mulch several inches away from the plant stems so as not to promote disease.

If you use a synthetic weed barrier fabric, cover it with straw or other light mulch to protect it from UV degradation.

If your garden soil is loose and rich, close planting—but not overly close—will enable your crops to occupy most of the soil habitat, inhibiting weed germination and shading out those weeds that do manage to lift their leaves above the soil line.

- **Limit water.** Where feasible, use drip, ooze, or furrow irrigation to water your garden. Drip and ooze irrigation systems place water directly in the root zone of plants and apply it slowly enough for plants to absorb most of it soon after it reaches the roots, so little moisture is left over to support weeds. By contrast, overhead irrigation systems apply water indiscriminately over the soil surface, providing water to both garden plants and weeds.

- **Manipulate soil fertility.** To prevent weed seedlings from getting a jump on slower-germinating vegetables, hold back on nitrogen at planting time. Instead, make sure there is adequate available phosphorous in the soil. This nutrient is key to root growth, which temporarily slows above-ground growth of foliage while a healthy root system is being developed. The vegetable plants will welcome ready access to phosphorous during the initial growth stages (as will the weeds), but the temporary absence of excessive nitrogen might help level the playing field for vegetables and weeds at the soil surface.

For more detailed information about soil nutrients, see p. 69.

If you make these strategies permanent components of your garden planning and operation, your battle with weeds will require less and less effort and expense. With these methods in place, the occasional weeds that crop up can be tolerated or easily pulled, hoed, mowed, or cultivated out.

Soil solarization is a nonchemical technique that reduces weeds and diseases. The basic premise is simple: Cover the soil with clear plastic and let the sun heat it up for an extended period of time.

Solarizing your soil kills weeds and diseases

If weeds and diseases are getting the better of you, a simple, nonchemical means of combatting them is soil solarization. This is a fancy term for the simple process of putting transparent plastic sheeting over tilled soil during the warmest and sunniest two months of the year. The plastic traps the heat of the sun, causing the top few inches of soil to get as much as 20°F warmer than uncovered soil. In this extra-warm environment, disease-causing organisms tend to flounder, while more-heat-tolerant beneficial microbe species increase in numbers. Also, the heat eliminates some pests, weed seeds, and seedlings. Solarization also appears to make more nutrients available to plants than are available in untreated soil. Soil solarization is an environmentally friendly alternative to soil fumigants and fungicides.

The only material you need to buy is a roll of clear plastic sheeting, like the kind intended for cheap and disposable painting drop cloths. Any thickness less than 5 mm will do, as long as the sheeting is transparent and will cover the area of your bed plus about 1½ ft. extra around all sides. Thin plastic works better than thick, and it doesn't need to be UV-resistant.

Weeds Controlled by Solarizing

Soil solarization may be more or less effective on a particular weed in your garden, depending on local weather conditions. Solarization has been shown to control the following weeds:

- Annual bluegrass (*Poa annua*)
- Barnyard grass (seed only) (*Echinochloa crusgalli*)
- Bermuda grass (seed only) (*Cynodon dactylon*)
- Common chickweed (*Stellaria media*)
- Common cockleweed (*Xanthium strumarium*)
- Common groundsel (*Senecio vulgaris*)
- Field bindweed (*Convolvulus arvensis*)
- Henbit (*Lamium amplexicaule* and *L. purpureum*)
- Lamb's-quarters (*Chenopodium album*)
- Large crabgrass (*Digitaria sanguinalis*)
- Nightshade (*Solanum nigrum*)
- Redroot pigweed (*Amaranthus retroflexus*)
- Shepherd's purse (*Capsella bursa-pastoris*)
- Wild oats (*Avena fatua*)

June and July are good months for solarizing, as the heating power of the sun is at its peak in most places in North America. In northern latitudes, it is best to keep the plastic on for about two months to ensure that high temperatures are maintained long enough to profoundly affect soil microorganisms, weeds, and weed seedlings. In areas farther south, four to six weeks of summer solarization suffices.

Solarization will kill many but not all weeds (see the sidebar above). Solarization is also effective against soil pathogens like verticillium wilt, crown gall, root lesion nematode, and phytophora root rot to a depth of almost a foot under the soil surface. If you have enough beds to fallow one each summer, solarization is a good nonchemical option for reducing diseases and pests.

Solarizing Soil Step-by-Step

Follow the steps here to prepare an area for solarization. After 8 to 10 weeks, remove the plastic and plant a green manure cover crop, or leave the plastic on until the following spring. Or you can plant crops and use the plastic sheeting as mulch. Just cut small Xs in the plastic and plant your starts. Take care not to mix up the soil from lower layers, as the effects of the process reach down only about a foot below the surface.

1. Remove or mow down the weeds in the area you want to cover with plastic. Rake up, remove, and compost or dispose of all the loose plant debris. Now, add any amendments you want to have in the soil before post-solarization planting. (You won't want to disturb the soil too much after solarizing or you might bring weed seeds to the surface.)

2. Next, till the soil and amendments. Break up large clods and work in any loose plant debris.

3. Rake the surface of the bed as smooth as possible to ensure close contact of the plastic with the soil.

4. Soak the soil to a depth of at least 1 ft. by running a sprinkler or soaker hose for 3 or 4 hours. Moist soil responds better to solarization than does dry soil, because water conducts heat.

5. When the soil is wet, dig a 6-in.- to 8-in.-deep trench around the bed, putting the clods of soil outside the raised bed.

6. Cut a piece of plastic the size of the bed, plus an extra $1\frac{1}{2}$ ft. all around. Put the plastic over the bed, pull it tight, then anchor it snugly in the surrounding trench with dirt clods, rocks, or bricks.

PART II
A Gallery of Vegetables & Herbs

ARTICHOKES

Artichokes prefer cool, moist summers and mild winters but they can be grown almost everywhere in the United States, except possibly Florida, where summers are too hot.

ESSENTIALS

- Artichokes need full sun. In hot-summer areas, some afternoon shade is beneficial.
- Grow in well-drained soil rich in organic matter. Before planting, work in 1 cup complete organic fertilizer or a shovel of aged manure per plant.
- Sow seeds 8 to 10 weeks before planting out.
- Plant out after soil has warmed and danger of hard frost has passed.
- Set seedlings 4 ft. apart; set rooted shoots and dormant roots 4 ft. to 6 ft. apart.
- Keep soil moist as plants grow.

SOWING & GROWING

You have three options for starting artichokes: from seed, from shoots taken from existing plants, or from dormant roots. Getting a head start is vital in producing artichokes the first year. Plants started indoors in late winter or early spring will be ready to harvest in late summer or fall.

In a cold climate, artichokes may survive a mild winter if well mulched. New shoots will arise on overwintered plants each year.

Starting from seed. Sow seeds in 4-in. pots. Fertilize with fish emulsion as they grow. Transplant seedlings after the soil has warmed and danger of hard frost has passed. About a fifth of artichoke seedlings will not be true to type. Plant extras so you can cull seedlings that don't appear true or that don't thrive. Cull again at the end of the season, keeping only plants that produce great-tasting chokes.

Starting from rooted shoots. To start artichokes from rooted shoots, you need someone with a plant to share. In early spring, use a knife to cleanly cut away a young rooted shoot, preferably less than 10 in. tall, then dig deeply with a spade to collect the root mass and replant.

Starting with dormant roots. Plant dormant roots in fall or winter in frost-free climates or in early spring elsewhere. Plant roots vertically, with growth buds just above the soil surface.

The most important factor for tender buds is water. Water also benefits the plant's fleshy roots. But soggy soil can cause disease problems like crown rot. Therefore, good drainage is essential. Mulch well to conserve moisture. An unexpected late frost can toughen or destroy developing buds.

Buds develop at the tips of 1-in.-thick stalks. The terminal bud is normally the largest and the first to mature. To encourage large, flavorful buds, remove all but one or two of the strongest shoots. Harvest by slicing through the stem just below the bud, which should be large, firm, and tightly closed.

GOOD VARIETIES

'Green Globe', reliable in cold climates, produces heavily and matures early enough to be grown in most areas as an annual. 'Imperial Star', developed to be grown as an annual, has round, tasty buds and produces slightly earlier than 'Green Globe'. 'Violetto' produces beautiful purple heads with a slightly elongated bud but is unsuitable as an annual.

ARUGULA

Arugula, rocket, roquette, or rucola—however you name it— delivers an earthy, peppery bite. This green is easy to grow and grows quickly. Keep it coming in your garden with successive small plantings.

ESSENTIALS

- Sow seeds directly into fertile ground, in shallow furrows 3 in. to 4 in. apart.
- Cover the seeds lightly and keep moist until shoots emerge.
- Seeds germinate in 10 to 14 days, and leaves are ready to harvest starting in 4 weeks.
- Successive small sowings are better than one big crop. Start planting in early spring as soon as soil can be worked, and sow repeatedly every 2 weeks through spring.
- Harvest at any age and size, until the plant goes to flower.

SOWING & GROWING

Generally, arugula is not fussy. A small plot of moist, well-nourished soil will grow a lush crop. If your soil is poor, add compost. When the seeds have sprouted, boost them gently with a liquid fertilizer. In good garden soil, further feeding is unnecessary.

PESTS

Flea beetles may riddle the leaves with pin holes. You can protect the plants with row covers.

HARVESTING

Arugula is ready to pick as soon as the leaves are abundant. The best picking is in the cool of spring to early summer and late fall, when the leaves are most tender and flavor most piquant. When daylight lengthens and hot weather hits, stems get tough and leaves sprout tiny hairs. The foliage is still edible but tastes harsher and is best cooked. Allow a few plants to go to seed, and when the plants are brown and very dry, harvest and shake out the seeds.

GOOD VARIETIES

Two types of arugula are generally available: common arugula (*Eruca sativa*) and wild, or Italian, arugula (*Eruca selvatica*). Wild arugula has more delicate foliage that forms a dainty cluster about half the size of common arugula, making it less suited to cooking. It is more heat-resistant than common arugula and therefore slower to bolt.

ASIAN GREENS

Hon tsai tai, autumn poem, mizuna, mibuna, tatsoi, komatsuna, and santoh are members of the genus Brassica *and are good representatives of the diversity and versatility of Asian greens. They are quick to germinate, grow vigorously, and are ready to harvest quickly. They all have the same basic cultural requirements, with slight differences in preferred growing season. Grow them together to harvest young as a mesclun mix—leaves come in a range of shapes and colors— or plant them individually to harvest as greens.*

Tatsoi

ESSENTIALS

- Asian greens require very fertile soil and plenty of water to support their rapid growth. Grow them in humus-rich soil generously amended with compost and aged manure.
- Irrigate during dry spells to keep the soil moist; these greens need 1 in. of water per week.
- To keep the soil cool and moist, plant closely and use mulch.
- Sidedress with compost in midseason.
- A shade cloth can keep Asian greens growing during hot spells.

SOWING & GROWING

For an early mesclun mix, broadcast seed, 5 to 6 seeds per square inch, in the garden or inside a cold frame. Thin seedlings to stand 1 in. apart.

When the danger of hard frost is past, sow seeds for late spring and summer harvest. Direct-sow 1 in. apart in rows, or start them in a seedbed or seedling tray for transplanting. Thin or plant mizuna, mibuna, hon tsai tai, and autumn poem 6 in. apart. Tatsoi, komatsuna, and santoh do better at 8 in. to 12 in. apart.

Make at least one midseason succession planting if you want to harvest young plants with tender and fresh-tasting leaves. Then plant again for fall and winter harvest in late August and early September.

HARVESTING

Begin harvesting 4 to 6 weeks after sowing. You can pick off all but the center leaves, which will regrow, or simply take the larger outer leaves as needed. It's possible for one planting to remain productive all season long, provided the greens are kept cut and watered.

PESTS

Flea beetles can be a serious problem on young seedlings. Use rotenone or pyrethrum dust, or cover the plant bed with a floating row cover. Another tactic is to delay planting until after the spring flea beetle invasion is past.

Cabbage moths will lay their eggs on the greens if they don't have other brassicas available. *Bacillus*

Mibuna

thuringiensis (Bt) is an effective and nontoxic substance that can be used to combat cabbage worms and loopers.

TYPES

Autumn poem. An all-green hybrid of hon tsai tai, autumn poem matures a little sooner and gives you more to eat: thicker stems and somewhat larger, deep green leaves. They are delicious stir-fried, steamed, or in salads. Both hon tsai tai and autumn poem are more productive when sown in June through September for harvesting summer through fall.

Hon tsai tai. Sometimes called purple bok choy or pac choi, this has a multitude of reddish-purple, budded flower stalks that quickly outproduce the leaves. Harvest the flower stalks just before the buds begin to open. The whole plant has a sweet, mild mustard flavor. Stalks are tender and pleasantly crunchy, and the yellow flowers make a tasty garnish.

Komatsuna. Often called mustard spinach, this green has tender, mild leaves that can be used in quantity like spinach. The leaves grow upright on juicy stems and will get quite large if not kept cut. Komatsuna is a good addition to spicy mesclun and salads. This green is both bolt-resistant and cold-tolerant, making it a reliable salad and cooking green in all seasons.

Mibuna. Mibuna is a close relative of mizuna, with narrow lance-shaped leaves and a hint of warmth that adds piquancy to salads and stir-fries. Vigorous growth makes mibuna well suited to cut-and-come-again harvest. Both mizuna and mibuna are superb winter salad vegetables for cold frames or hoop houses.

Mizuna. This green sends up dozens of thin white stems with fringed, deeply cut leaves. The taste is all crunch and no bite. Mizuna is an excellent, fast-growing ingredient for mesclun mixes.

Santoh. Also known as nonheading Chinese cabbage, santoh seems like two vegetables in one. The plant has ruffled, light green leaves on flat, bok choy–type stems. The large, round leaves have a delicate cabbage flavor, and the white stems are crisp and sweet. Santoh is a good choice for mesclun. Mature individual plants will reach 15 in. to 16 in. and produce abundantly for many weeks. The leaves are welcome in salads and stir-fries.

Tatsoi. Also called tah tsai, tatsoi looks like a flattened bok choy. Its thick, glossy, deep green leaves are spoon-shaped and grow in a dense rosette. Tatsoi has a mild brassica flavor, but with a wild-plant quality that wakes up the taste buds. Young leaves are perfect for salads, whereas mature leaves make a robust addition to soups, stir-fries, casseroles, or savory pies. Although the most cold hardy of these Asian greens, tatsoi should be planted after the last frost date to lessen the chance of premature bolting.

Komatsuna

ASPARAGUS

An asparagus patch can produce for decades, so when you prepare the bed, do it properly.

ESSENTIALS

- Asparagus needs full sun and well-drained soil with a pH of 6.5 to 7.5.
- Dig a trench and add compost or manure if needed.
- Set fresh, dormant crowns 6 in. to 8 in. deep and 15 in. apart, with 5 ft. between rows.
- Cover initially with 2 in. to 3 in. of soil; gradually fill the trench as spears emerge.
- Control weeds, asparagus' worst enemy.

GROWING

Asparagus plants are sold as dormant crowns—essentially a bundle of bare roots with some buds, or eyes, at the top. Plant as soon as the ground is workable, while crowns are still dormant and full of moisture. Avoid planting dried-out crowns—they will not thrive. Pull weeds or cultivate (but no deeper than 2 in.), or use mulch or weed-block fabric.

PESTS

Pests include the asparagus beetle, which nibbles on spears. If you see damage, look for dark eggs on the spear surface and scrape them off with your fingernail. Asparagus rust, a fungal disease that appears as reddish-brown spots on stems, can be treated with fungicides.

HARVESTING

Do not harvest any spears the first growing season. Vigorous new hybrid varieties can be harvested lightly for about 2 weeks the year after planting. A full harvest season may follow in the third year, provided the average size of the spears is larger than a pencil. In an established asparagus bed, harvest lasts for about 6 weeks.

If it's cool, asparagus may need to be harvested every 3 days; if hot, every day.

Harvest spears when they are 6 in. to 8 in. tall and the tips are still tight by snapping them off at soil level. If you plan to store the asparagus for a few days, cut spears just below the soil line, taking some of the white, woody base, which cuts moisture loss.

Stop harvesting when the tips turn feathery—fern formation is critical to next year's growth. Let the tops remain until the following spring; they'll act as a mulch, collecting leaves and snow to protect the crowns. More important, the ferns also transfer carbohydrates and energy to the roots, crucial to next year's harvest.

GOOD VARIETIES

'Mary Washington' is an old favorite as well as rust-resistant. 'U.C. 157' is heat-resistant. 'Jersey Giant' has high yields but tends to go to fern in temperatures over 80°F.

BEANS

Green or snap beans, runner beans, lima beans, and Southern peas (also called crowder peas and cowpeas) are all beans. All come in bush and climbing (or pole) forms. Despite the confusing terminology and bewildering array of choice, all have the same requirements: warm, friable soil of moderate fertility and adequate water. Most beans can be harvested in the snap (green), shell, and dry stages, although some, like limas and Southern peas, are harvested for fresh shelling.

ESSENTIALS

- Direct-sow when soil has warmed to at least 65°F. You can give beans a head start by soaking seed in water for 12 to 24 hours before planting.
- Loosen the soil at least 8 in. deep.
- Inoculate seed with a legume inoculant just before sowing.
- Sow bush beans 2 in. apart in wide beds or in rows spaced 18 in. apart; thin to 4 in. apart. Sow pole and runner beans 3 in. apart around a pole or along a trellis, and thin to 6 in.
- Water well and mulch to retain moisture.
- Don't touch plants when they are wet to avoid spreading rust disease.

- Harvest often to keep plants producing; optimal size depends on variety.

SOWING & GROWING

Bush beans produce for 10 to 14 days. To keep bush beans on the table, sow a new crop every 2 weeks. Grow 5 to 10 bush bean plants per planting for a family of four, plus extras if you plan to freeze or can beans or save seed. Many beans won't set fruit if the temperature is above 90°F. Flat-podded Romano types are more heat-tolerant.

Pole and runner beans produce until frost as long as you keep them picked. In addition to being more productive, pole beans are considered by many to have more flavor than their bushy brethren. These climbers can be grown on traditional bean tepees, trellised on nylon or metal netting, or trained up twine that has been firmly tied to a solid frame well anchored in the ground. One of the easiest supports is a cylinder of 5-ft.-high wire fencing.

Runner beans have showy scarlet, peach, or white flowers and come in three sizes: dwarf, intermediate, and pole. Runner beans aren't self-pollinating, so they can be less productive than common beans.

Like all legumes, beans can manufacture nitrogen. To help them do this—and to get a better crop—inoculate the seeds you're going to plant with nitrogen-fixing *Rhizobium* bacteria (available from some seed vendors and farm stores) just before planting. Keep the seedbed moist until the beans have sprouted; thereafter apply about 1 in. of water per week.

PESTS

Pest problems include Mexican bean beetle and various blights and viruses. If bean beetles are present, handpick and destroy both the beetles and their bright yellow egg clusters. To avoid disease problems, avoid working in the bean patch when plants are wet, and plant disease-resistant varieties.

continued on p. 194

HARVESTING

For the best flavor and texture, harvest snap beans when they're young, slim, and firm, at about 4 in. to 6 in. long. Depending on size and variety, beans may have strings, two tough strips of fiber that must be peeled from end to end before cooking (hence the traditional name of "string bean"). Harvest shell beans and Southern peas when the pods are bulging with seeds but still fresh and plump. They should be shelled out while still moist and glossy. The final stage of harvest occurs when pods are withered and brittle and the beans within are dry. Gather them into large paper sacks, write the variety name on the outside, and stash in a dry place until you have time to shell them.

TYPES

Bush beans. 'Royal Burgundy' and 'Purple Teepee' tolerate cool soil better than most and produce over a long period. 'Provider' germinates well in cool soil. 'Top Crop', 'Derby', and 'Venture' all have excellent flavor. 'Improved Tendergreen' and 'Contender' tolerate heat well. 'Roma II' and 'Jumbo' are favorite flat-podded bush beans and are heat-tolerant. 'Finaud', 'Tavera', and 'Nickel' are all tender and flavorful filet beans, the elegant, slender *haricots verts* so loved in France.

Limas. 'Fordhook' is a popular bush type, productive and good for northern areas; 'King of the Garden' is a favorite heirloom pole lima.

Pole beans. 'Kentucky Wonder' is famous for its delicious taste, and it preserves well, whether canned, frozen, or dried. 'Rattlesnake' is a colorfully mottled midseason bean. 'Harlan County Greasy' is an old heirloom with distinctive flavor.

Runner beans. 'Scarlet Runner' has red-orange blossoms; 'Painted Lady' is a scarlet and white bicolor; 'Sunset' has lovely peach-hued blossoms; 'White Dutch', 'Grammy Tilley', 'The Czar', and 'Desirée' all produce white flowers and plump, delicious white seeds.

Southern peas. 'Blackeye', 'Mississippi Silver', 'Mississippi Pinkeye', and 'Calico Crowder' are all flavorful favorites.

BEETS

Besides the sweet and suc-culent roots—what typically comes to mind when we think of beets—beets produce edible leaves. Larger ones can be cooked like chard or spinach, whereas smaller ones are delicious served raw in salads.

ESSENTIALS

- Beets need nutrient-rich, friable soil amended with lots of compost.
- Apply 3 lb. seed meal (6 percent to 7 percent nitrogen) per 100 sq. ft. of growing space.
- Sow 3 in. apart in rows or an offset pattern if in a wide bed.
- Keep soil moist but not saturated.
- Thin after germination.

SOWING & GROWING

The corky-looking beet seed is actually a cluster of several individual seeds. If your garden space is limited, sow seeds 3 in. apart in rows; if you have a larger bed, sow in an offset pattern. If you want well-developed beets, thin young seedlings down to one, leaving the most vigorous-looking plant in each group. Water afterward to settle the soil, so as not to leave air pockets that can dry out plant roots. Use the thinnings in salads. Don't transplant them unless you want just leaves; transplanted

beetroots end up rough, gnarly, and twisted. Sow beets every few weeks from spring to fall. Start harvesting about 60 days after seeding. Poke around in the soil, and pull those that are 2 in. or larger in diameter.

PESTS

Beets are usually trouble-free. Row covers will protect the plants from egg-laying adult flies of the leaf miner. Any leaves showing damage should be picked and destroyed. Prevent cercospora leaf spot and scab diseases with adequate spacing and by avoiding wetting the foliage when watering.

HARVESTING

Harvest when the roots are 1 in. to 2 in. in diameter. If need be, brush away soil from the shoulder of the root to check size. Then just grasp the stems and pull.

GOOD VARIETIES

Being a root vegetable, beets keep well longer than leaf and fruit vege-tables. Eventually, though, beets for fresh eating (which includes most varieties) will grow shaggy root hairs and lose sweetness and moisture. Long-storage beets are pretty much unaffected by time for a period of months, if held under proper conditions.

'Detroit Dark Red' is a popular, standard, red round beet. 'Cylindra' and 'Forono' produce long, cylindrical red roots, good for uniform slices. 'Golden' has full, sweet flavor but low germination rates. 'Touchstone' is a golden beet with good germina-tion and great flavor. 'Chioggia' has alternating rings of red and white, as well as very sweet flavor. 'Bull's Blood' also has red and white zoned roots and beautiful dark maroon leaves. 'Lutz Green Leaf', also called 'Winterkeeper', is a dual-purpose beet, grown for its large leaves and very large roots, which store well over winter.

BELGIAN ENDIVE

Belgian endive, those expensive, lime-tipped torpedoes found in the specialty produce section, are easy to grow. You need just three things: deeply dug soil; patience, because most of your time will be spent doing nothing; and an old nursery pot to force the final result—crisp, pale chicons.

ESSENTIALS

- Belgian endive requires friable, fertile, deeply dug soil to grow long roots.
- After the ground has warmed to 50°F, broadcast the seed across wide beds or in rows spaced 12 in. apart; keep the bed evenly moist.
- Thin seedlings to stand 6 in. apart. Mulch with 1 in. to 2 in. of chopped leaves or marsh grass.
- Water only when dry.
- Harvest when the roots are 1 in. wide at the top and about 7 in. long, sometime between late September and early November.
- To force, plant roots 2 in. apart in a deep pot. Water thoroughly. Cover with a larger pot and store in a dark location at 55°F to 68°F.
- Keep evenly moist.
- Harvest when the chicons are about 5 in. tall, cutting them off just above the root crown.

SOWING & GROWING

The goal of the growing season is to produce thick, healthy roots from which chicons can be forced in winter. Therefore, soil preparation is very important. Loosen soil to a depth of 12 in., and turn in 3 in. to 5 in. of compost and composted manure. Rake the bed smooth.

Belgian endive requires a long season, 120 days or more. If necessary, warm the soil for a week under clear plastic. When seedlings are up and growing, thin to 6 in. apart. Do not fail to thin, because unthinned plantings produce scrawny roots, which yield only scrawny chicons. After thinning, mulch the plants with 1 in. to 2 in. of organic matter. Thereafter, water only in very dry conditions.

HARVESTING

Harvest when the leaves are about 8 in. tall and the roots are about 7 in. long and 1 in. wide at the top. Carefully dig the roots with a garden fork, and cut the leaves back to 1 in.

Sort the roots and dispose of any whose tops are not at least 1 in. in diameter. Pick out a few to force immediately, and store the rest in perforated plastic bags or plastic-lined burlap bags. Lay the roots horizontally in layers in dampened sand, peat

moss, or sawdust. Put the container in a place that stays just above freezing—an unheated garage, basement, barn, root cellar, or if you have only a few roots, the refrigerator. Do not store Belgian endive above 45°F or it will sprout.

To produce chicons, take several roots out of storage and set them upright, 2 in. apart, in a deep nursery pot or lined cardboard box. Add soil or soilless mix up to the crowns. Water thoroughly. Cover completely with a larger pot or box and store in a cool (55°F to 68°F) and dark location; the chicons must grow in darkness or they will be inedibly bitter.

Resist the urge to monitor your crop daily. Instead, check weekly to make sure the soil stays moist. In 3 to 4 weeks, the chicons should be 5 in. tall. Cut them off just above the root crown. These same roots will produce a second, smaller harvest if stored again in total darkness.

BROCCOLI

Garden-fresh broccoli has loads more flavor than store-bought. After you harvest the central head, the plants will produce small florets along the stem.

ESSENTIALS

- Broccoli likes cool weather and plenty of moisture.
- Sow two seeds per cell, 6 to 7 weeks before the last frost date. Or direct-sow just before the last frost date.
- At 1 in. tall, thin to one seedling per cell and fertilize lightly.
- Work some 5-10-10 fertilizer into the garden before planting, and add compost to each planting hole.
- Set out seedlings 2 ft. apart just before the last frost date.
- Mulch to maintain soil moisture.
- Feed every 3 weeks with a 5-10-10 or similar analysis fertilizer.

GROWING

It's common to lose a few seedlings shortly after setting out, so start extra seedlings to replace any you lose. After the plants take hold, there's not much to do except water regularly, fertilize every 3 weeks or so, and deal with any insect problems.

PESTS

Protect newly planted seedlings from cutworms with a cardboard collar. Spread wood ashes around each plant to defend against maggots and slugs. To protect from cabbage worms and loopers, spray or dust the plants with *Bacillus thuringiensis*, getting the underside of the leaves too. If aphids show up, zap with water.

HARVESTING

Harvest when buds are tight and green. Once they begin to turn yellow, broccoli is past its prime and the taste becomes bitter. The central head is usually 3 in. to 6 in. across when ready. Cut 3 in. or 4 in. below the head, leaving plenty of the main stalk for florets to form, which will start to happen a week or so later.

GOOD VARIETIES

'De Cicco' and 'Calabrese' yield an abundance of small florets. 'Premium Crop' and 'Green Valiant' produce sizable central heads and lots of florets afterward. Try 'Packman' for early spring broccoli and 'Marathon', 'Waltham 29', or 'Emperor' for fall.

Romanesco Is Beautiful but Finicky

Growing Romanesco broccoli is worth the gamble if you're adventurous and a good loser. When you win, you'll have delectable chartreuse heads peaking in fascinating spirals. But in a bad year, you may get nothing at all. The taste of this Italian heirloom is exceptional—a blend of the best broccoli and cauliflower.

In some years, you may have heads in 3 months; in other years, it may take 6. Or you may get sprouts and no heads. Occasionally, the color is purplish rather than chartreuse.

Fertilizing every 2 weeks instead of 3, as for broccoli, helps. Aside from the extra fertilizer, the growing techniques for Romanesco are the same as for other broccoli.

BROCCOLI RAAB

Broccoli raab is extremely popular in Italy, favored for its slight bitterness, which is a little like mustard greens with a hint of broccoli. These comparisons fall short of capturing broccoli raab's unique flavor.

ESSENTIALS

- Broccoli raab likes cool weather and moist, fertile soil.
- Sow from early spring to late summer, broadcasting seeds evenly in a wide bed.
- Water seeds into the soil.
- When seedlings are a few inches tall, thin to 3 in. apart.
- Harvest shoots, leaves, and buds, cutting the main stem a few inches below the bud as soon as the bud forms.
- Leave the main stem and some leaves to produce a second smaller harvest.

SOWING & GROWING

Once sown, broccoli raab requires practically no care at all. Unseasonably warm weather may cause it to bolt too quickly, and deer can be a problem. In cold winter/hot summer areas, you can get two plantings per year. Sow the first planting in late August or early September for harvest from late October through November. Sow a second planting after a hard freeze; the seeds hunker down for the winter then produce an early spring crop. You can also allow some of the plants from the first planting to go to seed in late fall so that the seeds will germinate in the spring.

Don't bother to cover the seeds with soil, but do water the bed right after sowing—the water pushes the seeds into the ground. You'll get some dense patches—just thin them and eat the tender stalks and leaves.

PESTS

Broccoli raab shares the same pests as broccoli (see p. 197) but seems to be less susceptible. If flea beetles are a problem in your garden, protect plantings with row cover.

HARVESTING

Harvest broccoli raab as soon as the buds appear (plants will be 1 ft. to 2 ft. tall). Check the bed often, because the buds burst into flower soon after they form. With a knife, cut the main stem several inches below the bud, taking the bud and stem, along with side shoots and leaves, all of which are tender and edible. Leave behind the rest of the main stem, because the plant will send up another shoot, which produces smaller, more delicate leaves and buds. Broccoli raab tastes even better after it's been nipped by a light frost.

GOOD VARIETIES

'Spring Raab' and 'Cimi de Rapa' are recommended for spring and summer harvesting. 'Spring Raab' will overwinter in mild climates. 'Marzatica' is good for overwintering, and 'Sessantina Grossa' is recommended for fall through spring.

BRUSSELS SPROUTS

Although Brussels sprouts are not the easiest crop to grow—they need constant attention to keep pests at bay and to keep them growing vigorously—they're worth the effort. If you wait to harvest until they've been hit by frost you'll be rewarded with adorable little sprouts with a nutty, sweet flavor.

ESSENTIALS

- Brussels sprouts need full sun and fertile, well-drained soil with a neutral or slightly alkaline pH. They need regular, frequent watering to keep the soil constantly moist.
- Direct-sow or set out transplants 4 months before the first frost. Space plants 18 in. to 24 in. apart.
- Plants have shallow roots, so don't cultivate near them. Instead, use an organic mulch to control weeds, retain moisture, and keep soil cool.
- Brussels sprouts taste best after a light frost.

SOWING & GROWING

Brussels sprouts can be direct-sown 4 months before the first expected fall frost; sow in rows 24 in. apart, spacing seeds 4 in. to 6 in. apart. Thin seedlings to 18 in. apart. For transplants, sow in pots 5 months before the first frost and set plants out 1 month later. Feed with a balanced fertilizer, not one high in nitrogen.

PESTS

Like other brassicas, Brussels sprouts are subject to several pests, including cutworms, cabbage worms, flea beetles, cabbage root maggot, and aphids. An aphid infestation can wreck your harvest if they get into the sprouts themselves. Check plants diligently for aphids, hosing them off with a strong stream of water. Encourage beneficials that dine on aphids. Use floating row covers to exclude other pests.

HARVESTING

Start harvesting Brussels sprouts as soon as you've had a light frost. The plants are quite cold-hardy, so you can continue harvesting into winter. Cut or break off individual sprouts, working from the bottom up. It's customary to snap off the leaf before harvesting the sprout above it, but you should leave all the foliage on late-maturing varieties, to protect the sprouts from hard freezes. For maximum yield, don't harvest a whole stem at once; the sprouts at the top will be much smaller than those at the bottom.

GOOD VARIETIES

Hybrids include the old favorite 'Jade Cross', which is early; the midseason 'Falstaff', which has reddish sprouts; and the late-maturing, disease-resistant 'Diablo'. Two open-pollinated varieties are the early 'Rubine', with purple-red sprouts, and the English heirloom 'Roodnerf', a midseason sprout with excellent flavor.

CABBAGE

There are several types of common cabbage: the standard green (also called white) cabbage with smooth, tightly packed leaves; red cabbage; and the crinkle-leaved savoy cabbage. While they can all be used in a variety of ways, some types are best suited to certain preparations. For coleslaw and sauerkraut, you want a crisp, tight head of green cabbage. Red cabbage is superior for braised dishes, and savoy types are best for stuffing.

ESSENTIALS

- Cabbage needs cool temperatures, rich, well-drained soil, and regular, ample moisture.
- Start seed indoors 6 to 8 weeks before the last frost; set plants in the garden 2 weeks before the last frost.
- Plant 1 ft. to 2 ft. apart, with 1½ ft. to 3 ft. between rows.
- Mulch to conserve moisture and keep soil cool.
- Work aged manure into the soil before planting, or fertilize weekly with half-strength fish emulsion.

SOWING & GROWING

Early varieties mature in 60 to 80 days, midseason types in 80 to 90 days, and late varieties in 90 to

110 days. Time your planting so cabbage matures during those weeks with cool temperatures. In mild winter/hot summer areas, direct-sow in late summer for winter harvest. Thin direct-sown plants by cutting instead of pulling, so as not to disturb the roots. Cabbage's shallow root system can be damaged by cultivation, so control weeds with mulch.

PESTS

Cabbage is bothered by several insects, including cabbage butterflies, cabbage loopers, flea beetles, aphids, cutworms, root maggots, and slugs. Fortunately, there are low-impact controls for all. In climates where heat is not a problem, covering the entire bed after planting with spun polyester row covers will protect against butterflies, loopers, and flea beetles. If you see white butterflies or tawny moths hovering over your cabbages, check the underneath sides of

leaves for eggs and destroy them. Bt is an effective organic control for the larval stage of butterflies and loopers (see p. 173). Plants with 6 or more leaves can easily deal with 15 percent of the leaf surface being eaten. Aphids can be washed off with the hose. Collars and mats surrounding the stems protect against cutworms and root maggots, and saucers of beer will trap slugs.

HARVESTING

You can harvest cabbage anytime after the heads form. A heavy rain can cause heads to split, so be prepared to harvest all your cabbage and store it should you get a big storm. To harvest, cut the head off the plant with a sharp knife.

GOOD VARIETIES

Choose cabbage varieties based on how you plan to eat it. 'Early Jersey Wakefield' is good for slaw, 'Titanic' for both slaw and sauerkraut, and 'Early Dutch Flat Head' for sauerkraut. 'Scarlet O'Hara' is the best of the reds, for braised cabbage or borscht. Good savoy types include 'Famosa' and 'Deadon', excellent for stuffing.

CARROTS

Good soil preparation is necessary to grow great-tasting carrots. But sticking to a strict watering schedule, especially when seeds are germinating, is equally important.

ESSENTIALS

- Thoroughly mix ½ in. of compost into the top 5 in. to 7 in. of soil; break up any clods of soil.
- To facilitate sowing carrot seeds 1 in. apart, mix with coarse sand: 2 parts sand to 1 part seed.
- Sow in rows spaced 5 in. to 6 in. apart. Or, if your garden is weed-free, broadcast over wide beds.
- Water the seedbed thoroughly in the morning and evening every day during germination.
- Reduce watering to once a day until carrots are about half grown.

SOWING & GROWING

Carrots are moderate-climate crops; they grow best when soil temperature is between 60°F and 70°F. Plant carrots every 2 to 3 weeks for a steady supply.

If you've been adding compost to your garden on a yearly basis, your soil is probably fertile enough. If not, you may need to use fertilizer. Don't use a high-nitrogen type, which might cause carrots to fork, and be sure to mix it thoroughly into the soil.

If your garden has a history of weeds, planting in rows makes weeding easier. For planting in large containers or window boxes or in weed-free garden beds, you can broadcast seeds over the entire bed. After sowing, cover the seeds with a ½-in.-deep mixture of soil and compost.

Carrots germinate very slowly, usually taking 8 to 17 days. Water twice a day until carrot tops are 1 in. tall, then cut back to once a day. When carrot roots are 3 in. to 4 in. long (pull up a few to check the size), cut back to once every other day.

Pests are not a big problem with carrots. Amending your soil and rotating your crops will take care of most problems. Don't grow carrots in the same bed for at least 3 years.

GOOD VARIETIES

Smaller varieties are easier to grow. Fingerlings have consistently good flavor and texture, and they keep in the ground for a long time. 'Little Finger' is pointed and very crunchy and sweet. 'Minicor' is a stub-nosed carrot and tends to be more tender and juicy.

Round carrots like 'Planet' and 'Orbit' are not as sweet, but they have great crunch and flavor. Let round carrots grow to 1½ in. in diameter before harvesting—any smaller and they won't have much flavor.

'Nantes' and 'Chantenay' are two types of carrots that produce good, flavorful, medium-size roots, 6 in. to 8 in. long. There are many varieties. One of the best is 'Scarlet Nantes', a brilliant orange, almost coreless, juicy variety.

CAULIFLOWER

Up for a challenge? Try cauliflower. It requires careful timing, fertile soil, and constant moisture. Too much heat, too little moisture, or a cold snap at the wrong time will cause it to bolt. But if you can meet its needs, you'll reap full heads of tight, white (or green, purple, or orange) curds (what some people call florets).

ESSENTIALS

- Cauliflower needs full sun and fertile, well-drained soil with a pH of 6.5 to 7.5. Work in compost and a balanced fertilizer.
- Hot weather interferes with good head development. Grow as a spring or fall crop, and time your planting so it matures before or after summer heat.
- Start seed indoors and set out as transplants. Germinate at 70°F and grow on at 60°F.
- Never let seedlings get stressed by heat or lack of moisture.

SOWING & GROWING

For a spring crop, sow seed indoors 4 to 5 weeks before the last spring frost and set out plants after frost danger has passed. For a fall crop, sow seed in late spring and set out 4 to 5 weeks later. Once seed has sprouted, keep seedlings in strong light so they don't get leggy. Space plants 12 in. to 24 in. apart, in rows 2 ft. apart.

Do not cultivate around shallow-rooted cauliflower. Instead, mulch with chopped leaves, grass clippings, or straw to keep the weeds down. Be vigilant about watering.

White cauliflower needs to be blanched to keep its curd white. When the head starts to form, tie the inner leaves around it to keep the sun out. Self-blanching varieties have leaves that naturally grow up and around the head.

PESTS

Because cauliflower is a brassica, it is subject to all the cabbage pests: cabbage worms, root maggot, flea beetles, aphids, and cutworms. Use row covers to keep flying pests off, handpick or crush those you can, and hose off aphids. To avoid diseases, rotate crops, give plants adequate spacing, and avoid wetting the foliage when watering.

HARVESTING

Harvest while the curd is still tight. Use a sharp knife to cut through the stem below the head.

GOOD VARIETIES

For white cauliflower, try one of these: 'Fremont', good for summer and fall harvesting; 'Snow Crown', one of the easiest early varieties; 'Amazing', which is widely adapted and self-blanching; 'Early Dawn' and 'Minuteman', extra early and semi-self-blanching; 'Silver Cup', the earliest of all and good for spring or fall.

For a cauliflower of a different color, 'Panther' and 'Green Harmony' both have lime green curds; 'Cheddar' has a stunning yellow-orange curd; and the bright purple 'Graffiti' keeps its color when cooked.

CELERY AND CELERIAC

Garden-fresh celery is robust, with a sweet, spicy flavor. The knobby root of celeriac, or celery root, has fine-grained white flesh with a smooth celery flavor. Both crops need rich, loose soil and regular, abundant water.

ESSENTIALS

- Prepare soil deeply and work in lots of compost.
- Start from seed 10 weeks before the last frost; soak seed overnight before sowing.
- Barely cover seed with potting mix and cover the container with plastic only until seed sprouts. Germinate at 70°F, then grow on at 60°F to 65°F.
- Transplant to 1½-in. pots when seedlings are about ½ in. tall.
- Harden seedlings off properly.
- Set plants 8 in. to 10 in. apart and water in with fish or seaweed emulsion.
- Mulch deeply when plants are 4 in. to 5 in. tall.
- Every 2 or 3 weeks, fertilize with liquid fish or seaweed emulsion.

SOWING & GROWING

If your soil is heavy, dig a trench 1 ft. deep and wide and fill with well-decomposed compost. Or grow these

crops in raised beds with loose soil well amended with compost.

A week to 10 days before transplanting, start hardening off the seedlings. Wait until days and nights are above 55°F. Exposure to temperatures below that on 10 consecutive days causes bolting—you'll get flowers instead of the succulent stems or fat root you want.

HARVESTING

Celery. Harvest outer stalks of celery, a few at a time, starting 5 or 6 weeks after setting out. When plants have reached full height (about 12 in. to 18 in., depending on variety), you can mound earth around their bases about 6 in. high to blanch, or whiten, the stems. This makes them more tender and milder in flavor. Mulched celery plants can survive temperatures that dip into the low '20s with little damage. Harvest plants for storage before temperatures fall below 20°F, cutting them at the base with a knife. Whole plants store best at a temperature near 32°F with high humidity.

Celeriac. To get a smoother celeriac crown, snap off lateral leaf shoots as they appear. In late July, remove some outer leaves so the root grows larger and smoother, then cover with soil or mulch to keep it blanched and tender. Celeriac's flavor improves after a light frost. After digging the plant, shake off dirt and cut off rootlets and all but 1 in. of foliage. Hose off with a stiff jet of water, pat dry, then store in perforated, food-grade plastic bags in the crisper drawer or a root cellar. Stored at 35°F to 40°F with high humidity, celeriac keeps until spring.

GOOD VARIETIES

Celeries include 'Ventura', an early variety that thrives under less-than-ideal conditions; 'Golden Plume', which has a beautiful light yellow heart and delicate flavor; 'Florida', with a compact, bushy plant with well-formed hearts; and 'Red Stalk', an heirloom variety whose beautiful burgundy-red stalks are tender and spicy and retain their color after cooking.

Although you may find celery available as transplants, you will almost certainly have to sow **celeriac** yourself. Most catalogs offer only one variety of celeriac, usually 'Giant Prague', 'Brilliant', or 'Diamant'. The differences between them are subtle.

CHARD

Unlike many greens, chard thrives through the heat of summer and past the first frosts of autumn.

ESSENTIALS

- Chard prefers slightly alkaline soil, moderately enriched with compost, and regular moisture.
- Direct-sow ½ in. deep shortly before the last frost.
- When seedlings are 3 in. tall, thin the narrow-stemmed varieties to 6 in. apart and white-stalked chard to 12 in. apart.
- Mulch to keep soil moist.

SOWING & GROWING

The key to vigorous mature plants is regular watering when the chard plants are small. Never let the young greens struggle in dry soil for more than a day. Once mature, at about 1 ft. tall, the plants are far more tolerant of dry conditions.

For tender chard seedlings to use in salads, make successive plantings in spring and early summer. Then harvest the entire plant when young. Or if you prefer, make one spring sowing, enjoy the tender greens in early summer, and harvest the mature leaves and stalks all summer and fall.

PESTS

Slugs and leaf miners are chard's only garden pests. Use saucers of beer to trap slugs. Row covers protect against leaf miner damage by preventing adult leaf miners from laying eggs. The eggs develop into larvae that feed on the chard, leaving a distinctive, squiggly white line in the leaf.

HARVESTING

Harvest chard at any size from baby leaf on. Young tender leaves are good in salads, but older ones will need cooking. Pinch or cut individual leaves near their base, taking a few from each plant. Or harvest a plant at a time. However you harvest, be careful not to damage the crown at the center of the stalk, where new leaves form.

GOOD VARIETIES

The classic type of chard has thick white stems and medium green leaves. 'Fordhook Giant' and 'Barese' are examples of this type of chard. Both produce bountiful quantities of greens.

Narrow-stemmed chard comes in a range of colors. 'Charlotte' and 'Ruby', both with beet-colored stalks and red-veined leaves, look and taste great. Other stem colors range from deep gold to pale yellow to pink. Some seed blends, like 'Rainbow' and 'Bright Lights', combine the whole gamut. 'Bright Lights', which has mild-flavored leaves and stems in red, yellow, pink, gold, and white, works well for cut-and-come-again culture.

CHICORIES

The chicories—escarole, endive, radicchio, and Italian dandelion (or cutting chicory)—are sturdy Mediterranean greens that thrive in cool weather. From broad and wavy to fine and curly, creamy white to green to red, they offer crunch and a pleasant bitterness. Escarole, endive, and Italian dandelion (no relative of the lawn weed) are easier to grow than radicchio, which tends to be unpredictable and temperamental. Italian dandelion has a more pronounced bitter flavor than the other chicories.

ESSENTIALS

- Grow chicories like lettuce. They thrive in cool weather, short days, and with regular moisture. They need only moderately fertile soil.

- As with all greens, continuous, rapid growth is the key to producing quality chicories. Hot weather and dry soil are their enemies. Grow as either a spring or fall crop.

- Sow seed in 6-packs 4 to 6 weeks before setting out in the garden. For a continual harvest, make small, successive sowings every 2 weeks.

- Set transplants out in the garden starting 2 weeks before the last frost. Set plants in an offset pattern, spacing endive and Italian dandelion 6 in. to 8 in. apart, escarole and radicchio 10 in. to 12 in. apart.

- Water regularly, especially during warm weather.

- Endive is ready about 6 weeks after setting out; escarole in 8 or more weeks. Radicchio takes 11 weeks or more. Italian dandelion is fully grown in 6 to 8 weeks, but leaves can be harvested at any size.

- Five days before harvesting escarole, endive, or Italian dandelion, bunch the leaves together and secure them with a wide rubber band to blanch the inner leaves.

GROWING

You can direct-sow chicories, but they reach maturity faster if started indoors and set out as transplants. Escarole and radicchio, with their longer growing season, often do best grown as a fall crop. Optimum growing temperatures are between 45°F and 75°F. Adjust your schedule to your area so that the later stages of plant growth fall within this temperature range. Light frost doesn't hurt these chicories. In regions where winter temperatures stay above 10°F, radicchio can be planted in the fall and harvested in the spring. Newer hybrids have been developed

continued on p. 206

for spring planting and a shorter growing season.

Growing in early spring is possible but presents several problems. Cold spells can delay growth. Lengthening days lead to a tendency to bolt. And the weather often becomes too hot before the plants mature, resulting in an overly bitter flavor.

Cut Italian dandelion back when it starts to flower and it will regrow a new set of leaves. It is hardy to Zone 4.

PESTS

Chicories aren't much bothered by insects. Slow-growing escarole is susceptible to bottom rot, especially in cool, wet weather. Growing under plastic—in a hoop house for instance—keeps the rain off and helps prevent bottom rot. Planting an upright, cold-weather variety like 'Perfect' helps.

Tying up a plant to blanch it can lead to problems with rot on the leaf margins of the internal leaves. Make sure the plant is dry before you tie it up, avoid overhead irrigation of blanching plants, and don't leave them tied up longer than necessary.

If your soil lacks calcium, tip burn can develop, especially on fine-leaved, curly endives. Tip-burn shows up most often during spurts of growth when wet, warm conditions follow cool, dry ones. Provide adequate soil calcium and try to keep soil evenly moist.

HARVESTING

You can harvest endive and escarole at any stage, but to get a blanched effect you need full heads. Blanching produces a bright, yellow-white, tender heart that makes the plant less bitter and visually irresistible. Five days before harvest, when the head is very close to fully grown but still growing vigorously, pull the leaves together and place wide rubber bands around the plant. The new growth that occurs will be whitened, as sunlight never reaches it. An alternative method is to place a 1-gal. plant container over the whole plant, again about 5 days before harvest. Endive is traditionally blanched, whereas escarole is used more as a cooking green. But blanched escarole is a superlative salad ingredient.

Harvest radicchio when heads are tight and firm and leaves are red. Newer cultivars have been bred to be red without the need for cold weather.

Italian dandelion can be harvested at any stage from baby greens on, either leaf by leaf or as an entire head. Cut it just above the crown; the plant will sprout new leaves. It can also be blanched like escarole and endive, producing a milder flavor.

GOOD VARIETIES

Escarole. 'Salad King' is adaptable, disease-resistant, and vigorous. 'Coral' and 'Perfect' escaroles have more of an upright habit and are less susceptible to rot.

Curly endive. 'Tosca' is a large variety, with very fine-cut, thin leaves.

Radicchios. 'Castelfranco' and 'Red Treviso' are Italian heirlooms. 'Fiero' is a hybrid that produces elongated heads. 'Indigo', a round hybrid, doesn't require cold temperatures to turn an intense red. 'Red Verona' and 'Chioggia' both produce round red heads.

Italian dandelion. 'Catalogna', the most widely available variety, has dark green leaves. 'Clio' is similar but higher yielding and very uniform. 'Red Rib' has deep red stems and green leaves.

CHINESE CABBAGE AND PAK CHOI

Chinese cabbage forms tight, cylindrical heads. Napa types have leaf ends that fold over each other at the top; Michihili types have open heads. The thick, ribbed stems are juicy and crunchy, and the pale savoyed leaves have a mild flavor. Pak choi (or bok choy; there are various spellings) forms a looser, vase-shaped plant. It has smooth succulent stems and spoon-shaped leaves from light to dark green.

ESSENTIALS

- These plants need fertile, well-drained soil and abundant moisture. They can tolerate some afternoon shade.
- Exposure to frost or a string of 50°F nights can cause plants to bolt. Wait until weather has settled before planting.
- Best sown directly into the garden; transplanting can cause plants to bolt. If starting indoors, use peat pots and try not to disturb the roots when setting out.
- Chinese cabbage requires a longer growing season than pak choi but is more heat-sensitive. For that reason, it's best grown for fall harvest.

SOWING & GROWING

Chinese cabbage. Best grown during the shortening days of late summer and early fall. For spring growing, choose early varieties and time plantings carefully to avoid frosts on the early end and heat later on. Sow seeds 2 in. to 3 in. apart; thin to 12 in. to 18 in. apart.

Pak choi. Grows well as a spring or fall crop. Sow after danger of spring frost is over, or 6 to 8 weeks before the first fall frost. Space seeds 1 in. apart; thin seedlings to 6 in. to 12 in. apart, depending on the variety.

PESTS

Both crops are subject to the typical cabbage pests, including aphids, cabbage worms, cabbage loopers, cutworms, and flea beetles. Use collars against cutworms and floating row covers to protect from flea beetles, cabbage loopers, and cabbage worms. You can also handpick cabbage worms. Aphids can be hosed off with a stream of water.

HARVESTING

Cut whole heads of Chinese cabbage and pak choi at ground level. Chinese cabbage is ready when heads are firm and well-packed. Harvest pak choi heads at any size but before the stem starts to elongate in preparation for flowering; cut baby varieties at 4 in. to 6 in. Individual leaves of pak choi can be harvested while small to use in salads and stir-fries.

GOOD VARIETIES

Chinese cabbage. 'China Express' (Napa) forms bolt-resistant, stocky, barrel-shaped plants that hold well in the garden in cool weather and withstand light frosts. 'One Kilo' (Napa) forms narrow, elongated heads. 'Soloist' (Napa) is an early, small variety, producing 1-lb. heads. 'Jade Pagoda' (Michihili) grows 16 in. tall and only 6 in. wide; it's slow to bolt and ready in 72 days.

Pak choi. 'Joi Choi' is a quick grower, with very dark green leaves. 'Ching-Chiang', a very early dwarf pak choi with greenish stems, tolerates both hot and cold. Good for early planting. 'Mei Qing Choi' is bolt-resistant and early. 'Toy Choi' is a baby pak choi with dark green leaves and white ribs; it's ready at 3 in. to 5 in. tall, after only a month or so. 'Brisk Green' matures in about 50 days, producing smallish heads, with greenish stems and medium green leaves.

COLLARD
GREENS

Collards are grown as cooking greens, and together with mustard and turnip greens fall under what's known as Southern greens. All are easy to cultivate. They tolerate both cold and heat well, and their flavor improves with frost, making them ideal for gardens from Maine to Dixie.

ESSENTIALS

- If you have sunshine, water, and a nitrogen-rich fertilizer, you can grow collards.
- Although tolerant of indifferent soils, these deep-rooted plants do best in fertile, deeply worked ground with good drainage.
- Sow in 6-packs in late winter. Seeds germinate in temperatures between 45°F and 85°F.
- Plant out 4 to 6 weeks before the last frost, when seedlings have three true leaves and daytime temperatures reach 50°F. Space them

18 in. apart, with 3 ft. between rows.
- Greens can be grown in large pots 2 ft. deep, three seedlings to a pot.

SOWING & GROWING

Work composted manure and fertilizer into the soil just before planting. If you have extra seedlings, set them 9 in. apart. After a few weeks, cut every other plant, using the tender leaves in salads and stir-fries.

Collards and their kin are undemanding, but they like a sidedressing of nitrogen-rich fertilizer about a month after they're planted and every couple of weeks thereafter. Keep them consistently moist.

PESTS

Traditionally, the greatest threat to these plants' survival is the Southern family reunion, where greens are a main attraction. Cabbage worms, cabbage moths, and grasshoppers will also savage collards if given a chance. If you have trouble with cabbage worms, use the biological control Bt to keep them in check. Mustard greens are less bothered by pests than collards and turnip greens.

HARVESTING

Begin harvesting when the leaves are a little larger than your hand. Start

at the bottom of the plant and gently break the leaves at the stalk. Take 3 or 4 leaves per plant, and water the plant afterward. For subsequent harvests, every week or so, continue to take leaves from the base of the main stalk, working your way up.

Production continues until a very hard freeze leaves plants limp and exhausted. In the South, this means greens often produce through the winter, and they actually grow sweeter after the first frost. In fact, they can survive temperatures as low as 15°F if the temperature drops gently over several days. At season's end, pull up the spent plants and compost them.

GOOD VARIETIES

'Georgia', 'Vates', and 'Morris Heading' are the most popular collard varieties. 'Georgia' produces large blue-green leaves; 'Vates' has dark green leaves and resists bolting. 'Morris Heading' does not grow quite as tall, eventually forming a loose head.

Mustard varieties include the frilly 'Southern Giant' and two mustard-spinach crosses—'Savannah Hybrid' and 'Tendergreen'—which have milder flavor and more tender texture.

'Seven Top' is the turnip green of choice.

CORN

Sweet corn kernels may be golden, white, or a combination. The golden varieties tend to contain more vitamins, whereas the white ones are often more tender. However, this does not begin to describe the total number of sweet corn varieties. They fall into three groups: traditional, supersweet, and sugar enhanced or extended harvest. And despite genetic innovations, there still is only one way you can taste corn at its peak of flavor and sweetness: grow it yourself.

ESSENTIALS

- Corn needs full sun all day.
- Corn feeds heavily. Dig 2 in. of compost or manure and lots of chopped leaves into the soil in the fall before sowing the following spring.
- Sow when soil is at least 60°F.
- Sow four seeds together every 8 in.; space rows 18 in. apart. When plants are up, thin to three plants per hole.
- Make sure corn gets at least an inch of moisture every week.
- Once plants are up and growing, fertilize weekly with manure tea or seaweed extract.

SOWING & GROWING

Newly planted corn must never be allowed to dry out. A first watering with dilute seaweed extract or vitamin B1 will help to establish young corn plants.

Corn is wind-pollinated, so you need high-density plantings for good pollination. In small patches, grow corn in blocks of at least four or five short rows planted close together rather than a few long rows. Allow three plants to grow per "hill." A hill of corn—or beans or squash—is not a mound, but rather a close planting of several seeds designed to maximize garden space. If your soil is sufficiently fertile and you keep up with the watering, you can expect to get about two decent ears per hill. You will get fewer ears on the outer rows where pollination usually is weakest. That's why you should plant multiple short rows rather than fewer long ones.

PESTS

Ear worms, larvae that enter the silk end and eat young kernels, rarely eat a whole ear, and it's easy to remove the damaged areas prior to eating the corn. They don't pose a big problem, except in areas where field corn grows. If a problem does flare, apply Bt to young corn silks. Birds may eat seed or sprouts but can be kept away with netting. Deer and other grazers love corn as much as you do. By far the worst pest is the raccoon. These critters know all too well the smell of ripening sweet corn and are drawn to it irresistibly.

HARVESTING

Sweet corn is ripe at the "milk" stage, when a kernel pierced with a fingernail squirts a milky fluid. With most varieties, this coincides with the silk shriveling and turning dark brown. Ripe ears feel noticeably fatter when gently squeezed, and the individual kernels can be felt through the husks.

GOOD VARIETIES

Multiple varieties of corn cannot be grown in the garden without guarding against cross-pollination. With most vegetables, one variety pollinating another is a problem only if seed is to be saved for future plantings. But because corn is grown for its edible seed, the effects of a cross show up at harvest. If you want to grow more than one variety, select ones whose maturity dates differ by at least 2 weeks.

Traditional varieties. Traditional varieties of sweet corn stay at their ideal ripeness for only a short time

continued on p. 210

before becoming starchy, whether the ears are harvested or left on the plant. Some good traditional varieties are 'Golden Cross Bantam', 'Silver Queen', 'Seneca Chief', and 'Country Gentleman'.

Supersweet corn. So-called supersweet corn, sometimes called "shrunken gene" due to the shriveled appearance of the seed, carries a mutant gene that considerably slows the conversion of sugar to starch inside the kernels. The result is sweeter corn that retains its sweetness much longer than traditional varieties. Unfortunately, supersweet corn, known in shorthand as sh2, is also extremely susceptible to problems with cross-pollination. Cross it with another variety, and the result is field corn. Also, sh2 varieties are more susceptible to rotting in the ground. As a result, seed treated with a compound to prevent fungus is common. Supersweets require lots of water to germinate. They are more tender and also much less milky than traditional varieties. Two good sh2 varieties are 'Illini Xtra Sweet' and 'Early Xtra Sweet'.

Sugar enhanced. A more recent development is the group of varieties called sugar enhanced or extended harvest, abbreviated SE or EH. Although not as sweet as sh2 varieties, this type maintains its sweetness much longer, both on the plant and after picking, than traditional

varieties. The milkiness of this type is closer to traditional varieties. These varieties are much less affected by cross-pollination than sh2 varieties. Some favorites include 'Kandy Korn', 'Butter and Sugar', and 'Peaches and Cream'.

CUCUMBERS

There are several kinds of cucumbers: slicers or salad types, picklers, trellising or greenhouse cucumbers, and beit alpha (also called Middle Eastern or Persian) cucumbers. There are also novelty types, like lemon and Armenian cucumbers. Most are great for fresh eating, but for making pickles, be sure to choose a pickling variety.

ESSENTIALS

- Cucumbers like a light, fertile soil. Lighten heavy clay soil with compost.
- Direct-sow cucumbers 2 in. apart after soil has warmed to 65°F. When plants are 2 in. high, thin to 8 in. apart.
- Cucumbers need a steady supply of nutrients. If you use commercial, granulated fertilizer, mix a generous handful into the soil at planting and sidedress (see p. 283) at least once during the season.
- Adequate moisture is critical. Cucumbers need a deep soaking at least once a week.
- Mulch to keep soil moist and control weeds. Pulling weeds by hand or cultivating with a hoe might damage cucumbers' sensitive roots.

SOWING & GROWING

Cucumbers have grasping tendrils and willingly climb a fence or trellis. Vining cucumbers grow larger than bush varieties, and they produce more fruit. If you grow them up a trellis, you can grow vining cukes in the same space as more compact varieties.

Cucumbers are naturally monoecious, which means that they have male and female flowers on the same plant. Gynodioecious varieties produce only female flowers, and therefore can produce nearly twice the number of fruits as monoecious varieties, because only female flowers produce fruit. You will need a few male flowers to provide pollen. Seed companies take care of this by including in the packet a few seeds of a monoecious variety, which are usually dyed a vivid color so you can be sure to plant a few along with your gynodioecious cucumbers.

Another class of cucumbers is parthenocarpic. The varieties in this class require no pollination and produce seedless fruit.

PESTS

The cucumber beetle is the worst enemy, especially in the Midwest and East. Adult beetles feed on flowers and foliage; their larvae feed

on roots. Worse, the beetles may infect the plant with a disease called bacterial wilt, which blocks the flow of water through the plant's stems. Cucumbers are especially susceptible to bacterial wilt, for which there is no remedy. Infected plants will wilt and die within days.

You can protect young plants from cucumber beetles with a row cover, but unless you are growing parthenocarpic varieties, which need no pollination, you'll eventually need to remove the cover to let bees and other insects pollinate the flowers.

One defense against beetles and bacterial wilt is to plant cucumbers several times a year. If the plants are protected until they need pollination, chances are they will produce a

continued on p. 212

'Rocky' produces miniature one-bite cucumbers.

Picklers. 'Calypso', 'Royal', 'H-19 Little Leaf', 'Pickalot', and 'National Pickling' are all good varieties. 'Cool Breeze' is supposed to produce over a long period. 'Alibi' is highly rated for both pickling and slicing. 'Parisienne Cornichon de Bourbonne' is perfect for making *cornichons,* those tiny French sour pickles.

decent crop before the wilt strikes, if it strikes at all. Planting successive crops a few weeks apart ensures fresh cucumbers all season long, even if the beetles do in one or more of the plantings. (For more on cucumber beetles, see p. 153.)

most slicers. They produce intensely for only about 10 days, as opposed to several weeks for other types. For best quality, harvest picklers at 2 in. to 3 in. long, and don't let the fruit grow to more than 4 in. or 5 in. long.

Slicers. 'Diva' has nonbitter, seedless fruits with thin skin. 'Marketmore' is disease-resistant and burpless.

Slicing cucumbers. Best harvested at 6 in. to 8 in. long. They have dark green skin that usually needs peeling.

Trellising Cucumbers. 'Suyo Long', mild and burpless, does well in hot areas and is good for fresh eating or pickling. 'Orient Express' produces long green fruits like those sold in plastic sleeves.

HARVESTING

Cucumbers don't keep long—a week or so at most—because they lose moisture through their skin.

Beit alpha cucumbers. So-called Middle Eastern or Persian cucumbers are very juicy and mild, with thin, spineless skins that don't need peeling. Harvest most varieties at about 6 in. long and about 1 in. wide.

Trellising cucumbers. Usually burpless and seedless, producing long fruits that need to be trellised to grow straight. Harvest them at 12 in. to 15 in. long and not much wider than 1 in.

GOOD VARIETIES

Pickling cucumbers. Thinner skin and crisper, crunchier flesh than

Beit alphas. 'Amira', 'Sultan', and 'Babylon' are good for full-size fruits;

EGGPLANTS

Eggplants can be finicky, but if you can get them off to a good start, keep them warm, and keep pest damage to a minimum, an excellent harvest awaits you.

ESSENTIALS

- Eggplants need full sun, warm conditions, and fertile soil. Amend the planting bed with compost or manure, and work in slow-release organic fertilizer with an analysis of 7-1-7.
- Sow indoors 8 weeks before planting out. Germination takes 1 to 2 weeks. You'll get best results at temperatures of 80°F to 90°F.
- Don't allow eggplant seedlings to dry out or become rootbound. When seedlings have 2 sets of true leaves, transplant into 4-in. to 6-in. pots.
- Once night temperatures stay above 55°F, plants can go into the garden. Plant 1½ ft. to 2 ft. apart in rows spaced 3 ft. apart.
- Make sure plants get at least 1 in. of water per week; otherwise the fruit will be bitter.
- Feed established plants every 2 weeks with fish emulsion and a foliar spray of seaweed extract to increase fruit production.

SOWING & GROWING

To create a warm environment for germinating eggplant seed, provide bottom heat and cover flats to get adequate warmth. If your seed-starting mix doesn't include fertilizer, feed seedlings with half-strength fish emulsion twice weekly.

If you purchase seedlings, transplant them into 1-gal. pots. Set them outdoors during the day and indoors at night until the weather warms sufficiently.

You can speed soil warming in the garden by putting down a layer of black plastic or special infrared transmitting plastic mulch (see Resources on p. 284). You can't

hurry the air warming, however; you'll just have to wait until nighttime temperatures stay above 55°F before planting out.

Feed eggplants once or twice during the growing season with a light application of fish emulsion, manure tea, or compost tea. This supplies potassium, which the plants need to keep producing fruit.

To prevent stems from breaking under the weight of the fruit, stake and tie side branches, or grow eggplants inside tomato cages.

PESTS

Healthy plants resist attack better than plants that suffer from deficiencies.

Eggplants are very susceptible to flea beetles, which make pin holes in the leaves and can cause considerable damage. Cover plants with row covers early in the season to help prevent the first wave of flea beetles. (See pp. 169–172 for more on combatting flea beetles.)

Spider mites attack during dry weather and feed on the undersides of the leaves, causing the plant to turn yellow and sickly. Get rid of mites by spraying the leaves daily with a strong stream of water.

Yellow- and black-striped Colorado potato beetles can defoliate

continued on p. 214

plants in no time. Pick off by hand and remove masses of yellow eggs on the undersides of the leaves. Spun poly row covers can help protect plants from the ravages of insects.

Verticillium wilt is a soil-borne disease that can kill eggplants. The tricks to beating this disease are establishing healthy, fast-growing plants early on and keeping eggplants and other members of the tomato family on a 3-year rotation. Clear the garden of plants at season's end to reduce disease organisms in the soil.

HARVESTING

To get larger eggplants, once the plant has set six to eight fruits, pick off all remaining blossoms and let the fruit mature.

Eggplants are sweetest and most tender when picked young. Picking also stimulates the plant to keep producing. Harvest eggplants when they are bright and shiny—dull-skinned fruits mean mature seeds and tough skin. Eggplant stems are tough, so use a knife or scissors to avoid breaking branches when harvesting.

GOOD VARIETIES

'Taiwan Pingtung Long', 'Slim Jim', 'Thai Green', and 'Waimanalo Long' are all great stir-fry varieties.

White-skinned varieties are best for dips like baba ganoush and caponata, where purple-skinned eggplants can create a muddy effect. 'Casper', 'White Beauty', and 'White Sword' are good whites.

For grilled eggplant, stuffed eggplant, or moussaka, choose traditional globe-shaped eggplants with firm-fleshed fruits. 'New York Improved', 'Harris Special High Bush', 'Pompano Pride', 'Fort Myers Market', 'Rosa Bianca', and 'Listada de Gandia' are excellent choices when large eggplants are needed.

For marinated eggplant, 'Rosita' and 'Diamant' yield slices that fit neatly in a pint canning jar.

FALSE SPINACHES

These five spinach imitators—New Zealand spinach, Malabar spinach, leaf amaranth, Aztec red spinach, and orach—can be used like true spinach. Some have a spinach-like flavor, others don't. All thrive in or at least tolerate hot weather. The best of these are Malabar spinach, New Zealand spinach, and leaf amaranth.

ESSENTIALS

- Direct-sow or set out plants when soil has warmed to at least 60°F.
- Germination can take 1 to 3 weeks, depending on genus.
- Water regularly. Although some are drought tolerant, flavor is best with regular moisture.

SOWING & GROWING

If starting indoors, plant in 4-in. pots. Allow two or three plants of New Zealand spinach per pot; thin all others to a single plant per pot. Pinch the central shoot of Malabar spinach and leaf amaranth after the second set of leaves to promote branching and fullness. Do not pinch orach and Aztec red, which need to be encouraged to shoot straight up.

If direct sowing, thin all but Aztec red to at least 6 in., whether in patches or rows. Aztec red needs 15 in. or more to achieve its full drama.

Once established, all are exceptionally easy if watered regularly.

PESTS

These plants are practically disease- and pest-free. Foil flea beetles by covering plants with row cover; if aphids show up, hose them off.

HARVESTING

New Zealand spinach (*Tretragonia tetragonioides*). This New Zealand native has a crawling habit. Its succulent stems and leaves have a mild spinach flavor and are delicious raw or cooked. Germination is slow (up to 3 weeks) and uneven. Soak seed overnight before sowing.

Malabar spinach (*Basella alba* or *B. rubra*). This showy stand-out is available in green- or red-stemmed varieties, though most seed companies sell a mixture of both. Leaves look a lot like true spinach but the taste and cooked texture are slightly "seaweedy." Give it a strong tepee or trellis to climb. Scarify seed to help germination, which takes 14 to 21 days at 65°F to 75°F.

Leaf amaranth (*Amaranthus*). Also called vegetable amaranth. 'Pinang' looks much like spinach and has a sweet, mild taste. 'Puteh' (also called 'Besar') has tender, flavorful, spade-shaped leaves. 'Merah' is a show-stopping beauty. Its crinkly, dark-green leaves have vivid red to purple veins, similar to a coleus, and a slightly sweet, walnut-like flavor. Germinates best at 70°F to 75°F. Don't apply nitrogen fertilizer because leaves can build up excess nitrates.

Aztec red spinach (*Chenopodium berlandieri*). This relative of true spinach has red leaves near the bottom and green leaves above on each plant. Its single stalk can reach an amazing 8 ft. to 12 ft. tall, but the plant, including leaves, is only 1 ft. across. Each plant can produce a whole pound of delicious "spinach." The leaves steam up in less than a minute and retain their beautiful red color.

Orach (*Atriplex hortensis*). Orach, or mountain spinach, comes in red and green varieties. This is another relative of true spinach. The leaves are good steamed or raw, and the red varieties retain their color when cooked. Orach is a liberal self-sower. Germinate at 50°F to 65°F; sprouts in 7 to 14 days.

FAVAS

The fava, or broad bean, is actually not a bean but a vetch. Its flavor is rich and meaty with a background taste of bittersweet. Favas are usable at different stages, from the immature pod to the fresh bean to dried. Unlike heat-loving New World beans (like snap beans and limas), favas thrive in cool, wet weather.

ESSENTIALS

- Favas need 2½ to 3 months of cool weather. They grow best at temperatures of 60°F to 65°F and in moist soil.
- Dampen seeds, coat with inoculant, and plant immediately. Push the seed, eye downward, 1 in. to 2 in. deep and 4 in. apart. When seeds have sprouted, thin to 8 in.
- To keep plants from keeling over, plant in blocks of three rows 12 in. apart. Encircle the planting with twine once favas are 18 in. tall.

SOWING & GROWING

In mild-winter areas, plant favas in fall through late winter for spring harvest. In cold winter/hot summer areas, plant as soon as the ground is workable for early summer harvest. Favas can also be started indoors.

Being a legume, favas manufacture their own fertilizer by converting atmospheric nitrogen into a form their roots can use. To aid them in this task, inoculate favas with rhizobium bacteria.

Full-grown favas heavy with pods have a tendency to flop over, and stems can break if it's windy. To lessen potential damage, stake the perimeter of the bed with two rows of twine, starting 18 in. above the ground. Hot weather can bring serious aphid infestations. If the plant is in its later stages of pod development, just cut off tops of plants where aphids congregate.

Young pods can be cooked like green beans. Shelled, the beans are delicious any size from small and tender, to full size and meaty, to dry and brown.

GOOD VARIETIES

Favas are often listed in the bean section of seed catalogs. 'Windsor' is a good choice and widely available; 'Aquadulce' is a Spanish heirloom with large, tasty beans; 'Aprovecho Select' has very large beans; 'Sweet Lorane' is a productive small-seeded variety with very good flavor; 'Loreta' is heat-tolerant.

FENNEL

Warm weather and long days encourage this crisp, licorice-flavored vegetable to bolt, so grow it in spring or fall.

ESSENTIALS

- Fennel needs 3 to 4 months of cool to moderate temperatures.
- Sow seeds in cells 6 to 7 weeks before setting out. Seeds may take 2 weeks to sprout. Bottom heat gives faster and more uniform germination; ideal temperature is 70°F to 75°F.
- Transplant into fertile, nitrogen-rich soil. Space plants 6 in. to 10 in. apart; allow 18 in. between rows.
- Don't let the soil dry out and keep weeds down.
- Harvest anytime after the bulb forms, before the flower stalk emerges.

SOWING & GROWING

Fennel does best in moderate temperatures—45°F to 75°F—particularly once the bulb starts to form. For a spring crop, set plants out when the danger of hard frost is over, and start harvesting bulbs in June. For a fall crop, sow mid-June to early July, set out in early August, and harvest in October and November.

After seeds have sprouted, snip all but the strongest plant per cell at

the soil line. At all times, avoid disturbing the roots, which causes the plant to bolt. Spring seedlings need about a week to get acclimated to outside temperatures and light. The fall crop can go right into the garden.

In the garden, space plants 6 in. to 10 in. apart in rows. In wide beds, plant equidistant from each other in an offset pattern. The closer spacing will yield smaller bulbs. Plant seedlings deeply, to where the leaf stems begin to flare out from the short main stem.

Fennel that has grown quickly and continuously has a sweeter flavor than fennel that has suffered setbacks. To keep it growing unchecked,

be vigilant about watering and weeding. When the soil is dry below the top 1 in., it's time to irrigate.

Fennel suffers from few pests. Surface damage from slugs and earwigs is only aesthetic and can be trimmed away.

HARVESTING

Once fennel has started to form a bulb, you can harvest it at any size. The bulb continues to enlarge until a seed stalk begins to develop. The bulb will warn you that this is about to happen by changing its shape. Seen from the side, the upper portion of the bulb goes from a round to a triangular shape before the flower stalk emerges. If this happens, simply harvest the bolting plant and enjoy it. Bulbs can tolerate light frost but not hard frost. Use a knife to cut the thick stem just below the bulb.

GOOD VARIETIES

'Zefa Fino' forms slightly flattened bulbs and grows well in a wide range of conditions. 'Orion' has rounded bulbs and is bolt-resistant. Both mature in about 80 days.

GARLIC AND GARLIC SCAPES

A good harvest will yield about 10 times what was planted. You'll want to eat some succulent, fresh garlic and cure the rest for later use. But be sure to save the best heads for planting. The biggest cloves yield the biggest heads.

ESSENTIALS

- Garlic grows best in rich, well-drained soil with plenty of organic matter.
- Plant in late fall—about 1 month before the ground freezes for northern gardeners, November through January in the South.
- Plant unpeeled cloves, pointed end up (so blunt end down), 1 in. to 2 in. deep, and 8 in. apart.
- Mulch soon after planting and keep weeded.
- Harvest when nearly half of the leaves have yellowed. Cure in a cool, well-ventilated area, away from sun.

GROWING

At planting time, work in soybean meal, 1 oz. per sq. ft. Break garlic bulbs into unpeeled cloves no more than a day ahead. After planting, mulch deeply with chopped leaves, dried grass clippings, or pine straw.

In the spring, tops grow, then a round bulb develops, and finally the bulb divides into cloves. Feed twice with a liquid fertilizer such as seaweed emulsion shortly after tops begin active growth and again about 4 weeks later.

Taper off watering as the bulbs form. Check garlic development by gently brushing soil away from a bulb without exposing the roots or damaging the bulbs. When they have formed completely, stop watering altogether and leave the bulbs to dry in the soil for a week or more

before pulling. Because a garlic's maturation date determines when you should cut back on watering, you should not mix early and late varieties within a plot.

HARVESTING

Hardneck garlic produces two crops: scapes and heads. Harvest scapes soon after they've formed a loop, cutting just above the top leaf.

It's important to harvest garlic heads at the right time. Over-mature bulbs split open, leaving them susceptible to mold and dehydration. Garlic leaves begin to yellow and die, one at a time from the lowest leaf up. When approximately 40 percent of the leaves have yellowed, it's time to harvest.

Cure garlic in a cool, well-ventilated area, out of direct sunlight. Most people hang the garlic in bunches from string. Garlic is fully cured when there's no apparent moisture in the stem when you cut off the bulb. Before storing, cut the stems back to ½ in., trim the roots, and place the bulbs in net or paper bags. Garlic stores best at room temperature and 50 percent to 70 percent humidity. Hardneck garlic keeps for 3 to 6 months; longer-lasting softnecks keep for 6 to 9 months.

Sorting Out Garlics

It's easy to get confused about the classifications of garlic. Here's some help.

- Species and subspecies—All garlics are members of the same species, *Allium sativum,* but they fall into two subspecies. Hardneck garlics are *A. sativum ophioscorodon.* "Ophio" refers to the undulating, snakelike quality of the scape. Softneck garlics are in the subspecies *A. sativum sativum.* "Sativum" means domesticated. Many softneck garlics also develop scapes, but they are usually weak.

- Varieties—The two subspecies are further compartmentalized into varieties. Hardneck garlics are divided into Rocambole, Purple Stripe, and Porcelain varieties. Softneck varieties include Silverskin and Artichoke.

- Groups—Some varieties are subdivided into groups. Creole is a group of Silverskin garlics, whereas Asiatic and Turban are groups of Artichoke garlics.

- Strains—Finally, there are strains, named garlics like 'Inchelium Red' or 'Siberian'.

GOOD VARIETIES

Softneck garlic. The heads have a cluster of very small cloves at their core. Softneck garlics are generally better keepers than hardnecks.

'Inchelium Red', a softneck that forms huge heads, has a well-mannered flavor but is not the best keeper. 'Nootka Rose', a Silverskin subvariety with a hot flavor, is one of the best keepers.

Hardneck garlic. This garlic tends to have fuller flavor. Hardnecks have a stiff stem at their core, which grows into a curlicue scape. The scapes make good eating.

'Chinese Purple'—part of the Turban group—is very early. 'Ajo Rojo' is easy to peel and very hot when raw, but mild and creamy when roasted. 'Asian Tempest' matures early; flavor is powerfully hot when raw but very sweet when cooked. 'Burgundy' stores better than most other hardnecks. 'Chesnok Red' is a late variety and one of the best keepers of the hardnecks. 'Siberian', late to mature, forms large heads with five to seven large cloves. 'Armenian',

also late, has a somewhat fruity flavor with good garlic punch. 'Metechi' forms large heads with five to seven very large, easy-peeling cloves. It is very late, and one of the better keepers (almost until February) among hardnecks.

HERBS

For making an impact on the taste buds, nothing beats fresh herbs. They can brighten any meal of the day, with flavors ranging from subtle to assertive. So it's great news that herbs are among the easiest edibles to grow. What's more, you can even grow them without a garden, because practically all of them can be raised quite easily in pots. For many herbs, a single plant will suffice, so you can grow a whole range of flavorings in a small amount of space.

Most want full sun but a few tolerate or even thrive in shade. Pay attention to soil and water requirements—some herbs like rich living but many, especially the ones that originate in Mediterranean regions, need lean soil and a mulch of pebbles or small stones. When grown under their preferred conditions, most of these plants will be disease-free, and most are little bothered by pests.

Herbs taste best if harvested just at the point when they begin to flower. To hold back flowering as long as possible—and therefore increase the size of your harvest—simply snip off all developing flower buds as soon as you see them. Unless otherwise noted, harvest simply by snipping sprigs.

BASIL

Basil ranks right up there with tomatoes as a must-grow crop. As long as you follow a few simple rules, it's easy to grow an abundance of this summer favorite.

Basil

ESSENTIALS

- Start seedlings about a month before the frost-free date in your area, and don't set them out until the weather is thoroughly settled.
- Each basil plant needs 1 sq. ft. of growing space.
- Basil leaves are tender, so harden off seedlings adequately.
- Transplant into rich, well-drained soil in full sun, protected from cooling winds and driving rain. If the soil needs improvement, add compost, but don't use fertilizer.
- After transplanting, pinch out the growing tip. This causes the plant to bush out, and increases both the quantity and the quality of the harvest.
- Water only if the weather is unusually dry. Prolonged moisture leads to limp, flaccid plants that are prone to disease.
- Pinch off all flowers until you are ready to harvest.

SOWING & GROWING

Basil is a warm-weather plant. It germinates best at high temperatures—over 85°F—and will not grow well at temperatures below 65°F or so. A period of weather in the 50s will set it back significantly. You can transplant your basil seedlings at about the same time you set out your tomatoes—after all danger of frost is past. Lemon-scented basil doesn't transplant as well as other basils, so take extra care not to disturb the roots when setting out. Because basil is a leaf crop, you might be tempted to fertilize heavily. If you do, you may indeed get large plants but at the expense of flavor.

PESTS

In a home garden, basil isn't subject to much insect trouble. A few diseases that are problems include fusarium wilt, botrytis or gray mold, root rot, and leaf spot. The only real defense is a combination of crop rotation, good garden cleanup, good air circulation, and avoiding overhead watering.

HARVESTING

Snip off developing flower buds—you'll recognize them by their stacked, nearly leafless structure. Freshly cut basil keeps well for up to a week simply sitting in a glass of water. If you have only leaves with no stems, seal them in an airtight plastic bag in the refrigerator, with a few paper towels to absorb excess moisture. Don't put fresh basil in the refrigerator unprotected, or it will turn black.

GOOD VARIETIES

'Sweet Genovese' is the classic Italian pesto basil. 'Fine Green' has small leaves that are ideal for salads. The hand-size leaves of 'Mammoth' are perfect for wrapping fish for grilling. The purple leaves of 'Opal' and 'Purple Ruffles' make colorful vinegar. Good lemon-scented basils include 'Mrs. Burns' and 'Sweet Dani'. 'Nufar' is a wilt-resistant variety.

BAY

You don't need bay's native Mediterranean conditions to grow it successfully. Bay does quite well in a pot, which means you can put it on a patio in warm weather and bring it inside when winter comes. With its glossy, elegant leaves, Laurus nobilis *will crown any arena with an air of nobility.*

ESSENTIALS

- Grow bay in either full sun or partial shade, in well-drained, fertile soil that stays evenly moist.
- Common sweet bay is rated hardy to between 20°F and 25°F, but well-established plants can survive temps in the teens.
- In Zones 6 and colder, grow bay in a container and bring indoors for the winter.
- The ideal indoor spot is cool—0°F to 60°F—and bright; give bay at least 4 hours of direct sun or bright reflected light.
- Never let the soil in the pot get bone dry; a waterlogged plant is just as bad. A slightly pot-bound plant is at less risk from too much water.
- When moving bay back outdoors, gradually acclimate it to strong sun to avoid sunburning the leaves.

GROWING

Choose a soil mixture high in organic matter that retains moisture, adds fertility, and drains well. Mix in a balanced time-release fertilizer.

You can maintain bay at a certain size by clipping it, and you can keep it growing in the same pot for years. In spring, lift the plant from its pot and cut off 1 in. to 2 in. from around the root ball, including the bottom. Tease the roots apart with your fingers to get as much of the old soil out as possible. Repot in a fresh soil mix, adding more time-release fertilizer. Trim top growth by a quarter to compensate for root loss, and keep sheltered from wind until new roots grow and anchor the plant.

PESTS

The biggest problem is scale, aphid relatives whose armored shells can be smooth or crusty, depending on the species. Scratch the occasional scale off with a fingernail. With large populations, pick a cool, cloudy day and spray a fine horticultural dormant oil on the entire tree. Small plants can be dipped into a bucket of the oil solution.

HARVESTING

The best time to harvest bay leaves is mid- to late summer, when the essential oils are at their peak. For optimum flavor, use the leaves within a few days. Bay leaves placed in the flour bin will deter flour or grain beetles. A leaf placed under paper in a drawer or among the pages of a book releases hydrocyanic acid, which repels silverfish.

GOOD VARIETIES

There are some attractive cultivars. The new growth of golden bay, 'Aurea', has appealing reddish stems and leaves tinged yellow in the spring. Unfortunately, the gold color turns dark green as summer progresses. Willow bay ('Angustifolia', sometimes labeled 'Salicifolia'), with long, narrow, and paler green leaves, is slightly hardier than the others.

CHERVIL

Chervil (Anthriscus cerefolium) is a hardy annual, in the same family as parsley and carrots. The bright green, frilled leaves have a delicate, anise-like flavor that dissipates with cooking.

ESSENTIALS

- Moist, fertile soil and cool temperatures suit chervil best. A month before planting, work aged manure and compost into the soil.

- Chervil doesn't need full sun; it will thrive in high shade or dappled light.
- Chervil must be direct-sown, because its fragile, taprooted seedlings won't withstand transplanting.
- Sow twice a year, around the last frost date, and again when summer heat has started to wane. Broadcast the seed, rake it in, and water well. Seeds from packets germinate in about 2 weeks and freshly harvested seeds a little sooner.

SOWING & GROWING

Sow chervil thickly, scattering a packet's worth in an area about 3 ft. by 4 ft. Don't bother to thin. Later, the crowded stems will help each other to stay upright, discourage

Chervil

weeds, and keep soil from splashing up on the leaves.

The spring crop usually bolts at the first sign of summer heat. Let some of the plants flower. Like other members of the umbelliferous clan, chervil has flat, lacy flowers that attract beneficial insects.

Sometime in August you'll end up with a crop of ripe chervil seed, looking just like caraway seed. To harvest it, hold the cut stalks inside a large bowl or a paper bag and rub the seed heads. Then clear out the patch, dig over the soil, and resow in the same place. The second crop is usually much better than the first. The plants thrive in the cooler nights, yielding abundant harvests all fall. Plants sown in late summer will overwinter in Zones 6 and warmer, and you can harvest again from the same planting in early spring. Overwintered chervil tends to flower earlier than spring-sown plants, so start a new planting in another spot each spring.

PESTS

Pests are rare on chervil. If you see aphids, wash them off with a stream of water.

HARVESTING

Begin harvesting leaves about 4 weeks after plants sprout, by pinching or cutting the stems. Densely grown chervil may not need washing, but if it seems gritty, swish it in cool water and lay it between the folds of a paper towel to dry. To store it, refrigerate the leafy stems in a plastic bag with a damp paper towel, and they'll keep nicely for a week or more.

CHIVES

Uncommonly carefree, chives are one of the garden's first spring treats. Chives give two harvests— zesty leaves and pretty, edible flowers with a mild onion flavor.

ESSENTIALS

- Both the common chive and the garlic chive are hardy perennials.
- Chives like average soil, very good drainage, and 4 to 6 hours of sun.
- They don't require a lot of water— once a week if they're in the ground and there's no rain, or two to three times a week if they're in a pot.

GROWING

Chives don't thrive on neglect, but it's certainly easy to keep them content. To get started, buy plants from a garden center or herb supplier, or

Chives

get some from a friend. Occasional feedings of fish emulsion make them vigorous. They spread rapidly and can become overcrowded; where there's one plant at the start of the season, there will be a cluster of plants at the end. If the leaves start to yellow, divide the plants into 1-in. clumps in the spring or fall.

After the summer bloom, cut chive plants all the way back to encourage new foliage. In warmer climates like those found in Florida and southern California, chives will grow year-round, albeit slowly. In cold climates, pot up some chives and move them indoors onto a cool windowsill without a lot of sun.

HARVESTING

To keep the plant looking good, snip whole leaves rather than cutting off only the upper portions. Once plants begin to initiate flower buds, you can

continue to harvest, but be sure to cut above the juncture where the bud is forming or you'll lose the pretty, edible blossoms.

GOOD VARIETIES

Mostly, you'll find the common chive, *Allium schoenoprasum,* which has narrow tubular leaves, and the garlic chive, *A. tuberosum,* which has flat broad leaves. Common chives have lavender blossoms in late spring, and garlic chives bear white flowers in mid-summer. There are a few different cultivars of common chives available, including 'Grolau', 'Forsgate', and 'Profusion'. This last is a sterile cultivar and doesn't set seed, which means the flowers last longer and stay tender.

CILANTRO

Cilantro flourishes in cool nights and sunny days, like those found in autumn. Virtually unfazed by brief cold snaps and only slightly rumpled after a hard freeze, it rallies again with fresh growth at the first hint of spring. The fresh green growth goes by multiple names, including cilantro, coriander, and Chinese parsley, but the seeds are always coriander.

Cilantro

ESSENTIALS

- Cilantro does not abide hot weather and bolts when temperatures climb above 75°F for a few consecutive days, so grow it from fall through spring.
- Ideal growing conditions are rich, loose, well-drained soil, adequate water, and cool to moderate temperatures. Afternoon shade can prolong the season slightly.
- Direct-sowing is best. A pot of young seedlings from the nursery can be transplanted successfully, but don't try to separate the plants. Cilantro develops a long taproot, so don't try to move established plants.
- Make successive sowings from fall through spring, starting as soon as summer heat begins to wane. Young plants will winter over in Zones 6 and warmer.

SOWING & GROWING

Don't fertilize cilantro or it will lack flavor. Instead, work some compost or leaf mold into the soil. Scatter seeds on the prepared soil, rake lightly, and water in. Because cilantro doesn't take up much room, it's nice to have a few plants in several areas of the garden.

The glossy leaves of young plants resemble those of Italian parsley, but when it heads toward flowering, it becomes spindly, with small, sparse, and lacy secondary leaves. Once cilantro has made a home for itself in your garden, it willingly reseeds.

HARVESTING

Harvest individual leaves by pinching off at the base, or cut the whole plant back to an inch or so above the crown; it will resprout. The succulent stems are as edible as the leaves. The newer, greener leaves are preferable to the feathery secondary leaves, which have a tendency to be bitter. The flowers and green seeds are edible, too. The ripened seed is the spice coriander.

Harvest the coriander seeds before they dry out in the hot sun by hanging the long stems of the plant upside down in a paper bag in a dark, well-ventilated room. The seeds will fall off their stems when shaken.

Store in an airtight jar because weevils are fond of them.

GOOD VARIETIES

There are a few named varieties that are slower to bolt, including 'Santo' and 'Delfino', which can extend the season by a few weeks.

DILL

Dill takes its own sweet time to germinate, but once it's up, it grows fast. And it's so easy to grow that it's perfect for someone new to gardening or wanting to try growing herbs.

ESSENTIALS

- Dill grows readily in average soil as long as there is good drainage.
- In most soils, dill requires no supplemental feeding; in poor soil, water with weak manure tea every 2 or 3 weeks.
- In hot summer areas, dill can be grown in part shade.
- Direct-sow in spring starting about 2 weeks after the last frost. Make successive plantings every 3 weeks.
- Keep soil steadily moist until dill sprouts. Germination is best at soil temperatures of 60°F to 70°F.

SOWING & GROWING

Sow dill in rows spaced 6 in. apart for leaf dill and 1 ft. if growing for seed because the plants can get quite large when fully mature. Mixing dill seed with a little dry sand makes sowing easier. Germination takes about 10 days. Thin plants to 2 in. to 6 in. apart, depending on soil fertility. Dill is a light feeder, but after a heavy harvest, a dose of manure tea helps the plants recover.

Dill

PESTS

Dill is such a quick crop that it is usually up, cut, and gone before pests have time to find it. If dill matures to the seed stage, it might be afflicted with tomato hornworm, aphids, or even carrot rust fly. Hornworms are big enough to be handpicked, although their camouflage makes them hard to find until your eyes get used to spotting their bulk amid the delicate ferny leaves of the dill.

Aphids are best dealt with by snipping off the affected plant. To outwit carrot rust fly larvae, don't grow dill where carrots were the last crop. In fact, it's best to keep carrots and dill far apart if you plan to let your dill self-seed, because carrots grow poorly if they mix with a certain chemical in dill seeds.

HARVESTING

All parts of the plant are usable, from the fresh, tender leaves (dill weed) to the stems, flowers, and seeds in pickling.

GOOD VARIETIES

'Dukat' (aka 'Tetra') has abundant and sweet foliage. 'Superdukat' is said to have more essential oil than 'Dukat' and grows straighter and more uniformly for easier harvesting. 'Long Island' or 'Mammoth' dill, different names for the same plant, is a reliable producer. 'Fernleaf', a 1992 All-America Winner, has dark blue-green foliage and resists bolting.

FENNEL

The herb fennel, also known as sweet fennel, is a cousin to the plant that produces the vegetable fennel. They are very similar, but herb fennel produces all feathery top growth—and lots of it—instead of the succulent, bulbous stem of vegetable fennel. The leaves, stalks, and seeds of herb fennel all have a sweet licorice flavor.

ESSENTIALS

- Herb fennel is hardy to Zone 6. In colder zones, it can be grown as an annual. Fennel grows best in full sun, but the plant can cope with up to three-quarters shade.

- The soil should be rich, moist, and well drained for ideal growth, but fennel, like many herbs, has a way of keeping itself going almost regardless of conditions.

- Sow seed directly into garden soil about the time of the last frost, or start indoors 4 weeks earlier. Seedlings can be transplanted until they are about 6 in. high.

- Do not grow near dill, or do not let both dill and fennel flower at the same time.

Fennel

GROWING

In early spring, fennel starts as a feathery mound of green or bronze foliage. As it grows, the plant's profile changes to a vertical and dominating accent in the landscape. At full size in late summer, it can reach 8 ft. tall, and its value in the landscape changes to one of screening, dividing, or hiding parts of the garden.

Be wary of where you put your fennel, because it crosses easily with dill, and the results are poor. It's best to keep them far apart or to prevent them from showing flowers at the same time. Fennel seedlings can be transplanted without problems until their tops are about 6 in. high. Larger plants have long taproots that re-establish themselves with difficulty.

Where fennel is hardy, it develops woody stems after several years and should be divided. Do this when top growth starts in late winter. Make sure you dig out the deep roots, unless you want the fennel to grow back in the same place. Separate individual growth shoots. Those shoots with many root hairs can be immediately replanted. Any with skimpy roots can be potted up and kept in the shade for 2 weeks until they develop further. Water relocated plants frequently until they are established. Then water only in droughts or after cutting back to grow new shoots.

Rather than attracting pests, fennel helps fight them by attracting two species of beneficial flies, the syrphid fly and the tachinid fly. In the Pacific Northwest, fennel is also a primary host for the anise swallowtail.

HARVESTING

If the leaves are your main harvest goal, grow three or four plants so you can cut one down every few weeks for new shoots to develop. After cutting back a plant, water deeply with fish emulsion.

If it's the seeds you want, leave plants uncut until the seeds are ripe. When the seed heads are brown and dry, harvest by cutting them into a paper bag. Store in a dry place. The seeds separate easily from the heads when rubbed lightly between your fingers.

GOOD VARIETIES

Fennel comes in two forms, green (*Foeniculum vulgare* 'Dulce') and bronze (*F. vulgare* 'Rubrum'). Beyond color, little differentiates the two types.

LAVENDERS

Most lavenders are native to the Mediterranean, a region of cool, moist winters and hot, dry summers, so it's no coincidence that they do best in similar climates, like those in California, and struggle in places like the southeastern United States. The diversity of lavenders offers some range of adaptation for different growing conditions. The flowers of all types of lavender except the lavandins can be used in cooking.

ESSENTIALS

- Lavenders love full sun—at least 6 hours a day.
- Well-drained soil is a must. Lavenders prefer soils with a pH of 6.5 to 7.5.
- Add a small amount of balanced fertilizer to the soil around plants in spring.
- Don't use organic mulch close to lavender plants. Instead, use pea gravel or sand.

- Water regularly but not heavily—lavenders need 1 in. of moisture every 2 to 4 weeks. Avoid overhead watering in areas of high humidity.
- Prune twice a year, lightly in early spring just before new growth begins and again when harvesting flowers. Avoid severe pruning.

GROWING

The biggest killers of lavender plants are root-rotting diseases, which proliferate in high humidity and wet soil. These are especially a problem for English and spike lavenders and the lavandins. If you live in a humid area, give your plants as much air circulation as possible. Don't crowd them with neighboring plants, and don't grow a lavender hedge in a humid climate.

You can increase the drainage around lavenders by planting in raised beds or mounds. Well-composted organic matter will also help to improve soil texture. For real problem soils or areas with high humidity, add chicken grit, which is a crushed granite material fed to chickens.

To prevent disease, don't use organic mulches close to the plants. An alternative is pea gravel or white sand, which reflects sunlight up into the foliage, creating a dryer, warmer microclimate around the stem.

Lavender

Keep soil moist, but not wet, around young plants until they have developed good root systems which takes 1 to 2 years. Established plants can survive very dry conditions but do better if the soil doesn't dry out too much. Make sure they get 1 in. of water every 2 to 4 weeks. Overhead watering is risky in humid climates.

All lavenders can be propagated from stem cuttings. Nonflowering stems, 2 in. to 3 in. long, work best. Use a rooting hormone and add bottom heat in cool weather.

HARVESTING

Lavender can be harvested anytime but it is most fragrant just before the flowers open. Cut the wands at their base, just above the leaves.

GOOD VARIETIES

English lavender (*Lavandula angustifolia*). Sweetly scented, English lavender is the most sought after. It also is one of the hardiest, to Zone 5, but it doesn't thrive in wet, humid summers. 'Hidcote', 'Loddon Blue', and 'Royal Velvet' have the darkest flowers. 'Irene Doyle' and 'Sharon Roberts' bloom again in the fall.

Spike lavender. The fragrance of spike lavender (*L. latifolia*) is more resinous and camphor-like than that of English lavender. It blooms late and for a long time, from early August until mid-September. It's hardy to Zone 6.

Lavandin. Also hardy to Zone 5, lavandin (*L.* x *intermedia*) is a hybrid between spike and English lavenders. The darkest lavandin is 'Grosso', with a neat habit and good fragrance.

Spanish lavender. Hardy to Zone 8, Spanish lavender (*L. stoechas*) forms a low, sprawling plant, with squat flower spikes and a hint of pine fragrance.

French lavender. Both flowers and foliage of French lavender (*L. dentata*) are thickly resinous with the scent of lavender and camphor. It is a tender plant, hardy only to Zone 8, but always seems to be in flower, blooming all year if given enough light and warmth. If you live in a humid climate and can't grow lavandin or English lavenders, give French lavender a try.

LEMON BALM

Lemon balm, with its pretty heart-shaped leaves and scalloped edges, looks like nature's valentine. No wonder the 16th-century herbalist Gerard believed that drinking balm in wine "driveth away all melancholy and sadness." Another name for lemon balm is Melissa, from the Greek word for bee, and bees are indeed attracted to the cream-colored blossoms.

ESSENTIALS

- Lemon balm is hardy to Zone 4. In areas where the ground freezes, mulch the plants over winter to protect from frost heaving.
- It does best in part shade, but will grow in full sun.
- Lemon balm grows very readily and is not particular about soil.
- This member of the mint clan likes to spread, although it's not as aggressive as a true mint.

SOWING & GROWING

Lemon balm (*Melissa officinalis*) grows easily from seed. Sow in spring or early fall and cover lightly—the seeds are quite small. However, you'll harvest much sooner if you start with a nursery plant or a rooted cutting

Lemon Balm

from a friend's garden. Lemon balm grows 1½ ft. to 2 ft. in height and width. It is not quite as unruly as its sister mints, but it does have a tendency to spread. Lemon balm makes an attractive border plant or a nice potted specimen. In the spring, propagate with root cuttings made by lifting small sections from the mother plant. Seeds sown in spring germinate easily when soaked overnight before planting.

Cutting the long stems for harvest also helps to ensure a healthy plant, especially after flowering. Snipping flowers will prevent their setting seed when you want to limit regeneration.

A bronze discoloring of lemon balm's leaves results from too much heat or too much water. Feed lightly.

PESTS

Spider mites can be a problem during hot, dry summers, and aphids sometimes bother lemon balm. Both may be discouraged by frequent hard sprayings from the hose or by insecticidal soap, if necessary.

GOOD VARIETIES

'Aurea', a gold and green variegated type of lemon balm, is hardier than the standard type in cooler climates; it reverts to green in warmer areas.

LEMON VERBENA

Lemon verbena is reliably hardy only in Zones 8 and warmer; elsewhere, you'll need to protect it, bring it indoors, or grow it as an annual. But its citrusy perfume and delightful flavor make it worth the trouble. Be sure to plant it where you'll brush past it frequently.

ESSENTIALS

- In frost-free zones, lemon verbena is an evergreen shrub. It will survive light frosts but will drop its leaves. If cut back hard and protected heavily, it will survive temperatures in the single digits.
- Give lemon verbena a spot in full sun. It thrives in light loam, with good drainage and a near-neutral pH. If soil is heavy, work in an abundance of compost.
- Water regularly and fertilize with manure tea or fish emulsion for vigorous growth.
- Container-grown plants can be brought indoors for the winter.

Prune back hard, taper off watering, and let sit dormant until time to move it back outside.

GROWING

Start with a bushy, nursery-grown plant. Although lemon verbena tolerates dry soil, for good growth it needs regular moisture and benefits from regular nourishment. Water with compost tea or fish emulsion several times a summer.

Lemon verbena develops rapidly, easily growing 2 ft. to 3 ft. in a season. It tends to get lanky if not heavily harvested; cutting it back by about half its growth every 6 weeks keeps it looking good.

To carry an in-ground plant through the winter, cut it back to within a few inches of the soil line and pile mulch over the stem stubs. Start with about 4 in. of shredded leaves, then add another 4 in. after the first covering settles. Finally, cover with heavy-weight row cover and secure the edges with stones or soil.

Another option is to grow lemon verbena in a container, and move it into a cool, bright room before the first frost. Expect the plant to drop its leaves when you bring it indoors. Once this happens, cut back on the water until the soil is just barely moist. Come spring, be patient. It might be

Lemon Verbena

mid-May before the plant begins to leaf out. Check for life by cutting a stem to see if it is still green inside.

PESTS

In the garden, lemon verbena is bothered little by pests or disease. But in a greenhouse it is a whitefly magnet, and can also be plagued by spider mites. If whiteflies grow troublesome, you can spray them and their eggs off leaves with a water stream. Yellow sticky traps aid in measuring the population of whiteflies and also help slow down their reproduction. Hot, dry air encourages spider mites. Mist the plant frequently to raise humidity.

HARVESTING

During the growing season, harvest lemon verbena as you need it by cutting sprigs. Store any extra cut stems in a jar of water. Do not refrigerate

because cold blackens the leaves. Before frost threatens, or anytime the plant's shape warrants it, do a major pruning, cutting back up to one-third of the plant. Lay the stems on a tea towel in an airy spot and let them dry thoroughly, then store in a closed container protected from dust and light.

LEMONGRASS

Lemongrass has a haunting flavor that is at once perfumed and citrusy. If you love Southeast Asian food, try growing this herb. It's easy to grow in the ground or in pots.

ESSENTIALS

- In Zones 10 and 11, where it is completely hardy, lemongrass (*Cymbopogon citratus*) is an evergreen grass. Its roots are hardy to Zone 8b. Elsewhere it can be easily grown in a pot.
- It thrives in warm temperatures and rich, well-drained soil with regular moisture. It prefers full sun but can be grown in light shade.
- Start with a nursery-grown plant, and plant it outside after all danger of frost is past. You can also root a stalk from the supermarket by placing it in water.

GROWING

Native to the tropics of Southeast Asia, lemongrass thrives in rich, moist, well-drained soil but adapts to drier conditions, though the stalks will not be as flavorful. Lemongrass's long, bluish-green leaves grow in tufts from fibrous stalks attached at a common base. It reaches 3 ft. to 5 ft. in height, and a well-grown plant can increase to more than 2 ft. in width in one season.

In Zone 9 and the warmer parts of Zone 8, you can overwinter plants by mulching them heavily. Gardeners in areas where temperatures fall below 20°F should dig up their plants and bring them indoors for winter or grow lemongrass as an annual.

HARVESTING

To harvest or propagate the stalks, carefully divide them by cutting the bulbs away from the clump with a sharp knife, leaving some of the roots intact. Where lemongrass isn't hardy, harvest all stalks with some roots, trim the tops back to 6 in., and repot some indoors for wintering over.

Lovage

LOVAGE

Lovage looks—and tastes—like celery on steroids, with a flavor that's deeper, richer, and somewhat pungent. This hardy perennial forms an attractive plant that works well at the back of a perennial border.

ESSENTIALS

- Lovage forms a bushy plant that can grow to 3 ft. across. It has celery-like stems and leaves, and flowering stalks that reach 4 ft. to 8 ft. tall. The flower heads look like those of dill.
- Lovage grows readily in average soil. For more abundant leaves, work in some compost.
- Plant in full sun; in hot summer areas, afternoon shade is good.

- Divide plants every 4 years during dormancy to keep lovage vigorous.

SOWING & GROWING

Start lovage from fresh seeds, and provide bottom heat. Lovage is slow to germinate—even fresh seeds take 12 days or more, so cover the flat with plastic until seeds begin to sprout. If you're looking for plants, the better nurseries usually have them in the spring. You can also get a start from another gardener by digging out a rooted stem as the plants are emerging in spring.

Although lovage needs good drainage, it does like moist ground. In dry times, if you can give it up to 2 in. of water a week, lovage will maintain its vibrant appearance and growth pattern. Where summers are hot, lovage appreciates some afternoon shade. So if you can, tuck it into the back of a perennial bed that gets full sun only until early afternoon.

Removing the flower stalks as they appear will increase your yield of leaves. But you will miss out on the seeds, which are good as a garnish in many dishes.

PESTS

Lovage is pretty much disease-free. It isn't much bothered by insects, although leaf miners can be a problem. Cut away affected leaves.

HARVESTING

The best flavor is in the young, pale, inner leaves, which are mild enough to be used in salads. Larger, older leaves have a powerful flavor that can be overwhelming, but you can use them to rub the interior of a serving dish to add lovage flavor. The larger stems, which are round and hollow, make neat straws for tomato-based drinks.

MINTS

No garden should be without at least a few mint plants. But mint can be one of the most invasive plants in the garden, so to avoid starting an herbal jungle you'll want to keep it in check.

ESSENTIALS

- Start with cuttings or plants, not seeds.
- Plant in containers to keep mint from spreading.
- Water the soil deeply occasionally, rather than lightly and often.
- For bushier, healthier mint, pinch off the top two sets of leaves regularly.
- Cut plants to the ground as winter approaches.
- Divide and repot root-bound plants.

Mints

- Peppermint loves partial shade and moist soil. Spearmint tolerates more sun and drier soil than peppermint.

GROWING

Plant mint individually in pots at least 8 in. wide, or put three plants in a single large pot. Fill the container to within 1 in. of the top with rich potting soil and work in a little time-release fertilizer. Tuck in the mint and pack the soil firmly around it. Water in the plant well. Finally, pinch off the top two to four leaves on each stem to make the mint branch out and become bushy.

Water mint deeply and heavily once in a while, rather than watering it lightly more often. To help prevent the spread of leaf diseases, such as rust, water the soil and not the foliage.

When winter approaches, cut mints right to the ground. This will make them more prolific the following year. In cold climates, protect the roots by piling mulch around the pots or by bringing the pots into the garage until spring. The same severe pruning works on leggy plants at any season. They'll quickly send up new shoots.

In about 3 years, your mint will probably outgrow its container. A sure sign that the plant is root-bound is when the center of the plant dies. Then it's time to pry your mint from the container and cut the root mass into thirds. Then replant each portion in new soil in a separate container.

PESTS

Pinch off any leaves that have small brown spots on them—these could be rust. If your plants become heavily infested with rust, pull them up and throw them out. If this seems too drastic, try cutting the plants back to the ground and sprinkling the surface of the soil with a liquid sulfur compound.

HARVESTING

Mint plants stay healthy and produce better if you pick them regularly and often. If you need just a little mint or want an attractive garnish, pinch off the top two sets of leaves. If you need a lot of mint, cut the stems near the soil, leaving just a couple of leaves. Don't worry—your mint pots will soon be full of lush new growth.

GOOD VARIETIES

The two cornerstones of any kitchen mint collection are peppermint and spearmint. Peppermint (*Mentha piperita*) has a head-clearing aroma and expansive, menthol-cool flavor. The flavor of spearmint (*Mentha spicata*) isn't as overpowering. Spearmint tolerates more sun and a somewhat drier soil than does peppermint.

Chocolate peppermint is a good choice for desserts and confections. True mint and curly mint can substitute for spearmint. Orange mint has an intense perfume reminiscent of Earl Grey tea and a strong citrus flavor. Exotic mints, such as pineapple mint, lemon mint, apple mint, and ginger mint, are often more aromatic than the two mainstays but are usually less flavorful.

MUSTARD

- - - - - - - - - - - - - - - - - -

Mustard is an ancient plant that's full of appeal for contemporary gardeners. The plants are easy to grow and produce seed in a couple of months. The types grown for seed are black mustard, brown mustard, and white mustard. Brown mustard greens can be eaten, too.

Mustard

ESSENTIALS

- Plant mustard in full sun. It grows well in most soils but will produce the most seed in rich, well-drained, well-prepared soil with a pH of no less than 6.0.
- Mustard thrives with regular moisture. It likes cool weather; a light frost can even improve the flavor.
- All mustards are easy to grow, but black mustard is the easiest.

SOWING & GROWING

For best results, add 2 lb. to 3 lb. of 5-10-10 fertilizer per 100 sq. ft., or the organic equivalent. Thoroughly work the amendments into the top 2 in. to 3 in. of soil just prior to seeding.

In the springtime, sow the seed in shallow furrows about ⅛ in. deep and 15 in. apart, as the last frost deadline nears. In the South, you can also seed in September or October for harvest in the fall and winter. Once the plants are up, thin to 9 in. or 10 in. apart, and then you can almost ignore them. If you're interested in harvesting a lot of seed, however, feed the plants regularly with soluble fertilizer. The hotter and drier the weather, the faster the plants go to seed—30 to 60 days, depending on the variety and the climate.

PESTS

Mustard isn't much bothered by pests. Flea beetles can be a problem; use row covers to protect young plants. Remove before the plants flower.

HARVESTING

Pick brown mustard leaves for salads or stir-fries when they're small, young, and tender, or use the larger leaves for sautéing or stewing.

To harvest seeds of any species, pick the pods just after they change from green to brown, before they are entirely ripe; otherwise they will shatter and the fine seed will blow into every corner of your garden. All brassicas, if left to drop seed, can be weedy, but the mustards, particularly black mustard, can become invasive if left to self-sow. Harvest all the plants before seedpods dry. Spread the pods out on a clean cloth or fine screen, and let them dry for about 2 weeks. Once dry, gently crush the pods to remove the seeds and hulls. Store seeds in an airtight jar.

GOOD VARIETIES

Brassica nigra, B. alba, and *B. juncea* produce black, white (really a yellowish-tan), and brown seeds, respectively.

Black mustard. Seeds are moderately spicy. These are the seeds used in the famous Dijon mustard, and fried until they pop for West Indian dishes. Some seed sold as black mustard is actually brown mustard; one source for the real McCoy is Richters Herbs (see p. 285).

White mustard. The primary ingredient in traditional ballpark mustard; also the mildest of the three. The white seeds are the best choice for pickles, relishes, and chutneys. Neither white nor black mustards produce desirable greens.

Brown mustard. The hottest of all, brown mustard seeds are used for curries and Chinese hot mustards and frequently for Dijon-type mustards. If you're growing mustard for the greens, choose brown mustard or an Oriental variety like 'Giant Red' (for information on growing mustard greens, see Collard Greens on p. 208).

Grind mustard seeds in a coffee grinder, or use a mortar and pestle and sift the powder through a fine sieve. Most commercial dry mustard is cut with flour and colored with turmeric, and will not look—or taste—the same as your homemade version.

Keep your distance when grinding seeds. The substance that makes mustard hot—allyl isothiocyanate—will irritate your eyes and nose if you get too close. When mustard seeds are crushed and mixed with water, they release volatile oils that act like capsaicin, the hot component of chili peppers.

OREGANO & MARJORAM

The genus Origanum *includes both oregano and marjoram. They are similar and often confused. Marjoram has small, soft, light green leaves with a sweet, floral fragrance. Oregano has larger, stiffer, dark green leaves*

with a more pungent, slightly minty flavor. Oregano is grown as a perennial, whereas marjoram, a tender perennial, is grown as an annual. Otherwise, the culture for the two are the same.

ESSENTIALS

- Oregano and marjoram grow well without much fuss. These Mediterranean plants do best in fairly dry, alkaline soil, with good drainage and plenty of sun, but they also grow well in slightly acidic, humusy soil.
- Grow in full sun.
- Both plants take well to being grown in pots.
- Most oreganos aren't invasive, but one to watch out for is wild oregano (*Origanum vulgare*), which seeds itself profusely.

GROWING

Start with nursery-grown plants. Because the flavor can vary from plant to plant, it's a good idea to sniff and taste a leaf before you buy.

Apply compost around oregano plants in spring, which makes it easier for new shoots to root and grow. When growing in pots, fertilize every 6 weeks during the growing season and every couple of months during the winter.

continued on p. 234

PESTS

When well grown, oregano and marjoram are rarely bothered by disease. Aphids, spider mites, and whiteflies might attack but usually aren't a noticeable problem in a home garden situation.

PROPAGATING

Oregano is easy to propagate from rooted side shoots that develop in early spring when the plants start the new season. Established plants generally send out new growth all around their edges. If you lift these side shoots, you will find that some have developed roots. Clip off the baby plants that have begun to root. Put them in pots or replant them in the garden.

HARVESTING

Marjoram is best fresh. If you're going to dry oregano, pick it just before flowering. Drying oregano concentrates the flavor and improves taste.

GOOD VARIETIES

For pungent, zesty flavor, nothing beats 'Greek' oregano, which also goes by the names *O. vulgare hirtum* and *O. heracleoticum*. 'Kaliteri' also has great flavor. Some oreganos that combine good flavor with ornamental virtue include 'Golden' (aka 'Aureum'),

'Norton's Gold', 'Golden Crinkled' (aka 'Aureum Crispum'), and 'Variegated' oregano.

The best marjoram for cooking is the standard species *Origanum marjorana*.

PARSLEY

This cold-tolerant herb is so much more than a garnish. Its refreshing, zesty, and unassuming flavor and vibrant color really dress up a dish. Grow several plants so you can use it lavishly. Some parsley varieties are grown for their long white roots, which look like carrots and can be used the same way. The roots have a sweet, parsley-like flavor but the leaves are stronger flavored than regular parsley and somewhat bitter.

ESSENTIALS

- Parsley thrives in full sun but will also do well in partial shade. Give it rich, moist soil.
- Sow parsley seeds indoors 8 weeks before the last frost. Soak the seeds in hot water for 24 to 36 hours before sowing.
- Start seeds in cell packs, with five or six seeds per cell. Cover the pack loosely with a clear plastic bag to keep the medium moist.

- Once seedlings develop their first true leaves, use scissors to thin each cell to the strongest plant. Parsley doesn't like having its roots disturbed.
- When the plants are 5 to 6 weeks old, transplant 12 in. apart in the garden, handling the plants carefully.
- Wait to harvest leaves until stalks are at least 6 in. long.
- Parsley is a biennial, but you should grow it like an annual.

SOWING & GROWING

The hardest part to growing parsley is starting the seeds. A hot-water soak softens parsley's tough seed coat. Even so, germination takes 2 or 3 weeks. When transplanting the seedlings, be careful not to disturb the vulnerable root system. Dig in rotted manure before transplanting, mulch with straw afterward, and fertilize with liquid fish emulsion several times during the growing season.

Parsley seedlings can take a bit of frost, but too much cold weather will convince this biennial that it is going through winter, causing it to go to seed its first season. Sow parsley afresh each year because first-year plants taste better. Once parsley flowers and sets seed early in its second

Parsley

growing season, the flavor becomes somewhat bitter and grassy.

For parsley root, follow the same directions as for growing carrots (see p. 201).

PESTS

You may encounter the parsley worm or caterpillar, a large, green caterpillar with black stripes and yellow spots, which eats the leaves. You can handpick them, or just leave them alone—after pupating it emerges as the beautiful black swallowtail butterfly.

HARVESTING

To use parsley with a free hand, you'll need at least six plants for a family of four. Harvesting leaves regularly encourages new growth. Pick outer stems first. Parsley keeps well for a day or so in a glass of water on the counter. For longer storage, cover the parsley, glass and all, with a plastic bag, and store in the refrigerator. It will keep for a week or more if the water is changed every few days.

Parsley, especially the curly type, can harbor a lot of dirt, so wash it well.

Before frost, gather a large basket of Italian parsley. In the kitchen, rinse and dry the leaves in a salad spinner. Then stuff them into a 1-quart plastic zipper bag and suck the air out with a straw, forming a mat about 3/4 in. thick. Seal quickly and pop the bag in the freezer.

GOOD VARIETIES

There are two common types of parsley: Italian (or flat leaf) and curly. Curly parsley is very decorative in the garden and in pots, and is the traditional type for tabbouleh. Flat-leaf parsley has a deeper flavor and is easier to mince.

'Hamburg Half Long' and 'Arat' are two varieties for parsley root. Both produce roots about 6 in. long.

ROSEMARY

Wherever you plant it, be sure to set rosemary where you will brush against it so you can enjoy its wonderful aroma.

ESSENTIALS

- Rosemary is a tender perennial shrub. If you live in Zone 8 or warmer, you can grow most varieties in your garden with no

problem. There are several varieties suitable for Zone 7 and a couple that might survive a mild Zone 6 winter.

- Where rosemary is hardy, it is easily grown in a garden with 6 or more hours of full sun and good drainage. Elsewhere, rosemary thrives outdoors in pots.

- Where growing conditions are ideal, rosemary does not need fertilizing. If rosemary seems to be struggling, feed annually with liquid fish emulsion and kelp solution.

- Plant rosemary in light, alkaline soil. Keep it slightly moist until the plant is established (perhaps a full season); then keep it on the dry side, although the roots should never completely dry out.

GROWING

Hardiness varies. In addition to temperature, drainage and exposure to wind play a role. Planted in well-drained soil, in a spot protected from wind, perhaps sheltered by a south-facing wall, most rosemary varieties are hardy to 20°F or even 15°F. Where rosemary is marginally hardy, it must be well-established before going into winter. Plant out before the end of May, or grow the new plant in a pot the first season, overwinter it indoors, then plant it out in a sheltered spot in spring after hardening it off, which is important.

If water doesn't quickly drain from a test hole where you would like the plant to grow, dig in sand or even pea gravel and turn that spot into a mound or raised bed.

Transplant potted rosemary once or twice a year. When the plant finally gets too big to move to a larger pot, unpot it and shave off 2 in. of roots and soil from all sides of the root ball. Be sure to cut the top of the plant back to compensate for the root pruning. Repot in the same container with fresh soil.

Most rosemary grown in pots will survive light freezes, but you should bring the pots indoors before the temperature drops below 30°F. Successfully growing rosemary indoors requires good sunlight—the more the better—and ideally a southern exposure. If the plant is large, rotate it weekly so all sides of the plant receive sunlight. Wiry growth often indicates inadequate light. If you can't increase natural light, consider using artificial light. Rosemary grows best indoors at cool temperatures, 55°F to 60°F.

PESTS

When rosemary is planted outdoors, insects usually aren't a problem. But in the house, aphids and spider mites are more likely to cause trouble. If leaves become stippled with yellow or white specks, they probably have spider mites. If lots of leaves turn yellow and drop off, it may be whiteflies. Aphids attack dwindling plants.

Spraying frequently with strong streams of water to knock off those nasties is the first step. If the problem persists, spray with insecticidal soap, following the directions. Do not harvest leaves from such plants until they have regained their health and are free of spray.

Powdery mildew is often a problem indoors. Spraying affected plants (all parts) with a solution of 1 tablespoon baking soda in 1 quart water will help manage this fungal disease but won't get rid of it.

HARVESTING

Snip sprigs as needed, cutting from fresh, young, pliable stems.

GOOD VARIETIES

Shrub varieties come in dwarf, medium, and tall sizes, with compact, open, or spiraling habits of growth. Prostrate forms grow outward and will trail over the sides of a pot.

When grown in ideal conditions, the hardiest varieties are 'Arp' and 'Hill Hardy'; both can survive subzero temperatures. 'Dutch Mill', 'Nancy Howard', and 'Salem' are nearly as tough. Rosemaries hardy at least to 15°F include 'Tuscan Blue', 'Gorizia', and 'Mrs. Reeds Dark Blue'.

SAGE

Sage is a gardener's dream plant. It's useful, good-looking, and easy to grow. It offers a long season of harvest and holds its flavor well when dried. It sports lovely flowers in early summer. To top it off, sage comes in a variety of sizes and colors.

Sage

ESSENTIALS

- Sage leaves are typically gray-green with a leathery or pebbly appearance.
- Sage does best in gritty soil that isn't too fertile, so don't plant it among vegetables. Instead, grow it with other perennial herbs. Good drainage is key.
- Full sun and good air circulation result in healthy plants that resist disease.
- In early spring, before growth starts, cut plants back by at least one-third.
- Replace plants every few years, as they become straggly. Propagate new plants by taking cuttings or by layering.
- Most of the culinary sages are hardy at least to Zone 5 or winter lows of 10°F to 20°F.

GROWING

Sage is an easy herb to grow, putting up with conditions that are far from optimum. However, the closer you can imitate its native habitat, the happier it will be. Ideal conditions are full sun, good drainage, and a soil of moderate fertility.

Prune the stems by at least a third in early spring, after the danger of freezing is past but before new growth really gets started. Through summer, the light pruning that results from harvesting sprigs for the kitchen helps plants stay bushy.

PROPAGATING

Sage needs to be replaced every 4 or 5 years, when the plant becomes woody and straggly. The easiest way to do this is to start new plants by layering, or rooting the upper portion of a stem while it's still attached to the plant. Bend the branch to the ground, and pin it about 4 in. below the tip with some wire to keep it in contact with soil. Leave it until roots form, about 4 weeks, then cut it from the branch and transplant it.

PESTS

Diseases and pests normally aren't a big problem. Good drainage and good air circulation prevent root rot and mildews. If mildew does appear, apply Sunspray horticultural oil or a sulfur spray.

HARVESTING

The best leaves come from the last 4 in. of a branch. Sage leaves tolerate a fair amount of frost. In mild climates, you can harvest fresh leaves all year. If you plan to dry sage for the winter, take your main harvest just before the flowers begin to form. Plan to dry sage rapidly so it doesn't acquire a musty flavor. Remove the leaves and dry them flat on a screen.

GOOD VARIETIES

Common or garden sage (*Salvia officinalis*) forms an upright bushy shrub 30 in. tall. 'Holt's Mammoth' is a much bigger plant with very large leaves. Two nonflowering varieties that do especially well in cooler climates are 'Berggarten' and 'Woodcote Farm'. Sages of different colors include purple sage; golden sage, with light green leaves edged and streaked with bright yellow-gold; and tricolor sage, with leaves mottled in shades of white, cream, pink, purple, and green.

SALAD BURNET

----

*Salad burnet (*Poterium sanguisorba*) has a graceful, arching habit and toothed leaflets that have a surprising cucumber taste. Enjoy its fresh taste in pitchers of ice water, with wine, or even as a tasty addition to tomato-based beverages. It can also be added to salads or hot dishes, making this herb useful.*

ESSENTIALS

- Salad burnet is hardy to Zone 4. In mild-winter areas, it is evergreen through winter, but may die back

Salad burnet

in summer heat. In the North, it grows from spring through fall and dies back in winter. In the north, grow salad burnet in full sun. In hot-summer areas of the South and West, give it afternoon shade.

- Give salad burnet fertile, well-drained soil and steady moisture.
- The soft cucumber flavor is at its best during cooler weather.
- Remove blossoms before they open; after the plants flower, the taste becomes bitter.

SOWING & GROWING

Salad burnet is easily grown from seed; it can be sown directly into the garden or started in pots and transplanted. Starting in pots gives better control over moisture. Sow seed at the beginning of salad burnet's growing season in your climate—early fall in the South and hot West, early spring elsewhere. Fresh seed

germinates in about 5 days, quickly followed by frilly leaflets. The leaves are ready for picking about 8 weeks after sowing the seeds. For maximum yields, fertilize every 2 or 3 weeks and after heavy harvesting with half-strength fish emulsion.

PESTS

Salad burnet is virtually pest free.

HARVESTING

Harvest only the tasty, tender central leaves because the older leaves on the outer stems can be bitter and tough. Grasp all the central leaf stalks in one hand and cut them about 1 in. above the base of the plant. Fertilize the plant lightly and within days it will begin to flush out with new leaves. To harvest seed, roll the dried flower heads between your fingers and the seeds will fall out.

SAVORY

Summer savory and winter savory are two species of the same genus. Summer savory is the milder-tasting of the two. Its flavor is a little like thyme, with a slightly peppery aftertaste; use it raw or cooked. Winter savory has a spicier, more pungent flavor; use it in cooked dishes only.

ESSENTIALS

Summer savory. An annual, summer savory (*Satureja hortensis*) is easily started from seeds in spring.

- Summer savory thrives in the rich soil, regular moisture, and full sun of a vegetable garden. Give plants 6 in. of space all around.
- Individual plants can be grown in a 12-in. pot of compost-enriched potting mix.

Winter savory. A perennial, winter savory (*Satureja montana*) is hardy to -20°F (the warm end of Zone 4).

- Propagate winter savory by division, layering, or cuttings, or buy nursery plants.
- Plant winter savory in full sun and well-drained soil.
- Winter savory works well as an edging plant for herb gardens or mixed borders and can be sheared. Planted 10 in. to 12 in. apart,

Winter savory

winter savory plants will grow together to make a soft, low hedge of fragrant foliage.

SOWING & GROWING

Summer savory. Easy to start from seed sown indoors about 6 weeks before the last spring frost date (when sown directly in the garden, germination isn't reliable). Scatter seeds on top of sterile, soilless mix. Don't cover them; they need light to germinate. The seedlings are ready for hardening off when conditions are reliably frost-free.

Summer savory performs best if watered before the soil becomes dry. After harvesting, water with fish emulsion fertilizer to jump-start growth.

Winter savory. Slow to start from seed. Instead, buy husky nursery plants. Spring planting is best in cool climates, but fall planting works well in regions of hot summers and mild winters.

In spring, cut winter savory back hard and sidedress with a little compost. Well-established winter savory plants will survive a moderate drought without difficulty. After a few years in the garden, plants can get excessively woody. Lift, divide, and replant only the youngest sections.

Summer savory

PESTS

Under good growing conditions, savories are seldom bothered by pests or diseases.

HARVESTING

For freezing or drying, harvest just before the flower buds open, when the levels of essential oils peak. Otherwise, just snip stems as you need them.

GOOD VARIETIES

Summer savory. An annual and the milder tasting of the two, summer savory grows into a loose, bushy plant about 18 in. high.

Winter savory. A perennial, winter savory has a more pungent flavor and grows into a thick, bushy, semi-evergreen mound about 12 in. high. The foliage, which is narrow and needlelike, covers the stems more thickly than summer savory's, giving the appearance from afar of a deep green carpet. The neat, bushy growth habit makes it a popular plant for knot gardens.

SORREL

Sorrel's sword-shaped leaves pack a citrus tang. They have a nice crunch when raw and a velvety texture when cooked. Usually classified as an herb, sorrel can be used as a salad green and like spinach in cooked recipes.

ESSENTIALS

- Sorrel is a hardy perennial that grows well in most climates. It likes sun but will tolerate partial shade.
- The more fertile the soil, the better sorrel will grow. Add organic matter to the bed.
- Garden sorrel likes a moist soil; the French variety prefers a drier one.
- Set out plants soon after the last spring frost.
- Begin harvesting when the amount you need won't leave the plant looking sparse.
- For more leaf production, cut off flower stalks as soon as they form.

Sorrel

TARRAGON

*French tarragon (*Artemisia
dracunculus *var.* sativa*) has a
sweet anise flavor. Don't confuse this delicious herb with the
closely related but completely
flavorless Russian tarragon
(*Artemisia dracunculoides*).
Although French tarragon grows
easily, it needs a certain amount
of care to keep it flavorful.*

GROWING

You can start sorrel from seeds, sown
indoors or in the garden, but you'll be
able to harvest leaves much sooner
if you set out a plant. As a perennial,
sorrel grows much more slowly than
leafy annual herbs like basil.

Once sorrel is established, there's
little to do but harvest. A sorrel patch
will increase in girth for at least
4 years. After that, the leaf production may wane. To keep it growing
vigorously, dig up the plant, divide it,
and replant the heartiest sections.

PESTS

Irregular holes in the leaves are a
telltale sign of slugs and snails. Hand-
pick them, lure them to drown in
saucers of beer, or use copper strips,

mesh, or sheeting to keep them away.
If aphids are a problem, blast them
with a garden hose.

HARVESTING

Pinch off individual leaves. The young
leaves are more succulent, but larger
ones also can be eaten after removing
the stems.

GOOD VARIETIES

There are two species, garden or
common sorrel, *Rumex acetosa,* and
French sorrel, *R. scutatus.* Garden
sorrel produces leaves up to 2 ft. long.
French sorrel's leaves are smaller
and rounder in shape. 'Silver Shield',
a cultivar of French sorrel, has
delicate, silver-tinted leaves.

ESSENTIALS

- To have good flavor, tarragon
  needs fast-draining soil with a
  neutral pH and steady watering.
- Tarragon grows in Zones 2 to 9. In
  Zone 2 it benefits from a mulch of
  straw or dead leaves.
- Set out nursery-grown plants in
  4-in. pots that have at least three
  green shoots. If you're planting
  divisions of an older plant, check
  that the roots are attached to
  green shoots.
- Where summers are moderate,
  tarragon does best in full sun. It
  will grow well in half-shade, but
  may not have maximum flavor. In
  hot-summer areas, on the other
  hand, some shade is beneficial during high summer.
- Water young plants every 2 days
  during dry weather. Mature plants

Tarragon

are drought-tolerant, but regular moisture is necessary for a continual supply of fresh leaves.

GROWING

Although tarragon is drought-tolerant and will grow in so-so soil, certain conditions are important for it to have good flavor: well-drained, fertile, pH-neutral soil; regular moisture; and regular dividing to keep plants growing vigorously. If in doubt about your drainage, plant tarragon in a raised bed. Top-dress plants yearly with compost.

Every few years, divide plants in very early spring. Carefully remove the soil from the roots, saving only those with green shoots attached. Trim roots to fit into a 4-in. pot and

pot up in a fast-draining soilless mix. Leave in a shaded spot for 2 weeks. Once root hairs have developed, the new plants are ready to be set out 9 in. apart.

Container growing works well for one season, but then tarragon needs repotting or transplanting into the garden.

PESTS

As long as it's given good drainage, tarragon isn't bothered by pests and disease. Poor drainage can encourage root rot.

HARVESTING

Because Russian tarragon is similar looking to French tarragon and often mislabeled, taste a leaf of a plant before you buy. Tarragon lovers will need three or four plants to provide a continuous supply of leaves until late fall. Individual stems can be shortened and stripped of their leaves. For a continuous supply into fall, cut back about half of your plants in late June to about 6 in. high, leaving the remaining half for harvesting while the cut ones regrow. With careful watering, the plants will be ready to harvest again in 6 weeks.

THYMES

The world of thymes is vast, but only about half a dozen are considered suitable for cooking. The four most useful are French thyme, lemon thyme, oregano-scented thyme, and caraway thyme. For best results in the garden, mimic thyme's Mediterranean habitat as closely as possible, and prune correctly.

ESSENTIALS

- Thyme needs full sun; well-drained, gritty soil; and good air circulation. Soil that is good for vegetables is too rich for thyme.
- For container-grown plants, use a clay-based soil to help retain moisture and water regularly.
- Fertilize only at planting time with a time-release, balanced formula that contains trace elements.
- Mulch with light-colored stone chips, pebbles, or sand, which reflect light and keep plants healthy and thriving.
- Prune after flowering and again a month before frost.

GROWING

One of the single most helpful things in growing thyme is to mulch it with light-colored gravel, preferably one

Thyme

of limestone composition. The mulch reflects light onto the branches, helping the thyme to resist fungal diseases in humid climates; it keeps the stems and leaves clean; and it looks wonderful.

Set out plants in the spring, after all danger of frost is past, or in the early fall, as long as the plants have 3 or 4 weeks before the first frost to become established. Oregano-scented and caraway thymes are the hardiest of the four, thriving in areas where winter lows drop to the single digits. French thyme is the least hardy. If your winter temperatures stay below freezing for extended periods, either

protect French thyme or replace it come spring. Thymes are shallow rooted, so are subject to being heaved out of the ground by frosts; press any frost-heaved plants back into the ground with your foot.

Prune thyme twice during the growing season. Right after the plant has finished blooming, cut off the dead flower heads and generally shape up the plant. Prune again about a month before the first expected fall frost to encourage new growth, which is hardier than mature stems. When pruning, do not cut back into the older, woody part of the plant. The soft, green stems put on more and sturdier growth than do woody stems.

PROPAGATING

Stem cuttings root easily in clean, unscented, clay-based cat litter or vermiculite. Clip non-flowering stems 4 in. to 5 in. long, making the cut just above where the stem becomes woody. Strip the leaves off the lower two-thirds of the cutting, and stick the stems deep into a pot of vermiculite or the right kind of cat litter. Thoroughly moisten the medium and place the pot in a shaded area. Keep it moist; in a few weeks the cuttings will have rooted enough to be transferred to small pots or a

cold frame. The following year they're ready to set out in the garden.

GOOD VARIETIES

Thymes vary plant to plant in how much flavor and fragrance they have. Always pinch and sniff and even taste a sprig before deciding which specimen of French thyme or lemon thyme to put in your garden.

French thyme (*Thymus vulgaris*). The best known culinary thyme. 'Dwarf Winter' is an excellent variety of French thyme, with a shorter, bushier habit and stems densely packed with leaves.

Lemon thyme (*T. x citriodorus*). Lemon thyme has dark green leaves; golden lemon thyme has green and gold leaves.

Oregano-scented thyme (*T. pulegioides*) and caraway thyme (*T. herba-barona*). Use these varieties in the same dishes, respectively, that you'd use oregano or caraway seed.

KALE

Kale, with its rich dowry of nutrients, is good for you. It is also delicious, easy to grow, and beautiful to look at, both in the garden and on your plate. Although a couple of frosts will make kale sweeter, gardeners in mild climates can grow sweet-tasting kale by choosing the right varieties.

ESSENTIALS

- Enrich soil with compost or manure.
- Depending on your climate, sow kale once or twice a year.
- Sow seeds in cell packs or scatter in rows 18 in. apart. Cover with ½ in. of soil.
- Place paper-cup collars around new seedlings to deter slugs, snails, and cutworms.
- Thin seedlings 12 in. to 18 in. apart when they are 6 in. high.
- Harvest outer or lower leaves when plants are well established.

SOWING & GROWING

In mild-winter areas, sow kale twice a year, once in midsummer for fall through winter harvesting and again in late winter for spring harvesting. If you live in a colder climate, sow kale just once, in midsummer, for a fall harvest. You can also plant kale in

'Scotch' kale

early spring and harvest it until the leaves toughen in the heat and the plants go to seed.

Dig in 1 in. to 2 in. of compost with some slow-release fertilizer. Where the soil is overly acidic, a little wood ash is good for kale. If your plants look peaked during the growing season, water with fish emulsion.

Direct-sow plants or transplant seedlings. You may get a crop quicker by direct-sowing. On the other hand, you can protect tiny plants from snails and slugs better if you start them indoors.

PESTS

Protect transplanted seedlings and young sprouts from slugs and snails with a collar made from a waxed paper cup with its bottom trimmed off. This foils cutworms, too. Cabbage loopers and cabbageworms can be serious pests. As soon as the weather warms and you see the first brown or white moths flying frenziedly over your greens, begin inspecting both sides of the kale leaves and removing

or crushing the tiny white or orange eggs. 'Red Russian' and 'Lacinato' kale are also susceptible to aphids. Crush with your fingers or spray off with the hose.

HARVESTING

Harvest leaves from the bottom up by snapping them off at the stem.

GOOD VARIETIES

'Scotch', with curly, thick, blue-green leaves, benefits from light frosts, which sweeten the flavor. 'Red Russian' and 'Lacinato' are delicious from the get-go. 'Red Russian' has toothy blue-green leaves tinged purple. 'Lacinato', also called 'Tuscan Black' and dinosaur kale, is an Italian heirloom with narrow, pebbled, midnight green leaves.

'Lacimato' kale

KOHLRABI

Kohlrabi has a delicate flavor and crunchy raw texture. Depending on how it's cooked, its fine-grained interior can retain its integrity or it can be made into a velvety purée. The leaves can be eaten steamed, sautéed, or used in soups and stews. They taste somewhat like collards or kale.

ESSENTIALS

- Start seeds indoors 8 weeks before the last frost. Seeds germinate in a week or less at 75°F to 80°F.
- Feed seedlings weekly with a dilute solution of fish emulsion fertilizer.
- Two weeks before the last frost, transplant seedlings into the garden, 4 in. apart, in rows 12 in. to 15 in. apart.
- At the same time, direct-sow additional rows for later harvest. When their leaves begin to touch, thin direct-sown kohlrabi plants to 4 in. apart.
- Cover transplants and direct-sown rows with floating row covers.
- Mulch to retain moisture.

SOWING & GROWING

The primary rule in growing kohlrabi is the same as for any brassica: cool weather combined with a moisture-retentive soil rich in organic matter. To produce steady growth, mulch with straw to maintain soil moisture, and water when soil begins to dry out. Although kohlrabi is more tolerant of heat than other cole crops, high temperatures and dryness cause bulbs to be woody and to split. In most areas, kohlrabi is best grown as a spring and fall crop, harvesting in June and October when the bulbs have reached 2 in. to 2½ in. dia.

For a fall crop, start seeds in late July for transplanting. Two weeks later, direct-sow a second fall crop. Flea beetles like tender young brassicas, so delay transplanting until there are at least four true leaves.

If it is not grown under ideal temperature and moisture conditions, kohlrabi reacts to stress by splitting, making it difficult to peel. Hybrid varieties resist splitting.

PESTS

Floating row covers will protect against flea beetles and early cabbage worm infestations; keep covered until direct-sown kohlrabi is at least 4 in. high. Later in the season, control cabbage worms by spraying with Bt or handpicking.

HARVESTING

Harvest kohlrabi either by grasping the bulb and yanking the root out of the soil and then removing it or by snipping off the bulb and leaving the root behind. Kohlrabi keeps well, up to 3 months in the refrigerator.

GOOD VARIETIES

Purple and white varieties taste the same, like a very mild cabbage with a touch of sweetness. Recommended hybrids include 'Kolibri', 'Winner', and 'Grand Duke'. 'Early Purple Vienna' and 'Early White Vienna' are classic nonhybrids. 'Gigante' is a Czechoslovakian heirloom that stores well and can exceed 10 lb. 'Kossack' is a hybrid giant.

LEEKS

Leeks have a mild, almost sweet, onion flavor. At the market, they are pricey and often have short shanks. It's easy to grow your own beautiful, long leeks.

ESSENTIALS

- Leeks thrive in cool, moist climates, but will grow anywhere if you give them plenty of moisture and deeply dug, nitrogen-rich soil well amended with compost.
- For fall and winter harvest, sow indoors 8 to 10 weeks before the last frost, or direct-sow 4 weeks before the last frost. For spring harvest, sow in flats or direct-sow in late summer.
- For long, white shanks, plant leeks deeply. Make a 6-in.-deep trench and plant seedlings 6 in. to 8 in. deep within the trench.
- Hill up seedlings as they grow, until the trench is filled in.
- Lots of nitrogen makes for large, succulent leeks. Water weekly with manure tea or half-strength fish emulsion solution.

SOWING & GROWING

Leeks are cold-tolerant and they need a long growing season, so start them early. In the northern half of the country, sow them indoors in February or March. Elsewhere, you can direct-sow them in trenches, which saves the tedium of transplanting. Transplant seedlings when they're about the thickness of pencil lead.

Watering well is important. Soak the bed twice a week. Leeks that suffer from lack of moisture grow unevenly and have a stronger taste and pithier texture.

For spring leeks, sow seed in August or September. If using transplants, set them out well before frost, then bury them completely with straw or leaves. When a hard frost threatens, cover the whole bed with row cover or an old sheet to keep the mulch in place, and leave it on until early spring, when hard frosts are no longer a threat.

HARVESTING

Harvest leeks when the shank is large and firm or earlier for baby leeks. If you've planted as described, there are 12 in. to 14 in. of leek below the soil surface. Just pulling on the top is liable to break the leek. Instead, loosen the soil with a garden fork, prying up just what you need. Grasp the shank and pull, then shake the leek to free it of excess soil. Rinsing with a garden hose is a good idea. Leeks hold lots of dirt.

You can leave hardy varieties to overwinter in the ground, digging only as you need them, but you may need to mulch them heavily to prevent the ground from freezing. Or harvest them all before the ground freezes, clean them up but leave the roots on, and layer in damp builder's sand. Stash the box in a dark, very cool place, and be sure to rinse thoroughly before using to get rid of every grain of sand.

Nonhybrid leeks are good candidates for seed saving. Leave a couple of plants to go to flower next spring. When the seed heads are dry, cut them off and store in a paper bag.

GOOD VARIETIES

'King Richard', 'Lincoln', and 'Lancelot' are good for late summer and fall harvest. 'Giant Musselburgh' (aka 'Large American Flag') is a superb heirloom, long in the shank, firm, and good for overwintering. 'Blue Solaise', a French heirloom, also produces long shanks that overwinter well.

LETTUCES

The world of lettuces is large and varied. Heading lettuces range from crisp and crunchy Batavians and romaines to velvety, tender butterheads. Leaf lettuces are even more diverse, in colors from pale lime green to deep bronzy red, and shapes from simple to frilled and flounced. Altogether, lettuces are easy to grow, lovely to look at, and give you a lot of harvest from a small space.

ESSENTIALS

- Lettuce thrives in humusy, fertile soil with a near-neutral pH.
- Direct-sow or set out transplants starting in early spring. Plant a second crop in mid-spring. Sow fall crops starting when summer heat begins to abate.
- Keep lettuce plants moist to encourage regular growth and sweet-tasting leaves.
- Fertilize several times with a weak fish or seaweed emulsion or manure tea. For cutting lettuces, do this right after harvesting a section of the planting.
- Shade cloth and daily watering can help delay bolting during hot spells. If hot weather continues, harvest the whole crop before it bolts.

SOWING & GROWING

When sowing indoors, scatter lettuce seed thinly, about ½ in. apart. Cover lightly and keep the medium moist. Lettuce germinates best at 60°F to 70°F. Transplants are ready for the garden when they are a few inches tall.

Cutting lettuces. Plant in fairly dense bands because they are harvested when very young. Sow in rows 3 in. apart, spacing seed ½ in. to 1 in. apart. The easiest way to get the spacing right is to mix the seed with dry builder's sand (not beach sand), using twice as much sand as seed.

Heading lettuces. Need room to grow, so set transplants 4 in. to 6 in. apart. Do a final thinning to 12 in. apart when plants are about 5 in. tall.

Plan a late-summer planting because autumn-grown lettuce stands beautifully without bolting or getting bitter.

Mesclun. A blend of cutting lettuces and sometimes other greens, mesclun is harvested when still very young.

Lettuce seed is not a reliable keeper. Store extra seeds indoors in a cool, dry place and sow a little thicker the following season. Discard seeds after two seasons.

PESTS

Birds eat seeds and young lettuces; string reflective foil tape above the lettuce bed to deter them, or use bird netting to exclude them entirely. Row covers also work. Lettuces are prone to slugs, mainly because they have high water needs; plus the leaves create hiding places. Handpicking earwigs, slugs, and snails after dark for several days is usually an effective way to deal with these pests. Shallow saucers of beer are a good trap for slugs.

HARVESTING

For any type of lettuce, you can begin harvesting individual outer leaves once the plant has several leaves at least 4 in. long. Cut whole plants of head lettuce once they are the size you like. For cutting lettuce, use

Romaine leaves are sweet and crunchy with lots of substance. They hold up well to heavy dressings and in sandwiches. 'Rouge d'Hiver' does well in spring, early summer, and fall plantings. 'Rosalita', 'Majestic Red', and 'Cimmaron' were all developed from 'Rouge d'Hiver'. Outstanding green romaines include 'Jericho' and 'Olga'. 'Little Gem' (aka 'Sugar Cos' or 'Sucrine') is a miniature romaine. Each head makes a complete salad.

Leaf Lettuces. Some of the best include 'Red Oakleaf', 'Green Oakleaf', 'Lollo Biondo', 'Lollo Rossa', 'Red Sails', and perhaps the most famous of all (and justifiably so), the heirloom 'Black Seeded Simpson'.

scissors to harvest all the leaves from individual plants or a section of a row. Cut carefully, at least 1 in. above the crown, so new leaves will sprout.

GOOD VARIETIES

Head Lettuces. Batavians combine the sweet crispness of romaine with a more open butterhead-like shape. Some are remarkably resistant to bolting. 'Nevada' is resistant to tip burn, bottom rot, and bolting. 'Sierra' is a fine warm-weather choice. 'Cardinale' is another good Batavian.

Butterheads (aka Bibb, Boston, or limestone lettuce) form softly folded, smooth-leafed rosettes. 'Merveille des Quatre Saisons' is superb. 'Nancy' is disease-resistant and forms a classic green butterhead with a pale, tightly folded, creamy heart. 'Juliet' has green leaves blushed with burgundy on the edges.

MÂCHE

Mâche, sometimes called corn salad or lamb's lettuce, is a remarkably hardy salad green with a delicate, nutty flavor. Sow it in the fall; it will overwinter to provide the spring garden's first crop.

ESSENTIALS

- Mâche thrives in cool weather in moist soil. It produces best in soils amended with nitrogen-rich compost or manure.
- In Zones 6 and warmer, sow mâche once summer heat has abated, from mid-August until late September. In colder areas, sow as soon as the soil can be worked in spring.
- Sow three or four seeds per inch, in rows spaced 10 in. apart, or broadcast seed in blocks. Regardless of how you sow, tamp with a rake.
- Thinning is optional but doing so will yield larger rosettes.
- Mâche makes an excellent green manure and soil conditioner if you turn under what's left after harvesting.

SOWING & GROWING

Mâche survives temperatures of 5°F. In colder climates, a cold frame or a mulch of straw or evergreen branches can provide significant protection. Alternatively, cold-climate gardeners can enjoy a late-spring harvest from seed planted as soon as the soil can be worked, in late winter.

Mâche comes in small-seeded and large-seeded varieties. In general, large-seeded types resist heat better; small-seeded types prefer cool, moist conditions and do best when grown only in winter.

HARVESTING

Robust growth in good conditions should provide a harvest of thinnings in 2 months. Overwintered plants reach their peak size and flavor in late winter. To harvest, grasp the plant and cut near the base for whole rosettes, or trim an inch or two higher for cut-and-come-again leaves. Unwashed mâche stores well in a plastic bag in the refrigerator for a few days. Wash it well just before serving.

Harvest leaves until the plants bolt to seed. Harvest seed for next year's crop by shaking flower stalks into a paper bag. Hoe remaining stalks and stems into the soil as green manure.

GOOD VARIETIES

Large-seeded varieties produce light green rosettes 4 in. to 8 in. wide, with narrow, elongated, spoon-shaped leaves. Highly productive, easy-to-harvest large-seeded cultivars include 'Grosse Graine', 'Piedmont', and 'Valgros'.

Small-seeded varieties produce plants 2 in. to 5 in. across, with rounder and darker green leaves. Though more finicky to pick and clean, small-seeded choices such as 'Coquille de Louviers', 'D'Etampes', or 'Verte de Cambrai' are definitely more flavorful than large-seeded varieties.

MELONS

Locally grown melons are so luscious, they expose store-bought ones as flavorless imitations. There are two main types of melons—those in the muskmelon species and watermelons. Muskmelons include a range of fruits, with some of the most familiar being cantaloupes, honeydews, Cranshaws, and Charentais. Breeding has reduced watermelons' demand for huge space in the garden. They can even be trellised.

ESSENTIALS

- Melons need fertile, well-drained soil. Form planting mounds 3 in. tall and 12 in. to 18 in. wide to improve drainage. Use black plastic mulch to warm the ground, prevent weeds, and retain soil moisture.

- Start seeds indoors 3 to 4 weeks before the last frost date—no earlier. Plant two seeds per 2-in. container, and do not thin. Set plants out when frost danger is past and soil has reached 70°F.

- Use row covers to protect newly set plants from insects and harsh weather. Remove the covers as soon as the first flowers appear.

- To direct-sow, wait until soil has warmed to at least 70°F. Plant two seeds 1 in. deep in each mound.

- Space muskmelons 3 ft. apart with 5 ft. to 6 ft. between rows. Icebox watermelons can be grown 2 ft. apart with 4 ft. between rows.

- Melons are heavy feeders. Work in 3 lb. of 10-10-10 fertilizer or the organic equivalent per 100 sq. ft. just prior to planting. Sidedress (see p. 283 for more on sidedressing) lightly twice—first when the vines begin to run and again after the first fruit is harvested.

- Melons need steady watering throughout the season, at least 1 in. per week.

SOWING & GROWING

Seedless watermelons, which, despite the name, do contain soft, white seeds, don't produce their own pollen. They require the company of a pollenizer, which can be any seeded variety. Every third plant in a row of seedless watermelons should be a seeded variety. Choose a pollenizer with different surface markings so it's easier to tell at picking time which have seeds and which do not. Seedless varieties are fussy about germinating. The seed coat tends to adhere to the cotyledons and needs to be removed so growth isn't hindered.

continued on p. 250

PESTS

To protect against cucumber beetles, drape melons with a row cover immediately after planting, anchored every 3 ft. with a half-shovel of dirt. Remove it as soon as the first flowers appear so bees can pollinate the blooms. Melons started under row covers mature a week or two early.

Powdery mildew is a talcum-like growth that appears on leaves. Because it reduces photosynthesis and thus sugar production, powdery mildew causes melons to be less sweet. The best defense is planting resistant varieties, rotating crops, and spacing plants to permit good air circulation.

Blossom-end rot, caused by a calcium deficiency during fruit development, can be a problem. Maintaining the proper soil moisture makes calcium available when it's needed.

A yellow patch on the top of the melon is sunburn, not disease. A light sunburn (also called sunscald) is merely cosmetic, but a bad case can cause the flesh to deteriorate. Cover the fruit with a basket or cloth.

HARVESTING

Muskmelons. Turn from green to beige, and then to beige with yellow undertones as they ripen. The melon is ripe when a gentle tug releases the

fruit. This stage is called half slip. A dead-ripe melon will eventually disengage itself from the vine. This is full slip. The time from half slip to full slip is, at most, 2 days. Expect to get four to six muskmelons per plant.

Charentais. Unlike other muskmelons, charentais will not slip, but they will start to separate from the vine. Pick them when the skin has a beige undertone and a hard tug detaches the fruit.

Watermelons. Each watermelon plant will yield about two fruits per plant. It takes a lot of experience to truly detect a ripe fruit by thumping a watermelon. Instead, check the curly tendril near where the watermelon attaches at the stem; it should be dead or brown. Second, the underside of the watermelon

should be creamy-white for seeded varieties and golden yellow for seedless ones. And finally, an enlarging watermelon's rind has a shiny, bright green color that becomes dull when the fruit is ripe.

GOOD VARIETIES

Long-season muskmelons taste best. For cantaloupe, 'Gold Star' and 'Ambrosia' are tops in flavor. 'Passport' and 'Morning Ice' are excellent honeydews. 'Savor', a French Charentais, produces small fruits with exceptional flavor.

Full-size watermelons need about 25 sq. ft. per plant. For small gardens or short seasons, stick to icebox types such as 'Sugar Baby', 'Yellow Doll', or 'Tiger Baby'. 'Garden Baby' is a bush type needing only about 2 ft. by 2 ft.; it can even be grown in a container.

OKRA

Okra will produce in any climate where tomatoes, corn, and melons can be grown. The beautiful, hibiscus-like blossoms are a fringe benefit. A few days after the flower drops, the tender okra pod is ready to pick.

ESSENTIALS

- Okra needs warm soil and air temperatures, lots of sun, and well-drained, humus-rich earth.

- In long-season climates, okra can be direct-sown; harvest begins about 2 months later. Northern gardeners should start seed indoors 4 or 5 weeks before the last frost.

- In a cool climate, use black plastic mulch and row covers to give okra the warmth it loves.

- Harvest pods while small and tender, no more than 4 in. long.

SOWING & GROWING

Soak seed overnight before sowing, and provide bottom heat if possible. Sow three seeds per cell. Germination takes 3 to 5 days. When the first true leaves appear, nip off all but the strongest plant in each cell.

Cool temperatures set okra back. Harden off seedlings in a cold frame, or when outside temperatures are reliably above 60°F.

Okra tolerates a variety of soils but does best with lots of humus and average pH. Don't add too much nitrogen before the plants have set fruit or you'll have lots of foliage but fewer flowers.

Plant seedlings 12 in. apart, disturbing the roots as little as possible. If you have room, plant rows 2 ft. to 3 ft. apart. If space is limited, plant 12 in. apart in an offset pattern. Expect okra to grow 3 ft. to 5 ft. tall in the North, taller in the South. For a family of four, 6 to 12 plants is ample.

Water the seedlings with a high-phosphorus solution to encourage flower production, and fertilize monthly with a foliar fish spray. Be sure okra plants receive an inch of water a week.

PESTS

Cutworms can be a problem. In a small garden, a collar around each seedling will foil them. If you have a lot of plants, this can be cumbersome. Instead, raise extra seedlings

continued on p. 252

to replace any downed by cutworms. Police the okra patch every morning. If you find a plant severed at the base of the stem, dig around until you find the cutworm and kill it. Then fill the bare spot with another seedling. In a few days, the cutworms will have been thinned out.

Root knot nematodes also afflict okra, so don't plant it where there has been a nematode problem in the past without first treating the soil.

HARVESTING

An okra pod is ready to pick about 4 days after the flower drops, when it's 3 in. to 4 in. long. Ideally, the seeds will not yet have formed and the skins will be crisp but not tough. Tender okra makes for tasty okra. Pods left on too long become tough; cut them off anyway to encourage more to form. The harvest will continue until frost, and you should pick every other day or so.

Harvesting okra is an itchy business. Even spineless varieties have scratchy leaves, so wear long sleeves and gloves if your skin is sensitive, or just grin and bear it—the itching lasts about 30 minutes. Use a knife or scissors to cut off the pods, including about an inch of stem. Just-picked okra makes the best eating, but it'll keep in the fridge for a few days.

GOOD VARIETIES

'Clemson Spineless' is an All-America Selection (AAS) winner (see p. 278 for more on AAS), with dark green, meaty pods. 'Annie Oakley' is also spineless and produces well in cooler climates. 'Burgundy' has beautiful red pods. 'Cajun Delight' is another good choice for northern climates.

ONIONS

Onions can be grown from seed or from tiny onion bulbs, called sets. Sets are easiest, but you won't find much choice of variety. Diversity aside, onions grown from seed are less prone to disease, they store better, and they bulb up faster.

ESSENTIALS

- Onions need a long growing season.
- Plant in a fertile, loose soil high in organic matter, with a pH of 6 to 6.5. Give onions adequate potassium or their necks will thicken and the bulbs won't store well.
- Start onions in flats indoors 8 to 10 weeks before the last frost. Thin to 1/4 in. apart. When seedlings are 5 in. to 6 in. tall, gently separate and transplant individually into 6-packs. Trim tops back to 4 in. Water seedlings with half-strength soluble fertilizer.
- If direct-sowing, wait until soil has warmed to 50°F. Plant transplants and sets into the garden 2 weeks before the last frost.
- Sidedress with fertilizer, compost, or aged manure when bulbs begin to swell.

SOWING & GROWING

Transplant seedlings 1/2 in. deep, 4 in. to 6 in. apart, depending on the variety's mature bulb size. Cut the leaves back to 6 in. You can plant closer and thin them as scallions.

Keep onions weeded during the growing season. As they start to mature, onions stop producing new leaves and their tops begin to fall over. When you see these signs among your plants, ease up on water to encourage dormancy. Pull the soil away from most of the bulb, leaving only the roots and lowest part of the bulb in contact with the dirt. This aids the drying process by keeping moist soil away from the papery skins.

PESTS

Onions are virtually pest- and disease-free. If onion maggots are a problem in your area, don't plant too early in the spring, and use row covers to discourage the egg-laying flies.

HARVESTING

At full maturity, onions go dormant: The inner leaves stop producing blades, and the hollow-centered neck weakens, causing the tops to bend over. It is important to let the plants go dormant before harvesting, or they won't store well.

continued on p. 254

Harvest during dry weather. Cure onions in a warm, dry, airy location out of direct sun for up to 3 weeks before storing.

When onions are adequately dried, cut the foliage back to 1 in. to 2 in. (keep the tops on if you intend to braid them). Store in a cool, dry location with good air circulation. Onions can be stored in the traditional onion bags or in a shallow box with newspaper dividing the bulbs. Or place onions in a pair of pantyhose, tying a knot above each onion. When you need an onion, just cut below the knot above the lowermost onion.

Not all varieties are meant for long-term storage. Large, sweet onions must be used within a couple of months of harvest. Typically, onions with thick necks should be used soon, as well. Keepers have firm, dry bulbs with tight necks and layers of protective yellow or brown skin. These onions are usually pungent and sweet and become milder over time.

TYPES

When choosing seed, be sure to find types suited to your climate and zone. Onion varieties differ in the length of daylight and the temperature required to make a bulb.

Short-day types. Ideal for the South, where they grow through cool southern fall and winter months. They're triggered to bulb by the 12 hours of sunlight that come with the return of warm, early-summer weather.

Long-day onions. Best grown in the North, where summer days are longer. These onions require at least 14 hours of light to bulb up. The plant grows foliage in spring, then forms bulbs during warm summer weather, triggered by the long days.

Short-day onions grown in the North will bulb too early, then languish and never get to good size. This is fine if your goal is scallions (green onions), or tiny bulbs for pickling onions. On the other hand, long-day onions grown in the South produce lots of leaves, but no respectable bulbs.

Day-neutral onions. Can be grown anywhere.

GOOD VARIETIES

Short-day onions. 'Yellow Granex' produces flattened, very sweet bulbs. This is the type planted in Georgia for Vidalia onions. 'Desert Sunrise' is a red-skinned storage onion.

Long-day onions. 'Copra' is an early, medium-size onion, unrivaled for storage. It has the highest sugar content of the storage onions. 'Sweet Sandwich', a long keeper, has globe-shaped bulbs that are very sweet, especially after 3 months of storage. 'First Edition' is a medium-size onion with pungent flavor that's good for storage. 'Red Baron' has large, purple-red bulbs that store well. 'Ailsa Craig Exhibition' is a huge, round, snow-white, mild onion that stores into late fall. 'Lancastrian' is nicknamed the football onion. Its crisp, sweet bulbs, averaging 5 lb., are great for stuffing or for onion rings. They're good for short-term storage only.

Day-neutral onions. 'Candy' and 'Super Star' are both All-America Selection winners. 'Stockton Red' is a day-neutral red onion.

Bunching onions. Although any kind of onion can be harvested young as scallions, or green onions, bunching onions are specifically intended for this purpose. Some become bulbous if left in the ground. For scallions, harvest while still straight. 'Southport White Globe' forms a classic scallion with mild flavor.

PARSNIPS

Be sure to let parsnips stay in the ground until frosted; this helps them develop their sweet, nutty flavor. Parsnips are very hardy and can be left in the ground over winter and harvested as needed, even as late as spring.

ESSENTIALS

- Parsnips require clod-free, deeply dug soil to develop long roots. Work the seedbed to a depth of at least 12 in.; 15 in. is better. Once the soil is loosened, do not step on the seedbed until after harvest.
- Grow parsnips in soil that isn't overly fertile. Too much nitrogen results in forked roots with lots of root hairs. Add fertilizer to the seedbed the previous fall, or add only compost in the spring.

- Sow directly in the garden from early spring until early summer. Parsnips take 2 to 4 weeks to germinate. Sow radish seed along with the parsnips to keep the soil surface from becoming hard.

SOWING & GROWING

It's important to keep the seedbed moist and to prevent a crust from forming on the surface. Sow radishes along with the parsnips—they will sprout quickly and keep the soil loose for the tardy parsnips. Cover the seeds with sifted compost instead of soil to help retain moisture. When seedlings are a few inches high, thin to 4 in. apart by snipping instead of pulling.

PESTS

Parsnips are bothered by carrot rust fly maggots. Keep the pests out with row covers until the seedlings are at least 4 in. tall.

HARVESTING

Wait until after a good frost to harvest. Use a digging fork to loosen the soil. Harvest as needed, and keep the soil from freezing with a deep straw mulch. Or dig the whole crop before the ground freezes, trim the tops off, and store the roots in a root cellar or packed in damp sand at 34°F.

GOOD VARIETIES

'Cobham Improved Marrow' is ready to harvest in 120 days; 'Gladiator' is relatively quick to germinate and ready in 110 days; 'Panache', with longer roots, has good flavor even without being frosted and is ready in 110 to 120 days.

PEAS

Freshly picked peas are so tempting that many never make it from the garden to the kitchen. There are three types. English peas are the traditional shelling pea. Snow peas are grown for their tender flat pods, which contain only miniscule peas. Snap peas are a cross between the first two; they look like shelling peas, but both pea and pod are crunchy, sweet, and delicious.

ESSENTIALS

- Dig 1 in. of compost or manure into the beds.
- Plant peas when the forsythia is just starting to bloom. Make a second and third sowing at 2- or 3-week intervals.
- Inoculate seeds with rhizobia bacteria just prior to planting.
- Sow peas ½ in. deep in 3-in.-wide swaths, spacing seeds 1 in. to 2 in.
- Peas need moist soil during germination and again when they are blooming.
- Provide a trellis for tall peas; dwarf varieties may not require it, but they will benefit from having something to cling to.

SOWING & GROWING

Peas aren't particular about soil, but they will benefit from added organic material, like compost or leaf mold. Don't add lots of manure or any fertilizer.

Peas will germinate in soil as cool as 40°F, but it can take weeks; at 60°F it takes 9 days. But you don't need a thermometer to know when to plant. Sow peas when the forsythia is just beginning to bloom.

Because peas are legumes, which convert atmospheric nitrogen into nitrogen compounds in the soil, they don't need much fertilizer. If you want to enhance their nitrogen fixing, coat seeds prior to planting with a pea inoculant, a natural bacterial powder that you can find at most garden centers.

Peas stop producing when daytime temperatures stay above 80°F. Although peas do best as a spring crop, if a long, warm autumn is typical for your area, try planting a fall crop 60 to 90 days before your hard frost date.

PESTS

Birds will eat pea seeds and newly sprouted peas. Protect your plantings with netting until the plants are a couple of inches tall. Aphids can be hosed off the vines.

Pea enation virus causes the vines to turn pale and the pods brown and warty. Fortunately, it doesn't appear until the summer really gets warm and the pea harvest is almost over. To prevent powdery mildew, choose resistant varieties, don't sow too thickly, avoid wetting the foliage late in the day, and give the plants something to climb on. There are other viruses and wilts that affect peas, but by delaying planting until the soil is warm and by planting resistant varieties, you can usually avoid these problems.

HARVESTING

Once the vines start blooming, check the plants daily because pods form very quickly. Keeping pods picked extends production.

Pick shelling peas just as the peas have filled out the shells but before they start getting too mature and starchy. Test a pod or two regularly and pick them when they are bright green, full size, and still sweet.

Harvest snow peas when the pods are bright green and firm, with a ridge of barely visible peas along one edge.

Snap peas are at their best when the pods are well rounded and filled with plump peas but before they start to yellow or fade. You can pick them when they're smaller and flatter, but they won't be as sweet.

GOOD VARIETIES

Peas vary in height from 15 in. to more than 6 ft. Dwarf varieties produce more per square foot, but taller varieties make for easier picking

Shelling peas. 'Maestro' grows 2 ft. tall and is resistant to pea enation. 'Olympia' has good flavor, grows vigorously to 16 in. to 20 in., and is resistant to mosaic virus. 'Waverex', a tiny-pod variety with lots of flavor, grows 15 in. to 20 in. tall. 'Improved Laxton's Progress' is a better version of an older variety. It has large pods but grows only 16 in. high. Open-pollinated 'Oregon Trail' produces

many dark green, double pods on vines about 30 in. tall.

Snow peas. 'Oregon Sugar Pod II' is a nonclimber that grows to 30 in. tall and is resistant to pea enation virus, common wilt, and powdery mildew. 'Goliath', an All-America Selection winner, bears stringless pods on 5-ft. vines. 'Oregon Giant' bears large, broad, thick pods on 3-ft. vines that

are resistant to pea enation virus and powdery mildew.

Snap peas. 'Super Sugar Snap' grows over 5 ft. tall and resists powdery mildew. 'Sugar Ann' and 'Sugar Bon' grow 18 in. to 24 in. tall and require little or no help to hold themselves off the ground. 'Cascadia' is early and almost stringless.

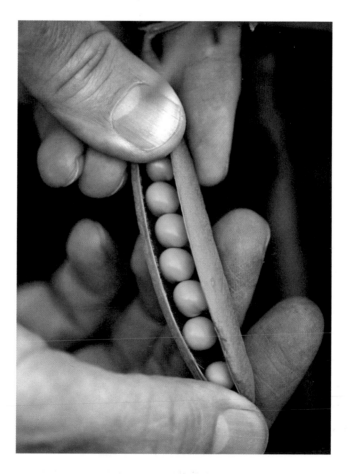

PEPPERS

Huge variety makes peppers fascinating to grow. The fruits comes in all sizes, shapes, and colors. Their flavors range from sweet to mildly spicy to hotter than many people can stand. The main thing to know about growing them is not to rush things—peppers need warm soil and air temperatures.

ESSENTIALS

- Peppers need full sun and well-drained, fertile soil.
- Start seeds in 6-packs 8 weeks before you want to transplant them outside. Provide bottom heat; peppers germinate best at 80°F.
- After 4 weeks, transplant to small pots. Keep warm.
- Plant outside when the garden soil is warm, 65°F. Plant in double rows 12 in. apart, with 18 in. between plants. In raised beds, space plants 14 in. apart in all directions.
- In cool areas, plant under a mulch of black, woven landscape fabric to warm the soil and control weeds.
- Stake plants to prevent tipping. A leaning plant puts fruit at risk of sunscald.
- Give peppers a nitrogen boost in mid-July to keep plants bearing until frost.

SOWING & GROWING

Peppers grow best in well-drained loam or sandy loam. The heavier the soil, the more organic matter you should add. Test the soil every few years to keep tabs on nutrient levels. In particular, peppers need adequate potassium and calcium, which help produce thick, meaty fruits that taste better and resist fruit rot.

In the middle of summer, when the leaves begin to lose their dark green color, peppers benefit from some extra nitrogen, either sprayed on the leaves or watered in. Don't give them too much nitrogen early on, though, or you'll get lots of plant and not much fruit.

PESTS

Practicing crop rotation, planting disease-resistant varieties in raised beds, and providing good air circulation take care of most pest problems.

That leaves the major antagonist, caterpillars, both the European corn borer and the corn earworm, which fly in as moths and lay eggs on the peppers. They become a problem in midsummer. If borer damage goes beyond your tolerance, you can spray with Bt.

Blossom end rot is caused by calcium deficiency and exacerbated by uneven watering. Good soil nutrition and regular irrigation are the answer.

HARVESTING

Most pepper varieties are green when mature, but turn vibrant colors when fully ripe. Their flavor changes at full ripeness, too, becoming more complex and sweeter or hotter, depending on the type of pepper.

Begin picking peppers 50 to 60 days after transplanting. A mature (but unripe) pepper should be full-size, heavy, and feel thick and hard. Cut, don't pull, the fruits from the plant to avoid breaking off whole branches.

For sweet bell peppers, you should be able to pick at least one or two peppers per plant each week until frost. Don't let the first, low fruits on the plants ripen, or you risk fruit rot setting in. By early August, stop picking immature green peppers to let them ripen.

GOOD VARIETIES

When it comes to peppers, what thrives in one part of the country may not in yours. Try different varieties until you find which works best for you. All peppers can be used either mature (green) or ripe.

Sweet peppers. 'Camelot' and 'Galaxy' produce blocky, four-lobed fruit, good for harvesting green. 'Elisa' has elongated fruits that ripen red; plants have good disease resistance and continuous fruit set. 'Orobelle' has blocky, thick-walled, four-lobed yellow fruit. 'Valencia' is the sweetest orange. 'Islander' produces beautiful lavender fruit. Long, narrow, thin-skinned and thin-walled peppers like 'Aruba', 'Biscayne', or 'Corno di Toro' (bull's horn) are good for salads, sautéing, and grilling.

Chili peppers. Not all chilis are hot; some are quite mild. Don't confuse the hotness of a chili with its taste. Taste and heat are two separate sensations, and all chilis have both.

New Mexican, or Anaheim, chilis are only mildly hot, with meaty, thick-walled pods. They are used fresh as green chilis, but they ripen red and get sweeter and hotter.

Poblanos are large mild chilis with thin walls, which makes them good for stuffing and perfect for drying. The plants are not particularly productive. Dried poblanos are called anchos.

Hungarian wax chilis are bright yellow, with a mild flavor more like a sweet pepper than a hot chili. The productive plants set pods early, making them good for northern gardens. Most will ripen to luscious reds and oranges that are deliciously sweet.

Cayennes, both red and gold, are best for adding just plain heat to anything. The plants are small, but they produce plenty of chilis that ripen early. Their thin skins make them excellent drying chilis.

Jalapeños are the best middle-of-the-road chilis—not too hot and not too mild. All jalapeño varieties are productive, growing around 75 pods per plant.

Serrano chilis are little bullets of heat. They can be used green, but are even better and sweeter after they ripen to a bright red.

Habaneros are considered the hottest chili in the world. Many habanero chilis have small squarish pods with lots of folds and crevices. The Scotch bonnet, a type of habanero, has some of that wonderful fruity habanero flavor but is a little less hot.

POTATOES

Potatoes are a rewarding crop to grow. They produce one of the highest yields per area planted of all food crops. Harvesting them is like going on a horticultural treasure hunt.

ESSENTIALS

- Plant in spring, when soil has reached 50°F, using only certified disease-free seed potatoes.
- Dig a trench 6 in. deep in soil well amended with compost, well-aged manure, or leaf mold. Allow 3 ft. between rows.
- Plant 12 in. apart for full-size potatoes, closer if you plan to harvest the whole crop as new (or young) potatoes. Cover with 3 in. of compost.
- When plants are 4 in. to 6 in. tall, mound soil to cover most of the leaves—a process called hilling. Plan to hill again 3 weeks later.
- Control weeds with frequent cultivation and provide adequate moisture, especially shortly before and during flowering, when tubers start to form.

GROWING

Potatoes grow from an actual piece of potato, called a seed potato. To avoid diseases, buy certified disease-free seed potatoes. Planting small, whole seed potatoes further reduces the risk of disease, but medium to large seed potatoes can be cut into pieces. Each piece must have at least two eyes and weigh about 2 oz. If sprouts have already started growing from the eyes, take care not to break them off. Supermarket potatoes have likely been treated with a sprout inhibitor and might carry disease, so don't plant them—even if they've already started to sprout.

Shallow planting allows the soil around the seed to warm quickly, encouraging faster sprouting. As the plant grows and the tubers start to form, hill them up with soil to encourage tubers to form. Hilling also protects the tubers from sunlight, which turns them green, making them bitter and mildly toxic.

PESTS

Planting certified seed potatoes and rotating crops are important to control insects and diseases. Never plant potatoes where their fellow nightshades—tomatoes, peppers, and eggplants—grew the previous year.

The potato's worst enemy is the Colorado potato beetle. Handpick the adult beetles as they emerge from their underground winter hideouts, and check under leaves for their orange eggs. Crushing the egg masses will keep them from hatching into ravening larvae, which then turn into adults.

Lightweight floating row covers are great for controlling potato bugs, leafhoppers, aphids, and other insects that like potatoes. After planting the seed potatoes, cover the rows with the thin polyester fabric and seal the edges thoroughly by shoveling small amounts of soil along the entire length of the fabric. The cover should stay on as long as possible, coming off when the weather is very hot or when the plants outgrow it. (For more on the Colorado potato beetle and its control, see pp. 151–153.)

HARVESTING

Potatoes can be harvested at any size. New potatoes can be harvested starting about 7 weeks after the plants break ground, or about the time potato plants blossom. But not all potato plants flower. Uncover the sides of the mound to check on tuber size. If they're too little, pack the soil back around the roots and wait a while.

If you are going to eat all your potatoes when they're new, it's easiest to uproot the whole plant. Dig straight down a good 1 ft. away from the middle of the plant to avoid slicing into any of the tubers. Then lift the plant gently while prying it

out with a fork or spade. Most of the potatoes will hang off the roots. Dig around with your hands to rescue any stragglers. If you want to poach a few small potatoes but leave the rest to size up, use your hands to feel around for the little potatoes and cut them off. Then pack the soil back around the disturbed roots and water the plant well.

For storage potatoes, harvest 2 weeks after a killing frost, when the ground is dry. Store only dry, undamaged potatoes at 40°F to 50°F at high humidity—75 percent to 90 percent.

GOOD VARIETIES

'Red Norland' is early, with red skin and moist white flesh. 'Yukon Gold' is early, with thin, golden skin and creamy yellow flesh. 'Rose Gold' is similar but with red skin and produces 2 weeks later.

Fingerlings like 'Russian Banana' and 'Rose Finn Apple' are elongated, finger-size tubers with exquisite flavor and texture. The flesh is yellow, the skins tender, and the texture smooth and dense.

'Cranberry Red' has red skin and light red, moist flesh. 'All Blue' has blue flesh.

RADISHES

Spring radishes are the quickest crop you can grow, and their crisp texture and jeweled colors are a welcome treat. Winter radishes are starchier, larger, and stronger flavored than spring radishes.

ESSENTIALS

- Plant seed in cold soil, as soon as it can be worked.
- Thin seedlings to 1½ in. apart.
- Keep soil evenly moist.
- To prevent flea beetles, cover beds with floating row covers right after planting.
- Hollow radishes indicate irregular watering or too-hot weather. Oddly shaped radishes are due to stress from lack of water or heavy soil.

SOWING & GROWING

Radishes are best when grown quickly in cool weather with constant moisture. Being root vegetables, they're potassium users, but a minimally fertile soil is adequate. Too much nitrogen results in more greens than root. More important is a light, airy soil. Clay soil can result in hotter, muddy-tasting radishes, particularly with daikons. Sow winter radishes in late summer for fall and winter harvests. Sown in spring, they'll bolt without making a radish.

Be sure you know which type of radish you're growing for the best result.

HARVESTING

Spring radishes are ready 3 to 4 weeks after sowing, when round varieties are about the size of a large marble or elongated ones no bigger than a little finger. Once they're ready, pick and eat them within a few days. Winter radishes mature in 6 to 8 weeks and can be used at any size. With tougher skins and denser flesh, they keep well for months. To harvest, grasp the leaves and pull up the plant.

GOOD VARIETIES

'Champion' stays firm at maturity. 'Marabelle' produces beautiful, marble-size roots. 'Sora' handles warm weather better than other varieties. 'Easter Egg' is a mix of red, white, and pastels. 'French Breakfast' forms mild red and white cylindrical roots. 'White Icicle' is long, white, and spicy.

The mild daikon is the best known winter radish. 'Red Meat' and 'Green Meat' are spicier, with white skin and colorful flesh. Black Spanish radishes have an ebony peel and peppery white flesh.

RHUBARB

Rhubarb is a vegetable, botanically speaking, that's used as a fruit. This perennial is easy to grow, and it doubles as a great foliage plant.

ESSENTIALS

- Rhubarb likes deep, well-drained, fertile soil in full sun or a mix of sun and shade.
- Dig a trench 3 ft. wide and 8 in. deep. Put 4 in. of manure in the bottom and cover with 2 in. to 3 in. of loam. Plant crowns 3 ft. apart.
- Dig and separate crowns every 4 to 5 years in early spring when a few sprouts appear.

GROWING

Because rhubarb will stay put for several years, choose its place wisely. It's a good idea to give it a bed of its own, where its roots won't be disturbed by nearby cultivation. If you're only putting in a few plants, you can plant in 18-in.-wide holes instead of a trench.

Rhubarb is ready for dividing when each original plant has generated several new crowns. When sprouts appear in early spring, cut around the plants with a spade, pushing the spade as deep as possible to get beneath the roots. Gently push down on the spade handle to raise the rhubarb crowns out of the soil.

Each crown resembles a gnarly carrot or pair of carrots grown together. It's okay to break or cut the little root connections between crowns when separating them. Very large crowns can be cut in half lengthwise, separating each leg. Just be sure there are buds on top of each piece, or the crown won't sprout.

To allow the new crown to gain strength, do not pick from new plantings during the first season and only lightly the second. When you divide rhubarb, leave two plants undisturbed so you won't have a year without rhubarb.

Although it's not necessary, mulching the beds with manure or leaves in the late fall after the rhubarb's leaves die back will help enrich the soil. To save plant strength, cut off the flower spikes when they appear.

HARVESTING

The harvest season for rhubarb is relatively long, from the time the stalks have grown long until midsummer. The stalks get stringier as the season wears on. Harvest by pulling the stalks sideways and away from the center of the plant rather than cutting. If you cut them off, the stubs remaining can be susceptible to decay and infestation. Store unwashed stalks in a plastic bag; they'll keep for about a week.

Rhubarb leaves contain oxalic acid, which makes them mildly toxic. Cut them off and add to your compost pile or spread them out as mulch.

GOOD VARIETIES

The best place to get rhubarb is from a fellow gardener. You may find crowns at your local nursery, but be sure they have buds on top; otherwise they won't grow. Red stalks are the most sought after, but the green stalks are just as tasty. There are several good varieties; a few are 'MacDonald', 'Valentine', and 'Victoria'.

RUTABAGAS

Rutabagas, also called swedes, are closely related to turnips— they look like a large, yellow-fleshed turnip, and their flavor is similar, although much sweeter. They are easy to grow, not picky about soil, very hardy, and store well.

ESSENTIALS

- Rutabagas need well-drained soil of moderate fertility. They will tolerate a little shade.
- The best rutabagas are grown for fall harvest. Direct-sow 3 months before the first expected frost.
- Sow seed about 2 in. apart. When seedlings have two sets of true leaves, thin to 6 in. apart.
- Rutabagas grow best with between 1 in. and 1½ in. of water per week during active growth.

SOWING & GROWING

Rutabagas don't do well on a rich diet—soils high in nitrogen and organic matter grow poor-quality roots—so this is a good crop to plant if you've got a patch of unimproved ground. Although they're best when grown as a fall crop and harvested after frost, you can also grow rutabagas in the spring. For a spring crop, choose early varieties and sow as soon as you can work the ground. For a fall crop, sow 3 months before the first expected frost.

PESTS

Like turnips, rutabagas are bothered by carrot root maggots and flea beetles; use row covers to exclude these pests. Root spot disease is caused by boron deficiency, which can be corrected by applying agricultural borax. Regular additions of good homemade compost usually prevent this problem.

HARVESTING

Wait until the garden has been hit by a couple of hard frosts before digging rutabagas. Cut the tops off to within about 1 in. of the root and store the unwashed roots in a chilly basement or garage. They keep best at 32°F to 34°F for 4 to 6 months.

GOOD VARIETIES

'Wilhemsburger' is an early variety, good for spring or fall. 'Marian' is resistant to clubroot. 'Laurentian' is an old favorite, with fine-textured, good-tasting roots. 'American Purple Top' has light yellow roots with purple tops.

SALSIFY AND SCORZONERA

*Salsify (*Tragopogon porrifolius*) and scorzonera (*Scorzonera hispanica*) are obscure vegetables in North America, but they deserve to be better known. Also called oyster plant or vegetable oyster, salsify looks like a whitish carrot and has a subtle, delicious flavor that will remind you of artichokes and oysters. Scorzonera is similar but with black skin. These root vegetables are delicious sautéed, baked into a gratin, or added to soups.*

ESSENTIALS

- To develop their long roots, salsify and scorzonera need deeply dug soil, but it shouldn't be particularly rich. Too much nitrogen results in hairy roots, which have a poor texture.
- They grow best in loose, somewhat sandy soils with a neutral to slightly alkaline pH.
- Salsify and scorzonera require 4 months to reach harvestable size.
- Direct-sow in early spring, as soon as the ground can be worked.

SOWING & GROWING

Loosen the ground to a depth of 12 in. to 16 in. and rake smooth. Sow seeds about ½ in. apart in rows, leaving 18 in. between rows. Both vegetables can be slow to germinate. They also are slow-growing crops, so make the most of your garden space by growing a quick crop like radishes, turnips, or salad greens in between the rows.

Stepping into the salsify bed compacts the soil and inhibits good development of the roots. If you must get into the bed, put a board down and walk on that.

PESTS

Salsify and scorzonera can be bothered by the carrot rust fly. Protect seedlings with row covers.

HARVESTING

Dig in the fall, after the first frost. These plants have long, brittle roots. To avoid breaking them, loosen the soil carefully and thoroughly with a garden fork, then lift the roots out. Trim the tops to 2 in. and store the roots as you would parsnips or carrots. Stored at 34°F in high humidity, salsify and scorzonera will keep for several months. Compost the tops.

GOOD VARIETIES

About the only salsify variety you're likely to find is 'Mammoth Sandwich Island', which grows roots about 8 in. long. 'Hoffmanns Schwarze Pfahl' scorzonera grows about 10 in. long. 'Belstar' scorzonera is a heavy producer.

SHALLOTS

Shallots are so easy to grow that any home gardener can have a supply on hand year-round. Just be sure to find out which varieties are best suited to your local soil and climate.

ESSENTIALS

- Shallots grow well in Zones 4 through 8. They grow from sets, or last year's bulbs.
- In Zones 5 to 8, plant shallots after the first frost of autumn. In Zone 4, plant as soon after spring thaw as possible.
- Shallots are prone to rot in moist soil. Amend the soil so it drains well. Plant the shallots in raised ridges, and allow 2 ft. between ridges. Set shallots about 6 in. apart and 2 in. to 3 in. deep, with their tips just emerging. Do not fertilize.
- Dust the newly planted shallot bed with wood ashes. Walk on either side of the planted ridge, pressing the soil into a gully to improve drainage.

GROWING

Exposure to winter freezing usually results in larger and better-flavored shallots. On the other hand, shallots are sensitive to severe winters, especially if they remain unprotected

by a straw mulch. The ridge-planting technique is almost fail-proof, but don't attempt it in Zone 4, where extreme freezing and thawing will heave the shallots out of the ridges in the spring, when they are most vulnerable. If you must plant in the spring, choose a variety known for its storing qualities, so the bulbs don't sprout over the winter before you plant them. Firm, small bulbs store best; large bulbs tend not to keep as well.

PESTS

Shallots are hardly bothered by pests. If onion maggots are a problem in your area, use a row cover to protect shallots from the flies.

HARVESTING

Harvest shallots once the tops die back. Spread out on a screen in a shady, dry, well-ventilated place and

let cure until the skins and necks are dry, about 3 weeks. Pull the dried tops off and store in a cool, dry place. The flavor softens in storage.

GOOD VARIETIES

There are three types of shallots. The so-called French shallot is the most common and produces clusters of small bulbs, typically with coppery skins and tear-shaped bulbs with rose-colored flesh. The second type is the so-called potato onion or multiplier onion, which is a shallot that forms a bulb one year, then divides into a cluster of bulbs the next season. This type of shallot is ideal for hot climates and is widely grown in the South. The last group is the top-setting shallot, which sends up a pseudo-flower head that forms a small cluster of bulbs.

The 'Gray' shallot is the aristocrat of the shallot world and is also one of the best storage varieties.

Yellow shallots tend to be hardier than the red varieties.

SPINACH

Spinach is a mainstay of the spring garden, but its harvest season is short. String it out by making successive plantings, using a combination of both cold-tolerant and bolt-resistant varieties.

ESSENTIALS

- Spinach thrives with regular moisture and cool weather. It grows best in temperatures of 45°F to 75°F. Young plants can withstand frost.
- Spinach likes well-drained, humus-rich soil in full sun or partial shade.
- Direct-sow spinach starting in early spring, as soon as ground can be worked. Sow small patches every 2 weeks until early summer.
- For early spinach, sow indoors 7 weeks before the last frost for planting out 1 month later.

SOWING & GROWING

Most spinach varieties mature in about 45 days, so to extend the harvest season, you need to stagger plantings. Work into the soil 1 in. or more of compost and enough fertilizer to add ½ lb. of nitrogen per 100 sq. ft. For earliest harvest, sow seed indoors in 6-packs 7 weeks before the last frost. Four weeks later, set the plants in the garden 4 in. to 6 in. apart. At the same time, sow more seed directly in the garden. Sow more plantings every 2 weeks through late spring.

For fall spinach, sow in late summer, either directly in the garden or indoors if the weather is still hot. For winter spinach, cover the fall crop with a cold frame and harvest all winter.

HARVESTING

Except for thinning, do not harvest whole plants. Instead, pinch or cut off individual, outer leaves when about 3 in. long, leaving at least six central leaves on the plant. For direct-sown spinach, harvest will begin a few weeks after sowing if you thin the plants. Thin twice, first to 2 in. to 4 in. apart, then a couple of weeks later to 6 in. to 8 in. apart, and enjoy the thinnings as baby spinach. After the second thinning, you should no longer remove whole plants.

PESTS

Leaf miners are spinach's only serious pests. They tunnel through the leaf, scarring and desiccating large portions of it. Pick off and destroy badly damaged leaves. To prevent the insects from reaching the spinach, use row covers from early May on.

GOOD VARIETIES

'Melody' and 'Tyee' are both cold-tolerant, with lightly savoyed leaves. 'Bloomsdale Savoy' is a bolt-resistant variety whose deeply savoyed leaves have good flavor. 'Indian Summer' and 'Steadfast' are bolt-resistant with flat leaves. 'Giant Spinach of Viroflay' (aka 'Monstrueux de Viroflay') and 'Giant Nobel' both have flat, tender leaves that are very large—12 in. long.

SUMMER SQUASH

Summer squash are notoriously easy to grow. The variety of colors (all shades of yellow and green, plus creamy white) and shapes (ridges, scallops, teardrops, balls, and S-curves) keeps things interesting, both on the plants and once harvested. Just be sure to pick them young for best quality.

ESSENTIALS

- Summer squash need fertile, well-drained soil in full sun.
- Allow the soil to warm to at least 65°F before planting.
- Dig in lots of well-aged manure or compost.
- Direct-sow to avoid transplant shock. Sow the seeds 18 in. apart in rows or hills 4 ft. to 5 ft. apart.
- Keep young plants weeded and don't allow the soil to dry out. Summer squash plants are thirsty, so water once or twice a week, even if there has been rain.
- Pick fruit often to ensure continued production.

SOWING & GROWING

Direct sowing is much better than setting out transplants. Direct-sown plants usually catch up quickly to transplanted ones. If you do choose to use transplants, set them out 2 weeks after germinating, when they have no more than two true leaves.

A month after the first planting, do a second sowing, which will give you strong, prolific plants until the first frost. When production of the first crop starts slowing down, you can pull out the plants and compost them. Doing this also gives you a chance to plant different varieties the second time around.

One trick for growing strong plants and keeping them well-watered is to sink a 1-gal. nursery pot in the soil, leaving 1 in. of rim out of the ground. Put a shovelful of compost into the pot, and plant squash around the pot a few inches away. As the plants grow, water directly into the pot, which delivers moisture and a mild compost tea right to the roots.

PESTS

Squash bugs resist most organic pesticides. Handpick the bugs every couple of days to keep them in check. Check the underside of leaves for clusters of shiny, orange-brown eggs, and scrape them off carefully.

Cucumber beetles spread bacterial wilt. If you're fast, you can handpick them. There's no cure for bacterial wilt. Spraying the leaves with a thin slurry of diatomaceous earth and water (about 3 tablespoons per gallon) helps deter cucumber beetles. The leaves will look whitewashed for 5 to 6 weeks. You can also protect plants with floating row covers, but you'll need to remove them once the plants start flowering in order to get a harvest.

Squash vine borer also causes wilting leaves. Look for a small hole near the base of the plant. Slit the vine from that point, destroy the borer, and then bury the stem under a mound of soil to promote rooting.

Whitish residue on leaves is most likely from powdery mildew. Affected plants will eventually succumb. Succession plantings are the best answer.

HARVESTING

Once fruits start developing, harvest early and often for continued production and best flavor. Crookneck and straightneck squash are best at 4 in. to 6 in. long and pattypans at 2 in. to 4 in. across. Squash blossoms are edible delicacies. Harvest them first thing in the morning; by afternoon they'll wilt. You can harvest both male and female flowers, but by taking only male blossoms—the ones without small fruit forming behind the flower—you won't diminish your squash harvest.

Use a sharp kitchen knife to cut the fruit from the plant. You might want to wear gloves, because the small spines on the leaves can be very irritating.

GOOD VARIETIES

Crookneck. 'Horn of Plenty' is a hybrid that produces delicate flavor and texture; bush plants typically carry fruit that's 5 in. to 7 in. long with thick necks. 'Dixie' is resistant

to cucumber beetles and is a good producer.

Lebanese. 'White Bush' is a Lebanese (also called Mid-East or cousa) squash bearing bulbous light green fruit with white speckles. It can be picked small but will not lose its flavor if left to get a little larger, around 7 in. to 8 in.

Pattypan. 'Sunburst', a pattypan or scallopini with stunning yellow color, has a nutty flavor, and tastes great when it's 2 in. to 4 in. wide. 'White Patty Pan' is creamy white in color.

Straightneck. 'Fortune' bears smooth, cylindrical fruit, perfect for grilling or stir-fries; early maturing

at 45 days. 'Lemondrop' produces high yields of 6-in. to 7-in., smooth, high-quality fruit.

Zucchini. 'Zucchetta Rampicante' has a vigorous, vining habit. It bears long, pale-green, S-shaped fruit with firm texture and mild flavor. 'Fiorentino' is a dark-green Italian zucchini with light green stripes and delightful ridges that develop on fruit 7 in. to 9 in. long. 'Condor' is a standard green zucchini known for its nutty flavor, perfect shape and color, and high yields. 'Burpee's Golden Zucchini' is a nice change from green zucchini. The heirloom 'Ronde de Nice' boasts fruits that are round, smooth, and pale green. 'Eight Ball' is similar but blackish green.

Cross-Section of a Squash Hill

To make watering easier, sink a pot in the ground at planting time and sow the squash seeds around the outside of the pot. When you fill the pot with water, it drains out the holes in the bottom, immediately reaching the roots of the plants.

SWEET POTATOES

Sweet potatoes (Ipomoea bata-tas) are part of the morning glory family and are native to the American tropics. They're not yams, a native of Africa, which come from an entirely different plant seldom grown here.

ESSENTIALS

- Sweet potatoes grow best in a moderately fertile, sandy loam. Dense soil produces stringy, misshapen potatoes.
- Apply a balanced fertilizer such as 10-10-10 or 7-7-7 in early spring so the nutrients will be readily available at planting time. Do not add extra fertilizer during the growing season.
- Plant sweet potato slips—shoots grown from a mature sweet potato—in ridges of soil 12 in. high and 3 ft. apart. Plant 12 in. to 18 in. apart, when soil temperature is above 65°F.
- Control weeds. Water as needed, backing off toward the end to prevent the sweet potatoes from splitting.

GROWING

Sweet potatoes are grown from slips, tender young shoots that grow from last year's potatoes. You can buy slips or start your own, which takes about 6 weeks. To start slips, plant whole sweet potatoes 2 in. deep in sawdust or potting soil. Keep warm, about 75°F. Each potato will sprout several tender, slim stems, or slips. When the slips have several leaves and are about 6 in. long, they can be pulled off and planted. You can hold them for a couple of weeks by keeping the roots moist.

It's a good idea to order slips from a sweet potato supplier every few years to safeguard against disease attacking your crop. Slips from professional suppliers are checked to make sure they're free of disease.

Make holes in the ridges, fill with water, insert the slips to half their length, then firm the soil. Keep well watered for a week, until roots start growing. Each plant should produce at least three potatoes.

HARVESTING

For the largest roots and sweetest flavor, harvest shortly before frost. The longer they grow, the sweeter the potatoes become. Begin by shearing off the vines. If local regulations permit, burn the vines to help prevent disease buildup.

Use a shovel or spading fork to dig into the ridge, being careful not to bruise the potatoes because the damage will encourage rotting in storage.

Harvested potatoes need to be washed and dried before storage.

Spread them on the grass in full sun, spray them with the garden hose, and leave them to dry for 4 or 5 hours. Store sweet potatoes in shallow containers in a shed or garage where they will stay dry and have good air circulation. For best keeping, cure them for 10 days to reduce their moisture and toughen the skin.

Store cured sweet potatoes in boxes in a dry, well-ventilated, cool area—about 60°F is ideal. They will keep for 8 or 9 months. Try not to handle them too much because they bruise easily. Wrapping each potato in newspaper helps them to keep longer.

GOOD VARIETIES

'Centennial' produces nicely shaped potatoes in about 90 days. 'Jewell' and 'Porto Rico' each mature in about 100 days. 'Porto Rico' has a bushy, compact habit. All three have moist, orange flesh. White-flesh sweet potatoes tend to be dry and not very sweet.

TOMATILLOS

Although related to tomatoes, tomatillos have not gone through vigorous breeding programs and as a result have all the hardiness and wildness of native plants. The compact fruit—which looks like a green cherry tomato—grows to maturity inside a papery husk. This Mexican native, also called husk tomato, is the primary ingredient in salsa verde.

ESSENTIALS

- Tomatillos grow well in all parts of the continental United States and in much of Canada.
- Tomatillos need lots of sun. They thrive in almost any soil but do need good drainage.
- In warm climates, sow seeds directly in the ground. In cooler areas, start seeds inside, 5 to 7 weeks before transplanting.
- In the garden, thin to one plant every 2 ft. to 3 ft. A couple of plants will supply more than enough tomatillos all summer.
- Every 2 weeks in the spring, spray the plants with liquid seaweed to encourage bloom.
- Tomatillos don't need a lot of additional water, but don't let them get too dry. If the plants wilt, give them a little water, and they'll perk right up.

- Trim stray stems to keep the plants in bounds.

SOWING & GROWING

Wait until the soil is thoroughly warm before planting tomatillos. Space your plants at least 2 ft. apart in the garden; 3 ft. is better in warm climates, where they'll grow faster and bigger. If you let them, tomatillos will grow over and through neighboring plants, and the branches will root wherever they touch the ground. Trellising or caging helps, but the simplest solution is to whack off the parts that get out of bounds.

HARVESTING

Harvest tomatillos when the fruit outgrows the husk and splits it open, but while the fruit is still firm. Left on the vine longer, the fruit gets pithy and bitter and doesn't keep as long after picking. Yellow fruit is overripe. Tomatillos will keep producing fruit at a steady pace throughout the summer and up until the first frost. If picked at the right stage, tomatillos keep for a long time, stored unwashed in a loosely closed plastic bag.

GOOD VARIETIES

In catalogs, tomatillo seeds are often listed under tomatoes, gourmet seeds, or unusual vegetables. There are only a couple of varieties. The most common is called simply tomatillo. 'Purple de Milpa' has slightly smaller, less abundant fruit and purplish skins.

TOMATOES

All-day sun, rich soil, and some TLC will reward you with juicy, tasty tomatoes. They come in varieties, colors, sizes, and shapes too numerous to mention. The hardest part will be deciding which to grow. The variety you grow is important for flavor, but how you grow your tomatoes will determine if you have loads of beautiful fruits or a few small ones on weak plants.

ESSENTIALS

- Tomatoes need full sun, warm temperatures, and fertile soil well amended with compost.
- Sow seed in 6-packs 6 to 8 weeks before the last frost. Provide bottom heat if possible; tomatoes germinate best at 70°F to 80°F. For a long harvest season, sow two or three batches of seeds 7 to 10 days apart.
- Transplant to 4-in. pots when seedlings have their first set of true leaves.
- Plant out hardened-off seedlings 1 to 2 weeks after the last frost, when night temperatures are consistently above 45°F. Be ready to protect early plantings if the temperature drops.
- Crowding increases the risk of disease. Set tomato seedlings 18 in. to 24 in. apart for trellised plants, 36 in. apart if using tomato cages. If growing in rows, allow 5 ft. between them.
- Provide support to keep plants off the ground, and use mulch to keep soil from splashing on leaves.
- During growth, deliver regular amounts of water, but scale back as tomatoes start to ripen.

GROWING

Tomatoes prefer a pH between 6.5 and 7.0, a little higher than for most other vegetables, and they need at least as much potassium (K) as nitrogen (N) to spur good fruit development. If a soil test indicates the need, add 3 lb. to 5 lb. of wood ashes per 100 sq. ft. At planting time, add 2 oz. soybean meal per plant.

Stakes, cages, or a trellis of some kind keeps plants off the ground and therefore healthier, and makes it easier to find and pick ripe fruit. The typical conical cages are too small for all but the smallest determinate varieties; you can make your own from 4-ft.-tall galvanized fencing with 4-in.-sq. openings—big enough for your hand and a nice, big tomato. Some support systems require tying; with others, you simply direct the growth. Either way, you need to monitor the plants frequently, at least every few days.

Mulch helps keep plants clean and lowers the incidence of disease. There are lots of options: straw, chopped leaves, landscape fabric, and a special red plastic mulch specifically designed for tomatoes and which reportedly increases yields.

Tomato plants—regardless of what size fruit they produce—are classified as either of indeterminate or determinate habit. Each has pros and cons. Indeterminate tomatoes keep growing and growing, so long as their health and the weather hold out. Their stems always end with another shoot, and the fruit clusters are spaced fairly wide apart on the stem (usually every third leaf). Being larger plants, they support more and larger fruit than do determinate tomatoes. The fruit also tends to taste better because more photosynthesis makes more sugars. Also, because indeterminate plants have more leaves, it takes longer for diseases to completely defoliate the plant. Indeterminate tomatoes need staking or trellising on supports that are no less than 5 ft. tall, and they should be pruned to no more than four main stems per plant.

Determinate tomatoes (also called bush tomatoes) have been bred to be shorter so they're easier to trellis. The stem ends with a fruit cluster, and the other fruit clusters are spaced closer on the stem, generally between every leaf. Determinates bear fruit early and in a concentrated period of 4 to 6 weeks, which is convenient for making sauce or canning. Determinate tomatoes do fine in

tomato cages (many of which are too short for indeterminate types) and shouldn't be pruned.

Semi-determinate plants, as the name implies, are somewhere between these two other types. Although there aren't many semi-determinate tomatoes, one of the most popular hybrids, 'Celebrity', falls into this category. Semi-determinates are best grown to three or four stems.

Pruning needs are based on the type of tomato. Determinate tomatoes don't need to be pruned, but other types simply produce more vegetative growth than is needed. So for indeterminate and semi-determinate tomatoes, you'll want to prune to one to four stems. About the time the plant starts to flower, it also starts to produce a new shoot, or sucker, at each leaf node. Pinch out all or most of the shoots when they are no larger than a pencil. In general, more stems means more but smaller fruits, which are produced increasingly later in

the season. A properly pruned and supported single-stem tomato plant produces larger fruit than a multi-stemmed plant of the same variety. You should also prune off any leaves that touch the ground.

PESTS

Tomatoes are subject to numerous leaf diseases, which can be especially bad in humid climates. Crop rotation, using disease-resistant varieties, and good air circulation should take care of most disease problems. Planting a second crop 5 to 6 weeks after the first lets you rip out and destroy diseased plants.

Insect pests vary with the region, but the worst include tomato fruitworm and tomato or tobacco hornworms. Beneficial insects help control both, and you can handpick hornworms. If the population is beyond your tolerance level, you can spray with Bt (see p. 173).

continued on p. 274

Blossom-end rot is due to calcium deficiency and irregular watering. Cat-facing is usually due to incomplete pollination in chilly weather.

GOOD VARIETIES

There are so many good tomato varieties that it's almost fruitless to make suggestions. Seek out tomato tastings during peak season—July to September—to learn what appeals to you and what thrives in your area. Heirlooms are usually not as disease-resistant or productive as the hybrids, but they offer the promise of great flavor. Here are some fairly universal favorites.

Cherry tomatoes: 'Sungold' (superb!) and 'Sweet 100 Plus'

Paste tomatoes: 'Roma' and 'San Marzano'

Slicing and beefsteak tomatoes: 'Celebrity', 'Big Beef', 'Beefsteak', 'Brandywine', 'Mortgage Lifter', 'Striped German'

Growing Tomatoes in Pots

Tomatoes are good candidates for growing in large containers (determinate, indeterminate, and semi-determinate all will work). You'll need something at least 20 in. in diameter, and you'll need to stake or cage the plants as they grow. Put 6 in. to 8 in. of potting soil well amended with organic nutrients in the pot and plant the tomato seedling. As the tomato grows, trim the lower leaves and add more enriched soil mix until the pot is full. This helps build root mass and allows you to plant earlier, because cold protection is as easy as covering the pot.

Be sure to provide plenty of nutrients in the right ratios (see the recipe below). You'll also need to be vigilant with watering, because pots will dry out much quicker than in-ground plantings.

- One 40-qt. bag potting mix
- 1 cup dolomitic limestone
- $\frac{1}{2}$ cup Perk® or other product containing iron and trace elements

Blend thoroughly and store the mixture in covered trash cans. Do this early in the year to give it time to mellow.

Meanwhile, mix together the following amendments and store.

- 4 cups soy meal (N)
- 2 cups blood meal (N)
- 3 cups bone meal (P)
- 2 cups kelp meal (K)
- 4 cups greensand (K)

At planting time, add 2 cups of the meal/greensand mix per 40 qt. potting mix. Blend thoroughly, and plant.

TURNIPS

Although you can grow them all summer long, turnips are at their best when grown in cool weather. Small, white "salad" turnips grow almost as quickly as radishes.

ESSENTIALS

- Turnips need fertile, well-drained soil that is kept regularly moist.
- Sow directly into the garden every 2 weeks, starting in early spring. Do not try to transplant turnips.
- Thin seedlings to allow adequate room for roots to enlarge.

SOWING & GROWING

For best quality, turnips need to grow quickly. Give them rich, loose soil with a neutral or slightly alkaline pH. For continued harvest, direct-sow every 2 weeks, beginning in early spring, as soon as you can work the ground. Sow in rows or wide bands, spacing seeds about ½ in. apart. When seedlings have their first set of true leaves, thin to 1 in. to 2 in. apart. Thin again a week or so later. Final spacing depends on what size you want the harvested roots to be—2 in. to 3 in. for small turnips or 3 in. to 4 in. for medium size.

PESTS

Turnips are subject to root maggots and flea beetles. Use row covers over seedlings to keep out both pests. To prevent diseases, don't grow turnips where other brassicas have grown during the preceding 4 or 5 years.

HARVESTING

Turnips are best when young and tender. Brush away soil from the shoulders of the roots to check on size. When they're right, just pull them up. Thinnings and tender young greens can be enjoyed in salads or sautéed or steamed. Turnips can withstand a light frost—and in fact that sweetens their flavor a little— but hard frost turns roots woody.

GOOD VARIETIES

'Golden Ball' (aka 'Gold Ball') has larger roots (3 in. to 4 in.) with yellow flesh; 'Purple Top White Globe' is a classic turnip with purple shoulders and creamy white flesh; it's best planted at 2 in. to 3 in. 'De Milan Rouge' is a red-shouldered French heirloom. Pick while small. 'Tokyo Cross' grows very quickly. 'Topper' is grown for greens. For more about growing turnip greens, see Collard Greens on p. 208.

WINTER SQUASH AND PUMPKINS

There are many types of winter squash; some of the most common are acorn, butternut, Hubbard, spaghetti, and delicata. The sizes and shapes vary, but they all have one thing in common— vines that sprawl far and wide. Pumpkin plants are even bigger. Nonvining bush varieties are available for most types of these squash and are much smaller, making them possible for the average home gardener.

ESSENTIALS

- Wait for the soil to warm above 70°F before planting.
- Plant two to three seeds or seedlings per hill or grouping. Space bush squash about 3 ft. apart, compact pumpkins 8 ft. apart. Traditional vining pumpkins need 10 ft. to 12 ft.
- Feed the soil lots of rich organic matter, and work in ½ cup of time-release fertilizer per hill before planting.
- Give growing plants 1 in. of water per week.
- Harvest before the first frost, a few weeks after squash have passed the fingernail test (see information under Harvesting).

SOWING & GROWING

Although in most areas you can direct-sow squash, transplants tend to fare better against cucumber beetles, which love emerging seedlings. Set out transplants when they have fewer than four true leaves, or else the plants will be stunted all season.

Squash prefer a well-drained, fertile, loamy soil with a neutral pH. A shovelful of compost and ½ cup of time-release 5-10-10 fertilizer worked into the planting hole does the job. Then mound the soil and compost mixture into a traditional hill and plant your seeds or seedling.

Squash and pumpkins like hot feet. The traditional small hill or mound (12 in. to 18 in. high) will warm up fast in the spring, encouraging vigorous root growth.

HARVESTING

To determine whether a winter squash is ready to harvest, poke the skin with your fingernail. If your nail leaves a mark, the squash is still immature. Even if no mark is left, wait a week or two before harvesting. Squash allowed to mature fully on the vine will keep longer in storage. For best flavor, cure squash for a week or two outside in a warm, sunny place, then store in a dry indoor spot out of direct sun with a temperature of around 55°F. The fruit from most compact winter squash plants keeps for 3 to 9 months, with butternuts keeping the longest and acorns the shortest.

For pumpkins, wait to harvest until the vines have been killed by frost and the stems are dry and shrunken. Pumpkins picked before they are mature will be "green" and won't store well. Wash with mild soapy water and rinse with a mild bleach solution to inhibit mold in storage.

PESTS

Cucumber beetles, squash bugs, and vine borers cause the most damage, but they are all manageable, especially in a small squash patch.

One way to deal with cucumber beetles, which arrive with the first days in the high 70s to low 80s, is simply to avoid them by planting a late crop.

Squash bugs winter over in garden refuse; a thorough garden cleanup is the first tactic. Planting late avoids the first few generations. You can use neem extracts, rotenone, or rotenone and pyrethrins to control

squash bugs. Handpicking is easy and effective.

Squash vine borer is the most destructive pest, especially of bush varieties, and also the hardest to control. The larvae burrow into the stem and feed on the stem tissue. If vine borers destroy the central stem of a vining squash, side stems that have rooted can take over. But if they destroy the only stem of a bush squash, then the plant is doomed.

Depending on what zone you live in, there may be ways to combat the problem of vine borers. The first indication of vine borers is a plant that wilts at midday. If you see sawdust-like residue at the plant base, split open the stem with a knife and remove the larvae, then cover the stem with moist soil. Wrapping the stem with breathable adhesive tape (from your first-aid kit) helps, too.

GOOD VARIETIES

Acorn. 'Table King' is a bush variety whose compact plants are as vigorous as those of most vining varieties. The best of the bush acorns is 'Table Gold', sometimes called 'Golden Acorn' or 'Jersey Golden Acorn'.

Buttercup. 'Gold Nugget' is a bush variety with flavorful fruits averaging 1 lb. to 3 lb. 'Emerald Bush Buttercup'

often sends out runners toward the end of the season.

Butternut. 'Burpee's Butterbush' is the best of the bush butternuts. 'Ponca' is an excellent semi-bush butternut that needs an area 6 ft. square, but it yields more full-size fruit.

Delicata. These pretty squash are either oblong or dumpling shaped. They have ridged, cream to yellow fruits striped green. 'Bush Delicata' bears 1½-lb. to 2-lb. oblong fruits with a nutty flavor. 'Sweet Dumpling' bears round and squatty ½-lb. fruits, each one right for a single serving. The flavor is sweet and nutty.

Pumpkins. Good pumpkins for cooking includes these with smaller fruits—in the 4-lb. to 10-lb. range: 'New England Pie', 'Rocket', 'Racer', 'Small Sugar', 'Howden', 'Montana Jack', and 'Long Pie', an heirloom that is harvested green and turns orange in storage. 'Rocket' makes a good carving pumpkin.

GLOSSARY

AAS (All-America Selection)
A variety that carries this designation means that it has been judged a variety of merit by a network of 27 judges scattered across North America. To be designated an All-America Selection, a new vegetable must be significantly superior to any similar variety already on the market.

Allium
The genus *Allium* counts onions, leaks, shallots, and garlic among its over 400 species, as well as many ornamental plants.

Bare-root
Bare-root plants are shipped from nurseries with no soil surrounding the roots, as opposed to sitting in a pot of soil. Plant bare-root stock as early as possible and be sure the roots remain damp until they are in the ground.

Beneficial insects
Insects that either eat or parasitize the insects that are bugging your plants are beneficial. The ladybug and the praying mantis are the best-known beneficial insects.

Biological control
A biological control is the practice of using one organism to suppress another. The control might be a beneficial insect that either feeds on or parasitizes its prey, or it might be a pathogen—a beneficial bacterium, virus, or fungus. If a biological is derived from a plant, for example a product containing neem or pyrethrins, it's called a **botanical.** If the active ingredient is derived from microorganisms like fungi, bacteria, and nematodes, it's called a **microbial.**

Blanch
In the garden, blanching means to whiten by excluding light. Certain vegetables taste better when blanched, like cauliflower, endive, and escarole, which are bitter if the edible portions are left exposed to sun.

Bolting
When a vegetable or herb grown for its leaves, shoots, or roots shifts from leaf production to flowering, signaled by the emergence of a central flowering stalk, it is said to bolt.

This is also known as going to flower (followed by going to seed). Plants bolt due to a change in day length, length of time in the ground, or the onset of high temperature or drought.

Bottom heat
This is heat applied to soil to enhance propagation of seeds or cuttings. Bottom heat increases soil temperature, which in turn enhances the rate of most biochemical processes, including respiration, shoot and root development, and the release of hormones.

Brassica
This large genus of vegetables and herbs from the mustard family are also known as cole crops. Cole, an old term for cabbage, is where cole slaw comes from. Another moniker is cruciferous vegetables or crucifer.

Cloche
Cloche is the French word for bell, and original cloches were glass bell-shaped jars that were placed over plants to protect them against the cold. Lighter-weight, less breakable material has replaced glass.

Cold frame
Essentially a bottomless box with a window for a lid, a cold frame is like a miniature greenhouse. The back "wall" of the frame is several inches higher than the front, so the glass or plastic-glazed "window" sits on a slope. A cold frame is oriented so the lid slopes to the south, thereby catching as much sun as possible.

Compost tea
Compost tea is a natural fertilizer and is made by filling a watering can with half water and half compost and steeping for several hours. The liquid goes on the plants, and the compost goes back in the pile.

Cover crop
Any crop grown for the specific purpose of soil improvement is a cover crop, also called green manure. There are two reasons to grow a cover crop: to hold soil in place and to add nutrients and organic material to the soil in the

form of decaying leaves and roots when it's turned under. The best cover crop plants have sturdy root systems, lush top growth that's high in water content and that breaks down rapidly, and a tendency not to reappear as weeds once they're turned under. Good cover crops include legumes like clover, field peas, alfalfa, and vetch, as well as rye, oats, wheat, barley, mustard, and millet.

Crop rotation

This is the technique of changing where you plant particular crops year to year to minimize disease and insects. Another benefit is that different vegetables draw minerals and nutrients from the soil in differing amounts, so rotating crops means these elements are used evenly.

Cultivar

A cultivar is a *culti*vated *var*iety, produced by selective breeding and given a modern name, usually set off by single quotation marks. Cultivars may result from the efforts of plant breeders or in nature when two plants cross by accident. Regardless, a cultivar has a new set of genes inside and a new set of traits outside.

Curing

Curing involves letting a winter storage vegetable rest in a location with good air circulation until its skin has hardened or thickened. Some vegetables cure in the sun, while others need shade.

Damping-off

If seedlings die within days (or even hours) of germination, the culprit is probably the fungal disease damping-off. You'll see a dark line on the stem of affected seedlings just at the soil line. To lessen the risk of damping-off, sow seeds in a sterile soilless mix. If you're reusing pots or flats, soak them in a very weak bleach solution briefly before seed-starting begins, and let them air-dry. If you cover containers to raise the humidity and temperature, uncover them as soon as seeds start sprouting. Encourage good air circulation, don't keep the medium too moist, and water from the bottom by setting the container in a pan of water.

Days to maturity

The number of days to maturity is the expected number of days for a crop to begin producing. The number starts either from setting out in the garden (in the case of transplants) or from germination (in the case of direct-sown crops). Consider days to maturity as a guideline.

Determinate and indeterminate

These two terms refer to plants having defined limits of growth (determinate) vs. those that continue to grow until they die (indeterminate).

Diatomaceous earth

Silicon is the chief element in diatomaceous earth, a fine white powder consisting of the skeletal remains of microscopic algae known as diatoms. Also known as silica dust, diatomaceous earth is used for its insect-controlling properties. Added to animal feed, stored grain, and sterile potting mixes, it has helped control a range of infestations by soft-bodied crawling insects like ants, fleas, earwigs, cockroaches, and slugs.

Direct-sow

Also known as direct-seeding, direct-sowing means to plant a seed in soil in the garden, as opposed to sowing in flats or pots and then transplanting seedlings into the garden a few weeks later.

Dormant

Like animals that hibernate, some plants take a winter nap, called going dormant. Growth ceases, tops wither and die or leaves drop, nutrients are pulled down into the roots, and the plant hunkers down to wait out winter.

Double digging

Double digging is the equivalent of deep tilling or subsoil plowing. To double dig is to remove a layer of topsoil to "spade depth"—8 in. to 12 in., roughly the length of a spade's blade—and set it aside. Then, the next spade's-depth layer of soil, the subsoil, is loosened, aerated, and often augmented by compost, manure, or other organic matter. Finally, the top layer is put back in place. Double digging relieves subsoil compaction and refurbishes the topsoil.

Drip line

A drip line is an imaginary line on the ground that encircles a plant and corresponds to the periphery of the leaf canopy. While the drip line is not an accurate delineation of a plant's personal space, at or below the ground, gardeners can use this periphery as a guide for where they should tread carefully, cultivate lightly, and fertilize sparingly.

Frass

Frass is the term for insect manure. As with other wild creatures, the size and shape of frass can give you clues to its origin and therefore to what is eating your plants.

Friable

Friable means crumbly and is a highly desirable trait in soils. If your soil is friable, clumps and clods are easy to break up, and air and moisture (and thereby nutrients) can move freely within its structure.

Frost dates

There are a few important frost dates: last spring frost, also known as the frost-free date, and the first fall frost date. The period in between is the frost-free season, or your growing season. There is a distinction between the **average frost date** (first and last) and the **safe frost date** (again, first and last). A reference to a frost date in a catalog or on a seed packet without specifying first or last likely means the last spring frost, since that is the frost most gardeners are concerned with. For growing fall crops, knowing when to expect the first fall frost is critical to calculating when to sow or set out the crop in summer so as to get a harvest.

Germination rate

Germination rate is the percentage of seed in any given batch that is likely to sprout; seed packets sometimes are labeled with a germination rate. If the germination rate is 90 percent, plan on sowing an extra 10 percent to make up for those that won't sprout. Germination rate diminishes with time, and with exposure to light, heat, and moisture; the rate at which it diminishes varies from vegetable to vegetable.

Harden off

Hardening off—acclimating a plant to outdoor conditions of stronger sun, temperature swings, and wind—is best accomplished over a period of one to two weeks, slowly increasing the amount of sun and the length of time left in it. Seedlings started indoors need to be hardened off, as do potted plants overwintered inside.

Hardiness zone

This term refers to a climate zone or growing area that shares similar extremes of temperature, though not necessarily any other climate aspect such as rainfall or wind or amount of sun. The USDA Plant Hardiness Zone Map (see p. 291) divides continental North America into 11 zones, based on average winter minimum temperatures. A plant's hardiness rating is based on which zones it will survive in, based on winter lows.

Hardpan

In some soils, particularly those heavy in clay, a rock-hard layer sometimes forms below the topsoil. This is hardpan, an almost cement-like layer impervious to water, air, and root penetration. Repeated tilling to the same level and growing crops with weak, shallow, fibrous roots can encourage hardpan to form. The answer is a combination of breaking the hardpan by double digging, increasing organic matter, and growing deep-rooted cover crops.

Heaving

The freeze-and-thaw cycles that happen in a typical winter can actually push plants right out of the ground. This is known as heaving, sometimes called frost-heave, and it is a leading cause of winter kill. Heaving occurs when ice crystals form in the soil and attract water. When that water freezes, it forces plants upward by displacement.

Heirloom

An heirloom variety is one that has been passed down from generation to generation without a trade name or a pedigree.

Hilling or hilling up

Hilling is a technique of mounding soil to cover some of the stem of a plant, and there are various reasons to do this, based on the vegetable. You hill leeks to blanch them, while you hill potatoes to get a bigger crop, because tubers will form all along the stems that are covered in soil.

Horticultural oil, summer oil, superior oil, or dormant oil

These are terms for ultra-refined petroleum or vegetable oils that can be sprayed on plants to kill insect eggs and disease organisms. The original, heavier-weight oils were used largely on trees and were only suitable for spraying in winter, hence the term dormant oil. Newer oils are light enough to be used in summer and on many kinds of crops.

Humus

The word humus has been wantonly misapplied as a label for a number of organic materials, including compost, leaf mold, and peat. Technically, humus is a brown or black, carbon-based material containing a variety of compounds. Humus results from partial decomposition of plant and animal matter and thus forms the organic portion of soil. It also serves as a substrate for microbiological soil activity. Soil is said to be fertile if it contains, among other things, 20 percent humus. Without it, most biological and chemical soil processes cease, creating dead or barren soil.

Hybrid

A hybrid is the result of crossing specific parent plants by controlling pollination. Hybrids are often designated F1 in seed catalog descriptions, a term meaning first generation. Hybrids are very consistent; think of them as the identical twins of the plant world.

Integrated pest management (IPM)

Integrated pest management is a multipronged approach to managing pests. It combines monitoring, prevention, and control, or perhaps better stated, management.

Integrated weed management (IWM)

Integrated weed management follows the same methods as IPM, with the focus on weeds.

Interplanting

This is the technique of mixing one or more crops together for one of the following reasons: to make the best use of space, to take advantage of microclimate conditions created by nearby plants, to make it harder for pest insects or diseases to find target crops, or to create a pleasing arrangement of color and texture.

Lashing

Binding two or more pieces of something together—like stakes or branches—is called lashing. Lashing calls for two types of material: spars (the stakes, sticks, branches, poles, or pieces of wood you're lashing together) and something to lash them with, like cord, string, rope, twine, or leather.

Lath

A lath is a thin, narrow strip of wood typically used in construction. Lath that is thin enough to be flexed might be used for laying out curves in a path or patio.

Leaching

Leaching is the release of substances either by percolation or by washing away or oozing. It most often refers to the loss of nutrients and other elements from the soil by means of percolation. Fast-draining sandy soils are more subject to leaching than heavier clay soils. However, a soil high in organic matter, while fast draining, will also hold onto nutrients.

Legume

A member of the pea family, including peas, beans, and vetches. Legumes have the capacity to convert nitrogen from the air into a form that is usable by plants.

Legume inoculant

A form of *Rhizobium* bacteria that takes nitrogen from the air and fixes it in the soil so that legumes can easily absorb it. Legume inoculant looks like fine, dark brown dust. You moisten the seeds, coat them with the inoculant, and sow. Inoculating legume seeds can boost yields by 15 percent to 20 percent.

Loam

The texture of a particular soil depends on the proportion of sand, silt, clay, and organic matter, and loam has relatively equal proportions of different sizes of all of them. As a result, it is adequately loose for root growth, drains well yet holds moisture, and is naturally fertile.

Minimum/maximum thermometer

A min/max thermometer records the highest and lowest temperatures since the last setting, giving you the most accurate records of what happens, temperature-wise, in your garden.

Monoecious vs. dioecious

A monoecious plant is one that has male and female reproductive parts on the same plant. Most vegetable and fruit plants are monoecious. With dioecious plants, male and female reproductive parts are found on separate individuals. For pollination and fruit set, you must have at least one or a few male plants for numerous female plants.

Mycorrhiza

This word, a blend of the Greek words *myco* meaning fungus and *rhiza* meaning root, refers to the symbiotic association of the mycelium of a fungus with the roots of a seed plant. Mycorrhizae form when tiny fungal filaments (known collectively as the mycelium) invade root tissue and serve as conduits between soil particles and root cells. The fungi dissolve soil particles by releasing enzymes and then send molecules of critical minerals directly into the root tissue. In exchange, the fungi extract from root cells the carbon-based starches and sugars they can't manufacture.

Nematode

A nematode is a microscopic worm. Some are plant pests infesting mostly roots, while others are beneficial insects that prey on soil pests. Nematodes can't be detected with the naked eye.

N-P-K ratio

The three numbers on a bag of fertilizer are called the N-P-K ratio or N-P-K rating, and refer to the percentages of nitrogen (N), phosphorus (P), and potassium (K) in the fertilizer. A balanced fertilizer, such as 6-6-6, is one that delivers an equal amount of each of these elements.

Open-pollinated (OP)

Unlike hybrids, open-pollinated (OP) plants are pollinated naturally, such as by insects or wind. Open-pollinated varieties have stable traits that persist, so you get plants similar to the parent. OP seed can be saved from year to year. Heirloom varieties are always OP, but not all OP plants are heirlooms.

Pea brush or pea sticks

A way of supporting peas is to thrust stout twigs or branches into the ground where you are going to sow peas. As the peas grow, their tendrils catch hold of the twigs.

pH

pH is a measure of the concentration of hydrogen ions in a given substance; in layman's terms, pH measures acidity and alkalinity. The pH scale ranges from 0 to 14; the lower the number, the more acid the soil.

Photoperiodism

The ability of plant physiology to respond to alternating periods of light and darkness is called photoperiodism. Most plants can tell when the sun comes up and goes down. In some plants, though, the length of time the sun is up or not up determines when and if they will produce flowers or drop their leaves.

Plants whose flowering is triggered by an increase in the number of hours of sunlight per day in early summer are called long-day plants. Plants that flower in response to waning sunlight in late summer and fall are called short-day plants. Day-neutral plants couldn't care less how long the sun is up.

Phytotoxic

This means both toxic to plants and a toxin produced by a plant.

Pinch back

Pinching out the bud at the end of a stem encourages a plant to grow fuller, because everywhere you remove one stem, two more grow in its place, one from each leaf node just below the pinch point. You can also pinch back to remove flower buds to delay a plant going to flower.

Pot on

Potting on means to transplant into a larger pot.

Pyrethrum

Pyrethrum is the dried, powdered flower heads of *Chrysanthemum cinerariaefolium*. Extracts from pyrethrum, called pyrethrins, are used as insecticides.

Raised bed

A raised bed is a self-contained area for growing plants built above ground level.

Rotenone

One of the most widespread botanical insecticides is rotenone, which is derived most often from the roots of the tropical plant *Derris elliptica*. Although relatively nontoxic to humans and other mammals, rotenone can be dangerous to fish and other aquatic creatures.

Row covers

Row covers are lightweight, nonwoven fabrics made of spun-bonded polypropylene or spun-bonded polyester used to protect plants from cold and, when adequately anchored, to keep pests from gaining access to plants.

Seed leaves vs. true leaves

When a seed first sprouts, it puts out one or two seed leaves, or cotyledons. These first leaves usually don't look anything like the true leaves of the plant, which start developing next. A plant that sprouts a single cotyledon or seed leaf is known as a monocot, and a plant with two cotyledons is a dicot.

Sidedress

The technique of applying a band of granular fertilizer alongside plants and working it in is known as sidedressing. If you use a dry fertilizer, this is the way to give your plants a midseason boost, as opposed to watering in a liquid fertilizer or spraying on a foliar spray.

Soilless mix

Using a soilless mix—a potting medium that contains no soil—for starting seeds indoors greatly reduces the risk of your seedlings succumbing to soil-borne diseases. Soilless mixes are light and fluffy, so plant roots penetrate them easily. You can buy soilless mixes or make your own from equal parts perlite, vermiculite, and peat moss.

Solanaceous crops

These are the members of the nightshade family: tomatoes, peppers, eggplants, potatoes, and tomatillos. Some produce solanine, a toxic compound that turns potatoes green.

Solarization

Soil solarization involves putting transparent plastic sheeting over moist, tilled soil during the warmest and sunniest time of year and leaving it in place for about two months, during which time the soil gets hot enough to kill disease organisms and weeds.

Sonication

Also known as buzz pollination, sonication is a technique in which certain kinds of bees attach themselves to a flower and rapidly move their flight muscles, thereby loosening pollen. Bumblebees are important sonicators; honeybees do not sonicate.

Square-foot gardening

Square-foot gardening is an adaptation of the natural behavior of plants, which is to grow as close together as they possibly can and take full advantage of the light, soil, and moisture conditions of the site. Not all plants are best grown this way. Narrow upright growers need regular cultivation between plants to discourage weeds, so rows wide enough to accommodate a hoe are necessary.

String level or line level

This is a small tool for finding a horizontal line or plane. The working part of it is a tube of nonfreezing liquid with an air bubble. To use it, you hang the level on a string stretched taut between two stakes and move one end of the string up or down until the bubble floats evenly between two lines marked on the tube.

Succession planting

This is the practice of growing a second (or third or even fourth) crop in the same space within a growing season, so as to maximize your garden's output. Succession planting, or staggered sowing or planting, refers to planting the same crop elsewhere in the garden on a staggered timetable so as to extend the harvest.

Terminal bud

The terminal bud is at the end of a stem. Buds found lower on a stem are lateral buds. The terminal bud at the very top of the plant gets a name all its own—the apical bud.

Thinning

Thinning is to remove some seedlings before they get very big to give the remaining ones room to grow.

Topsoil and subsoil

Topsoil is the upper layer of soil, which contains decomposed organic matter. Subsoil is what lies beneath. In the garden, topsoil is the area of soil that is cultivated and improved with organic matter.

Transpiration

Transpiration is the release of water vapor from a plant's leaf surfaces into the atmosphere. The transpiration process is how plants lose 99 percent of the water they absorb from the ground. It is also how plants obtain water. As water evaporates from leaf surfaces, it reduces internal water pressure throughout the plant and, as a consequence, draws water into the roots from the ground. Transpiration is thus a giant, coordinated sucking motion with the atmosphere as the sucker and the plant as the straw.

Tuteur

A tuteur, French for the word trainer, is a plant support. Tuteurs are multisided structures, but the ones you most often see are pyramidal, with four sides. The sides usually have crosspieces to provide toeholds for climbing plants.

Worm castings

Castings are to worms what frass is to insects—in a word, manure. Earthworm castings are rich in minerals because the action of the enzymes and bacteria inside the worms' guts helps break down soil particles and release nutrients.

SEED CATALOGS

Abundant Life Seeds
Cottage Grove, OR
(541) 767-9606
www.abundantlifeseeds.com

Bountiful Gardens
Willits, CA
(707) 459-6410
www.bountifulgardens.org

Burpee
Warminster, PA
(800) 333-5808
www.burpee.com

The Cook's Garden
Warminster, PA
(800) 457-9703
www.cooksgarden.com

Evergreen Y.H. Enterprises
Anaheim, CA
(714) 637-5769 (fax)
www.evergreenseeds.com

Fedco Seeds
Waterville, ME
(207) 873-7333
www.fedcoseeds.com

Gurney's Seed & Nursery Co.
Greendale, IN
(513) 354-1491
http://gurneys.com

Harris Seeds
Rochester, NY
(800) 544-7938
www.harrisseeds.com

Henry Field's Seed & Nursery Co.
Aurora, IN
(513) 354-1494
http://henryfields.com

John Scheepers Kitchen Garden Seeds
Bantam, CT
(860) 567-6086
www.kitchengardenseeds.com

Johnny's Selected Seeds
Winslow, ME
(877) 564-6697
www.johnnyseeds.com

Native Seeds/SEARCH
Tucson, AZ
(520) 622-5561 (fax)
www.nativeseeds.org

Nichols Garden Nursery
Albany, OR
(800) 422-3985
www.nicholsgardennursery.com

Ornamental Edibles
San Jose, CA
(408) 528-7333
www.ornamentaledibles.com

Park Seed Co.
Greenwood, SC
(800) 213-0076
www.parkseed.com

The Pepper Gal
Ft. Lauderdale, FL
(954) 537-5540
www.peppergal.com

Pepper Joe's, Inc.
Myrtle Beach, SC
pepperjoe1@sc.rr.com
www.pepperjoe.com

Pinetree Garden Seeds
New Gloucester, ME
(207) 926-3400
www.superseeds.com

Redwood City Seed Co.
Redwood City, CA
(650) 325-7333
www.batnet.com/rwc-seed

Renee's Garden
Felton, CA
(888) 880-7228
www.reneesgarden.com

Seed Savers Exchange
Decorah, IA
(563) 382-5990
www.seedsavers.org

Seeds of Change
Estaca, NM
(888) 762-7333
www.seedsofchange.com

Southern Exposure Seed Exchange
Mineral, VA
(540) 894-9480
www.southernexposure.com

Stokes Seeds
Buffalo, NY & Thorold, Ont., Canada
(800) 396-9238
www.stokeseeds.com

Territorial Seed Co.
Cottage Grove, OR
(800) 626-0866
www.territorialseed.com

Tomato Growers Supply Co.
Fort Myers, FL
(888) 478-7333
www.tomatogrowers.com

Vesey's Seeds Ltd.
York, PEI, Canada
(800) 363-7333
www.veseys.com

West Coast Seeds
Ladner, BC, Canada
(888) 804-8820
www.westcoastseeds.com

Willhite Seed Inc.
Poolville, TX
(800) 828-1840
www.willhiteseed.com

ASPARAGUS, RHUBARB,
HORSERADISH, SOFT FRUITS

Daisy Farms
Dowagiac, MI
(269) 782-6321
www.daisyfarms.net

Simmons Plant Farm
Mountainburg, AR
(479) 369-2345
www.simmonsplantfarm.com

Walker Plants
Pittsgrove, NJ
(856) 358-2548
www.walkerplants.com

GARLIC, SHALLOTS,
POTATOES

Artistic Gardens & Le Jardin du Gourmet
St. Johnsbury Center, VT
(802) 748-1446
www.artisticgardens.com

Filaree Farm
Okanogan, WA
(509) 422-6940
www.filareefarm.com

Gourmet Garlic Gardens
Bangs, TX
(325) 348-3049
www.gourmetgarlicgardens.com

Irish Eyes Garden Seeds
Ellensburg, WA
(509) 933-7150
www.irisheyesgardenseeds.com

The Maine Potato Lady
Guilford, ME
(207) 343-2270
www.mainepotatolady.com

Wood Prairie Farm
Bridgewater, ME
(800) 829-9765
www.woodprairie.com

HERB PLANTS

Companion Plants
Athens, OH
(740) 592-4643
www.companionplants.com

Goodwin Creek Gardens
Williams, OR
(800) 846-7359
www.goodwincreekgardens.com

Richters Herbs
Goodwood, Ont., Canada
(905) 640-6677
www.richters.com

Sandy Mush Herb Nursery
Leicester, NC
(828) 683-2014
www.sandymushherbs.com

The Thyme Garden Herb
Alsea, OR
(541) 487-8671
www.thymegarden.com

Well-Sweep Herb Farm
Port Murray, NJ
(908) 852-5390
www.wellsweep.com

SUPPLIES, TOOLS, DRIP
IRRIGATION, COMPOSTING

A. M. Leonard, Inc.
Piqua, OH
(800) 543-8955
www.amleo.com

Charley's Greenhouse & Garden
Mt. Vernon, WA
(800) 322-4707
www.charleysgreenhouse.com

Creekside Gardens
Chehalis, WA
(360) 748-4024
www.wormlady.com

Dripworks
Willits, CA
(800) 522-3747
www.dripworksusa.com

Gardener's Supply Co.
Burlington, VT
(888) 833-1412
www.gardeners.com

Harmony Farm Supply & Nursery
Sebastopol, CA
(707) 823-9125
www.harmonyfarm.com

Lee Valley Tools
Ogdensburg, NY & Ottawa, Ont., Canada
(800) 267-8735
www.leevalley.com

The Natural Gardening Co.
Petaluma, CA
(707) 766-9303
www.naturalgardening.com

Peaceful Valley Farm & Garden Supply
Grass Valley, CA
(888) 784-1722
www.groworganic.com

BENEFICIAL INSECTS AND
BIOLOGICAL CONTROLS

A-1 Unique Insect Control
Citrus Heights, CA
(916) 961-7945
www.a-1unique.com

Arbico Organics
Tucson, AZ
(800) 827-2847
www.arbico.com

Beneficial Insectary
Redding, CA
(800) 477-3715
www.insectary.com

BioLogic Company
Willow Hill, PA
(717) 349-2789
www.biologicco.com

Harmony Farm Supply & Nursery
Sebastopol, CA
(707) 823-9125
www.harmonyfarm.com

Hydro-Gardens
Colorado Springs, CO
(888) 693-0578
www.hydro-gardens.com

Kunafin "The Insectary"
Quemado, TX
(800) 832-1113
www.kunafin.com

Rincon-Vitova Insectaries
Ventura, CA
(800) 248-2847
www.rinconvitova.com

Troy Biosciences, Inc.
Phoenix, AZ
(602) 233-9047
www.troybiosciences.com

BOOKS
Some of these books are out of print but worth tracking down.

Seed saving
Saving Seeds, Rev. ed., by Marc Rogers, Storey Publishing, 1991.

Seed to Seed, 2nd ed., by Suzanne Ashworth, Chelsea Green Publishing, 2002.

Good bug references
Chemical-Free Yard & Garden by A. Carr, et al., Rodale Press, 1991.

Destructive and Useful Insects by R. L. Metcalf and W. P. Flint, McGraw-Hill Book Co., 1993.

The Gardener's Guide to Common-Sense Pest Control by William Olkowski, Sheila Daar, and Helga Olkowski, The Taunton Press, 1996.

Rodale's Garden Problem Solver by Jeff Ball, Rodale Press, 1988.

Weed information and identification
The Gardener's Weed Book by Barbara Pleasant, Storey Communications, 1996.

Rodale's Successful Organic Gardening: Controlling Weeds by Erin Hynes, Rodale Press, 1995.

Weeds by W. C. Muenscher, Cornell University Press, 1987.

Weeds: Control Without Poisons by C. Walters, Acres U.S.A., 1996.

Weeds: Guardians of the Soil by J. A. Cocannouer, Devin-Adair, 1964.

Weeds: The Unbidden Guests in Our Gardens by Mea Allan, Viking Press, 1978.

Weeds and What They Tell by Ehrenfried Pfeiffer, Bio-Dynamic Farming and Gardening Assoc., 1970.

Weeds of the West by Tom D. Whitson, University of Wyoming, 1996.

COOPERATIVE EXTENSION
To find your nearest cooperative extension office, visit the USDA's website at www.csrees.usda.gov/Extension

CONTRIBUTORS

Ike Adams

Helen Albert

Suzanne Ashworth

Keith Baldwin

Joan Bankemper

Robin Barnard

Judy Barrett

Melinda Bateman

Pat Battle

Ingrid Bauer

Jim Becker

Susan Belsinger

Yael Bernier

Pamela Bird

John Bray

George Bria

William E. Brown

Robert Bruleigh

Weldon Burge

Stu Campbell

Debora Carl

James Carr

Carrie Chalmers

Andrea Ray Chandler

Linda Chisari

Ron Clancy

Leslie A. Clapp

Peter Coe

Eliot Coleman

Sharon J. Collman

Sam Cotner

Paul D. Curtis

Sheila Darr

Jeff Dawson

Margaret de Haas van Dorsser

Leonard Diggs

Glenn Drowns

George L. Egger II

Frank Ferrandino

John C. Fisher

Fran Gage

Peter Garnham

Jan Gertley

Edward Giobbi

Sam Gittings

Jutta Graf

Mike Guertin

Garrett Hack

Rolfe Hagen

Sheryl Bills Heckler

Jean Hendrick

Clarke Hess

David Hirsch

Alex Hitt

Sandra Holloway

Lucinda Hutson

Elaine R. Ingham

Lee James and Wayne James

Janet Jemmott

Des Kennedy

James Kerr

Robert Kourik

Alice Krinsky

Louise Langsner

Lucy Apthorp Leske

Mimi Luebbermann

Marcia MacDonald

Mary Maier

Janie Malloy

Martin Mathes

Heather McCargo

Susan McClure

Roy McGinnis

Laura McGrath

Barbara Meidinger

Jo Meller

Richard Merrill

Theresa Mieseler

Ashley Miller

Ed Miller

Diana Morgan

Leslie Mosch

Shep Ogden

Bill Olkowski

Olga Olkowski

Mena Paton

Karen Pendleton

Cass Peterson

William Quarles

Joe Queirolo

Joel Reiten

David Rigby

Sandra B. Rubino

Gray Russell

Carol Savonen

Warren Schulz

D. Casey Sclar

Aurelia C. Scott

Jim Sluyter

Jack Staub

Lee Stoltzfus

Diana Stratton

Edward and Verna Streeter

Rexford Talbert

Harold Taylor

Maggie Stemann Thompson

Sylvia Thompson

Sheila Turnage

Stefanie Vancura

Andy van Hevelingen

Marc Vassallo

William Woys Weaver

Linda Wesley

Kris Wetherbee

John White

Ann Marie Wilson

Abigail Wiscombe

Nan Wishner

Tracy Wootten

Andrew Yeoman

Israel Zelitch

Ron Zimmerman

CREDITS

PHOTOS

Andre Baranowski
p. 40 (right), 54, 165, 215, 223, 245, 249 (bottom), 266

© **Matthew Benson**
p. 199, 255, 275

John Bray
p. 40 (left), 99, 241, 268

Jennifer Brown, © The Taunton Press, Inc.
p. 184, 185, 208, 238

David Cavagnaro
p. 197 (right), 225, 276

Skye Chalmers
p. 261

Ken Chermus
p. 139

Courtesy Ron Clancy
p. 27 (top right)

Frank Clarkson
p. 204

Barbara Damrosch
p. 132 (top)

Jaret Daniels
p. 142, 143 (bottom left and bottom right), 172

Jodie Delohery, © The Taunton Press, Inc.
p. 39 (bottom), 45, 50 (top), 230

J. F. Dill
p. 143 (top right), 144 (top)

Courtesy The Ephrata Cloister
p. 11

***Fine Gardening* staff**, © The Taunton Press, Inc.
p. 44

Roger Foley
back cover (far right),
p. 30, 31 (top), 56, 57

Stacy Geiken
p. 243 (bottom)

Adam Gibbs
p. 26, 27 (top left), 110, 226, 257

Boyd Hagen, © The Taunton Press, Inc.
p. v, vi-1, 2, 20, 21, 24, 25, 42 (top left), 89, 119, 120, 152, 193, 200, 210, 211, 212, 213, 217, 228, 231, 247, 258, 259, 262, 263, 271

Phillip Harvey
p. 232, 258

Cary Hazlegrove
p. 224, 267 (bottom)

© **Saxon Holt**
p. 4-5, 29, 41, 50, 66, 71, 104, 186-187, 192, 195, 216, 238, 239, 246

Kim Jaeckel
p. 65, 87 (left), 181, 219

Janet Jemmott, © The Taunton Press, Inc.
p. 39 (top), 201, 212, 214, 242, 243 (top), 248, 251, 253, 273, 274, 277

© **Andrea Jones/www. gardenexposures.com**
front cover

Susan Kahn, © The Taunton Press, Inc.
p. 235, 240, 249 (top), 250, 256

© **Lynn Karlin**
p. 10 (top left and right), 22, 23, 43 (top right)

Jefferson Kolle, © The Taunton Press, Inc.
back cover (center left), p. 75, 220

© **Robert Kourik**
p. 92

Larry Lefever
p. 12, 13

Ruth Lively, © The Taunton Press, Inc.
p. 19 (left), 31 (bottom), 39 (center), 63, 69, 122, 124, 130 (bottom), 132 (bottom left and right), 133, 146 (bottom), 147, 170, 189, 194, 205, 218, 267 (top)

© **Mark Lohman**
p. 8, 34, 91

Justin Machonochie/Hedrich Blessing
p. 53, 61

Allan Mandell
p. 18, 19 (right), 32, 33, 35, 51, 62

Charles Mann
p. 196

David McDonald
p. 236

Marcia Mcdonald
p. 14, 16

Mary Morgan, © The Taunton Press, Inc.
p. 82

© **Jerry Pavia**
p. 7, 138

Scott Phillips, © The Taunton Press, Inc.
back cover (center right), p. 67, 83 (bottom), 85, 86, 87 (right), 130 (top), 140, 174, 264, 270

Pam Pierce
p. 176

Bryan Reynolds
p. 143 (top left)

Gail Schumann
p. 179

© **Pam Spaulding**
p. 190, 191

Derek St. Romaine
p. 42-43 (bottom)

Marc Vassallo, © The Taunton Press, Inc.
back cover (far left), p. ii, 10 (bottom left and right), 15, 72, 83 (top), 84, 96, 97, 100, 101, 102, 103, 123, 127, 128, 146 (top), 148, 149, 150, 157, 158, 160, 161, 166, 197 (left), 198, 229, 244, 272

Robert Vinnedge
p. 47, 48, 49, 117, 129, 136

Rosalind Wanke, © The Taunton Press, Inc.
p. 36, 38, 68

Steve Wanke
p. 188

Linda Wesley
p. 203, 222, 227

Ron West
p. 141, 144 (bottom), 145, 156, 159, 162, 163, 164

DRAWINGS

Vince Babak
p. 135

Sally Bensusen
p. 30

Krista Borst
p. 23, 49

Michelle Burchard
p. 19, 27, 28

Susan Carlson
p. 159

Christopher Clapp
p. 178, 269

Wendy Edelson
p. 105, 106

Michael Gellatly
p. 55, 60, 90, 93, 95, 131, 156 (bottom)

Kim Jaeckel
p. 58, 59, 168, 183

Bob La Pointe
p. 33, 46, 62

Mindy Lightipe
p. 153,

Melanie Powell
p. 65

Roberta Rosenthal
p. 78

Mark Sant'Angelo
p. 133

Dolores Santoliquido
p. 144

Pat Schories
p. 112-113, 114

Redenta Soprano
p. 73 (top), 125

Peggy Turchette
p. 73 (bottom), 77

Marc Vassallo
p. 14-15, 17

Leslie Watkins
p. 52

Gary Williamson
p. 70, 108, 109

Eleanor Wunderlich
p. 111

Metric Equivalents

Inches	Centimeters	Millimeters	Inches	Centimeters	Millimeters
1/8	0.3	3	13	33.0	330
1/4	0.6	6	14	35.6	356
3/8	1.0	10	15	38.1	381
1/2	1.3	13	16	40.6	406
5/8	1.6	16	17	43.2	432
3/4	1.9	19	18	45.7	457
7/8	2.2	22	19	48.3	483
1	2.5	25	20	50.8	508
1 1/4	3.2	32	21	53.3	533
1 1/2	3.8	38	22	55.9	559
1 3/4	4.4	44	23	58.4	584
2	5.1	51	24	61.0	610
2 1/2	6.4	64	25	63.5	635
3	7.6	76	26	66.0	660
3 1/2	8.9	89	27	68.6	686
4	10.2	102	28	71.1	711
4 1/2	11.4	114	29	73.7	737
5	12.7	127	30	76.2	762
6	15.2	152	31	78.7	787
7	17.8	178	32	81.3	813
8	20.3	203	33	83.8	838
9	22.9	229	34	86.4	864
10	25.4	254	35	88.9	889
11	27.9	279	36	91.4	914
12 1/2	30.5	305			

USDA HARDINESS ZONE MAP

The zones stated in *Fine Gardening* are based on several sources and should be treated as general guidelines when selecting plants for your garden. Many other factors may come into play in determining healthy plant growth. Microclimates, wind, soil type, soil moisture, humidity, snow, and winter sunshine may greatly affect the adaptability of plants. For more information and to zoom in on your area, visit the map online at www.usna.usda.gov/Hardzone/ushzmap.html.

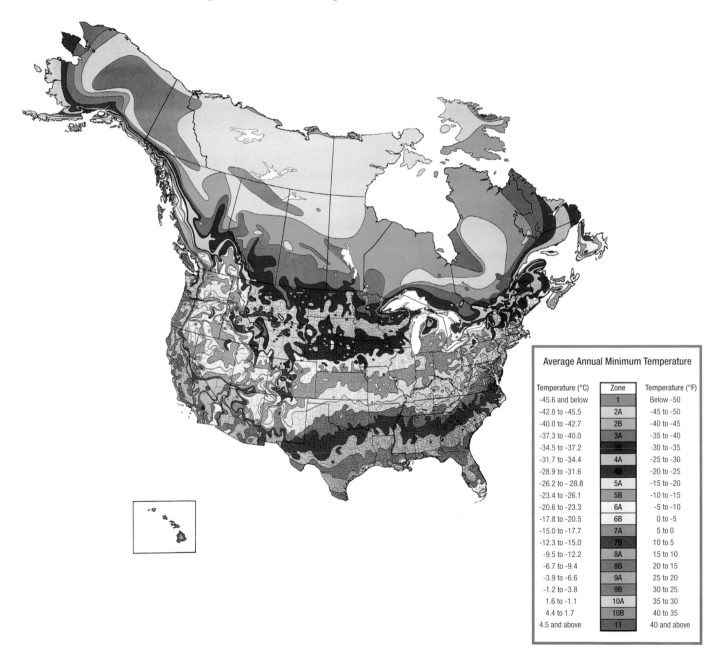

Average Annual Minimum Temperature

Temperature (°C)	Zone	Temperature (°F)
-45.6 and below	1	Below -50
-42.8 to -45.5	2A	-45 to -50
-40.0 to -42.7	2B	-40 to -45
-37.3 to -40.0	3A	-35 to -40
-34.5 to -37.2	3B	-30 to -35
-31.7 to -34.4	4A	-25 to -30
-28.9 to -31.6	4B	-20 to -25
-26.2 to -28.8	5A	-15 to -20
-23.4 to -26.1	5B	-10 to -15
-20.6 to -23.3	6A	-5 to -10
-17.8 to -20.5	6B	0 to -5
-15.0 to -17.7	7A	5 to 0
-12.3 to -15.0	7B	10 to 5
-9.5 to -12.2	8A	15 to 10
-6.7 to -9.4	8B	20 to 15
-3.9 to -6.6	9A	25 to 20
-1.2 to -3.8	9B	30 to 25
1.6 to -1.1	10A	35 to 30
4.4 to 1.7	10B	40 to 35
4.5 and above	11	40 and above

INDEX

nonchemical methods, 165
recording in journal, 140
repellents, **165**, 167–69, **168**
row covers, 122, 124, 154
See also Deer control
Pesticides
application of, 163, 165–67, **166**
bees and, 150
biological insecticides, 172–76, **174**, **176**
composting material treated with, 86
homemade sprays, 150, 163
least-toxic choices, 165–66
nonselective, 146
protection when using, **166**, 167
selection of, 140, 166–67, **174**
pH of soil, 73, 81–82, **82**, 282
Phosphoric acid, 71
Phosphorus (P)
application of, 71–72
availability of, 71
calculating amount needed, 79–81, **80**
crop rotation and, 111, 112, **112**, **114**
fruit crops and, 111, **114**
labeling of fertilizer bags and percentage of, 74, 80
plant growth and, 69, 70
sources of, 71, 75, 77, 111
superphosphate, 71, 72, 73, 74
weather conditions and, 70, 72
weed control and, 183
Photosynthesis, 69, 107, 123
Picket fences
four-square gardens, 11–12, **11**, **12**, **13**, **16**
individualized design of, **50**
octagonal garden, 30, **30**
style decisions, 50
wire-mesh lining for, 30
Pigeon manure, 77, 78
Pine needles, as mulch, 41, 97
Pinworms, 164, **164**
Piperonyl butoxide (PBO), 155, 175, 176
Pirate bugs, 145, **145**, 148, 151
Planning the garden
bed size decisions, 116, **117**
calendar, gardening, 106–107
days to maturity of plants, 106, 279
fertilizer requirements of plants and, 74–75
growing season and frost dates, 106, 107, 116, 280
journal, gardening, 107
planting schemes, 110–16, **112**, **113**, **114**
scale drawing of garden, 105
strategizing the garden, 105–107
sun vs. shade, 107–10, **108**, **109**
when to plan, 105–106
Plantation gardens, 30–31, **30**, **31**
Plant growth
days to maturity of plants, 106, 279
nutrients and elements for, 69–70, 72–73
Planting the garden
crop rotation, 106, 110–13, **112**, **113**, **114**, 139, 279

direct-sown seeds, **69**, 116, 122–24, **123**, **124**, 279
interplanting crops, 115, 155, 281
replacing harvested plants, 115–16
succession planting, 107, 115–116, 283
See also Cover crops; Seeds and plants
Plant protectors
cloches, 126, 129, **129**
plastic tunnel, 128–29
row covers, 122, 124, 127–28, **127**, **128**, 154, 282
shade cloth, 122
water-filled, 127, 130
Plastic edgings, for paths, 43
Plastic mulch, 97
Plastic tunnels, 128–29
Plate compactor, 48, 49
Plumbing in the garden, 44
Pole beans, 18, 54, 59, 193–94
Pollination of plants, 124, 149–50
Polypropylene fence, 52
Potassium (K)
availability of, 72
calculating amount needed, 79–81, **80**
crop rotation and, 112, **112**, **113**, **114**
labeling of fertilizer bags and percentage of, 74, 80
plant growth and, 69, 70, 72
potassium chloride, 72
potassium nitrate, 72, 76
potassium sulfate, 72
root crops and, 112, **114**
sources of, 72, 75, 77, 112
Potatoes
crop rotation and, 111, 113, **114**, 139
disease-free stock, 139
essential growing information for, 260–61, **260**
fertilizer requirements, 74, **75**
mulch and, 99
nitrogen and, **114**
pests and pest control, 151–53, **152**, 162–63, **162**, 170, 173
pH of soil and, 81
pollination of, 149
resources, 285
viruses, 170–71, 179
Poterium sanguisorba (salad burnet), 237–38, **238**
Poultry manure, 76, 77, 78, 80, 86
Pumpkins
essential growing information for, 276–77
frost dates and, 106
mulch and, 98
pests and pest control, 153–54, **153**, 156–59, **157**, **158**, **159**
pollination of, 149
saving seeds, 124
PVC edgings, for paths, 48
Pyrethrins, pyrethrin-oil formulations, and pyrethrum products, 155, 163, 169, 174–76, **176**, 190, 282
Pyrethroids, 174, 176